W9-AQL-293

the *kafka* problem

an anthology of criticism about franz kafka by auden · baum

bergel · brod · burgum · camus · daniel-rops · estrada

flores · fuchs · groethuysen · hardt · hoffman · jacob · kelly

landsberg · lerner · magny · neider · poggioli · saurat

savage · schoeps · spaini · urzidil · vašata · vietta · wahl

warren · weidlé · weiss · werfel · winkler · woodcock

Edited by Angel Flores

LIBRARY
BRYAN COLLEGE
DAYTON, TENN. 37321

the

Kafka

problem

GORDIAN PRESS
NEW YORK
1975

53872

Originally Published 1963
Reprinted 1975

Copyright © 1946
By New Directions
Renewal Copyright © 1974
By Angel Flores and New Directions
Published by Gordian Press, Inc.
By Arrangement

Library of Congress Cataloging in Publication Data

Flores, Angel, 1900–   ed.
   The Kafka problem.

   Reprint of the 1963 ed. published by Octagon
Books, New York
   Bibliography: p.
   1. Kafka, Franz, 1883–1924. 2. Kafka, Franz,
1883–1924––Bibliography. I. Title.
PT2621.A26Z7 1975   833'.9'12   75–32558
ISBN 0–87752–204–9

" The reason posterity's appraisal of a man is often more correct than that of his contemporaries is that he is dead. Only after death, only in solitude, does a man's true nature emerge. In death, as on the chimney-sweep's Saturday night, the soot gets washed from his body. Then it can be seen who did the more harm, his contemporaries to him, or he to his contemporaries. If the latter, he was a great man."

franz kafka

acknowledgments

Kafka has many friends, and they have lightened my labors. I wish in particular to thank three of them: Kate Flores, Lienhard Bergel and Charles Neider for help of almost every kind. I am extremely grateful also to Mr. and Mrs. John Urzidil for much invaluable background material and photographs, to Mr. Walter Nubel for the loan of several books and for sundry bibliographical items, to Mr. Anthony Tudisco for generous assistance in procuring out-of-print magazines and books, and to Mr. James Laughlin for encouragement and co-operation.

I am indebted to the Louisiana State University Press for permission to reprint Frederick J. Hoffman's essay in his *Freudianism and the Literary Mind;* to *Focus* (London) for the article by George Woodcock; to *The Central European Observer* for the article by Rudolf Vašata; to *The Sewanee Review* and *Focus* for the essay by D. S. Savage; to *The Menorah Journal, Life and Letters To-day* (London) and *Hemisphere* for material by John Urzidil; to *Partisan Review* for Camus' essay; to Dr. Robert Klopstock for Werfel's letter printed here for the first time; and to *Scrutiny* for Major Winkler's analysis. Quotations from Kafka are given in the Willa and Edwin Muir versions whenever possible.

To Mrs. Ruth Oakley of the Queens College Library I am thankful for procuring photostats and magazines from other libraries.

A. F.

contents

vii

exegesis and commentary

viii

foreword

I still vividly remember the enthusiasm with which I, then a graduate student, like so many others at the time, welcomed the appearance of this volume, back in 1946. It was like water from the rock for travelers thirsting in the trackless haunting land of Kafka's fiction into which we had newly entered without guides. Walter Benjamin was still as little-known as Kafka himself had been a few years earlier, and except for Brod's biography and a recent Kafka *Miscellany*, hardly anything existed to orient us in our bafflement. So we rushed to Angel Flores' anthology as to a revelatory guide. Our understanding of Kafka, we hope, has grown a good bit beyond the insights offered here; it would be sad if it were otherwise. Yet, this volume remains remarkable for the breadth, diversity, and lively challenge of its contributions. Austin Warren's article on "The Penal Colony," Lienhard Bergel's on "Blumfeld," and above all Camus' "Hope and Absurdity" remain fundamental texts in all Kafka criticism to the present day. Others like Kelly's and Schoeps' provide the clearest formulations of a once-dominant way of looking at Kafka which conveys to us the sense of an epoch stamping the history of Kafka reception for all time. For here we encounter the spiritual climate from which Kafka himself had grown and the tradition he helped to advance. Although there are many more dimensions from which Kafka speaks to us today, the first medium through which he appears to us can never be removed from the vast seminal force Kafka has since become.

ix

It is, therefore, an occasion of great joy to see the renewed availability of this classic. Apart from several individual contributions which remain most illuminating for the contemporary reader, the republication of Angel Flores' pioneering work is welcome as the repossession of a milestone in the history, not only of Kafka criticism, but with it, of our contemporary sensibility.

Walter H. Sokel

Chairman, Department of Germanic
Languages and Literatures,
University of Virginia

x

introduction

It has been told that Thomas Mann once lent his friend
Einstein a book by one of his favorite authors, Franz Kafka, and
that Einstein returned it with the comment: "I couldn't read it,
the human mind isn't complicated enough." I do not know how
true this is, but I think it would be safe to say, after some years
of research into Kafka criticism, that if Einstein finds Kafka beyond his understanding, he is the only man who has ever admitted it. Nearly everyone who reads Kafka, not to mention many
who don't, seems to have not the slightest doubt that he understands him perfectly, and moreover that he is the only one who
does.

Perhaps this is exactly what Kafka intended. The present book is designed to display this broad and sometimes mutually exclusive range of opinion. Sundry Kafkian facets are
analyzed and so explored as to offer the reader new points of
departure. In the course of exegesis and commentary nearly every
school of literary criticism, ranging from the extremely conserva-
tive (Martínez Estrada, Schoeps, Weidlé) to the socially conscious (Baum, Fuchs, Lerner) presents its argument. But despite
the excitement of juxtaposing such divergent strictures I have

tried to avoid the extravagances of bygone rages in literary criticism: the psychoanalytical nightmares of Helmuth Kaiser (Franz Kafka's *Inferno*), for example, and the trances of countless occult mystifiers.

A few of Kafka's friends are here, writing from personal knowledge of the man: Baum, Brod, Fuchs, Politzer, Urzidil, Ernst Weiss—the first and the last victims of the Nazi Terror which suppressed and burned Kafka's books and scattered his friends in every direction: Jerusalem, London, Bombay, New York. So, several expected contributions have not arrived in time, and others, alas, will never come. I have endeavored, too, to include critics of varied backgrounds and nationalities: from France, Poland, Czechoslovakia, Italy, Germany, Argentina and Austria, as well as from the United States and England. Unbelievable as it may seem, it has not been difficult to avoid repetition: every man who writes on Kafka somehow immediately becomes an individual.

The Kafka Problem has been planned to give a general view of the man and his works, to present various attitudes toward recurrent Kafkian themes, problems and influences. An effort has been made to include analyses of the literary, philosophical and social factors which left their mark on Kafka's work, as well as the reasons for his continuing and growing influence in the literature and thought of today.

When Kafka died in 1924 his reputation was solidly established but it was confined almost entirely to rather snobbish circles. It soon began to cross frontiers, but always in de luxe coaches. It came first to Madrid, where a Spanish version of *The Metamorphosis* was published in the *Revista de Occidente* in 1925. French, Italian and English translations of Kafka then appeared in the *Nouvelle Revue Française* (1928), *Il Convegno* (1928), and *transition* (1929), three of the foremost vanguard literary journals of Europe.

In the early 30's the impact of the publication in Germany of Kafka's three novels in 1925–1926 led to the appearance of *The Castle* (London and New York, 1930) and *The Great Wall of China* (London, 1933) in English, and of *The Trial* in French, Norwegian and Italian, all in 1933.

On the occasion of the tenth anniversary of Kafka's death in 1934, *The Literary World,* a monthly journal edited in New York by the present writer, published an "Homage to Franz Kafka" with tributes by Thomas Mann, Max Brod, Waldo Frank, Denis Saurat and others.

In 1935–1937 six volumes of Kafka's *Gesammelte Schriften* were published in Berlin, and subsequently (1937–1938) *The Trial, The Metamorphosis* and *Amerika* appeared in English translation, in book form. In France the *Nouvelle Revue Française* continued to present French versions of Kafka, culminating in *The Castle* in 1938; while in Buenos Aires the Spanish critic Guillermo de Torre persuaded the Editorial Losada to publish *The Metamorphosis* and *The Trial* in Spanish (1938–1939). New periodicals joined in making Kafka better known by means of critical analyses and translations: *Cahiers du Sud,* of Marseilles, from 1934 almost uninterruptedly until today; *Sur,* of Buenos Aires, since 1936; and, in the United States, *Partisan Review,* since 1938, and *New Directions,* since 1940, when it published *Amerika.*

As Mr. Toynbee pointed out in *The New Republic,* the World War II period witnessed an intensified interest in Kafka in France, with the publication of numerous translations and essays. Two reasons may be adduced for this. One is that the European world of the late 30's and early 40's with its betrayals and concentration camps, its revolting cruelties and indignities, bore a remarkable resemblance to the world depicted by Kafka in the opening decades of the century. History seems to have imitated the nightmarish background evoked by the dreamer of Prague. Readers who at almost any other historical period might have dismissed Kafka's works as far-fetched and inconceivable now recognized in them their own familiar world. A second and concomitant reason is the revival of interest in Kierkegaard and Existentialism, and the linking of Kafka with them. Most of the present-day exegetists and translators of Kafka in France—Jean Carrive, Pierre Klossowski, Jean Starobinski, Marcel Lecomte—are seeing in Kafka's works but a dramatization of their own Existentialism.

However this may be, Franz Kafka is being studied

and read. His influence is perceptible in some of our most gifted short story writers and novelists, and criticism of his work has become broader and more searching and vital. It may not be too rash to state that Kafka's exotic creations, regarded only recently as rare hothouse specimens, the property of esoteric literary cliques, now being exposed to sun and rain and wind, are becoming an organic part of contemporary letters.

Angel Flores

A Kafka sketch

biographical note *

kate flores

The name Kafka, or Kavka, was quite common among the Jews of the Czech regions of the old Austrian empire. Literally, the onomatopoeic word Kavka means "jackdaw" in Czech. And so a jackdaw, a small black crow, was the trade-mark of the firm of Hermann Kafka on Old Town Square in the heart of Prague. Hermann Kafka had come to Prague from the small Jewish community of Wossek near Strakonic in southern Bohemia, where his father was a butcher. Together with his wife, Julie Löwy Kafka, who belonged to an old rabbinical family steeped in Talmudic tradition, he had built up his establishment, a wholesale business in inexpensive ladies' wear: blouses, stockings, etc. Moderately prosperous, they lived in an apartment near their shop, like a hundred other small merchants of Prague, from whom they were hardly to be distinguished.

* This account is based largely on *Franz Kafka: eine Biographie* (Prague, 1937) by Max Brod. Quotations from Kafka's diaries and notebooks are in the translations of Willa and Edwin Muir, wherever available. Quotations from Kafka's letter to his father and *Autobiographical Sketch* are based on the translation of Sophie Prombaum. Dr. Lienhard Bergel made many suggestions, particularly regarding Kafka's literary preferences.

I

Their first child, Franz, born in Prague July 3, 1883, was given the Hebrew name of his mother's grandfather, Amschel, a pious, learned man with a long white beard. Amschel's rooms were lined with books. For religious reasons he bathed every day in the Elbe River, in winter chopping a hole in the ice for the purpose. His father had been a still more pious and learned man, highly esteemed by Christians as well as Jews. One of Amschel's brothers, a physician, became converted to Christianity. It was an introspective family, ruled by moral and ethical scruples, and imbued with the tragic sense of life characteristic of devout Jews. Amschel's wife, upon the early death of their daughter, Franz' grandmother, from typhoid fever, refused to eat or to speak to anyone for a year and then drowned herself in the river one day. One of their sons was known to Franz' mother as her "loony Uncle Nathan," and indeed each generation of this family produced at least one eccentric. Franz Kafka spoke of "recalcitrance, sensitiveness, a sense of justice, restlessness" as his maternal inheritance.

Julie Löwy Kafka, a sensible, extremely intelligent woman, her husband's devoted partner in all his enterprises, admired the robustness of the Kafka family, its vitality, its optimism and its aggressiveness. In contrast to the Löwys, who were impractical, dreamy, shy and delicate, an early death being not uncommon among them, the Kafkas were practical, realistic, self-confident and strong. Hermann Kafka was a man of heroic proportions, and his imperious personality dominated his household. Thus as in Goethe and Thomas Mann, two polar tendencies met in Franz Kafka, who regarded himself as "in brief, a Löwy, with a certain element of the Kafka which, however, is not actuated by the Kafka will to live, to do business, to conquer."

With both parents preoccupied with their shop, the boy was left mostly in the care of governesses. He had a lonely childhood. A brother Heinrich died at two years, a brother Georg at six months. There were then three girls, the eldest born when he was six. Very early he gave signs of being moody and afraid, to the consternation of his father, who had no patience with sensitive people. "I was a timid child," Kafka wrote in a long, never-delivered letter to his father (1919); "though stubborn, to

2

be sure, as children are, and spoiled by my mother, still I cannot believe that I was especially unruly. I cannot believe that a friendly word, a gentle guiding hand, a kindly glance would not have brought any response desired of me." But brusque, domineering Hermann Kafka saw no reason to be gentle with his cowering son; on the contrary, harsh treatment was what he thought he needed. Franz' mother, though "a paragon of reason" compared to her husband, never dared to oppose him openly; to the boy his parents seemed to form a unit against him, just as his three sisters did later.

Hermann Kafka would be considered an orthodox Jew. He attended synagogue on the high holy days, fasted on *Yom Kippur,* observed the various Passover rites, and had his son confirmed in the usual *Bar Mitzvah* ceremony. He expected his son to follow his example, "if only out of respect for tradition." But young Franz found all the outward forms of the Jewish religion ludicrous, "a joke, not even a joke." His conscience tormented him, and he was filled with "that ever-ready sense of guilt," at what appeared to be a betrayal of his father, but "it was impossible to convince a child, over-observant from excessive fear, that the few trifling rituals you observed in the name of Judaism, with an indifference corresponding to their emptiness, could have a higher meaning . . . This was no isolated phenomenon, being a common experience among the transitional Jewish generation which migrated from the relatively devout countryside to the cities. It was a natural development, but it added another bitter conflict to our already difficult relationship." (*Letter to My Father.*)

The German-speaking Kafkas gave their son a strictly German education. After elementary school he was sent to a German secondary school on Old Town Square famous for its severity, where he lived in meek terror of the school authorities but was a good student in spite of difficulty in mathematics, and even though he spent most of his time reading instead of doing his homework.

Kafka's experience in home and school, he wrote in a fragmentary *Autobiographical Sketch,* was that they strove to obliterate the individuality; and he describes the hopelessness of

3

all attempts to suppress aspects of his individuality such as his irresistible desire to read, and his remarkable but most characteristic reaction to such suppression. Every departure from the norm weighed upon his conscience, and overwhelmed him with a sense of guilt of which he seems to have been always conscious, and which he might almost be said to have nourished:

> For example, I had read all evening, although I had not yet studied my homework for the next day . . . this lapse could surely be no worse than my late reading itself, especially since its consequences were much restricted by my great fear of school and the authorities: whatever I neglected here and there by reading, I used to make up quite easily, with my good memory in those days, in the morning or in school. But the crucial point was that I myself shifted the condemnation suffered by my idiosyncrasy of reading late into the night to my secret negligence, thus arriving at a most depressing state of mind. It was like receiving a tap with a brush, not intended to hurt, but only as a warning; but one reacted by separating the bristles, drawing their points one by one into one's body and beginning to prick and scratch one's inside according to one's own design, while the other hand still calmly held the handle of the brush.

He divided his idiosyncrasies into two groups, secret and revealed, and found that as he grew older more and more of his idiosyncrasies were revealed; but even then his scrupulous conscientiousness prevented him from shaking off his burden of guilt:

> . . . this brought no release, however; it did not reduce the mass of secrets; closer scrutiny revealed that everything could never be confessed. Even that which appeared to have been fully confessed in the past left its root within. But even if that had not been the case . . . one secret peculiarity was enough to upset me, so that notwithstanding all other rectifications I might have made, I would feel cut off from everything. But

4

An early photograph of Franz Kafka

Left: Kafka soon after receiving his doctorate. Right: in the Tatre Mountains

worse than that. Even if I had kept no secret, but had cast everything from me so far as to be left quite clean, the next moment I would again be overwhelmed with the same entanglement, for I would suspect that the secret had not been fully recognized and apprehended, and so it would return loaded upon me anew by society. This was no illusion, but only a special form of perception that, at least among the living, no one can purge himself of his individuality.

While still in secondary school Kafka wrote plays for his parents' birthdays in which his sisters would act under his direction. He kept the extent of his writing secret; it was an "idiosyncrasy" in which he himself found something wrong. He had begun to write in his teens or earlier; in a letter to Oskar Pollak dated September 6, 1903, he speaks of sending him "a bundle containing everything I have written so far . . . Nothing will be missing but the pieces written in childhood (my curse, you see, has been upon me from the beginning), the ones I no longer have, those I consider of no value . . . and finally that which I cannot show even to you . . ."

In 1902 Kafka entered the German University in Prague, where he met Max Brod, his life-long friend and biographer, and where he decided, after fourteen days of chemistry and a semester of German literature, to study law. In his *Letter to My Father* Kafka explains his choice of law, which meant simply "feeding mentally on sawdust" for a few months before the exams: "Actually I was never free to choose a profession; I knew that compared with the main thing [writing] everything else would find me as indifferent as had all my subjects in secondary school; the point was to find a profession which would most readily permit me this indifference." This indifference, incidentally, he states was his "only protection against a nerve-destroying fear and sense of guilt."

Upon receiving his doctorate in jurisprudence on June 18, 1906, Kafka served the usual year of practical law training while attached without salary to a law court. He then accepted the first position that seemed susceptible to "indifference," a minor one with an Italian insurance company, the Assicurazioni

Generali. He continued to live with his parents, where he had his own room and the solicitous care of his mother, but there could be no thought of accepting further support from his father. In July, 1908, Kafka obtained a rather more desirable post with a large institution charged with the administration of the workmen's compensation laws of the Kingdom of Bohemia (Arbeiter-Unfall-Versicherungs-Anstalt für das Königsreich Böhmen in Prag). Here Kafka's duties consisted of making comparative studies of the hazards involved in different trades, drawing up reports grading the various industries accordingly, and recommending accident prevention measures. Relatively useful work in a bureaucratic organization was concerned, in effect, more with shielding the government from the consequences of its own laws than with dispensing any benefits accruable under them. Applicants were shunted about from one department to another as if to disprove their contention of disability. Eventually they might obtain papers to fill in, involving another search for someone capable of explaining them, after which someone who would accept them had to be found.

Dr. Kafka was a scrupulously conscientious employee. His superiors found his reports entirely satisfactory (judging from one quoted by Brod, dealing with the hazards of a wood-cutting plant, they must have been minor masterpieces), and his fellow workers liked him. But his work hardly permitted him "indifference." Mutilated, suffering human beings stared him in the face every day, people whose faith in the benevolence of their Habsburg rulers was often betrayed. "How modest these people are!" Kafka once exclaimed to Max Brod. "Instead of storming the building and smashing everything to bits, they come to us and plead!" Kafka's sketch "New Lamps" indicates the attitude of his organization toward suggested improvements in working conditions, an attitude of hypocrisy too smooth to combat. At one time Kafka drew up a utopian plan for a workers' collective society based not on organization or coercion but on individual ethical attitudes. Work would never lead to the accumulation of wealth, nor even to the acquisition of comfort. It would afford only the barest physical necessities, but even these had to be earned. The relationship between employer and employee would be one of mutual confidence. The support of the workers in illness and old age would be the only province of the state.

The "Kingdom of Bohemia" which in 1918 became Czechoslovakia after three centuries under Habsburg rule was the battleground par excellence of the German-Czech struggle. Like Joyce, Kafka belonged to a strongly nationalistic minority group while writing in the major tongue of the oppressing nation. Kafka sympathized with the Czech resistance movement which before the first World War sought to establish an autonomous Bohemian state within the Austro-Hungarian empire. While never politically active, he studied the Czech language and literature and attended mass meetings and discussions.

The earliest preserved piece of writing by Kafka is a long story of about forty pages, his first larger work, entitled "Description of a Struggle." Begun in 1902, it bears characteristic Kafka traits: the limpid style, the bewildered bachelor, the quest motif. In this story Kafka already manifests uncertainty about marriage, which seems a threat to one's orderly existence; love and fidelity are regarded as terrible unknowns.

There seems to be no trace of a novel entitled "Excursions into the Dark-Red" which Kafka read to Brod and Oskar Baum in 1904, nor of a story, "The Sky in Narrow Streets," which he entered in a contest sponsored by a Vienna newspaper, *Zeit*, in 1906.

Two excerpts from "Description of a Struggle," published in the Munich magazine *Hyperion* in 1909, marked Kafka's first appearance in print.

Later in the same year, the German Prague newspaper *Bohemia* published a long account of an experimental airplane flight which Kafka had made a special trip to Italy to witness, entitled "The Airplane in Brescia" (September 28, 1909). Inventions fascinated Kafka; hence, perhaps, his interest in Franklin's *Autobiography*. He attended moving pictures all his life.

On March 27, 1910, *Bohemia* published in its Easter supplement five slight experimental pieces which, together with thirteen others, comprised Kafka's first book, *Observations* (1913), published in Leipzig by Kurt Wolff and Ernst Rowohlt, who jointly managed the vanguard Ernst Rowohlt Verlag. Kafka

9

was most reluctant to publish this book, really a brochure of 99 wide-margined pages set in huge type, and did so only upon the insistence of Brod, who during a vacation trip in the fall of 1912 had brought him to Rowohlt Verlag and shown them his five *Bohemia* sketches; when they asked for more, Kafka had found all his manuscripts "worthless." The standards which Kafka set for his writing were so high that practically everything published during his lifetime—a few short stories—had to be prodded from him by his friends. He referred to his writings as "scribblings" and regarded them as tentative attempts to clarify his own problems and objectify his sufferings. Although he often read them to his friends, he thought most of them would be of little interest to anyone else. Perhaps this is one reason for his fragmentariness, another possibly being his feeling that everything he wrote about, no matter how trifling, was inexhaustible.

Although Kafka's working hours were comparatively short (8 to 2, six days weekly), his position was an almost insuperable obstacle to his writing. The six hours of monotonous, hateful work in his office drained him of his spirit and energy. "His weariness is that of the gladiator after the combat; his work was the whitewashing of a corner in a state official's office." (*Reflections on Sin, Pain, Hope and the True Way.*) In addition his parents expected him to assist in their shop whenever necessary, and he never declined despite his complete distaste and lack of talent for business matters. He took to writing at night, a practice which cost him his health. He began to suffer from insomnia and incessant headaches, his temples feeling the way a pane of glass must feel at the shattering point, he said.

In an effort to regain his health Kafka took up athletics, which he had always shunned in school, and became an excellent swimmer, rider and oarsman. He went boating on the Moldau, and hiked in the woods with his friends. He was known as a "fresh air fiend," and spent some time at nudist colonies in the Harz Mountains. The theories of nature healing which were new and popular all over Europe at this time greatly attracted Kafka. He became a teetotaler and a vegetarian, remarking one day before the fish in the Berlin aquarium: "Now I can look you in the eye with a clear conscience." When the celebrated anthroposophist Dr. Steiner visited Prague in 1911, Kafka attended his lectures and even paid him a visit, reporting his experiences in a diary entry of March 28, 1911. Judging from his ironic notations Kafka was under no illusions as to the Herr Doktor's powers, but still in his office, where he tried to show the humility he could not feel by finding some ridiculous place to put his hat, he set forth his problem with the utmost clarity:

> My happiness, my talents and every possibility of my being of some use in the world had always been bound up with literary activity. . . . Well, I could not devote myself to literary activity, as one ought to do, and for varied reasons. Leaving family considerations aside, I could never make a living out of literary work because of the slow rate at which I worked and the peculiar nature of my writings; besides, my poor health and my character hindered me from committing myself to a life which was bound to be uncertain even in the most favorable circumstances. So I had become an official in an insurance office. But literary and administrative work could never agree together or achieve a mutual happiness. The smallest success in the one profession involved grave set-backs in the other. If I did some good writing of an evening I was in a fever next day at the office and could do nothing right. This distractedness was getting steadily worse. In the office I met the claims of the outside world but not those of my inner world, and every unsatisfied inner claim became a rooted misery I could not get away from . . .

On September 2, 1911, Kafka wrote in his diary:

> Sleepless night. The third on end. I fall asleep all right but in an hour's time I wake up as if I had laid my head in the wrong place. I am wide awake, I feel as if I had not slept at all . . . And all night long till about five o'clock it goes on like this, I really do sleep, but vivid dreams keep me awake at the same time. My body lies asleep *beside* me, while I myself have to struggle with these dreams. At about five o'clock the

11

last trace of sleep vanishes and I do nothing but dream, which is more exhausting than lying awake. In short, I spend the whole night in the state a healthy man finds himself in just before he really falls asleep . . .

September 3:

The same kind of night, only a worse struggle to get to sleep . . . Again it was the vividness of my dreams that kept me from sleeping: even the drowsy interval of half-sleep is haunted by them. In the evening and in the morning I cannot help being conscious of my creative powers. I feel loosened out to the very depths of my being and can fish up from inside myself anything I please. This evocation of forces which one does not allow to function reminds me of my relationship to B. Here, too, there are outpourings which are kept in check and made to turn back and destroy themselves, only—and this is the difference—that more mysterious forces are here in question and that my life depends on them.

On August 13, 1912, Kafka met in Max Brod's house in Prague a young lady from Berlin, "Fräulein F. B." This "wholesome, merry, natural, robust young woman," as Kafka described her in his diary, tormented him for five years with the question of marriage, an agonizing problem for Kafka, one of the most insoluble of all his insoluble problems. Nowhere is the ambivalence of Kafka's nature more evident than in his vacillating attitude toward marriage. "One can try to understand the matter in two ways, or even in both simultaneously," to use his own expression in another context. First, Kafka on the one hand yearned to lead a normal, average existence, to be "a simple man of regular habits," a useful member of the community who neither questions nor is questioned about his role in society. On the other hand Kafka found these apparently simple ideals impossible of attainment. "Without forebears, without marriage, without heirs, yet with a wild longing for forebears, marriage, heirs. They all stretch out their hands to me, forebears, marriage, heirs, but too far away for me." Kafka lived in this torturing abyss between his

12

two incompatible selves. Second, Kafka's attitude toward his father was an important if not decisive factor.

Shortly after this meeting, on the night of September 22-23, 1912, "in one burst" from 10 P.M to 6 A.M., Kafka wrote his first work which he himself considered of value, "The Judgment" (*Das Urteil*), one of the very few stories which at the end of his life he described as "counting."

> My legs were so stiff from sitting that I could hardly move them from under the desk. Frightful tension and joy as the story unrolled itself before me, as if I were borne on by a flood. Over and over again this night I really brought it off. All things can be put into words, all one's ideas, even the strangest, find a great fire ready for them in which they are consumed and reborn. The light grew blue before my window. A wagon went by. Two men crossed the bridge. About two in the morning was the last time I looked at the clock. As the maid came through the hall I was writing the last sentence. Turned out the lamp and it was bright day. Slight heart pains. The weariness that vanished in the middle of the night. Then I went palpitating into my sisters' room. Read them the story. Before that stretched myself in front of the maid and said: "I've been writing until now." The look of my untouched bed, as if it had just been brought in. . . . This is the *only* way writing should be done, only in circumstances like these, with such a complete outpouring of body and soul . . . Many feelings carried over from the writing . . . thoughts about Freud, of course, at one point about a passage in "Arnold Beer," at another something in Wassermann, and something else in Werfel's "Giantess," and of course about my own "City Life."

Dedicated to Fräulein F. B., this story was published in Max Brod's yearbook *Arkadia* the following year.

A story of "A Simple Man of Regular Habits" who dies in his thirty-fifth year, entitled "Gustav Bleukelt" (the name probably based on Flaubert's), was begun at this time but never finished; it was apparently destroyed.

13

Kafka now spent several nights of "incredible ecstasy" on the first chapter of a new novel, "The Forgotten," or, as it was later called, *Amerika*. This chapter, "The Stoker," dealing with the adventures of a young boy sent to America after having been seduced, was finished October 3, 1912, and published in May, 1913. It was awarded the Fontane Prize in 1915.

A few weeks later, on November 24, 1912, Kafka read to his friends "The Metamorphosis," a remarkable story of Gregor Samsa who awakes one day to find himself turned into "some monstrous kind of vermin." This story, too, evidently has a basis in Kafka's complex relationship with his father and his life-long sense of guilt.

Kafka worked on *Amerika* during the winter of 1912–1913. All this intensive writing, most of it done at night, brought him close to a nervous collapse by spring; in the hope of relieving his tension he took up gardening and carpentry as hobbies, and decided to go to a sanatorium in Riva. In July, 1913, he made the following "Survey of the Reasons for and against My Marrying":

> I. Inability to bear life alone . . . I cannot withstand the assault of my own life, the aggression of time and of age, the vague compulsion toward the pleasure of writing, the nearness to madness—all these I cannot withstand alone. . . . Marriage with F. will give me greater power of resistance.
>
> II. All this sets me to thinking: of the jokes in the funny papers; the remembrance of Flaubert and Grillparzer, the sight of nightshirts spread out upon my parents' beds, Max's marriage. Yesterday N. N. said: "All my married friends are happy; I can't understand it." This remark also set me to thinking; again I was afraid.
>
> III. I must be alone a great deal. Whatever I may have achieved is the achievement of solitude.
>
> IV. Everything that does not have to do with literature I hate; conversations, even those concerned with literary matters, bore me; visiting bores me; the joys and tribulations of my family bore me to death. Con-

14

versation takes away the importance, the seriousness, the truth of all the things I think about.

V. The fear of a bond, of losing myself in it. Then I will nevermore be alone.

VI. Before my sisters, especially in the past, I have often been an entirely different person from the one I am before other people. Intrepid, naked, powerful, astonishing, moved as I seldom am except when I write. If only I might be thus, through the intermediary of my wife, before everybody! But would it not have to be at the expense of my writing? Not for the whole world! Not for the whole world!

VII. Alone, I might perhaps quit my job some day. Married that would be forever impossible.

Kafka first read Kierkegaard the following month, when he procured an anthology of his works entitled *The Book of the Judge*. From his diary entry of August 21, 1913, it appears that Kafka originally became interested in Kierkegaard largely because of the Danish philosopher's concern with the question of marriage.

Today I have got Kierkegaard's *Book of the Judge*. As I surmised, his case in spite of essential differences is very like my own; at least he belongs to the same half of the world. He comes to my support like a friend. I am drafting a letter to her father which I shall post tomorrow if I feel equal to it . . .

In this letter Kafka confined himself to arguments likely to dissuade his would-be father-in-law, describing himself as a "reserved, silent, unsociable, discontented creature," with no talent for family life, one who in the bosom of his family, "among the best and most lovable of human beings," lived more alien than any stranger, and who was bound to "come to a bad end and soon," because his office work could never absorb him but on the contrary might shatter him completely. "I am not very far from such a breakdown . . . You might ask me why I do not resign my post and try to support myself by literary work—I have

15

no private means. To this I can give only the feeble reply that I have not the strength."

Kafka went to a sanatorium in Riva alone in September, writing Brod: "The idea of a honeymoon trip appals me." In November Fräulein F. B. sent a friend to Prague to plead her case with Kafka; this failing, she evinced a loss of interest, whereupon he went to Berlin and became formally engaged in the spring of 1914. But by July he changed his mind and broke off the engagement, in a trying scene in her parents' home and another in a hotel near the Anhalter station. Determined to devote himself entirely to writing, he wrote his parents from Marienlyst, Denmark, that he had decided to resign his position and live in Munich or Berlin as a journalist, having saved 5,000 kroner, which would last two years.

But the war shattered all his plans, and he returned to his job in Prague. By September, 1914, he finished Chapter I of *The Trial*, a novel of a man pursued by an intangible sense of guilt, who seeks a trial which is never granted, a story of punishment without crime. This chapter was his first work after reading Kierkegaard, though he was apparently working simultaneously on "The Penal Colony" and "The Russian Railroad."

In October, upon receiving a letter from Fräulein F. B.'s friend, Kafka resumed seeing her on rare and painful occasions. "The Penal Colony," one of his most excruciating stories, was finished in November; "Exegesis of a Legend" (Chapter IX of *The Trial*) in December.

In order to work on *The Trial* Kafka occasionally took leaves of absence from his office; in February, 1915, he left his parents' apartment and took a quiet room of his own in Bilek Street, and later one "At the Sign of the Golden Pike," where he wrote Chapters V and VI. By now he was, like Proust, neurasthenically intolerant of noise. In July, 1916, after another brief engagement to Fräulein F. B., he retracted again, giving metaphysical and economic reasons.

Max Brod mentions Kafka's wide readings at this time —Pascal, the Bible, Kropotkin, Dostoyevsky, Herzen, lots of Strindberg, Beginning with his university days, Kafka's taste in modern literature was predominantly anti-romantic. He disliked the sentimental, the vague, the pompous, the picturesque and the fantastic as ends in themselves, the irresponsible playfulness of romanticism, and art for art's sake. Though in general he was a great admirer of Goethe, the sentimental vapors of *The Sorrows of Werther* repelled him. Of the German romanticists he liked only Kleist, particularly the matter-of-factness of his style, a quality which he found attractive in Hebel's *Anecdotes*. Kafka preferred the diaries of Hebel and Grillparzer to their works, probably finding interesting Grillparzer's eternal scruples about himself and his relations to his art and to women. Two of Kafka's greatest influences were Flaubert and Stifter, both opponents of the flight into the imagination, who attached significance to the minutest realistic details. All his life Kafka studied Flaubert, his antidote to romantic vagueness and effusion, particularly *Sentimental Education* and *Temptation of St. Anthony;* "Investigations of a Dog," one of Kafka's last stories, he regarded as a variation on the *Bouvard and Pécuchet* theme. Stifter idealized marriage and parenthood in his novels and stories, of which *The Descendants* was one of Kafka's favorites. Stifter's psychology of the bachelor is much the same as Kafka's; both these writers were unhappy in their relationships with women, in both cases for obscure reasons. Stifter and Kafka both suffered incurable illnesses; and each faced a bitter conflict between his art and his profession. Kafka's struggle, however, reached an unparalleled intensity.

In this basic conflict Kafka followed Stifter rather than Flaubert. It was impossible for Kafka to absolutize art as Flaubert did, not because he had a lesser concept of art but because he had a deeper one. The poignancy with which he lived this conflict between ethical and esthetic values, between life and literature, explains his predilection for Thomas Mann, to whom, of all his contemporaries, he probably felt closest. For the easy decision in favor of art, as represented by Oscar Wilde, he had no sympathy, nor for the Nietzschean titanism of Frank Wedekind. He liked the poets of childhood and youth in contemporary German literature, Hesse, Carossa, Emil Strauss, but disapproved of the baroque sensationalism of Gustav Meyrinck.

Of the three great German lyricists of his time he

17

admired the concreteness and simplicity of Hofmannsthal's lyrical prose. His interest in Stefan George can have been based only on their common anti-romanticism; in every other respect they are polar opposites. It is most surprising that Rilke is never mentioned by Kafka, nor does Rilke ever speak of Kafka in his letters, though some of his writings may have come to his attention, particularly since Rilke had early become interested in Werfel. The two greatest poets of Prague would have recognized their kinship. There was the common bond of their Kierkegaard studies, as well as Rilke's friendship with and Kafka's admiration for Rudolf Kassner. Brod's remark—"The category of sainthood (not that of literature) is the only one applicable to the understanding of Kafka's life and writings"—could apply as well to Rilke. It was a worldly sainthood, in conflict with traditional religion.

Kafka admired Tolstoy (in one of his letters he mentions "The Death of Ivan Ilyitch"), and he must have read Gogol. He was interested in the early Hamsun, and read Walt Whitman and Franklin's *Autobiography*. Strangely enough he liked Dickens, though with great reservations. In his diary he calls *The Stoker* "a plain imitation" of *David Copperfield*. His characterization of Dickens shows again his probing for the genuine: "The heartlessness behind his mannerisms which overflow with feeling. These bolts of coarse characterization which are artificially driven into every person, and without which Dickens could not build up his story even superficially."

Few other non-German writers were of great importance to Kafka with the exception of Kierkegaard, Flaubert and Pascal, on whose *Pensées* Kafka undoubtedly modeled his Aphorisms, some hundred of which were found in a note-book dated 1917–1919 entitled by Kafka's editors *Reflections on Sin, Pain, Hope, and the True Way*. Another small collection of aphorisms entitled *He* was written in 1920.

The privations of the war, coupled with the strain of earning his living while writing with a "grace-given surplus of power," told on Kafka's health. In August, 1917, he coughed blood; a catarrh of the lung was found and he was ordered to a sanatorium to avoid tuberculosis. But Kafka would consent only to a rest cure in Zürau, where his youngest sister had a farm near

Saaz. At Christmas he met Fräulein F. B. in Prague. It was their last meeting; his illness saved him all further excuse. She went back to Berlin, married another man fifteen months later, and had two children. Kafka returned to Zürau, the vague scenic background of *The Castle*.

Kafka attempted to resume his work in the summer of 1918, spending his mornings at the office, his afternoons gardening at the Pomological Institute in the suburb of Troja, and his evenings studying Hebrew and the Talmud. He now put together the largest work to appear during his lifetime, *A Country Doctor*, fourteen short stories running to 191 pages. But his poor health soon forced his retirement, and he lived for the rest of his life in sanatoria on a small pension, refusing any assistance from his parents.

In 1919 while living at Schelesen near Liboch, Kafka was engaged again for a brief period. In November of this year he wrote his long letter to his father, from whom he had been estranged for some time. In this letter, which ran to over one hundred pages but in which he felt he was oversimplifying things, Kafka dissected his life-long fear of his father, who he felt despised him and whom he dreaded and adored. Frau Kafka, who was to have delivered it, with a gentle word or two returned it to her son. *The Penal Colony* appeared this year, as well as *A Country Doctor*, dedicated "To My Father."

There was another short-lived romance at Merau, Austria, in 1920. The following year Kafka's illness reached a crisis, with pulmonary fever and shortness of breath, at a sanatorium in Tatranské Matliary, Tatra.

One of Kafka's and the world's finest short stories, "The Hunger-Artist," was published in the magazine *Neue Rundschau* in 1922, his last publication.

On March 15, 1922, Kafka came quietly to Prague and read Max Brod the opening pages of *The Castle*.

In the summer of 1923, his last summer, when Kafka was staying with his sister and her children at Müritz, a resort on the Baltic Sea, he discovered a Jewish vacation colony near by. He enjoyed their educational program, attended their evening gatherings, played with their children. One day he saw a young girl cleaning a fish. "Such delicate hands in such bloody, messy work!" he said. Dora Dymant, an accomplished Hebrew student who came of a prominent Chassidic family originally from eastern Poland, was only nineteen or twenty, Kafka forty. He decided almost at once to live with her in Berlin, tuberculosis notwithstanding. At the end of July, over the objections of his mother and father, he moved to the Berlin suburb of Steglitz, where he wrote one of his most "cheerful" stories, "A Little Woman," about his landlady, Frau Herrmann. Six weeks later they moved to a villa at 13 Grünewald Street, where, blissfully happy and living in the most idyllic circumstances, Kafka wrote "The Burrow" and "Investigations of a Dog," his last two stories.

The terrible Berlin winter of the inflationary year 1923, when Kafka hesitated even to accept parcels of food from his parents, was the immediate cause of his death. He suffered several serious attacks of pulmonary fever. On March 17, 1924, Max Brod brought Kafka and Dora Dymant to the Kafkas' apartment in Prague. His condition became steadily worse, and on April 10, in an open car under a pouring rain, with Dora standing over him vainly attempting to protect him from the weather, they drove him to a sanatorium near Vienna, where his case was diagnosed as tuberculosis of the larynx. As this sanatorium treated only lung patients, he was transferred to Professor Hajek's clinic in Vienna. Put beside a dying man for lack of an available private room, Brod appealed to influential friends; Franz Werfel interceded, but the Professor declared that Kafka was just another patient. Finally they found him a pleasant room, with flowers and a view, at the Kierling Sanitarium in Klosterneuburg, near Vienna, where he spent his last few weeks correcting proofs of *The Hunger-Artist*, a collection of four stories including "First Grief," "A Little Woman," "Josephine the Songstress" and the title story. It appeared shortly after his death.

Kafka asked to marry Dora, writing her father that although he was not an orthodox Jew, he was a "repentant Jew on his way back into the fold." But her father's rabbi forbade it. He died June 3, 1924, and was buried in the Jewish cemetery in Prague.

The following year *The Trial* was published, with an

"Epilogue" by Max Brod stating that among the mass of writings Kafka had left he had found two notes addressed to him, one in ink written not later than 1921, and an older one in pencil, requesting that he burn "unread and to the last page" everything his friend left behind him "(printed in magazines or newspapers, written in manuscripts or letters) without exception, so far as it can be got hold of, or begged from the addressees . . . and be sure not to forget the notebooks . . . all this, without exception . . . and that you should do it as soon as possible is what I beg of you." Max Brod, for cogent if supererogatory reasons which he carefully lists, did not honor his friend's request. Instead, though many in Kafka's intimate circle felt it was a betrayal, he gathered together and edited for publication nearly everything he could find by Kafka, including his three unfinished novels, *Amerika, The Trial* and *The Castle,* which incidentally had not been started at the time these notes were written. The *Collected Works* appeared in six volumes, 1935–37. More material has since been assembled; at present another edition is planned in ten volumes.

Perhaps Franz Kafka would not have been surprised at this, or even displeased. For is it not one of his Aphorisms: "One must not cheat anybody, not even the world of its triumph"?

recollections

john urzidil

I knew Franz Kafka for many years and conversed with him frequently. I grew up in his neighborhood, enjoyed the company of his friends and, since my early youth, devoted much time to his writings. Nevertheless I do not consider these advantages sufficient for a full perception of his work. It may easily be that others, not so close to him, show a far better understanding. I feel that my interpretation of Kafka, like any other, constitutes but a one-sided intellectual experiment. Kafka's greatness may be seen in the very fact that it lies within the power of any reader to attempt and to achieve his own deciphering of Kafka. Therefore it does not make much sense to play off one interpretation against the other, for all of them may be right.

One may compare Kafka's work with a very ingenious, intricate apparatus which produces astonishing results for hitherto undisclosed purposes. One feels the results are sublime and remarkable, the purposes important and significant, but still one lacks the adequate spiritual means to define them exactly. Thus one continues to interpret. This, of course, is bound to remain fragmentary and may even lead one astray. The privilege of

23

walking always on plain ground belongs to the very few. The others may be satisfied with occasionally reaching a glade.

Perhaps it would be useful if I set down some personal reminiscences of Kafka the man before discussing his works. Franz Kafka detested noise, and, although far from being phlegmatic, he never got excited. He was fond of understatement. Asked about his occupation, he never answered: "I am a writer," but always: "I work for an insurance company." His superiors thought well of his reports. They did not notice, of course, that those reports were ennobled by a unique prose style. Kafka merely intended to perform his duties satisfactorily. Occasionally, however, he compared the insurance business to the religion of primitive tribes who believe in the prevention of evil by means of various manipulations.

When, in 1912, his first book, *Betrachtung,* was published, he presented a copy to my wife with the significant dedication: "The advice, 'No flies will get into a closed mouth' [concluding words of *Carmen* by Merimée] has not yet been followed in this book. Therefore it is full of flies—best keep it always shut." Such was Kafka's comment on a work which marked a new phase in European prose. I remember an afternoon when Kafka talked to me about Flaubert and, as the strongest symptom of literary conscience, quoted Flaubert's remark about one of his novels just in the making: "This is not the way great works of art originate." In addition he mentioned Ibsen's *The Pretenders* where the poet is asked: "Are you always so sure that you really are a skald?" And, at the same time, there occurred to him some words from Goethe's Diary: "A few poems offered me the opportunity of trying whether there still remained something poetical in me." Goethe wrote these skeptical lines in 1812, long before many of his outstanding poetical works were even begun.

It was Goethe, whom Kafka admired so much, who coined the formula: "Let no one think himself capable of overcoming the first impressions of his childhood." This recognition was to become the foundation of a whole psychological school. Kafka's personality and work certainly testify to the correctness of this proposition. The rugged atmosphere in his paternal home, the threatening and depressing appearance of his bourgeois

24

father, were Kafka's heaviest mental burden throughout his whole life. His mind and work were deeply influenced by this unavoidable father-vision. He was unable to free himself of it, even though he wrote a hundred-page letter to his father, a document of utter frankness, an indictment of the tyrannical Father-God, an attempt at analysis, both militant and humble, of the fundamental conflicts between the two worlds of father and son.

Kafka is usually regarded as one of the outstanding and most peculiar German stylists. His style, however, was formed not only in the sphere of the German language, not only by the creative elements of Jewish ideology, but also by the Czech atmosphere in which he lived. He was born at Prague, in 1883, where he spent his childhood and youth, where he studied and worked, and where his best friends lived. Thus his style, from the beginning, was amalgamated with Slavonic elements. In my opinion, there is no doubt that Kafka's uncommon way of representation, his abundance of extraordinary metaphors, his allegorical and symbolical features owe much to the Czech forms of expression and to their particular realistic lyricism.

He looked at himself in a meditative, inquisitive, accusatory and judicial way; and you may safely say that all his writings are but the records of these procedures which he uninterruptedly instituted against himself. In those procedures, the whole world was at once the prosecutor, the juror, the witness, the advocate and the chorus-like public, and, in Kafka's person, the whole actual world in all its concerns, connections, developments, in all its multiplicity was brought to trial. His work consists of indictments, pleas, protocols, *corpora delicti* pertaining not only to Man but to God.

Once Kafka said to me: "To be a poet means to be strong in metaphors. The greatest poets were always the most metaphorical ones. They were those who recognized the deep mutual concern, yes, even the identity of things between which nobody noticed the slightest connection before. It is the range and the scope of the metaphor which make one a poet." You cannot, of course, be oblivious of the fact that every metaphor, by linking seemingly disparate subjects, is nothing but a religious or philosophical intuition of the unity of the world.

25

Is it surprising that this metaphysical and complicated mind favored the instinctive, pure and simple life and considered it a desirable and, so to speak, idyllic goal? The way, however, which leads to this simple life is like the way to *The Castle*. To attain this goal, far away from the cultured and refined strata of society, man has to undergo many initial tumults, has to make thousands of efforts of the most varied sorts. The contemplation of those manifold exertions astonishes and saddens one but, simultaneously, it provokes a smile. What, however, in man's multitudinous efforts to attain the pure and genuine life, is the moral turning point on which everything depends? It is the capacity for resolution, the ability to make up one's mind. No man knows beforehand when and how he is to reach this moral decision which pertains solely to him personally. Nobody else can reach it for him. Yet if he misses his decision he can nevermore make amends. His gate which had been kept open for no one but him will be locked and the Gatekeeper who had waited long to admit him disappears ("Before the Law"). Kafka addresses all his reproofs to himself, punishes himself, smiles at himself, weeps for himself, seeks by his work to atone for himself. It is precisely thus that he serves mankind, too. In the ethical bent of his thought and the wide sweep of his convictions one perceives an optimistic conception: the belief in man's goodness, in the possibility of his redemption, in the moral importance of his participation in his own destiny. Only superficial readers can accuse Kafka of artistic decadence. In fact, I do not know any other author who so scrupulously avoids valuing anything at zero.

Kafka was not a "poet" in the usual sense. No lyric line ever came from his pen; but throughout his works one is conscious of the imaginative rhythmic power of a poet. Nor is he an author in the sense of the "Grands Ecrivains" who conceive vast closely-knit literary edifices. Even in his extensive novels (*The Trial, The Castle, Amerika*) just as in his shorter prose works (collected under the titles *Meditation, The Country Doctor, The Hunger-Artist*) as well as in the stories "The Metamorphosis," "The Judgment," and "The Penal Colony" Kafka impresses one as a kind of aphorist. Yet he unquestionably ranks with the greatest figures in the narrative literature of the world. Again, he is no philosopher in the technical sense nor are we able to deduce any system of thought from his life work. Nevertheless, scarcely anywhere in recent literature can one find so much philosophical thought, such comprehension of psychology and ethics. Thus Kafka's prose works form a category of their own. He cannot be ranged and classified within any definite group of authors. Perhaps that is why he is in such high repute.

The look in Kafka's eyes was always a little puzzled, full of the wisdom of children and of melancholy slightly counterpointed by an enigmatic smile. He always seemed to be somewhat embarrassed. He did not belong to the people who have a retort in store at all times. It was impossible to salute him first in the street; he always forestalled it by one second. His whole person was like his prose: quiet, gradual, serene, free from adjuncts, difficult to comprehend sometimes, not always easy to manage, a task to his lovers, a problem to his admirers, seemingly simple, but certainly pure and, at the same time, so deep that in consequence of this indescribable purity one could never distinctly recognize how deep, in fact, one was looking.

recollections

oskar baum

Social problems like social poets are not peculiar to our own day and age. We all know that. Every really great thinker and creator of art in the past had moments of clear vision into the injustice and misery that oppresses the masses. So, too, the work of Franz Kafka, who more than anyone else sensed the desperate helplessness of the present-day world and gave prophetic expression to it in the inspired visions of his fear-dreams, is deeply rooted not only in his personal destiny but also in the social misery of his time.

Kafka was an employee of a government bureau which dealt with workmen's accident insurance. The documents in his department on which he did more or less mechanical labor surrounded him constantly and directly with the workers' suffering,

> "which is enlarged to virtually fantastic dimensions by the Taylor System and the 'conveyor belt.' How can it be endured at all? Perhaps all of us are only dreaming that it is being endured, this almost inconceivable suffering, for in reality we all know that it exceeds the limits of human endurance and (which in this case un-

fortunately amounts to the same thing) of human humiliation. . . ."

Kafka's social feelings were deeply aroused when he saw the mutilations which the workers suffered as a result of inadequate safety measures. "How modest these people are!" he once said to Brod with wide-open eyes. "They come to us and plead. Instead of storming this institution and smashing everything to bits, they come to us and plead."

Franz Kafka was pinned in between his despised profession, which in no way accorded with his capabilities and inclinations, and the overwhelming inspirational flood of his creative genius, which he was compelled to resist. The time and energy which remained to his delicate body, after his office duties, were so inadequate for his passionate and conscientious creative fantasy that this dilemma alone was bound to wear him down. Hence the exacerbating, disconsolate battle of his unique talent for natural opportunities of development, his striving for inward and outward freedom and purity.

Franz Kafka's financial situation was unfavorable, especially since he would not have recourse to the help of his parents (out of pride) nor would he prostitute his literary gift. Was a social and political order conceivable, consciously or in dreams, in which a man with so unique a literary talent would not be doomed to pencil-pushing and wide-eyed despair at the thought of the marriage he desired and the concomitant responsibility to a wife and children?

Max Brod's biography of Kafka, written by the poet's most intimate friend with sympathetic understanding and with a conscientious effort at objectivity—a biography with soft overtones of autobiography—is a poetic work of rare perfection and power of thought. Brod was especially eager to refute the widespread view that Kafka was a melancholy man, who had turned his back upon the world, and was hounded by lugubrious dreams and bizarre fantasies. Precisely the opposite was the case: no one who did not intimately know him and the tragic situation of his soul would have suspected anything of the sort in his indescribably charming character, which, to be sure, was often

29

quiet, but was always inspiring and inspired in the animated joy of receiving.

His graceful manner of expression and self-evident originality in every casual remark as well as in the most serious passages of his major works revealed that keynote of divine good humor which was independent of every situation and which is noticeable even in the translucent irony of his phantasmagorias. His kindliness and readiness for sympathetic consideration of even the most insignificant human being around him could appear cruel on occasion, to an unworthy observer, because it was not a conventional good-naturedness but something deeper. This kindliness was not pleasure or quiescence in the accidental present form of life, but an ethical and physical discipline, if necessary, if not so much called for, but suggested even stern self-denial—painful reorientation—as the almost self-evident, the most meaningful course of action. He even laughed often and easily, especially in discussions of striking facts or people and, when reading aloud, at startling oddities of the text. He even laughed very often instead of criticizing; it was a mixture of wonderment and worldly-wise knowledge of universal frailty, an uncommon, though not unreserved amiability, always ready with advice and help, whenever it accorded with his strict candor. The happiness of his last year in Berlin, its fulfillment of love and independence, creative work and publications, its letters filled with humor, prove that he was by no means inaccessible to the joys of life and the world.

Kafka's relationship with his father, this fateful dominant note of the development of his soul, is compared by Brod (this is an original deepening of the problem) with the family complex of Proust—these two contemporaries, who did not know each other, show many similarities of destiny and work—and of Kleist, whom Kafka admired so much. It is a sign of a more serious and more profound attitude toward the battle of self-assertion when a human being who is uncommonly conscious of his responsibilities takes issue from the very beginning with the opposition forces he encounters as a child and engages his first opponent in a life-long battle.

The story of this life reads like a moving, thoughtful

poetic work. His relations with the world, with his friends, the richly varying stages of his self-doubt, especially in the five years of his first engagement, the break-through of his artistic creative power, and the relation of his works to his personal life—all this is clearly portrayed by Brod with constant reference to entries in Kafka's diaries, and against the background of his uncompromising attitudes toward artistic, ethical, and religious questions, in which latter Kafka for a long time came very close to the viewpoint of the aged Tolstoy.

The lot of loneliness and the struggle to become a part of the community constitute the central problem which runs through all his works, the futile struggle of a man who strives honestly and indefatigably but is coolly rejected as an outsider by that close-knit organization society, and is stigmatized and pursued by a mysterious guilt which he himself cannot identify.

But Kafka's world of ideas is not founded upon a world-view of inescapable despair, as many assume. Even in the most cruel vision of the hopelessly tangled, endless jungle of human aberrations, in the eternally futile search for the right way, the existence of this right way nevertheless is an immutable certainty; and the wondrous, uncanny suspense in these narratives lies in good part in the fact that just one flash of correct insight, of the right application of will, would open the way. As Brod puts it significantly, we are constantly "one instant in advance of the creation of the world."

o o o

My own first meeting with Kafka, which Brod had arranged, still stands out clearly in my memory. On that autumn afternoon of the year 1904, when we were little more than twenty years old, Kafka read to us his just-finished novel *Excursions into the Dark-Red* (*Ausflüge ins Dunkelrote*). Of the enthusiastic exchange of ideas into which we were led by the problems of the story, I still remember Kafka's remark: "The temptation to distract attention from the plot by means of tricks of style is greatest when the need is least."

Kafka's first gesture upon being introduced to me by Brod left a deep impression upon me: though he knew he was in

31

the presence of a blind man, still he bowed silently, a senseless formality, one would think, toward a man unable to see it, but as I bowed his smoothly combed hair touched my forehead, perhaps because I had bowed rather deeply, producing in me an indefinable emotion. Here was the first person I had ever met who treated my defect as something that concerned only me, requiring no adjustment on his part, or special consideration, or the slightest change in his conduct.

That was the way he was. That was the way his cool, austere aloofness, in its deep humanity, surpassed the usual manifestations of friendliness on the part of people being introduced to me: a needlessly exaggerated warmth of speech, of intonation and handshaking.

Kafka had a way of fitting every involuntary gesture, every common word into his very personal view of the world—in spite of the abstract conflicts which continually dominated his mind—which made his behavior and outward appearance extraordinarily individual. When he read aloud—this was his special passion—the enunciation of each separate word, in spite of the utter precision of each sound and the sometimes dizzying speed, became completely subordinated to a broad musical flow of phrases, phrases of long breath and dynamic crescendi. These crescendi were also part of his prose; the finished pieces, as for example "The Bareback Rider" (*Die Zirkusreiterin*), sometimes have the miraculous structure of *one* sentence.

The exceptional position of Franz Kafka and his literary work in our contemporary life can be explained, but only he who has experienced the profound natural agreement that existed between his shortest remarks, his words, his intonation and the action and physiognomy of the characters in his tales—he alone can understand to some extent the anguish of his creative mind.

I remember when Kafka was working on a philosophical drama—a drama which nobody was ever to read. It was to be called "The Cave" (*Die Grotte*) or "The Tomb" (*Die Gruft*) and, judging from hints which he sometimes gave unintentionally when joy over his work loosened his tongue, it was to take place among shepherds and shepherdesses before the entrance to open tombs: a struggle against and for death, a serene play of emotions combating one another both in their force and in their sweetness. One is ashamed of death as of something almost inappropriate and indecent, for it is regarded as a punishment; yet it is impossible to learn for what kind of sin the death sentence is pronounced, for indeed other punishments are also meted out. If young people become guilty of death, they regard it as being particularly shameful. The reverence for old people stems from the fact that they have been alive for so long and still have not deserved death. Yet the idea that nobody ever *does* deserve it, occurs to no one; but it is certain that always to be on one's guard against it, always to think only of how not to sin is the worst and most dangerous sin.

He never revealed anything about the action of the drama. He only told how, during the time he wrote it, he always, after work, in utter bliss quasi-floated down the endless row of steps that led from the Alchemists Lane to the Klaarplatz. There he used to pass by a bookstore where a new Shakespeare edition was on display. The beginning of *Hamlet* was exhibited as sample pages. And there, every day, he read the discourses of Horatio and his friends down to the line which the book below it hid from view. He racked his brains to remember how it went on; he would have given anything to know; he searched his memory, it tormented him to reconstruct this ideal of a dramatic speech— but, to reach up to his bookshelves at home? No, no! That would indeed have spoiled any possibility of reflecting on this passage.

When the play was completed he refused to read aloud from it. We knew from several previous works what it meant when *he* declared a work to be a failure. He repulsed our most fervent, shrewdest and roughest attacks. "The only non-amateur quality the play possesses is the fact that I won't read it to you," he said. It probably was among the great pile of manuscripts he slowly threw into the fire, one after another, before leaving Berlin for the place where he was to die.

At the time when this work was being written he had three apartments. He, who was such a fresh-air fiend, chose for his work one of those low, narrow, dwarf houses of only one room in which, according to tradition, the alchemists of the Emperor Rudolph had lived. The stove smoked, but here it was absolutely quiet: complete solitude. For sleeping he rented an extremely high, airy and hall-like room with enormous windows, belonging to an old palace of the nobility, which, however, no stove in the world could have heated in winter. For the inevitable routine of life, for meals and social intercourse, a room in his parents' apartment served. This very strict division was beneficial to his work, but it cost him his health.

Early in 1918 I spent a week with him in Zürau, at that time a deeply snowed-in village near Saaz, where his courageous sister managed a farm. During the long nights, which we often spent in conversation, I learned more about him than in the previous ten years or in the subsequent five. Perhaps in the future I may succeed in giving a connected account of his state of soul at that time, which was bitter and indifferent to life.

Of the many sketches and plans about which he spoke to me during those nights—without any hope or even intention of ever executing them—I should like only to give the outline of a little fantastic story: A man wants to create the possibility of arranging a soirée, which assembles without anyone ever having been invited. People see, converse with and observe one another, without knowing each other. It is a dinner for guests, each of whom may choose for himself according to his own tastes and without disturbing anyone else. One can appear and again disappear whenever he pleases, one has no obligations towards a host and yet, without hypocrisy, one is always welcome. When in the end this bizarre plan is successfully executed, the reader realizes that this attempt at overcoming solitude has only produced—the inventor of the first café.

Translated by H. Lenz and Annelore Stern.

recollections

ludwig hardt

The last time I saw Franz Kafka, about a year before his death, he was grievously ill. When I suggested that he join me on a trip to Italy, he gave me as a parting gift a description of Siberia which he happened to be reading, with the inscription: "To prepare you for our trip to Italy."

Could there be any gentler way of pointing out the hopelessness of plans? Does not one feel the scar of his smile in this inscription? This smile of his may well have been a mask thrown over his inner depths—and not in the presence of strangers alone. It was an invitation to approach more closely, and at the same time a smile that came from his heart, one which was intended in passing to release him from himself and lend him an almost commonplace insignificance. What a release was there! To silence the driving spirit within him with a roguish wink, and still to preserve a pleasant outward countenance in the process! What a feeling of well-being his presence gave!

There was, for example, the little hunchbacked servant-girl who was his housekeeper when he used to work on his great novels in a small house in the Alchemists' Lane, in Prague. Of Franz Kafka the poet she was as little aware as anyone. Nevertheless, she respected him as a person to such a degree that she collected every little scrap of paper that bore his hand, and could not be moved for anything in the world to give up a single one of them, notwithstanding her needy circumstances and the considerable sum she was offered. These little scraps of paper bore in each case some friendly or jocular phrase with which Kafka accompanied his wishes with regard to the housekeeping. "I slept in my easy chair tonight; don't think for a moment I made my bed myself!" one of them goes, in Czech (the girl understood no German). He had, as a matter of fact, spent the whole night writing.

This sort of shyness is revealed, too, in the soft answers he was capable of giving. I went to his office once to find him; he was not in, and only his hat lay on the table. When he entered, I told him his hat had substituted for him quite adequately. Kafka's laughter was something to hear—laughter in which his skeptical estimate of his accomplishment as a petty official played only too plain a part. And then, when I let slip the question why he, a writer, should have to work as a petty official, he replied: "I think the director likes me."

At this point I should like to repeat a remark made by Kafka, which Brod tells in different form in his biography, because there this episode is not rendered correctly, and because it reveals Kafka's whole personality. He was a vegetarian by conviction, but on medical advice he had to eat meat again. Because of this he suffered an attack of fish poisoning; he must have been happy that he again was permitted to become a vegetarian. At this time he visited the Berlin aquarium. There he stepped close to one of the tanks and said softly to the fish: "Now I can look into your eyes with a clear conscience." St. Francis Kafka could not suspect that his companion overheard this remark—I ask his forgiveness that the world now learns what was intended exclusively for the fish!

"*Familien koennen nicht mehr zu Gott.*" There is perhaps no man on earth who has felt this line of Rilke's with greater depth and despair than Kafka. Once when I sat beside his sickbed reciting to him poems of Matthias Claudius, Kafka said: "Yes, if one could only be like him!" And in truth, Franz Kafka had much in common with this pious poet. The most stirring aspect of his genius still consists, however, in the fact that it rests on a foundation of modesty, of uprightness, of heartfelt sympathy, of naïveté, even of primitiveness—qualities which come very close to a piety of that sort, very nearly correspond to it, even though they may long remain hidden from a world which much prefers to engage in guessing games over the almost inexhaustible possibilities of interpretations of which Kafka's works are susceptible. The world nevertheless may surely do just that, if it would be forcibly reminded in all this that except for these properties his works would not be available in all their untrammeled purity and truth.

"I wish to thank you for these hours which made my heart beat faster," the poet wrote to me after an evening of recitations during which he heard me for the first time (although I had been giving selections from his works for years). This was in 1919, at the "Mozarteum" in Prague. The program included prose selections from Kleist, Johann Peter Hebel, Robert Walser and Franz Kafka. The first three were favorites of Kafka, as I well knew. Kafka was in the audience, so that I met him in person that evening for the first time. He confessed to me that he had been amused at the ironic solemnity with which I had clothed Robert Walser's lines: "Even if you do see the cashier eating bread or bologna, you needn't turn away in disgust; just remind yourself at once that it is supper which you see being eaten." I had actually pronounced the word *supper* (*Abendbrot*) as though it had been the word for *sunset* (*Abendrot*). He then added: "I've written something like that, too. The father speaking of one of his 'Eleven Sons,' says it is a delight to see him in a fencing pose, because in *delight* (*entzueckt*) appears unmistakably the *drawing* (*das Zuecken*) of the sword." When, after Kafka's death, I told this to his sister Ottla, she declared, "That isn't true! You've made that up!" When I still insisted on the truth of the incident, she said: "Forgive me, but it was just too incredible for me to believe. My brother never in his life quoted anything from his works by way of comparison. That was entirely contrary to his nature. If he made such an exception in your case, he must have been very fond of you."

37

This doubt on the part of his sister will appear understandable to anyone who recalls the following event: When Kafka was in the Hohen Tatra Mountains seeking a cure for his illness, there was a Doctor K—— who used to lie beside him. After they had encountered each other every day for many weeks, the latter inquired: "Tell me, aren't you the Franz Kafka who wrote 'The Country Doctor'?" Whereupon Kafka, shrinking into himself a little, turned mournfully aside, clasped his hands in despair and whispered: "On top of everything—this!"

It will be understood, from the foregoing, that he did not like to hear his works discussed. Nor did I therefore—though I sometimes bitterly regret it now—out of deference to this sentiment, ever ask him any question on this point. (How he would laugh and shake his head if he were to see a good forty authors in this "faraway part of the earth" pounce on him simultaneously! For "pouncing" is certainly what he would call it—on a defenceless man, he would probably add in that way of his.)

I am sure, then, that he would not have liked me to recite his works. Recitation to him probably smacked too much of an attempt at persuading, and persuasion was the very thing that was neither intended nor desired on the part of the poet. I hope he will forgive me for having done so regardless, from sheer compulsion and pure delight at an epic which holds grace in every word, at the great pure breathings of a prose wherein, beneath the serene surface motion, tormenting dreams move about in unfathomable depths and in a mysterious kind of order; wherein conundrums of lofty import are mirrored in the crystal of their own insolubility; and wherein the conscience sobs amid images and shapes of profound and distinct strangeness.

Opposed as he may inwardly have remained to my efforts to introduce to the world his then completely unknown works, his engaging friendliness appeared in other ways. The morning after our first meeting, he brought me an edition of Hebel's *Schatzkaestlein* which he used as a child; and when I asked him for a short dedication, the master-poet, without pausing to think, wrote at once: "For Ludwig Hardt, as a favor to Hebel." As jocular as these words may sound, are they not at the same time a high distinction? With these words he made me a brother of poets—the greatest honor to be awarded a reciting artist—and thus a brother of Franz Kafka, swearing fidelity to him and his works.

Will he take in this solemn vow with a smile? Or will he, pointing to his own breast with a hand that no longer trembles, repeat the phrase he once wrote for me: "The old law seems to be borne out, that we are all glad to help him who is beyond redemption"? In that case, I should like to reply to him with a poet's phrase which might well stand as a motto over the mighty edifice which bears his name:

Who talks of Victory?
To endure's the thing!

Translated by Christian D. Meyer.

Postcard sent Feb. 17, 1922, from the Bohemian resort Spindel-muhle. On it, Kafka thanks John Urzidil for Karl Brand's book of poems and alludes to Tolstoy's Death *of Ivan Ilyitch*

Kafka's last photograph, a few months before his death

recollections

franz werfel

A quarter of a century ago, when I met Franz Kafka for the first time, I knew instantly that he was "a messenger of the king." This feeling was always with me in his presence. My veneration and love for him was always accompanied by a strange awe. The others enjoyed at that time with esthetic delight his so-called originality—if I remember correctly, he was then giving readings of "The Metamorphosis"—I, however, felt instinctively that he was not so much a human being, as one to whose share had fallen, in a tragic way, too much of that which is beyond nature. Franz Kafka was a messenger from above, a great chosen one, and only the circumstances of our epoch led him to express his knowledge of yonder and his inexplicable experiences in the form of poetical parables. I have always remained conscious of this distance between him and me, for I am only a poet.

[Letter to Robert Klopstock, December 2, 1934]

Translated by Lienhard Bergel.

43

the human voyage

max lerner

Genius, wherever it crops up, is a strange and solitary plant; nor have we in literature had so many instances of it that we can afford to neglect one as authentic as Franz Kafka. There was about his genius a lonely and almost nihilist quality. It seems to have come from nowhere, to belong to nothing, even perhaps to lead to nothing. Kafka is part neither of the humanist nor the anti-humanist tradition into which we have come increasingly to divide the recent intellectual history of Europe. Yet unmistakably his books have left a scar upon our consciousness.

During his lifetime Kafka made no great noise in the world. He never sought recognition and never received it. He was born in 1883 of a Jewish tradesman's family of Prague. He grew up, sensitive and unhappy, in the shadow of his father's dominant personality. The memory of that (as we learn from his famous "Letter to My Father") and the sense of inadequacy that went with it, were to haunt and cripple him for life—make him set impossibly high standards for himself, make him reluctant ever to call a piece of work finished or to surrender a manuscript for publication, obsess him (as Thomas Wolfe was later to be ob-

45

sessed) with the search for a father and for justification before him. He studied law and became a functionary of the Austrian bureaucracy, in the workmen's compensation division. Here in an office he spent his days; his evenings he spent with the writing which he loved so and which so tortured him. He joined no movements, whether literary or political, and seemed more absorbed with the tempestuous voyage of the human spirit than with the turbulence of Europe in its chaotic war and post-war phases.

The last years of his life were broken by sickness and the search for health. His relations with women were troubled: he never married; twice he broke off his engagement; and only at the close of his life did he find some peace in such a relation. He died in 1924, at 41, of tuberculosis, leaving instructions (fortunately unfulfilled) that his manuscript writings be burned.

Since his death Kafka has become a force in our writing. Yet everywhere his influence has been confined to the smallish literary groups and their magazines. Talk of him there and you get as response the subterranean intensity of the early Christian fathers, wrapped often in incommunicable symbols. This catacomb Kafka is not healthy: it means the blocking of the channel that might connect him with the large body of potential readers; it means also that those who are left are forced often into uncritical acceptance and elaborate commentary—the cult and the canon.

For that reason the publication of American editions of his three major works was something of an event. Kafka published during his lifetime some stories and sketches comprising one of the six volumes of his collected works in German. The rest appeared posthumously under the ministering hand of his friend and executor, Max Brod. The three great novels fill three of the other five volumes. The remaining two contain further short stories (Kafka was a master of the short story in a form almost wholly alien to the Anglo-French-American tradition), parables, *pensées*, journals, letters.

Kafka is a philosophical and religious novelist. I mean this in a central and not marginal sense. He is not a novelist who happens to be dealing with these themes or, as Muir points out,

46

chooses to use religious characters. Kafka was absorbed with certain problems from an angle which made it impossible for him to treat them except through fiction, allegory, parable. He was a philosopher groping for a form rather than a novelist groping for a theme. It is fairly clear that the writing of these novels was, as their reading may be, an act of religious exploration. I use the term religion, of course, not in the sense of an institutional creed or a body of received dogma, but of a system of personal belief transcending experience—the sense that Carlyle meant when he said that the most important thing about a man was his religion.

But while the themes are grand themes, Kafka does not assault them in a magisterial way. He approaches them indirectly, through stories that for all their oppressive nightmare quality and their overtones of allegory, wear an aspect of innocence. *Amerika,* for example, is in form almost a picaresque novel —a twentieth century *Roderick Random.* It seems to be only a loose episodic narrative of what happens to Karl Rossman, a German boy of sixteen, when he sets out to make his career in America—his meeting on shipboard with a stoker, his adoption and abandonment by a rich uncle, his adventures in a country house, his career as lift-boy in a hotel, the misfortunes that befell him through two rascally knights of the road who later settled down in a ménage with a fabulous mistress, his employment by the "Nature Theater of Oklahoma." *The Trial,* less loosely wrought, is the story of Joseph K., who finds himself accused of a crime he did not commit and the nature of which he cannot even discover. He tries to get a hearing, deal with an advocate, find allies, reach the higher judges. He never succeeds. But he gets a warning of his sentence from a sermon preached in a cathedral to himself as a one-man audience; and in the end he is stabbed to death by two officials of the court.

The protagonist of *The Castle,* K. (note the progressive attenuation of name), comes to the village thinking he has a summons from the castle as surveyor. But he receives from the castle only denial or evasion. He spends his energy on successive stratagems and devices for getting near the officials of the castle, particularly one called Klamm. There are adventures with women, with village inhabitants and castle retainers, with K.'s two assistants; there is a harrowing story within a story; there is a comic note of high diplomacy in the alliances and alignments K. seeks to form in order to get even the smallest foothold in the village. In the end, Max Brod tells us, Kafka planned to have K. wear himself out in his efforts; but as he lies dying, a messenger arrives from the castle to say he can stay in the village on temporary sufferance.

Many a critic has tried his hand at interpreting the allegory. I don't intend to do that here. But some things may be said summarily. Kafka is dealing with the largest themes of the fate of man in a world whose meaning stretches beyond his experience. His starting-point is the inadequacy of the empirical and the rational. The purpose of life becomes thus an endless quest for the meaning of life. This quest, whatever its form, is always a search for an organic relation with something beyond ourselves. It may be, as in *Amerika*, only Karl's desire after his expulsion from the old world (he had been seduced in Germany by a servant-girl) to find roots in a new world—a job, a career, a home, independence—and thus fulfill himself. It may be, as in the cathedral scene in *The Trial*, a desire to find what lies beyond the door of our unique personality. Joseph K., dissatisfied with the rational routine of his life, was "accused"—a marked man. He haunted the court where lay his fate, yet he could make no connection with it. K., in *The Castle*, also wanders beyond his accustomed locus; he wants a connection with Klamm, even of the slightest and humblest. Even the agonizing rebuffs he receives do not make him think of retreat. His search for roots in the village, for a place near the castle, seems to come from a fatal inner necessity.

But with the sureness of the necessity there is also the sureness of failure—absolute failure in *The Trial*, failure relieved in *The Castle* only by the grimly ironic concession at the end. The quest must continue, but the one certain thing about it is the massive inaccessibility of the goal. I do not believe, as some of his critics say, that Kafka was content with this; that he resolved it with the old liberal cliché of Goethe and Tennyson that meaning lay in process rather than in end, in the search for the Grail rather than the Grail itself. Kafka was bitter. And anyone

48

who does not read his bitterness in his novels and stories misses, I think, half their quality. But the paradox from which grew bitterness yielded by the same token inexhaustible material for a sort of cosmic comedy. I have already mentioned the attempt to reach God by power-politics. Kafka's attitude toward God was that of the Greeks who constructed an entire theogony but kept them with human frailties. Klamm, the chief man of the castle, looks like a paunchy bourgeois and has barmaids as mistresses. The court officials in *The Trial* are old, wheezy, and generally decrepit; the attendants are lecherous and sadistic. The whole theme of bureaucracy as part of the cosmic is a persistent one in Kafka, no doubt because of his own experience in Austrian administrative officialdom. On shipboard, in the hotel, in the "nature theater" (although this is a genial and careless bureaucracy), in courtroom, village, and castle, red tape is king. Man is caught in a mechanism not of his own contriving—a mechanism, moreover, whose operations are gallingly slow, inefficient and even accidental. In fact, by a wild irony in this regime of order and law, it is accident that is decisive. Despite the oppressive anxiety of Kafka's protagonist to fulfill his quest and come to terms with his universe, despite his desperate straining to make even the slightest headway, he is hopelessly entangled in a network of casual incidents. The most irrelevant act may lead to the widest consequences; the trivial is canonized.

This is, of course, the stuff of dreams: and the most obvious thing about the Kafka world is that it is a dream world. There hangs over it the heavy blanket of anxiety that we know from our own dream existence. Will the protagonist make it? Will he, after roaming through corridor after corridor, find his way off the ship?—the passage that leads back to the living room of the country house?—the key that opens the door of escape from Brunelda's apartment?—the door, among all the myriad doors of the tenement house, that leads to the courtroom?—the way out of the cathedral before his name is called and the sermon starts? —the path in the snow that leads back to the inn before night falls? This nightmare world has also its comic aspect, and there is a Chaplinesque music-hall quality to Kafka that has several times been noted. But the other aspects are more persistent. As in a dream, events follow each other with the phantasmal logic of illogic. Granted the premises, the details have a certain cogency: but the premises are outrageous. Time plays tricks: K. starts out in the morning from the inn toward the castle; in a few hours, night comes and it is dark. Space plays tricks; the more K. presses toward the castle, the farther away it seems to get. There are changes of identity. In fact the whole Kafka universe seems to illustrate the principle of discontinuity. You go from A to C without having passed through B.

The uncertainty is underscored because Kafka's protagonist moves throughout in an atmosphere of intrigue and conspiracy. There is a crazy quilt of plot and counterplot, but with a wild subjectivism in it all: the dangers and malignancies that beset the path of Kafka's protagonists you see only through their own eyes. Kafka means you to see that subjectivism. In *The Trial*, for example, although Joseph K. is under arrest, he is not under detention. He is out on a sort of psychic bail, goes about his daily tasks in the bank and reports to court only from an inner necessity. And yet his world, like the world of K. and Karl Rossman, is none the less full of enemies and obstacles, like that of a savage in the jungle of his fears. In fact, the most important thing is that the enemy is never localized, and enemy and goal are one. The castle and the court are not only inaccessible; they carry on in their own remote and complicated way a campaign not to be reached. And the very allies that Kafka's protagonists hope to use in attaining their goal turn out to wear the badge of the enemy-goal. One gets a hint of Emerson's Brahma: "When me they fly, I am the wings"—except that this is pursuit rather than flight. What we seek with is part of what we seek. What we fight with is part of what we fight.

This sense of being implicated in a dualistic world is a strong sense in Kafka. It is to me even stronger than the feeling of the alienation of the individual from his world which the critics have tended to stress. Loneliness is the great fact of our mechanized life and has become one of the great themes of our literature; yet it will not do to see Kafka as a Sherwood Anderson writing another *Winesburg*, no matter how cosmic. Kafka's protagonists are not lonely because their social system is deadening:

they are lonely because they are caught midway between a good and evil whose contradiction there is no way of resolving, although each is part of the other. Max Brod has pointed out that Kafka was not tender-minded enough to think there is a synthesis for this polarity. His God is like the Jehovah god of the Jewish tradition, at once terrible and desirable.

Kafka's religion is thus far from the religion of consolation. He offers no cheap and easy endings, no safe harbor for the human voyage. It is rather a religion of unending exploration. It is to be sure, heavily laden with a sense of guilt and a sense of determinism, both of which go back to the tragic Greek conceptions. The scene in *The Trial* in which the executioners come for Joseph K. and find him waiting for them and link their arms in his, moves swiftly and with a sure fatality. Yet this is not characteristic. More so are the scenes in *The Castle* in which K. holds his intricate and casuistical conversations with Olga and with the various functionaries on how things work in the castle. It has often been pointed out that Kafka was influenced by the Chassidic movement, and there is throughout the books that feeling for the folk-mind and its inherent symbolism which characterized the Chassidic revolt against theological hair-splitting. And yet there is also an enormous amount of hair-splitting in the unwearying discussions in Kafka of the ways of God to man. Kafka was God-drunk; but in his intoxication his subtle and powerful intellect did not stop working.

It seems curious that a writer with preoccupations of this sort should be today one of the great influences in our literature. The reason lies, I think, in the state of that literature. We seem to have come to a dead end. Among the younger writers the emphasis has been social, the method realistic. And Kafka challenges both. He goes beyond the problem of man facing his society to the problem of man facing himself and the unknown and inaccessible within him. He belongs thus in a sense to the tradition which, in Freud's words, has sought to explore the "psychology of the depths." Yet always in his own way. For his is not the emphasis upon the irrational which is true of the Freudian group. What he has done has been to give the tradition of rationalism a new twist so radical as to transform it. Since the

51

seventeenth century our thinkers believed that to suppress the barbarian in man and thus make civil society possible, men must enter into a "social contract"—a compact with each other to preserve the fabric of civilization, and make law and order possible.

But for Kafka social constructions and even social reconstruction are not enough. His protagonists are seeking always not a compact with man but a compact with God. Hence it is not surprising that, as I have mentioned, so many of the speeches in Kafka seem exercises in ratiocination. Compacts are legalistic affairs, and Kafka's characters want to get their precise bearings in the universal frame of things. Yet whatever their mode of speech, what they are driving at—and what Kafka is concerned with—lies beyond rational and irrational, in the realm of the non-rational.

Similarly with Kafka's method. Realism as a method has been run to the ground. While I do not agree with MacLeish and Van Wyck Brooks that literature must nourish national morale, I do agree with Philip Rahv that the cult of experience in our literature has worn thin. What Kafka does is to stand realism on its head. He understands that the fictive world must somehow be made real, and that this depends upon great particularity of detail. But he applies this precision of method to a world of his own creating which has no correspondences to the world of our daily experience. Kafka has often been spoken of as an "abstract" writer. But that is to miss the whole point. He does not see his truth, as the abstract artists do, by generalizations and geometrical abstractions. He is nothing if not concrete. He loved Dickens, and there is something of Dickens in him. His people are so highly individualized as often to reach the comic.

This combination—realism of detail within a framework of symbolism—is Kafka's peculiar gift to fiction. The American tradition contains nothing quite like it, and even for distant resemblances we must go back to Melville's *Moby Dick* with its allegory of evil, and to Hawthorne. One may answer that most good writing today has overtones of symbolism. And that is true, even in the naturalistic fiction of Steinbeck, whose tortoise crawling across the road in *The Grapes of Wrath* is not only a tortoise but the whole mass of plain people. But there is a distinction between a novel with symbolic overtones and a novel whose essential material is symbolism. Or perhaps it is better to say that Kafka writes on several planes at once, and the planes are interconnected. One plane is that of real people doing and saying workaday things but in a dream world; the second plane is that of symbols and of the allegorical framework that furnishes a logic for the otherwise illogical actions of the people; the third plane is that of the philosophical and religious implications of people and symbols together.

It is this genuine complexity of Kafka and the enormous earnestness of his meaning that keeps his art from becoming —what much expressionist art has tended to be—an escape from the ugliness of social reality. Not that Kafka was much of a social thinker. I can agree with Harry Slochower that there are some acute insights into the nature of the social hierarchy in Kafka, but I cannot agree that they go much beyond isolated insights. It is the complex and the non-rational and symbolic in Kafka's vision that have so deeply influenced the younger writers, including Rex Warner, Dylan Thomas, W. H. Auden in his most recent phase, and the *New Directions* group. To many perhaps Kafka will prove a good escape from the current social weariness; to many he will offer what Spengler so uncannily foresaw in his term "the second religiousness." Kafkism is not in its inherent nature any sort of ivory towerism. It is not art for art's sake. It goes beyond the social but it remains within the problematic; and the problems of human belief and human destiny that it plots out are as worthy of exploration as almost any in our time. A book, Kafka wrote in one of his aphorisms, must be the ax that breaks the frozen sea within us. For the younger American writers he may himself prove to be that ax.

k.'s quest

w. h. auden

The full length novels of Kafka belong to one of the oldest literary genres, The Quest, and it may not be unfruitful, perhaps, to approach his work by comparing it with some earlier examples of this genre. For instance, what has been, at different times, the object of quest, and who has been its hero?

THE FAIRY STORY

The goal in the fairy story is either some sacred object which endows its possessor with magical powers, e.g., the Water of Life, The Golden Fleece, or marriage with a beautiful princess, or both, i.e., the acquisition of the object is the condition for marriage. The object has usually fallen into the wrong hands, having been stolen by some giant, or dragon, or witch who uses its powers for evil ends, for selfish aggrandizement of his or her own power. The rescue of the magical object, the marriage with the princess (who is often bewitched till she is cured by marriage) are of benefit, not only to the hero himself, but to society as a whole; as long as the magical object is in the wrong hands, the crops will not grow, the people are unhappy and their future is dark, for there is no heir to the throne. When the hero succeeds, not only he and the princess, but the whole country can live happily ever after.

There are a number of young men who set out on the quest and all but one of them fail, and the cost of failure is death. The successful one, the hero, is usually the last person one would have suspected, i.e., he appears to be no one in particular, to be less gifted than his unsuccessful rivals. He succeeds, firstly because, knowing that he is less gifted, he is willing to accept help from the humblest creature, the ant, the bird, etc., while his better endowed rivals believe that they can succeed by their own gifts alone, when as a matter of fact no human being, however gifted, could succeed without help; and secondly he succeeds because he is willing to risk failure to answer the call for help, to give away his last penny to the beggar who it would seem could not possibly assist him, yet, as it turns out, is precisely the one who can.

THE HOLY GRAIL

There is still a sacred object, the Hallows, but it has not been stolen by evil powers, it has been lost by sin. It cannot be owned, it can only be worshipped; although it is supernatural, it bestows no magical powers; to be permitted to behold it is the only reward. In theory anyone could discover it who led a life free from sin, though he could never bring it back to show to those who are sinful. In practice, to lead a sinless life is impossible without the supernatural gift of grace, and the Grail is attained by the predestined knight, Sir Galahad.

The temptations of the fairy story hero were to refuse to help others when to do so looked like delaying or even abandoning his final goal; the temptations of the Grail knight are to forget his goal for the sake of immediate pleasure or to accept what appear to be offers of help, but are really hindrances.

THE DREAM QUEST (e.g., *The Divine Comedy*)

The purpose of the journey is no object but spiritual knowledge, a vision of the reality behind appearances, while the dreamer when he wakes can henceforth live his life on earth.

56

The dreamer is, theoretically, everyman; i.e., it is not by any act or virtue of his that he attains this vision, for the vision is a gift of Divine Grace. It does not necessarily follow that the vision will change his life, but if he does not change, his responsibility is greater than that of those who have never been granted his vision.

PILGRIM'S PROGRESS

The journey is no longer a special journey within life, like the quest for the Grail or the Dream Journey, but earthly life itself from birth to death. The goal is salvation, and though this is a universal goal, for everyone has to take the journey, each journey is unique; the success of one pilgrim does not help another. Whether one succeeds or fails depends on one's own will to succeed; every mistake sets one back, but none are irrevocable except giving up. There are helpers and enemies; there are guide-posts and these are not equivocal; the Way may be difficult but it is not deceptive, so long as one keeps the goal clearly in mind and never stops willing to get there.

THE QUEST FOR NECESSITY (e.g., *Faust, Peer Gynt*)

The Quest is the journey through life, and the goal is still personal salvation, but the latter is conceived quite differently. In earlier salvation quests, the way was never doubtful. To be saved, i.e., to realize one's essential self, it was only necessary to obey the commands and directions of God which He issued to Man clearly and unequivocally in His church or His Bible, and to reject all possibilities that conflicted with them. But in these quests, the faith in religious authority is lacking, and what is sought is an individual and immediate certainty, without faith, that the subject is "in the truth." This can only be acquired by exploring *all* the possibilities of one's nature, good *and* evil, for it is only when a man knows them all, that he can be perfectly certain which is the right one; as long as there is a single possibility untried, he cannot *know* that it should be rejected, he can only *believe* it should.

The hero of such a quest must be willing and daring enough to try everything, however shocking; he must surrender

57

completely to whatever the immediate moment suggests; he must at all costs avoid making an irrevocable choice. The artistic difficulty in writing a quest of this kind is that, as the possibilities are infinite, the quest can never end, and any ending—for a book must end sometime—is arbitrary. The ending of *Faust* is artistically unsatisfying because the reader is not convinced that Faust is saved, nor indeed is Goethe, for the angels sing of Faust:

> Him in the pupa stage
> Gladly receive we so

i.e., his development is still incomplete. Ibsen is more honest, for *Peer Gynt* closes with the warning of the Button Maker that he and Peer will meet again.

THE QUEST FOR INNOCENCE (The Detective Story)

The formula is this: a group of people are living in what appears to be a state of innocence and grace, where there is no law since there is no need for it. A corpse is found under conditions which make it certain that one of the group must be the murderer, i.e., the state of innocence is lost and the law enters. All fall under suspicion but the hero-detective identifies and arrests the guilty one and innocence is restored to the rest, or rather what before was only an appearance of innocence, now becomes real.

The hero who identifies and removes the guilt is: (a) a total stranger to the group, (b) the exceptional individual who is, as an individual, what the innocent suspects can only be collectively, in a state of innocence and grace.

THE KAFKA QUEST

The Kafka novels are like the detective story and unlike all the earlier quests, in that while in the latter the movement of the journey is willed by the hero, and it is others who try to arrest or divert that movement, in the former it is the others who move, and the hero's efforts are directed towards stopping it. The hero of *The Trial* wishes to put an end to it; the hero of *The Castle* wants to be allowed to settle down in the village. The novels differ from all other forms of quest in that the hero's

58

problem is no longer "Can I do what I am required to do?" but "What am I required to do?"

The knight seeking the Holy Grail, for example, knows he is required to be chaste; he may, when tempted, fail but he knows in what way he has failed. Faust does not know where his journey will end, but he knows what he must do now, which is whatever the present moment suggests. The detective's course of action is given him from moment to moment by the evidence he discovers; he is often given false information which leads him astray, but he knows that his job is to distinguish truth from falsehood.

K., on the other hand, is not simply tempted, i.e., confronted with two alternatives which he knows are good and evil, nor is he carefree, so that movement is direction enough. He knows that it matters enormously what he does now, without knowing what it ought to be. If he *guesses* wrong he must suffer the consequences and feel just as responsible as if he had *chosen* wrong. Further, if the instructions and information he receives seem to him absurd or contradictory, he cannot, like the detective, take that as evidence of malice or guilt in others, but only as proof of his own.

In the detective story, the murder is certain and the guilty party is temporarily uncertain, in *The Trial* the situation is reversed; K. knows he is guilty, he does not know of what, and his whole efforts are directed not to proving his innocence but learning the cause of his guilt. In *Pilgrim's Progress* Christian has to win Heaven by doing the things that make him deserve it; in *The Castle* there is no question of K. being able to win a right to be the Land Surveyor; he can only ask the Castle to give him permission to be.

In a similar way, the nature of Kafka's hero is radically different from all previous conceptions of the heroic. Previously the hero is the exceptional individual, exceptional either by his inborn gifts or his acquired virtues. His goal is either to manifest or to achieve individuality; the hero who is saved achieves this positively, the tragic hero who is damned achieves it negatively but the guilt of the latter lies not in his being or wishing to become an individual, only in his going the wrong way about it.

59

K., on the other hand, suffers and fails to achieve his goal precisely because he *is* an individual. For example, he cannot become what he wishes, the Land Surveyor, because he cannot cease to be K. The comic contradiction is that K. is a single letter, and Land Surveyor a much more "heroic" sounding definition, but K. is the name of an individual and land survey is a definition of an occupation. The fact that he is K. is really the evidence of his guilt in *The Trial;* if he were innocent he would have no name, like the fawn in the wood in *Through the Looking Glass.*

Kafka's hero has a name consisting of only one letter and no position in the world; the other characters have names of many letters and occupations, or rather, perhaps one should say that they appear to have, when seen through K.'s eyes. For what Kafka seems to be saying is: "What is generally called individuality is nothing of the kind, but only the *persona* or mask of action which is all we can know about others; individuality is something that can only be known subjectively, and subjectively individuality is the simplest brute fact that the 'I' which feels and knows and acts can never be defined by what it feels and knows and acts; it can be reduced to the barest minimum of a single letter, but to nothing, never." Man, therefore, can never know the whole truth, because as the subject who knows, he has to remain outside the truth, and the truth is therefore incomplete.

From this follows the paradox that K.'s only guarantee that he is following the true way is that he fails to get anywhere. If he succeeded in getting his way, it would be a proof that he had failed.

truth for truth's sake

h. e. jacob

Someone who knew Franz Kafka when he was alive told about his meticulously neat, calligraphic handwriting. Yes! It fits his inner portrait, it fits this bureaucrat of life, that he should have written calligraphy, that he did a neat job of setting columns of numbers and myriads of letters. Neat in the smallest and in the complex that is common to all: handwriting. Not for love of beauty but for love of correctness. "Thus through these angles and curves," he might have thought, "there runs the ideal image of writing—let us not depart too far from it!" In his handwriting Kafka probably was not an esthete but a precisionist: no calligrapher but an orthographer. And making ever wider arcs around this little circle of pedantry—arcs comprising ever more reality—he finally became a writer of the true, an alethographer.

Kafka, the truthful! Read his writings and feel how this descriptive word, this prime word, issues from them to him. Easily, without the use of force—and withal as his only characteristic.

When I received the news of Kafka's death and the content and nature of his meager work in one painful lightning flash came poignantly to my mind, I felt that the essence of this

61

work is truthfulness: the striving for truth and for nothing else. Truth in *Observations,* truth in "The Stoker," truth in "The Metamorphosis" and in "The Judgment," in "The Penal Colony" and in "The Country Doctor." Truth of cognition, truth of expression as the innermost center, the innermost light. Psychology? Worldly wisdom? Humor? Melancholy? They too are present in Kafka's work, but only as externals, as windows. One could extract them or wall them up, these merely optical aids, these projection instruments of the will to truth—there would still remain in the radiant inner chamber the truth itself, disembodied.

Perhaps there are greater writers in our epoch—there has been and there is no truer writer. In his earliest book *Observations* (which like an arsenal already contains the themes of all his later works) we find a prose piece of only a few sentences, "The Misfortune of Bachelors," which in a calm crescendo makes one comprehend this very misfortune. "It seems so bad to stay a bachelor, and like an old man have to beg for acceptance, while struggling at the same time to preserve one's dignity, when one wants to spend an evening with people," he says, and the piece and the thought end there, sorrowful but harmless, with the observation that it will be necessary "to pattern one's appearance and one's conduct after those of one or two bachelors we remember from our youth." We feel: this is the end, this must be it. We feel that the poet, after having written this, sadly closes his writing-case. But no: he flings it open. To blast out one more, this final, this terrible sentence: "Thus shall it be, except that you will be such a person yourself, in reality, today and even after today, with a body and a real head—and that means that you will have a forehead, too, to pound with your hand." In all literature I have never encountered another sentence like that. When, I ask, where and when could it have happened that a poet jumped up from the table and cried like this man Kafka: "Well, then, I have spoken, I have written about a special kind of misfortune—but now I perceive that through my speaking and writing, through my expression of it, perhaps this misfortune has become fictitious. Nevertheless, believe me: it *is* a misfortune . . . beyond, beyond all speech, writing, expression, literature, we shall one day stand there, lonely, childless, with a body and a real head!" This attitude toward art and this attitude toward truth has, I say, no parallel.

Certainly: others too have recorded moods, feelings as small as one sixteenth, values as small as one thirty-second. But no one has recorded the truth of such situations as Kafka. There is that prose piece about "The Passenger" on a streetcar (that symbol of all daily motion). The passenger, relates Kafka, is completely insecure in relation to his position in the world, in the city, in the family. "I am utterly unable to defend," he continues, "the fact that I am standing on this platform, hanging on to this strap, letting myself be carried along by this car, that people get out of the car's way or walk quietly along or relax in front of shop windows. It is true, no one demands a justification from me, but that makes no difference." (He himself clearly expects it of himself.) Now a girl gets on. "She is dressed in black, the pleats of her skirt scarcely move." She stands there like that, securely reposing in her self-evidentness, satisfied with not having to inquire about her being born into this very second (about which Kafka inquires, however). She stands there like that, not in the least a riddle to herself—and, as if overwhelmed by astonishment, the poet concludes: "How is it that she is not astonished by herself, that she keeps her mouth closed, and says nothing of this sort?"

No indeed, this is no mere description of mood, these are not minute values, this is not an anecdote, in short, not prose by Peter Altenberg. Here we hear something absolute, an organ-point. The insecurity of Kafka's man in the streetcar suddenly becomes the only secure thing in this world: so reassuring is the phenomenon of a truthful human being, even when it represents something in itself disturbed.

Kafka, the devotee of truth. Kafka, the alethiophile. Zola, Ibsen, Strindberg, Björnson—were they greater than Kafka because they told the truth about greater matters? But the measure of truth in all matters can only be the truthfulness of the person expressing it, and not the large sociological or political complex to which it is applied. The truth of a miniature is a truth too, and by no means a mere "finesse." Whoever is so presumptuous as to see in Kafka a "delicate" or even a "dandy" writer,

63

misunderstands him. The world, painted in all its proportions on the shell of an insect is still the world, as much as (and sometimes better than) one spread over a colossal canvas.

Silently, noiselessly, the truth is served in Kafka's writings. He is not an esthete of his will for truth. He is not an exhibitionist about it—when, after all, in these days, all others are whip-cracking clowns of their own ethics. He is very quiet about it. He conceals his truthfulness for the sake of truthfulness.

Kafka is a poet who has sacrificed to his love for truth all those things which to others are the fiery darts that are needed to make them write at all and which, at best, afford an intellectual stimulus. He is a poet of ultra matter-of-fact reporting. A poet who did not love beauty (but without loving ugliness!). A poet who did not love ecstasy (but without therefore loving the Philistine!). A poet who desired simply nothing but the completely pure, completely faultless passage of truth through his self, who in this desired the deepest of things (and for whom it would have been unbearable to receive such praise in his lifetime since praise itself compels us to adopt some sort of untruthful attitude).

      ◦   ◦   ◦

Would it be possible for someone whose entire art is the will for truth to employ a technique for its expression? There would be only one: the technique of the dream.

If we look sharply we notice that all of Kafka's stories really are dreams. Not by any means dreams of that mistaken conception under which formerly poetic works were called dreams, not dreams in the sense of rose-colored lyricism, not fictions outside of truth, not uncontrollable gushings of a rampant fantasy. Kafka's stories are controlled dreams in a psychoanalytical field: dreams full of symbolical actions, dreams full of active symbols. There is no phase of Kafka's prose in which—easily visible to the initiated—the whole technical apparatus of the dream does not appear, with heavenly wish-fulfillments on the one hand, with long wonderful glides through and beyond logic and space, and on the other hand with dyspnoic spells, oppressive obstruction in the smallest of matters, inability to open doors

("The Law," "The Metamorphosis"), inability to find ways and objects ("The Stoker"). Not infrequently the emotional reactions in Kafka's tales are expressed as directly as in dreams: Karl Rossmann, for example (in "The Stoker"), although he is already in the presence of a large company of people, suddenly kisses the stoker's hand, and in the story "A Dream" the narrator suddenly begins to weep madly because the artist pauses in decorating a tombstone. The amazingly exact aperception of small, frequently trifling features which runs through all of Kafka's writings corresponds to our powers of perception in dreams, and, as if the similarities were not enough, we often find autonomous symbols which, wrought from the most secret depths of the soul, suddenly stand before us in a glaring and excessive light: for example the little rusty scissors in "Jackals and Arabs," the tangle of cardboard and yarn in "Worries of a Family Man." In this prose writing there is not a single line which is not recounted through a medium of the dream although there is only one occasion on which the anonymity of the dream is unmasked by the statement "he awakened" (in "A Dream"). All fear in Kafka is dream-fear, world-fear, success-fear, all joy is dream-joy, dream of friendship, wish for love. The doctrine of Freud and Adler that man is only true when he dreams is decisive for Kafka—yes, it even became the sole decisive thing in his life. For if it is true (and it is), then the truthful man cannot do anything but recount dreams.

But, oh contradiction!—as we dream we give form. There is no dream which in spite of all truth is not also a giving of form. This too must be considered by all who want to understand Kafka.

For the first time in a long time the Germans have regained in the work of Kafka a prose writing which is truth in the highest degree and also form in the highest degree. (Commonly these two factors are not found together.) I do not doubt that almost in the same breath with Eichendorff's romantic irony (after all "The Ne'er-do-well" too is one of these stories of highest reality which, not unlike Kafka's stories, at once yields up its entire substance to its own burning secret of form!) literary criticism will some day mention, praise and admire Kafka's psychoanalytical irony as an artistic form. Not, to be sure, as a proof of

65

its being related to any romanticist. That would be wrong, for Kafka's attempt to put himself to sleep, to make himself dream, thus to tell us the truth in dreams, is entirely new, is unheard of in the realm of truth, in the realm of form and in the realm of their union: art.

But—and this is the staggering thing—Kafka always dreams about matters of the mind. Or rather, the dreams dream themselves like living fountains in Kafka, who is merely their cavern. In "The Stoker," for example, justice dreams a dream of injustice upon the earth, in "The Penal Colony" humanity dreams of militarism, in "The Metamorphosis" and "The Judgment" inferiority dreams of active life, fear of life dreams death. In "The New Attorney" the unheroic epoch reproduces in dreams the heroic age of yore, in "Jackals and Arabs" the office of the justice of the peace feels how superfluous it is amid the eternal hatred of the nations, in "The Country Doctor" Christian conscience dreams the nightmare of its own failure. There is hardly a single moral problem that Kafka did not concern himself with very deeply. But he does not solve the problems, he does not want to solve them, his concern with them all is the mummy-like rigidity of the sleeper who dreams them. Staggering with heaviness which at the same time is lightness, dancing with hope that is despair, and vibrant with smiling anguish, the great wish-images which have inspired mankind for centuries rush through his soul. Kafka's relations to them is not that of an individual but that of all mankind which after all is only dreaming these problems too and is not solving them either.

That's how it is. And only that man understands the writer Kafka at all who realizes that he was no professional "queer fellow," no ego off on a tangent, no "original," but that in his anonymous and objective prose writing he was a mouthpiece above the plane of specialization, a speaker for common concerns. But still most people approach this classically simple man as though he had been an impressionist, a man of bizarre whims and notions, a man of the kind of Peter Altenberg. He who in truth recounted small affairs quietly and grandly like Tacitus, is considered a *pointillist*, a specialist of his own brand of humor and sorrow, a roving challenge to "make the molecules race," a second

Christian Morgenstern. For nothing can be so misleading as the sight of a rounded whole.

✿ ✿ ✿

But—and this may serve as an excuse—this simple and guileless writer is in fact hard to understand. Indeed, it is his very truthfulness that makes understanding him difficult. Kafka's striving for inner truth is so great that, to the displeasure and bewilderment of the average reader, conflict with the factual truth upon earth, yes, even with optical reality, is inevitable. For example, in the first lines of "The Stoker" we learn that sixteen-year-old Karl Rossmann sees in New York harbor the statue of the goddess of freedom "bearing aloft a sword." But, as everyone knows, the Statue of Liberty does not bear aloft a sword at all, but a torch. What has happened here, then? An embarrassing bit of carelessness by the author? No, something quite different. As I have already said, in the symbolical story of the poor stoker, justice dreams of the injustice upon earth—what, then, should the incongruous and untrue goddess of liberty do with a torch? She can't shed any light anyway. "Let us then rather give her a sword, give her the sword with which justice, this goddess of freedom of the wealthy, can beat down upon the righteous!" So thinks Kafka, so dreams the poet, so prompts the thought-dream in him. On the other hand, he would not have dared to omit the image of liberty entirely, for what does a sixteen-year-old like Karl Rossmann see when he sails into New York? The poet has only corrected optical reality a bit, in the interest of truth.

But this, well after all, is too much. This, multiplied by a thousand (for Kafka's work consists of a thousand such details, thousands of such sallies from more common reality into the truth of symbols) this is too much for his contemporaries. Never yet has a poet so protected himself from being understood as has Kafka. One can almost speak of a self-enjoyment of truth, of a *"manger-soi-même"* of truth in his works. Does this not border on estheticism after all? Perhaps. But today when every poet seems to have license for any lie, I cannot at all object if one exception among them all practices *"la vérité pour la vérité."*

Translated by Harold Lenz.

kosmos kafka

austin warren

> *"Nothing more deeply engrosses a man than his burdens ... We win by capitalizing on our debts, by turning our liabilities into assets, by using our burdens as a basis of insight."*
>
> —KENNETH BURKE

> *"James ne nous a pas apporté des ideés, mais bien un univers nouveau de pensée et de sentiment."*
>
> —T. S. ELIOT

Kafka's novels evoke a world with its own structure, mood, end—a world as self-coherent and recognizable as that of Dickens, of Dostoyevsky, of Proust, of Poe, of Hawthorne. Like Hawthorne's and Poe's, Kafka's is a limited, a lyric world. Not Balzac or Tolstoi or Scott, he is a metaphysical poet in symbolist narrative.

His is a city world. Even Kafka's Village must be a metropolitan fragment, a city overpopulated and extending beyond our sight. Like Dickens' London it flourishes in grotesques.

But they have not the vigor, the delight in their own salt being, of Quilp and Miss Mowcher; and they are chiefly unnamed and seen but momentarily. Old women look out of inquisitive windows; in the gutters sit leering irreverent mocking children; a young lad, his nose half eaten away, scrutinizes arrivals; the warden wears a gross body, ill-adjusted to his "dry bony face, with a great nose twisted to one side." If the hero enters a house it affords people and darkness. "Anyone coming in from outside could make out nothing at first. K. stumbled over a washing-tub; a woman's hand steadied him. The crying of children came loudly from one corner. From another, steam was welling out and turning the dim light into darkness."

It is an overcrowded, airless world, within which it is difficult to sustain faith in the dignity of the human soul, the weight and worth of the individual. One remembers Georg Salter's illustrations for *The Trial,* cuts in which most persons except the introspective hero are shapes of shadow. Kafka's solipsism is intelligible, is defensible, as the illusion necessary to sustaining, in the populous and anonymous city, the belief that the soul and its choices matter.

Even Kafka's imagined America is not a land of broad cornfields shining in the sun and facilely convertible into gold but a chiefly metropolitan affair, already stratified, weary, and hopeless—a land of vast hotels for the rich and noisome slums for the poor. "Karl thought of the east end of New York which his uncle had promised to show him where it was said that several families lived in one little room and the house of a whole family consisted of one corner where many children clustered around their parents." He read Franklin's *Autobiography,* we are told, and admired Walt Whitman, and liked the Americans because he believed them to be "healthy and optimistic." But his imagination does not so present them: surely Kafka's first novel is misinterpreted by those who find it cheerful. A "WPA" Theater opens hospitably at the end, to be sure; yet the novel follows Dickens, not Alger. Karl is the young Copperfield, the young Oliver Twist, the sensitive boy ejected from his home on charges which puzzle him. He finds America gleaming but hard. Before landing, he encounters social injustice in the case of "The Stoker";

70

his uncle, who suddenly appears and assumes his support, as suddenly and less plausibly renounces responsibility; he is deceived and maltreated by his chance travelling companions; for no fault of his own, he is discharged from the hotel; he comes near to ending as a slavey in the crazy apartment of delirious Brunelda. America is a world where elevators whiz up and down, phonographs play incessantly without anyone's attending to them, political candidates get lost in the crowds which "choose" them. It offers the image of the ascent to Brunelda's apartment: long stairs moving up into squalid darkness; beside the stair-railing, a little girl weeps; then rushes up the steps gasping for breath.

Kafka's is also a world we have known in dreams or nightmares—a rational unnatural world in which unnatural situations are rationally worked out, in which everyone is able, like Lewis Carroll's creatures, to argue long, ingeniously and convincingly. It is a nightmare world in which the "I," all innocent and eager to submit, all desirous to propitiate, is pushed about, pursued, regimented by potencies veiled of visage, in which one is forever being orally examined by dignitaries who forever flunk one. These are novels in which the self and the world are juxtaposed in opposition. If one is not being pursued by the world or carried off by the world one is running after it. There is the image of the old father trying to catch the ear of the Castle dignitaries—trying in vain, for the officials go at a gallop, their carriages "race like mad." It is the world of a Mack Sennett comedy —one of chase and pursuit, of intense movement, horizontal and vertical, of running and climbing. It is a world of mystery and uncertainty and insecurity, of fear and trembling.

It is a world of hierarchy, created by Kafka in the parodic imitation of the Austrian bureaucracies under which he lived, within which, as under-official, he worked. In its chief traits it could be a feudal estate or it could be an American department store or a chain of restaurants or the Boston Public Library. Hierarchy provides, negatively, for deferment of responsibility or indefinite retreat. One's complaint always reaches the wrong office; one stands in front of the wrong window; one is passed on from office to office, in general moving up the scale of delegated authority toward the mysterious ones "higher up," only

71

to find that the proper official to handle the complaint is out of town or the necessary documents are lost or one's claim is outlawed. Wonderful is the efficiency of an order so complexly gradated that every expert is inexpert at satisfying a simple need for justice. Kafka's own image for this order is the long process of law; but experiences with the great systems of chain stores and chain restaurants will do. If one's dinner isn't good (i.e., isn't as one ordered it) there's no gain but only cruelty in scolding or otherwise penalizing the waitress: she is not responsible. Nor is the "hostess." Nor is the assistant manager in charge of the evening. Nor the manager of "all our Boston restaurants." Who is responsible? The wondrous system cannot answer; and the poor diner is left helpless and recourseless and all stifled within, while the wondrous system, rising by finely efficient ranks, operates upon its own transcendent notion of what the American diner needs and shall have.

As F. H. Bradley's maxim runs: "The world is the best of all possible worlds, and everything in it is a necessary evil." Of course even the most wondrous system must be operated by human beings; and in such a system there must inevitably be errors and malpractices the more difficult to rectify in proportion as the system is elaborate. There are other difficulties. Hierarchic order is necessary in a universe densely populated, whether with atoms or souls, yet in an order so intricate, instrumentalities must, almost unavoidably, turn into ends: readers exist in order that librarians may make card catalogues and bibliographies, pupils in order that educationalists may write books on methods of teaching, worshippers in order that janitors may sweep and lock churches. Under-officials, those who administer the rules to the public, can scarcely be expected to understand the spirit of the rules or what, as formulated by unseen and doubtless long dead "higher-ups," the rules aimed at. A teeming universe must, of course, be a "planned," even if an ill planned or a too fussily planned, society. The easy improvisation which fits the New England village—the teaming of neighbors, farmers, and shop-keepers in the menial business of the town—cannot endure transportation to the city. Indeed, by one of his most sustained boldnesses, Kafka imagines that even the Village cannot really be a village:

72

if its multiple needs are adequately to be taken care of, there must be business enough to require busy attention from a whole Caste of officials.

It would be easy to take Kafka's novels as burlesques of bureaucracy, and satiric they of course are, but without sharp definition. They are provided with no satiric norm, no contrasting model of elegance and humanity, but only with a hero too uncertain of himself to sit in judgment on them, and too intent upon learning their ways to bother with criticizing them. As for bureaucracy, it is even at its worst a corruption of order; and order is a state so blessed, so indispensable, that one must respect even its parodies. And as for bureaucrats, the charge against them generally is that they are too insistent upon the importance of their work, too narrow in their conception of it; but surely it is the duty of officials to be officious, and narrowness and even scrupulosity are marks of their being dedicated to their profession. The work of the world is carried on by experts not by *honnêtes hommes;* and if we want to deepen the sense of "work" and "world" we must add, "strait is the gate and narrow the way"; the price of salvation is the forced sale of all that one has.

Hierarchy is pyramidal. Is there, for Kafka, any Reason, any Supreme Will, at the top and the end? Or is hierarchy a staircase which ends not in a dome or a tower but in a walk off into darkness? The answer is uncertain; the top is covered with mist. Of a Chief Justice, a head of the judiciary system, we never hear, nor of a proprietor or even head manager of the Hotel. In *The Castle,* we hear for a preliminary moment of the "Count West-west," but soon he and any direct view of the Castle itself are lost or forgotten. Doubtless there is an ultimate authority, but we never reach it except through its intermediaries: there is no direct, no mystical vision. In "Before the Law," the lowest door-keeper can see a few doors ahead of him in what he believes to be a vast series of ascents: "From hall to hall keepers stand at every door, one more powerful than the other. Even the third of these has an aspect that even I cannot bear to look at." Of the ascending series we can say that there is no point at which we observe it to stop. Olga explains to K.: "Who it is that Barnabas speaks to there [in the Castle] I have no idea,

73

—perhaps the clerk is lowest in the whole staff; but even if he is lowest he can put one in touch with the next man above him, and if he can't even do that he can refer to somebody who can give the name." They are men set under authority; and "Does not the least degree of authority contain the whole?"

In both *The Trial* and *The Castle,* under-officials, advocates and villagers spend much time in speculating upon the ways of the "higher-ups." In the latter we hear Amalia ask, "Is it Castle gossip you're at? . . . There are people in the village who live on it; they stick their heads together just like you two and entertain each other by the hour"; to which K. replies that he is just such a person, "and moreover people who don't care for such gossip and leave it all to others don't interest me particularly." So the talk goes on. We "gossip" or speculate about Klamm, attempting to adjust to coherence the glimpses we catch. A man like Klamm "who is so much sought after and rarely seen is apt to take different shapes in people's imaginations"— to give rise to angelophanies or theophanies very diverse each from the other.

Yet Kafka's officials, however otherwise various, have in common a certain obtrusive trait, a certain perversity. They are not Hellenic or elegant: just as the rooms in which the courts sit have none of the grandeur or even decent neatness we might presume; just as the Castle is unimpressive and the schoolmaster assures us that strangers are always disappointed in it. The officials are less balanced and humanistic and virtuous, surely, than the villagers; they are, instead officious, pompous and pedantic. But the "virtues of the pagans are splendid vices," and "officious, pompous, and pedantic" are dyslogistic terms which may honorably be transvaluated as "conscientious, dignified, and painstakingly and properly accurate."

These paper-reading officials are scholars, intellectuals; and their scholarly life bears no discernible relation to their biological and affective lives: they have their mistresses, and they have their papers. Like the highest academics, they are specialists; and they have an elaborate command of their own dossiers without seeing them in relationship to the rest of heaven and earth.

74

"Papers" bless and curse. They are not only the records of law, the registers of the probate court, the ledgers of business but the annals of history and the bibliographies of scholars and the memory of the race, the possibility of preserving and interpreting our past experience. They represent also the effort of the intellect to understand by dissection, arrangement, systemization. "Papers" constitute civilization; without "papers" we remain barbarians. Yet "papers" clutter up the world; "papers" menace our freedom. They may be "busy work" to amuse the old children, to keep scholars from thinking and the timid from knowing themselves afraid. It is an academic malady to play with books and papers and notes, in order to avoid existential thinking; to preserve records without selection, to multiply distinctions and discriminations till one is incapable of singleness of mind and simplicity of action. Papers assemble, by the most laudable of intentions, into libraries; yet for every man who, like Arnold, fears he may know more than he feels, a great library is an object of terror, a monument to the futility of past speculation, a deterrent to action through its marmoreal suggestion that one must read yet another book before one knows enough to do.

There are some rich, fantastic scenes in which Kafka's papers become objects in themselves, figures in a Disney cartoon.* The search, in the superintendent's bedroom for a missing document, in the process of which papers half cover the floor and go on mounting: or the description of Sordini's office, every wall of which is covered with columns of documents tied together, piled on top of one another; "those are only the documents that Sordini is working on at the time, and as bundles of papers are continually being taken away and brought in, and all in great haste, those columns are always falling on the floor, and it's just those perpetual crashes, following fast on one another, that have come to distinguish Sordini's workroom."

The copiousness of the papers has an approximate correspondence in the volubility of official speech. Addiction to argument characterizes almost all Kafka's people, not merely his

---

* Some of Kafka's most brilliant scenes are animated cartoons. Best of all, perhaps is the scene in *Amerika's* Porter's office, with its spectacle of perpetual motion.

lawyers and secretaries. In these novels, all are dialecticians; all are conscious of *pro et contra*, fertile in "various lections." They do not—like Mann's great controversialists, Naphtha and Settembrini—argue in abstract terms; they are existential thinkers and deploy their subtlety on the obscure and difficult matter of living aright.

The Trial and The Castle are composed very largely of dialogues, and dialogues dialectic. Indeed, the characteristic excitement of later novels (written by a student of Plato and Kierkegaard) lies in the wit, the intellectual suspense, of the dialogue. The thoughts, no more than the papers in Sordini's office, stand still; like action in a detective story, they are full of sudden shifts of direction, convincing evasions of the foregone conclusion.

What does Kafka mean us to make of his argumentation? Is it ridiculously specious, or—so far as it goes—true? "Both" would have to be the answer. It is absurd to speculate about the nature of the highest, for of course we can't know; we can't even know how near we come to knowing. Yet it is man's true nature and highest function to engage himself upon these speculative questions concerning the nature of reality; and there is no delegation of duty to others.

Kafka's world is one of mystery.* *Omnia exeunt in mysterium.* In stories like "The Country Doctor" and "The Metamorphosis," the unnatural erupts itself into the orderly sequence of nature. The horrible redaction of a young clerk into a bug does not allow of being sterilized through allegory, nor is it presented as a dream. The chief horror of the story is, perhaps, that no one within it sees what happens as "impossible": it is horrible, to be sure, but in various ways these people, who are obviously sane and simple, adjust themselves to a painful situation. There are occasional bits of near or sheer magic in Kafka: in The Castle, Barnabas disappears with the rapidity of an elf or a thought; the first day passes and it grows night, within an hour or two after

---

* If you don't find it genuine, you will at least find it a *mystification*. Einstein is said to have returned a novel by Kafka to Thomas Mann, its admirer, with the remark: "I couldn't read it for its perversity. The human mind isn't that complex."

76

morning; after a few days of living with K., Frieda, formerly "unnaturally seductive," is "withering in his arms." But it is not Kafka's ordinary or best practice to deal in legerdemain. He secures his sense of mystery chiefly through his device of multiple interpretation.

There is, in method, a superficial analogy with the practice of Hawthorne, who frequently offers substitutionary readings of a fact. With Hawthorne the alternatives are usually supernaturalism or some form of naturalism. Thus, preliminarily, at the elaborate ending of *The Scarlet Letter*, we are tendered the alternative of supposing that there was, or was not, a scarlet letter imprinted upon the breast of the minister, and then a choice of three methods for the possible production of the stigmata: some said by the natural means of penance; others said by means of magic and drugs; others said by the out-going operation of the spirit. "The reader," says Hawthorne, "may choose among these theories."

Kafka offers no such invitation; nor is it his method thus to contrast a supernatural with a natural reading. Indeed this is precluded by the very nature of his method and conception. It is, for him, in and through the natural that the supernatural operates and, with whatever intermittence and illusion, is revealed. He relishes detail, for the highest is not vague in itself but precise.

Kafka's world is neither a fantasy nor the world of the average sensual man. It is the world seen slightly askew, as one looks through his legs or stands on his head, or sees it in a distorting mirror, or dreams it. Nor does his adjustment take, like Swift's in *Gulliver*, the method of segregation. With Swift, the fantastic is safely corraled and tucked away in the initial assumption; with Kafka, realism and fantasy move in more close and sensitive relation. In *The Trial* and *The Castle*, the whole sequence is so improbable as to suggest some kind of pervasive allegory, but at no point (or almost no point) does there occur the downright impossibility. It is improbable that, in a large and wealthy city, there should be law courts lodged high up in dingy tenement houses, or that a village should require the service of a vast staff of busy, hurrying officials, or that, upon looking into a lumber-room in one's own office building, one should discover two court-wardens being flogged. Yet there might be an explanation; these things "could be": they are not like centaurs, oceans flowing with lemonade, and trees growing greenbacks. And Kafka's multiple interpretations are all possible options within one world. They represent the same fact or situation read from successive views as the operations of a mind which keeps correcting or reversing itself. Common sense and intuition know at once what to think; the skeptical intellect offers and rejects view after view, each plausible.

Kafka delights to offer a convincing interpretation; then, with rapidity, to substitute another which seems yet more convincing. A scene in *Amerika* shows Robinson, his face and arms swathed in manifold bandages. "It was horrible to see him lift his arms to his eyes to wipe away his tears with the bandages —tears of pain or grief or perhaps even of joy at seeing Karl again." Then we see the horror dissolve. "The trivial nature of his wounds could be seen from the old rags of bandages with which the lift-boys, obviously in jest, had swathed him round."

The Castle abounds in more subtle shifts. A woman sits in a chair in a kitchen. The pale light gives a "gleam of silk" to her dress; she seems to be an aristocrat, "although of course illness and weariness give even peasants a look of refinement." To a question from K., the woman replies disdainfully, but "Whether contemptuous of K., or of her own answer was not clear." If one is self-conscious or otherwise fearful it is necessary and difficult to interpret the looks of others. Thus K. sees the peasants gazing fixedly at him: he thinks it done out of malice—yet perhaps they really wanted something from him but could not express it, or perhaps, on the other hand, they were simply childish. But if the first view of the peasants and their attitude was mistaken, what about the first view of Barnabas? One doubt, one disillusionment, infects one with a general mistrust of his own judgment. "Perhaps K. was as mistaken in Barnabas' goodness as in the malice of the peasants. . . ." Frieda's hands "were certainly small and delicate, but they could quite as well have been called weak and characterless." After Olga's account of Amalia's defiance of Sortini, K. says, "Amalia's act was remarkable enough, but the more you

78

say about it the less clearly can it be decided whether it was noble or petty, clever or foolish, heroic or cowardly. . . ." Longer, more structural examples are the discussion concerning K., and the Superintendent concerning the meaning of Klamm's letter, and K.'s talk with Frieda about the landlady, and Olga's discussion with K., concerning the nature of Barnabas' relation to the Castle.

Kafka's "mystery" is, then, the apparent sign of how elusive is the truth. What happens is tolerably easy to ascertain, but what it means is the important and exacting business.

Such scrupulosity of interpretation recalls a characteristic feature of hierarchy everywhere prominent in Kafka's novels —the connection between promotion, pleasing and propitiation. Kafka's worlds are theocracies, not legal utopias. One's success or failure depends on one's skill in divining the wishes of the great man; and among underlings there develops a necessary skill in calculating his mood by his complexion, step, tone of voice. Cases there naturally are in which the signs allow of ambiguity of differing interpretation as between experts of equal experience.

The interpretative complexity recalls also the elaborations of rabbinic and patristic commentary. John Mason Neale's commentary on the Song of Songs offers, out of innumerable Fathers, Doctors and Saints, all manner of conflicting yet severally edifying glosses: on the text, "his left hand is under my head, and his right hand doth embrace me," for example. What is the distinction between the hands, and why their position? According to some, the hands distinguish temporal from spiritual goods; according to another view, the left hand equates the law, the right hand the Gospel; according to another, the left hand indicates punishment, the right, blessings and rewards. Other comments differentiate mystical states, the left being the Illuminative as the right is the Unitive Way. And "the loveliest interpretation of all," says Neale, is that which sees in the left the Manhood of Christ, and in the right his Godhead.

It was not till late in his life that Kafka began to study the *Talmud;* but already, in the discourse of the priest in the Cathedral (in "Before the Law"), Kafka shows his ingenuity and depth as the exegete of a given fable. The priest's whole com-

79

mentary cites the studies of innumerable rabbis who had already concerned themselves with the story. Says the priest, "I am only showing you different opinions about it. You mustn't have too much regard for opinions. The text is unchangeable and opinions are often only an expression of doubt about it." Like Plato, whose myth images a reach beyond dialectic, like Kierkegaard, whose *Fear and Trembling* starts from and repeatedly returns to the story of Abraham and Isaac, so Kafka, delighting in speculation, yet offers his story as an imaginative construction the meaning of which is anterior to and not exhausted by any commentary offered within it.

Kafka comes closest to allegory in "The Penal Colony," a myth which, though full of literal horror is obviously not a companion piece to "The Pit and the Pendulum." An allegory is a series of concepts provided with a narrative, or a narrative accompanied by a conceptual parallel. Strictly, it is a philosophical sequence which calculatedly and systematically works itself out in images. But allegory is rarely as rigidly pure as *Pilgrim's Progress* or *The Romance of the Rose* or *The Celestial Railroad*: it deviates from purity in two directions—by losing its systematic character, becoming a series of intermittent symbolisms, or by keeping its system but abstaining from offering a conceptual key to its parable.

Kafka's novels are not, in any strict sense allegorical; and it is puzzling to find his method compared to Bunyan's. From his diaries and aphorisms and his friend Brod's commentaries we know that he intended the novels to give creative expression to the mysteries of Justice and Grace; that they are metaphysical novels we should surely have made out; but Kafka provided them with no conceptual chart. They require none, and it is their special richness that they have much particularity untranslatable into generality. Indeed, we need not, for either intelligibility or interest, keep reminding ourselves that the Castle is Heaven and K.'s disappointments but symbols of the mysterious ways in which God moves. The ways of men are, for those who seek to understand them, baffling enough.

Kafka's symbols are, indeed, capable of more than the religious interpretation. As Brod indicates, K. symbolizes the

Jew in his exclusion from society and his eagerness to find a place within the community, a home and a shop, as well as the seeker after the Kingdom of Heaven. But K. is also the bachelor in search of marriage and companionship; and K. is also every man in respect to his final aloneness.

Kafka's novels all, significantly, remained unfinished. Of them he wrote: "What sense would there be in reviving such . . . bungled pieces of work? Only if one hoped to create a whole out of such fragments, some complete work to which one could make a final appeal . . ." He was not himself, then, in agreement with the judgment of Brod and others that the novels would not gain substantially by completion and revision.

We have in each case a notion of the ending. *Amerika* was to conclude with the young hero's finding, within the Nature Theatre of Oklahoma, his freedom, "even his old house and his parents"; *The Trial* concludes with a scene, written out in at least a preliminary version, in which the hero is executed; *The Castle* was to end with permission being given to K., then dying, to live in the Village. But the exact articulation of scenes between the opening sequence and the end remains indefinite. The ending, in each case, could be applied after any number of intermediate chapters; it follows after, but only generally from, them. The arrangement of the chapters in *The Trial* is Brod's work, and a chapter like "The Whipper" could only vaguely be placed. It should be observed also that parts of the novels—for example, "The Stoker" and "Before the Law"—were published separately.

With some plausibility, one might call these books novels of the spiritual picaresque. Yet they are not completely episodic: even in the loosest, *Amerika*, the two rascals, Delamarche and Robinson reappear after we fancy we have seen the last of them; and in *The Castle* there is a very considerable integration of the materials; one notes in particular the fashion in which the matter of Chapter I (the teacher, the Laseman family, Hans Brunsurck and his mother) is subsequently developed. Each novel begins in substantially the same way: the hero breaks with his past. In two of them, he has left his home and we meet him as he enters a new world; in a third, his thirtieth birthday and his summons collaborate to start a new life.

The question of method is: Can there be a logic of composition when one's matter is the irruption of the irrational? There might, of course, be a psychological unwinding; the episodes might grow more elaborate or complex, deeper or more wry. In the unfinished state of the novels, no such progress is obvious. If one compares these novels with mystical documents like the books of St. Teresa and St. John of the Cross we find no such obvious symmetry and development as that of *The Interior Mansions*. Such systematic structure would doubtless have struck Kafka as simplifying: we don't know that much about the workings of Providence. And because of that pious skepticism it seems unlikely that Kafka could have written a novel with the close composition of *The Golden Bowl*.

In terms of narrative method, Kafka writes (with occasional lapses) from within the mind of the hero; and the introspective hero, through whose eyes we have glimpses of other persons, static figures, is drawn from the author. He is man alone, man hunted and haunted, man confronted with powers which elude him, and with women with whom he is never at ease, man prosecuted and persecuted; man in search of a job; man the outsider who wishes to come in. He is the man eager to do right but perpetually baffled and thwarted and confused as to what it is to do right—the man for whom the sense of duty, of responsibility, the irreducibility of "ought," has survived the positive and particular codes of religions and moral systems—the man in search of salvation.

A narrow, moving writer, Kafka is (as he would have desired) less artist than symbol. The appeal of this "narrow" symbol has been extraordinarily wide to Europeans and Americans of the last decade. One secular hope after another has failed the liberals and the communists: the German republic, the Spanish republic, the Maginot line. Kafka can be the symbol for what remains. He is illiberal, unrelenting, unsentimental; as Spender has said, he combines the power of the visionary with the self-criticism of the skeptic, so that he communicates the sense of there being something to believe without the claim of being able to define what it is. It is difficult today to believe in the reality of a world of comfort, good sense and progress; we doubt that we shall ever see such a world again; we think it wise to prepare ourselves spiritually for worlds more exacting and brutal and metaphysical; and of such worlds Kafka is initiate.

Kafka is, curiously, not a revolutionary. That is to say, he is not a moralist and reformer but an artist and a man of religion. The problem for him is one of accepting the universe. The painful complexity of living can be transcended aesthetically by reducing mystery itself to a kind of pattern, and religiously by acknowledging one's finiteness, learning to live in fear and trembling, by faith.

the objective depiction of absurdity

claude-edmonde magny

Few modern writers have the power to forge myths capable of rousing in us the violent emotions which the myths of the ancient religions arouse. Kafka is such a writer. About his slightest tale, once the first impression has been mastered, it is possible to talk indefinitely without wringing it dry, almost as one can talk about some object, person, or real event. For this reason, none of the abstract theories and philosophical exegeses about them is satisfactory. When Max Brod and others would have us see in *The Castle* solely the drama of the gift of Grace, which is for some incomprehensible reason denied and in the end obtained when it is no longer hoped for, we feel that we are being cheated. In those abstract schemes, in those structures of concepts, we refuse to recognize what we love in Kafka: the objective character (ordinary to the point of banality) of what transpires, which is the stuff of everyday life whose commonplace tenor stands in sharp contrast with its essential absurdity. Therefore I should like in this essay to stand before his work as before a flower, or some mysterious, gesturing idol, turning it and turning it about in my fingers, not in order to grasp its meaning, but rather to point out its manifold aspects.

85

In the foreground is the extraordinary density of his narratives, a reality as compact as the flakes of that thick snow which falls in the opening pages of *The Castle,* and whose presence we feel throughout the book. Never are we aware of the author pulling strings, crouching behind his puppets, moving among them to set ambushes, or to modify their fate. Kafka's stories do not in any way give the impression of "literary pieces," written by a man; rather they are like meteorites, surprising yet familiar dark blocks which force themselves upon our attention. In few works is the author so absent. He is never hidden behind the mask of narrator or confidant, interpolating his hypotheses and surmises. He has been identified with K., his anonymous hero—the initial invites identification, as does also the fact that, according to Max Brod, *The Castle* was begun as an "Ich-Roman," a story related in the first person. But even when we adhere to this interpretation, still it is K. who absorbs the author Franz Kafka and dominates him. K. does not know himself; he does not know who he is or where he is going. He derives no privilege from his identity with the author, contrary to what happens in Proust, for example—and in nearly all autobiographical novels— where the author seems to possess a truly privileged knowledge of the states of consciousness of "Marcel," his creature and pseudonym. Kafka does not know the end of his novel and the fate of his characters any more than the reader and the characters themselves. It is not he who guides the play. And therefore he succeeds in making us feel in the heart of the story that mysterious force which emanates from the Castle, and which we know very well was not created by the author, a person like ourselves. Kafka simply manifests the force. He is its instrument, along with the Superintendent, the landlady from the Bridge Inn, the barkeeper, Frieda, K., and the rest.

Hence we ought not to do what Kafka himself always refrained from doing: provide dialectical constructions for the unfolding of events which should be taken as a *real* account. Otherwise Kafka is quickly converted into a kind of frustrated philosopher who needs to be explained to himself and to others for lack of sufficient power of analysis and abstraction. That would imply a gratuitous insult: Kafka chose exactly the mode of expression that suited him. To deprive his narrative of the tense reality which is its great quality ° is to transform poetic myth into abstract allegory. Nothing could be more opposed to the spirit of Kafka and to his conception of existence.

The world, for Kafka, is essentially *turmoil*, something that is not *rational*, and whose essence therefore only a fantastic tale can express. To derive from his work a philosophy (even one which embraces turmoil and paradox, like that of Kierkegaard), is to render it too rational and, therefore, to falsify it. Only the gratuitousness of the event itself, of the *contingit*, can reveal the essential absurdity of things.

The brutality of the event immediately indicts as vain most human notions of morality: that of the "justice of fate," of "personal merit," even that of "responsibility." A fundamental idea of Kafka is that we are responsible not only for what we have expressly willed and for what we have *done*, but also for our indiscretions, our secret desires, our very misfortunes. To him, the notion of commitment must be taken in a passive sense: we do not commit ourselves to something; we find ourselves already committed to something—in a situation where, whether we have sought it or not, we will be punished if we default. Such a conception of responsibility, which considers neither the intention nor the act, is shocking but profound. No "lay" morality with rational pretensions has been willing to accept it (not even that of Kant, whose critique of the purity of intentions would at certain practical points come close to Kafka's morality), but it is at the basis of all primitive religions, as witness, among manifold examples, the "ancestral guilt" of the Old Testament, the "stigma" of the Greeks, in fine, the predestination to crime in certain accursed families, as in the case of Oedipus and the Atridae. There

---

° We shall not insist here on the profoundly realistic character of Kafka's work, since Landsberg has done it so adequately in his article; nor is the drama of Grace what Kafka wishes to relate in *The Castle*, but rather the story of a poor devil of a Land Surveyor who is made to come from afar off with the promise of a job, and of his disappointment when he learns that there has been a misunderstanding, and that, out of charity, they will employ him as school janitor. One can, certainly, discover *a posteriori* a philosophical significance, but it is not primary and results more or less arbitrarily.

87

weighs on Kafka's characters as on the characters of Greek tragedy, the sense of hidden guilt, stronger than simple "uneasy conscience": something analogous, perhaps, to the sense of original sin, with the difference that it is we who have committed the sin, no matter if we committed it unwittingly, no matter if we have forgotten it. In Kafka, the sin is almost always relegated to the past; often its nature is never clarified: the tale begins with the punishment, and what one has done to deserve the punishment, and even whether he does deserve it,* remains unknown. The judgment also belongs to the past. We are *already* judged. The sentence is behind us, and one may question whether modifying our actions, "mending our ways," would change it in any respect.†

This idea of a responsibility antedating the action is found in nearly all of Kafka's tales, even those where it does not constitute the essential theme, for example the short story "A Country Doctor," in which there appears—together with the theme of nightmare, the inhuman helplessness before the predestined event—the theme of the gratuitous catastrophe for which we are nevertheless responsible. And it is the profoundly irrational, *unacceptable* nature of this idea that makes his stories wound us so deeply: we feel it confusedly behind every recital, and our esthetic indignation reveals the protest of our reason.

Here it will be said, no doubt: this is an idea which we know very well in certain philosophers, Kierkegaard for example. It is the idea of *Fear and Trembling,* according to which

* Thus, in "The Metamorphosis" no justification whatsoever is given for the frightful catastrophes (transformation into a loathsome insect, solitude, suffering, sickness and finally death) which rain down upon the hero. Likewise in *The Trial;* in the short story "The Penal Colony," the police official charged with the execution of the sentence explains that the condemned does not know what he has done, nor what the sentence is. He has not been permitted to defend himself because he would only have "muddled things with his lies."

† Which is shown very well in "A Dream," where Joseph K., the hero of *The Trial,* and doubtless of *The Castle* as well (though the first name, Joseph, does not figure in the last work) sees himself, in dreams, inside a grave prepared beforehand, with his name already inscribed on the tombstone.

there is no common measuring-stick between God's justice and man's justice, and none, therefore, between morality and religion: God can order acts which appear unjust and even culpable to our eyes, such as the sacrifice of Abraham. We could go still farther and invoke the Cartesian theory of the Eternal Verities which—applied to moral commandments instead of to mathematical propositions—gives exactly the theory of Kierkegaard.° But the peculiar characteristic of Kafka is that he does not go in search of God to explain: Kafka does not explain; he affirms. This is the fact. *Es ist so.* Not once does he mention God in all his work. If he would introduce him expressly, all would be clear. We would believe we understood, we could accept, as does Job. But this he did not wish. The cup must be drunk to the lees, we must suffer without comprehending the inhuman sentence through which, like the condemned man in "The Penal Colony," we attain the ecstasy of the sixth hour.

There would be no shock for the understanding in the tales of Kafka if he were a philosopher. If instead of telling us the story of "The Judgment," he would say simply: "The understanding of God is incommensurable with our own," we would believe ourselves falling again into one of those truths made trite by Christianity, such as "The designs of Providence are inscrutable," and we would cease to pay him any attention. The message of Kafka would have been lost. To recur to Kierkegaard or the theory of the Eternal Verities for commentary is to deaden the impact of Kafka's tale, to try to escape the brutality of the real by explaining it away. And this is precisely what we must not do. Philosophy, like common sense or conventional religion, tends at times to be no more than a means of better enduring the world, of cushioning what in reality is shocking and intolerable. Because he is not a philosopher, Kafka wrenches us out of that weak-kneed wisdom. He hurls the unacceptable before our eyes and obliges us to look on it. He stands at the antipodes of all soothing, comfortable literature, as remote from the escape mechanisms of the romantics as from ordinary realism, which presents us with

° Cf. the critical disquisitions of Leibnitz at the beginning of his *Discourse on Metaphysics.*

the image of the world to which we are accustomed. In that sense, one could say he is a surrealist and that his tales have more reality than the novels that are allegedly realistic.

There is in Kafka a double value of irrationality and of nightmare as well. First a value of nightmare *per se,* to jerk open our eyes, to fling to earth the screens of philosophy and ideas that we interpose between ourselves and reality.° And in this the reading of Kafka accomplishes a *catharsis* which at first does not seem fundamentally different from that procured by reading *Alice in Wonderland* or some surrealist text. But in Kafka, nightmare and fantasy have *content* values as well: they are a revelation of truths beyond our understanding, indeed, unacceptable to it, that could be revealed in no other way. Herein lies Kafka's superiority over an author like Lewis Carroll, and also over the philosophers because he has added insanity to the conceptual content, because he has written nightmares and in that form is able to penetrate more deeply the essence of reality. If Kafka did not possess this "deep truth," "The Metamorphosis" or "The Penal Colony" would be merely "horror stories," † instruments, simply, for a kind of surrealist release in which it matters little whether the thing that frees the emotions is kept in sight, since the important thing is the release. In Kafka, the irrational, the horrible (as in "The Metamorphosis" or "The Penal Colony"), even the grotesque ("A Report to an Academy"), are never introduced for the sake of the literary effect produced, but for the sake of the mystery to whose door these proceedings bring

° In this sense, a conventional notion: moral, juridical, etc., for example, that of responsibility as defined by law or common sense ("One is only responsible for what he has done and done with full knowledge and consent, deliberately") is a sort of absolution given by society, a barrier set up for protection against the feeling of unconditional guilt that is in the depths of our conscience and is expressed in the old myths—that of Oedipus, that of Orestes—but which would make life intolerable if we abandoned ourselves to it.

† Here I am unjust perhaps to the horror story: cf. what Landsberg says in *Pierres Blanches* about the resemblances between the Marquis de Sade and Kafka. But although that linking is ingenious and sound, one cannot deny that the will to *reveal* is more conscious and expressed in Kafka than in Sade.

90

us. They are not alone designed to arrest our attention, but to express a depth of reality. They are inscribed in the essence of things.

*   *   *

Kafka tries, if not to justify, at least to give a sort of psychological translation to the shocking idea of our initial, almost pre-natal, guilt, trying to discover and expose it in the heart of actions that are in appearance most innocent. That is what he does, for example, in "The Judgment," one of his most extraordinary short stories, perhaps, because of the slow and gradual intrusion of the fantastic into a reality that is completely trivial and everyday (while in "The Metamorphosis" we find ourselves from the first moment installed in nightmare). We think we know whom we have loved? Can we know? . . . How dare we guarantee the purity of our intentions, of our love?

The hero of "The Judgment," George Bendemann, is a nice fellow who together with his father directs a prosperous business, and who has become engaged some months before. It is a Sunday morning and George is trying to write to one of his friends, established for some time past in Russia, where his affairs are not going well, and with whom George has gradually lost touch. He has not even informed him of his engagement (above all, it seems, in order not to sadden the friend by the spectacle of his own good fortune). He does not know what to say to him; everything he fancies useless: to counsel him to return to his fatherland would imply considering his failure irremediable; besides, he may be too late, perhaps the friend is no longer to be found at the address to which he is writing. Nevertheless, George finishes his letter, announces his engagement to the friend and invites him to the wedding. Afterward, he goes to his father's room to show him the letter. It appears that it is months since he has entered his father's room—which is a perfectly natural thing, of course, since he sees him every day at business. At the end of a series of rather surprising Jeremiads in which he complains of his old age, of his helplessness, the father says with sudden harshness: "I beg of you, George, do not deceive me. . . . Do you *really* have this friend in Petersburg?" The question does astonish

91

us, but we think the old man is falling into second childhood. And this impression seems confirmed by the exceedingly painful and irrational scene which follows between the father and son. The father, raising himself on his elbow in the bed, accuses the son of having plotted his friend's perdition, and reveals that he, happily, has secretly informed the young man—who is like a son to him—and has defended his interests; and the end of his speech, when he solemnly condemns his son to death by drowning—"*Ich verurteile dich jetzt zum Tode des Ertrinkens!*"—only astounds us proportionately, as one proof more of the old man's insanity.

And at this point a surprise effect occurs, something like that in a detective story at the moment when it is unexpectedly revealed that the guilty one, the "villain" of the piece, is not the person we thought. The different happenings *reclassify* themselves before our eyes and quickly take on entirely different meanings from those which they had had till then. George feels himself immediately put out of the room. He heads toward the river, and *really drowns himself.*

This denouement, however *unacceptable,* is convincingly set forth in exactly the same tone of truth and reality as the beginning of the story: George jumps the railing of the bridge "like the excellent gymnast he had been in his youth, to his parents' delight." Meanwhile the horrible and mysterious is interwoven as in a continuous weft. "Something" * pushes him to the water, a force without countenance, all the more mysterious because we are not even told it is a force, something that has no name, against which George struggles without being able to resist: "he was gripping the rail as a starved man seizes on food." He dies making protestations of love for his parents and with the last sentence everyday reality closes over him—and over the entire story with its web of the horrible and familiar—like the water of the river: "The traffic over the bridge at that moment was endless."

Behind this irritating—and captivating—enigma, behind this defiance of reason, we feel the presence of something

* *Ueber die Fahrbahn zum Wasser trieb es ihn."*

more than the arbitrary act of an author intent on astonishing at any cost. Nothing in Kafka's style suggests the desire to astound. On the contrary, by his extreme restraint, he is perhaps the most "classic" of German authors. And owing to that, we ask ourselves what in the conduct of George could have justified the sentence which punishes him, as little as we would question ourselves about a mishap, apparently unmerited, which might strike one of our friends. And, little by little, certain circumstances come to memory: we feel ourselves capable of "reading between the lines." A more exact analysis of George's sentiments reveals to us from the very first pages the self-satisfaction, the latent Pharisee-ism, the hypocrisy, which make him *deserve* his sentence. He sits down to write the letter to his friend as one makes an arduous sacrifice: is this true friendship? He stops with complacency to contrast the failure of the other with his own triumph on the sentimental plane and the social plane as well as in business: his fiancée belongs to one of the "good families" of the city. Similarly, his sentiments toward his father are far removed from filial piety, he treats him with a condescending manner; he would like, at bottom, to have him retire from business "to rest"; in reality, to be able to run the business alone. But he dissembles all this to his own eyes and to ours as well—at least the first time that we read the story. The shock we receive at the end incites us to justify it by a reflection on the real intentions of George. As the story proceeds, the Pharisaic attitude of George toward his father becomes more and more sharply defined: for example, when try-ing to undress him to put him to bed, he notes that his linen is not especially clean, that the old man is deteriorating and does not take care of his person, and that he George will have to pay more attention to him from now on. Then he disposes of his father as of a child or a thing: and brusquely, without consulting him, and even without the least idea of doing so, he decides to take him to live with him when he is married.

The extraordinary thing is that this overweening air of superiority does not emerge into the open at the first reading. The reason is that at the same time, from a certain point of view, George is right; his father actually is in the process of relapsing into childishness, and when he says that he, the son, has no friend in Russia, that he never has had, George is not mistaken in thinking what he does. The evidence of the father's insanity neutralizes in a way the evidence of Phariseeism in the son; and this duality of planes constitutes precisely the strength of Kafka. But the fact that the father is insane does not justify the conduct of the son with respect to him. That one is wrong does not mean the other is right: we live in a world in which we are all wrong. A Truth that we tend too much to forget each time, for example, that we commit the moral fallacy of treating someone who has acted badly toward us as if he had put himself "outside the pale"—a fallacy that Kafka refuses to admit. He will not let anyone be right; he confines himself to establishing the duality of the points of view of his characters, without taking part, without declaring either superior to the other, nor in any way more *truthful*. There is in this a discovery of the profound significance of insanity (as a paramount manifestation of the fundamental irreducibility of all points of view) that is lacking in Pirandello who is, nevertheless, so obsessed with the theme.

The work that "The Judgment" recalls is not *Henry IV* nor the disputes between Signora Frola and Signor Ponza, but the short story of Sartre called "The Room," * in which insanity is described somewhat in the same manner as in Kafka and suggests the same train of thought. Pierre is actually insane; the author leaves us no doubt of it; but the fact that his point of view differs fundamentally from that of the people called "normal" is not enough to establish the superiority of those latter nor does it authorize his father-in-law Monsieur Darbedat to treat him condescendingly. As to Kafka, he will hardly say the father is insane; but he *suggests* it now and then, by a few horrible details. For instance: when George deposits him on the bed, the old man amuses himself playing with his son's watch-chain and clings to it with so much strength that the latter has hard work freeing it. Here insanity makes its appearance under a physical and "objective"—almost medical—aspect, about which there can

* In John Lehmann (ed.): *New Writing*, New Series, Vol. II, Spring 1939, pp. 6-28, London: Hogarth Press: 1939. *(Translator's note)*

be no doubt; * but that does not imply that the sane man is in the right, the insane in the wrong, and the denouement of the story sanctions the condemnation of George.

❄   ❄   ❄

The critical examination of intentions in the "clear conscience," so evident in "The Judgment," likewise constitutes one of the major themes of *The Castle*, along with the theme of the irreducibility of points of view which is of course tightly bound up with it. On that account K.'s † conduct is the object of extremely diverse interpretations (but seldom flattering to him) on the part of the different characters, from the landlady of the Bridge Inn to Momus, the secretary at the Castle office, who draws up a formal charge against him: his relations with Frieda are explained, for example, by grossly sensual motives but above all by a more or less conscious Machiavellism which would make him use her as a tool to reach Klamm, her chief of service, and so, the Castle. There is no way of gauging exactly the veracity of those accusations: all the denials of K. do not persuade his enemies, nor perhaps ourselves, of his good faith. It is not a question of establishing whether a certain material action did or did not take place, but of the motive that should be attributed to K.'s acts: ‡ and on this score it is only possible to convince those

---

* In like manner, at the end of "The Room," the definite proof of insanity in Pierre is given by the fact that he starts to stutter; the madness ceases to be an almost willful play of the spirit, a "voluntary alteration of all the senses" as in Rimbaud (what we would call myth-mania), and becomes sickness, a psychological change: true insanity—as Rimbaud puts it, "the kind that shuts itself in."

† K. is the Land Surveyor who is trying to establish himself in the village at the foot of the castle and who seduces Frieda, a barmaid at the Herrenhof who has been the mistress of Klamm, a Castle official.

‡ Here it should be pointed out how Kafka achieves by simpler means an effect identical with Pirandello of the absolute impossibility of arriving at knowledge of the truth. For example, in *Right You Are*, Pirandello is obliged to resort to an extremely complicated hypothesis; in *The Castle*, on the contrary, it is a question of extremely simple, ordinary acts whose true import, nevertheless, eludes us. The doubt is not rooted in the historic reality of a deed, in the problem of knowing whether such and such a particular act took place, but in something infinitely more profound. The

who are convinced beforehand. K. himself is not one of these: when Frieda takes up the accusations of the landlady, K. for a moment is overwhelmed, but he refrains from protesting the purity of his intentions. As he himself recognizes, almost everything in that charge is the truth: he has never concealed his desire to reach the Castle and see Klamm, if necessary through Frieda or no matter whom. The deeds they challenge him with are correct: only the hostile interpretation which is given them can be discussed, though not broken down definitively.* One can argue, if one wishes, that if K. has chosen precisely that night to make himself Frieda's lover, it is because, for some reason, he wants to pass the night in the place where the master of the Castle lodges, and this was his only means of achieving his object: but this is a grave imputation only in the event that Frieda does not love K.; if she loves him, surely she knows he did not throw himself on her like a beast of prey to make her serve his purposes, but that in large measure, it was she who came to him.

All the less can K. defend himself from those accusations because the deep Machiavellism of which they accuse him is exposed even in his least premeditated acts, those which have most surprised himself, such as his love for Frieda and his sudden departure from the Bridge Inn. The others, then, appear to know his secret intentions better than he himself. And then too, it is not his sincerity which is under suspicion, so that if K. were to protest, his protests would be worthless: they would answer that per-

---

superficiality of Pirandello's play stems in large part from the fact that everything could be reduced in the final instance to determining a precise historic fact, establishing whether the daughter is crazy or has died. Now then, this determining of historic fact is difficult; it may even be impossible in certain circumstances, for example, in consequence of a lacuna in our records: as it is impossible for us to know the exact date of death of Atala III of Pergamos, but that kind of knowledge is not essentially and under all circumstances impossible, as it would have to be for Pirandello's thesis to be really disquieting, something like determining what a being *is*, what, for example, was Atala III. Pirandello has indeed perceived the fundamental ambiguity of all that exists, but he has given us only an uncertain and contingent expression of it, therefore a superficial one.

* "*Alles, was du sagst* (he says to Frieda) *ist in gewissem sinne richtig, unwahr ist es nicht, nur feindselig ist es.*" *Schloss,* 305.

haps he himself is unconscious of his sinister purposes. The landlady of the Bridge Inn makes it clear from the start that she does
not accuse him of a lie (thus depriving him of all recourse): on
the contrary, she finds him "open as a child," *kindlich offen*. But
it disturbs her that K. is so different from the people of the village: these latter cannot understand his real motives; so they will
not be persuaded to believe him even when he speaks frankly.*
The true ambiguity is rooted not in what K. *says* or *does* but in
what K. is deep in his heart, and because of that it cannot be
settled by abstract speculations about his conduct, nor above all
by the speculations of strangers, of people who speak another
language.† What Momus and the landlady try to arrive at beyond the motive for K.'s acts is an estimate of his personal worth,
and about that, K. himself cannot pronounce. And here is clarified
and justified our statement at the beginning that responsibility
in Kafka does not depend on the intentions, and scarcely on the
acts: it matters little whether we have done something purposely
or not, even whether we are materially guilty, since we are not
charged with having done this or that but with being this or
that. In the first pages of the book, the landlady of the Bridge Inn
says that they do not reproach K. with being a stranger, a rolling
stone, whose purposes are vague: K. is what he is, and can do
nothing about it. The landlady only confirms the fact and de-
plores that Frieda has imprudently linked her fate with his. But
he is none the less a dangerous person, whom they have to combat. And here we have the reason why critical probing of intention can remain implicit in Kafka: he reaches beyond the intentions themselves, he reaches through them to the essence of
the being, his inner void, his fundamental guilt and perversity.

* And here we find a new manner of combining doubt about
the motive with the irreducibility of points of view: Since K. does not hold
the same point of view as the people of the village, they will appreciate
his sincerity of bearing inopportunely; they will not believe he is telling the
truth, for example, when he declares himself disposed to enter the Castle
by any means whatsoever.

† On the contrary, as Kafka says, the ambiguity is dispersed
instantly the moment Frieda loves him, because this love is a sort of immediate contact with his innermost being.

97

Why, then, quibble over motives? The accused can no more make a valid defense than can the rebel soldier in "The Penal Colony"; his guilt is indelibly graven in him, in his innermost being; it is his being.

Hence the critique of intention, through probing too deep, ends in a blind alley. It cannot arrive at any certainty, even the certainty of our guilt. On that account, we ought not to attribute to it in Kafka a role which it does not play: that of a Theodicy, in the Leibnitzian sense—*a justification of God,* to which one has recourse to explain condemnations apparently unmerited, the chastisement of the innocent, and all the injustices of fate. The impurity of our heart does not warrant the misfortunes that wound us (moreover, is not the greatest of these this impurity itself?). At best, it is a manner of softening the sentiment of our condition, an attempt to explain it, in order to help us accept it, without the explanation pretending to be complete. Likewise the Pascalian critique of the notion of merit serves simply to make the layman accept the Jansenist doctrine of predestination, to make it less offensive to his eyes by leading him to look into his own heart and perceive to what degree it is "hollow and full of wretchedness," but it would be folly to conclude from this that the theological doctrine of predestination is founded on psychological or moral considerations. Likewise, though the courts take into account whether or not a deed was committed deliberately, this consideration of the will to wrongdoing on the part of the culprit serves only to justify to society the sanctions whereby society sits in judgment. Originally these sanctions did not take into account the intentions of the culprit: it was in the beginning a simple defensive reaction, and the culprit is always, at bottom, a scapegoat. Kafka does not fall into such gross error: even if K. were perverse to the core—he seems to us, on the contrary, clearly sympathetic—that would not justify his misfortunes, just as the insanity of George's father does not justify his son's attitude toward him.

The true meaning of this critical revelation of the intentions must be sought in another direction: it is a manner of expressing what for Kafka constitutes one of the essential aspects of our condition as men: the irreducibility of points of view. Thus, when K. nears the Castle, which from afar seemed to answer well enough to his preconceived idea, though it looked more like a village than a Castle, the disappointment begins: it is nothing, in truth, but a jumble of tumbledown fortifications, notable only because they were built of stone; indeed the whole exterior is crumbling. Likewise Klamm, when K. looks at him through the keyhole, appears to him a very ordinary sort of man, of middle height, a bit fleshy, his features already set with age, and who sleeps a great deal; but K. has not really seen him; he cannot see him as he is, and the landlady tells him so. Just as, not being native to the place, he cannot comprehend the prestige which surrounds the Castle in the villagers' eyes. The villagers, for their part, are well aware of it; as soon as the teacher meets K., he asks him: "You don't like the Castle?" (K., on the contrary, is somewhat astonished by the question, and all the more when the teacher seems to expect a negative response) and adds: "Strangers never do." They take into account the fact that K. is not one of them: but that in nowise helps them to understand him better. In a misunderstanding there is always one who is aware of the barrier which separates him from the rest, and owing to that, believes himself superior. But what good is this awareness? In that respect, the world of Kafka resembles the world of Racine, in which lucidity is vain and only imposes one torture more.

The conflict between points of view incompatible but equally legitimate (or illegitimate) is one of the themes of "A Report to an Academy," the story of the ape who transforms himself into a man. Here the opposition does not arise, as in "The Judgment," between the demented man and the Pharisee, but between the animal and the "rational" being.

An ape who has succeeded in raising himself by a kind of self-education to the human state, delivers to an Academy the very scholarly report of his experiences. For the rest, from the beginning of his report, he excuses himself for being able now to bring only very rudimentary data on his former state as an ape, his *"äffisches Vorleben."* In proportion as he has become acclimatized to the world of men, return to apishness has become difficult, even if he should desire it.° Here the metamorphosis is complete, as complete as that of Gregor Samsa ("The Metamorphosis") who, when he tries to speak, believes himself pronouncing articulate, intelligible, human words while actually they are the indistinct cries of an animal.

One cannot hold two points of view at once. Nor does the passing from one condition to the other constitute a superiority: the new state limits no less than the old. Here can be seen the meaning of Kafka's predilection for the infraconceptual, the infrarational: for the sleeper, the mad; lower still, for the ape and the insect; here are particularly manifest the incompatible points of view of the different beings who inhabit the world and, at the same time, the condition of man is revealed as a limited state no less than that of insect or ape.

The dominant emotion of the ape after his capture, when he is locked up in a cage on the bridge of the ship, is "There's no way out" ("*Kein Ausweg*"), and he has only one idea: to get out, get out at any price. He does not want liberty— which so many men desire and which is in most cases nothing but a bitter gibe—but a way out no matter where it leads, as one buried alive wishes simply that the wall might be a little farther away, the ceiling a little less low, even if this way out is illusion. But flight is not the way out since breaking out would only make things worse; it would be an act of desperation; no; what is necessary is to remain where he is and try to better his condition by rising above it, using the most humble means. Because the way out which he seeks is modest, it does not matter much if it should turn out to be an illusion; the disillusionment will not be serious, since he was not looking for anything of much im-

---

° But all through the report, there are details which remind us continually that it is an ape who is speaking and not a man: he relates, for example, that a reporter has had the impudence to present as a vestige of his ape-nature the fact that he often takes off his trousers in public (when he was doing it, in reality, to show visitors the scar of the wound he received at the time of his capture), and adds that they ought to cut the fingers off the hand that wrote those words.

portance; on the contrary, if he had sought liberty,* not to achieve it would be terrible. There is in Kafka a very strong sense of the humility of all human triumphs which recalls Pascal expounding the argument of "the wager": on this account, the essential difference between man and ape does not inhere in the possession of reason or language but in the custom of shaking hands, which attests a frankness of character.

In the foregoing there will have been recognized, no doubt, certain themes with which philosophers and poets have made us familiar and which we would call, abstracting them to banality, the sense of our solitude in the midst of men and in the midst of the world, anguish in the face of the limitations of our state, the sense of the impossibility of all escape and of the vanity of every act. But Kafka, thanks to the mythical transposition that he offers us, recovers and communicates a sort of primary sensation, irreducible, ineffable, that our man's-words betray and dilute in trying to express: that "old ape-truth" that we have forgotten, in part voluntarily, in our desire to get out of it, to find a way out, whatever it may be; that perhaps is lost for us in its original crudity and horror, but which nevertheless lies hidden in us and which we stumble upon in nightmare or anguish: the proof that there is "no way out." Pascal's argument of "the wager" appears almost an abstract expression in the face of the brutality of this immediate experience; soothing, calming and comfortable alongside this wordless pang, this impotent terror of insect or beast.† We think of the insect which has fallen

* The word "liberty" is used, of course, ambiguously to cover at the same time its meaning for the ape and for the man. Perhaps there is in Kafka the idea of an intermediate state in which liberty is not yet desired, as in the ape, or in which it is still not desired, as in certain men, wherein one's condition is accepted bravely, with all the limitations it entails.

† We must beg to be excused for insisting so strongly on this point as a reaction against the opinion, unfortunately too widely held, of Kafka as a frustrated Pascal, frustrated because he was not a Christian. For instance, Daniel-Rops, seeking what is lacking in the universe of Kafka to make us accept it as complete, says: "Upon reflection, it seems to me to lack a sense of responsibility" (sic); and farther on: "this man always threatened by punishment, and whose efforts are always futile, is like a vapid reflection of the Christians' sinner. But the religious teaching of good

101

into a cup and never succeeds in climbing out again, up the slippery wall of glass,* of all those old myths sunk deep in us, of all the old metaphors that each one finds again instinctively to express his affliction. But in Kafka, they are deeds, things that happen, and not simple metaphors.

Our whole civilization is only an effort to turn our backs on that original pang and forget it. And those among us who preserve the memory, who still hark back to that apish past, make of it reports to Academies: the philosophers and the writers, they take their anguish or their nausea and make a novel, or philosophy.

One must not look on Kafka merely as a spirit of denial, who ridicules all human ambitions because he cannot comprehend their nobility: he feels on the contrary very strongly the nobility of any aspiration or effort, whatever its object. The end of the ape's Report is full of legitimate pride, the pride of the life that has attained exactly the goal it set and which does not admit the suggestion that "perhaps it was not worth the trouble." Kafka simply refuses to consider the ontological value of the end toward which man aspires and gives us only the most humble, and usually grotesque and vulgar, expressions of it. In Kafka our loftiest aspirations become the ambition of the ape to escape from the zoo and reach the music hall, or, better still, the ambition of K. to obtain an interview with a petty official of the Castle. His work resolves itself into a kind of mysticism without God, in which the hero seeks, almost always in vain, and by most strange and sorrowful means—at times against his will—an ecstasy which circumstance withholds from him. The most typical story in this respect is "The Hunger-Artist," the story of a professional "hunger-artist" who shows himself in a cage from circus to circus, for

---

and evil, of sin and forgiveness, gives a deeper meaning to life. Kierkegaard, Pascal, starting from similar observations, sink roots much deeper into the mystery of existence. . . ." It seems to us on the contrary that the importance of Kafka derives from the fact that he has uncovered very strong, very primitive, absolutely irrational feelings that we carry driven deep in us, of which religious fables, philosophical systems, poetic myths are merely expressions—attenuations, maybe.

    * Cf. Gregor, in "The Metamorphosis."

whom fasting the longest time possible is his life purpose, an end in itself, yet with no idea of accomplishing anything else through the fast. The spectators see merely a circus stunt, a means of earning a living in which it is natural to try to cheat. The most humane among those set to watch him turn their backs, so to speak, in the night and play cards in the corner, leaving him the chance to eat on the sly. The fatality of his existence is that they never permit him to fast as long as he would like, never more than forty days, and that only in the large cities; not for medical or humane reasons, but because the interest of the public would fall off over a longer period. When they do bring him out of his cage, with great pomp, the professional faster is ready to faint, not from hunger, as the public believes, but from rage and humiliation that they will not let him fast longer. He ends by passing out of fashion and dying forgotten, without the public or anyone bothering to count the days of his fast. Here we find the theme of fundamental solitude symbolized materially by the cage (as in the story of the ape) and, morally, by the lack of understanding on the part of the public. A rejuvenation, if you wish, of the theme of the "loneliness of the artist," of the "ivory tower" or of the "Albatross," with the difference that this aloneness holds nothing poetic (it is, on the contrary, terribly vulgar, at once horrible and grotesque); it is the aloneness of the Mount of Olives with the spitting, the insults and the sponge soaked in gall; nor is it due to the public's *hostility*, as in Baudelaire *— merely to its indifference, and the inability of the crowd to understand anything; in the last analysis, it is nowhere said that this aloneness constitutes superiority: † before dying, the mystic faster gives the key to the enigma: if he fasts, it is because he can do nothing else; it is a fate, not a vocation; he has never found the food he could savor; if he had, he would have gorged himself with it as all of us do. So the insatiable hunger, the divine nos-

* The sailors, for example, do not despise the ape, do not ridicule it or try to hurt it, as Baudelaire's sailors do with the Albatross: on the contrary they tickle him where he likes to be tickled, and busy themselves with his education.

† In the story of the ape it is even said expressly that the effort to make life viable must consist in getting out of it.

talgia that possesses the mystic or artist perhaps is at bottom only some lack, something unsatisfiable, a fundamental maladjustment, the sign of an imperfect soul.

This union of realism and mysticism gives Kafka's work its exceptional value and is what we must try to plumb to discover his "message." Kafka is capable of seeing at the same time what a thing holds of the commonplace and marvelous, and expressing it. When K. cohabits with Frieda for the first time, he does it under the counter of the tavern where she serves, in the midst of barrels of beer; nevertheless, it is for both an incomparable experience. Similarly, the condemned man in "The Penal Colony" begins to vomit, up to the instant preceding the ecstasy of the sixth hour. Kafka appears to insist with some determination (though aside from this, without coarseness, almost without seeming to notice) on the scant brilliance life can hold. But such a realism is not a simple literary method; neither is it solely designed, as we pointed out in the beginning, to make us accept the improbable happenings it relates; it produces this effect to be sure, but that does not exhaust its meaning; the *everyday* seems to have here a more profound significance: Kafka perceives, in the most trivial things, meanings we no longer perceive because we have let ourselves be blinded. We do not have the hardihood to open wide our eyes; being alien to the world, we cannot understand it, any more than K. can truly see Klamm or feel the beauty of the Castle. And, for Kafka, the goal of a work of art is to make us see as in transparency, to make us "read between the lines," a meaning that in any other manner would escape unnoticed.* We are in the world as K. in the town (which he nevertheless must survey in his capacity of Land Surveyor), in the midst of things whose interest we do not perceive at all, nor, with greater reason, their meaning, which appears to us trivial and commonplace until the day when some unaccustomed event (or reading) arouses us, forces us to open our eyes and gives us a foreboding of what lies behind them. But to convince us, the writer's point of departure must be the real and he must not

* Cf. the deleted part of *The Castle* cited in the final note of this article.

diverge from reality. The immanence must subsist absolute, like that of certain poetry; with this difference: the transfiguration of the real does not consist in seeing in things the beauty they enclose (as in Keats), nor in a communion with the essence of each particular thing (as in Rilke), but in reading in life, *meaning*— for the most part sinister or inhuman meaning, since what one becomes aware of has in it nothing reassuring or comforting. Then can be seen how fragile is the crust of civilization and reason which separates us from the atrocious, from the barbarous, from the unthinkable; as thin as the cloak of earth which disguises the grave, dug for him beforehand, that Joseph K. sees in his dreams. Kafka has strongly the sense that human life is entirely bordered by the inhuman. That is what "An Old Page" expresses, the fragment of an anonymous account, jotted down on a fluttering leaf of paper which floats as the last trace of a civilization. Some nomads encamp in the square of the capital, facing the imperial palace; nobody understands them; not even their gestures; at times they grimace; then one sees the whites of their eyes and foam lathers their mouths. It is not that they wish to speak; nor even to frighten; that is, simply, how they are. They take what they need, but without using force; they eat raw meat in the company of their horses; they end by feasting on a live ox. The emperor, powerless, follows the spectacle with his eyes from behind the windows of his palace, and more and more withdraws to the interior.* We are surrounded on every hand by what is horrible, monstrous; here it is, at our side, in the frame and structure of our life. Its intrusion is not exceptional, it is the rule, and it is enough for the crust to crack in any place to make us aware of it.† Wherever, wheresoever we may look

* Here we find the same theme of the man overwhelmed by his destiny, the man charged with a mission he knows he cannot fulfill, but for which he will nevertheless be held responsible, for whom this calling, of which he is unworthy, instead of lifting him above himself, becomes a fate that crushes him. Cf. "An Imperial Message."

† Cf. Sartre's *La Nausée*, 199-201, the moment in which Antoine Roquetin returns from Paris: the prophetic vision he has of the Cities invaded by vegetation. What constitutes the ground of Sartre's work is, as in Kafka, the impression that life is essentially without rules, without laws, that a day might bring forth anything at all; that life lacks necessity,

round about us, shadowy things are to be glimpsed, that we could glimpse if we had the strength to hold our eyes well open and look them in the face. But it is almost unbearable; so we give up, we shut our eyes; and all falls back into obscurity.* Perhaps it is better so.

Translated by Angel Flores.

---

that it is fundamentally *monstrous*. The revelation of what might come to pass is only an extension of something *already there*, if we knew how to see it: "All those pairs of eyes which slowly devour a face will be there, no doubt, for good measure, but they will be no more numerous than the first pair. It is life I fear."

     * Kafka says so himself in a deleted part of *The Castle*, cited by Max Brod: "If you have the strength to look at things steadily, without, as it were, blinking your eyes, you can see much; but if you relax only once and shut your eyes, everything fades immediately into obscurity."

kafka and dostoyevsky

renato poggioli

The search for a habitation which we know under no
other form but that abstract and conventional one of an address
can sometimes assume the dimensions of a discovery or an adventure. Thus once when I was wandering in that section of
Prague which is enclosed between the Old City square and the
banks of the Moldava, the whereabouts of the domicile I was
looking for seemed to me an allusive and encouraging prelude
to the acquaintance and conversation that I was so impatient to
begin. The person who was expecting me was Max Brod, a Jew
by birth and a German by tongue, a journalist and a writer,
legatee to the work and memory of Franz Kafka, and the impulse which moved me toward him was the piteous anxiety to
visit the spiritual relics of a departed confrère. His house was
half way along the last building of an ugly and twisting little
street which grew wide only to shelter in a little square a few
steps away the old Synagogue with its little roof of bricks loom-
ing over your shoulders like the top of a dormer window, and
the seat of the ancient Jewish community, as charming and comic
as a carillon or a cuckoo clock. Indeed a sweet and polished little
remnant of the ghetto, one of those corners which must have been

preferred in the Middle Ages by the most fanatical and reflective Israelites, in that ancient and curious Prague which has been revealed to us by Meyrink.

The sound of the bell, a dark corridor and the sweet and warm voice of the hairy little man who cordially offered me his hand, aroused me from my reveries and recalled to me at once the object of my visit and the questions to be asked him. The little man answered me less with words than with documents and with facts, and exhibited a small and tattered collection of photographs; they were all pictures of Kafka. Franz as a baby, a grammar school pupil, and at the university; Franz in sports, on a walk with his friends, in the country; Franz sick, in a sanatorium, dying. Within me now from the sight of so many mementos there remains only a single and confused recollection: a typical face of a Jewish schoolboy of Central Europe, with the lineaments which express the characteristic *"refoulée"* impudence of the race. But the forehead, under the brushcut hair, radiated a sweet and precocious sense of old age from the noble and anxious furrows which gave to the face a strange sense of harmony and beauty, while the vivid and dreamy eyes under the wide and neat curtain of his eyebrows revealed traces of a devastating and monomaniac reflectiveness. I remember well that Brod guessed my thought and anticipated a hesitating and still unexpressed question from me. "Franz was very happy and used to laugh very often. He used to talk a good deal, and in a strong voice, and he died of tuberculosis of the larynx." Then I endeavored for a moment to imagine the sound of that voice and of that laugh, and I was astonished when, as if by an illumination, I felt they must have been like the laugh and the voice of Svidrigailov. And then I understood that the world and the art of Kafka could not be explained except by Dostoyevsky's myth.

Remember one of the most obscure and deceiving passages of the dialogue of Raskolnikov with Svidrigailov? Svidrigailov enters like a phantom into the room where Raskolnikov is feeding on rancor and solitude. He presents himself to him, tells him of his own life, speaks to him of the continual apparitions of his dead wife, and says to him, "Who knows that the other world is not peopled with spiders or with something of the same sort?

108

. . . For us eternity is only an incomprehensible idea, a thing enormous and immense. But why immense, I ask? And if instead it were only a dark recess, a sort of bathroom crammed with spiders in all the corners? I sometimes imagine it to myself in exactly that way." And when Raskolnikov asks him: "Is it possible that you don't know how to imagine anything less desolate and more just?" Svidrigailov responds, "More just. But it can also be granted that an eternity so constituted is very just; nay, if I have to say so, that's exactly the way I would make it." To which Dostoyevsky adds that Svidrigailov pronounced these words with "an abstracted smile."

The first revelation that the thought and image of Svidrigailov are flashing into the reader's mind is that a similar idea of eternity as a little gray and dusty room full of spiders is nothing but a metaphysical projection of the scenario in which all the characters of Dostoyevsky live. In fact all the critics of his work from the positivist Mikhailovsky through the mystic Merezhkovski, who was the first person clever enough to contrast the myth of the author of *The Brothers Karamazov* with that of the author of *Anna Karenina,* have noted that the pages of Dostoyevsky never disclose to us the rustic and natural landscapes of Tolstoy, and that the only background on which his creatures live, act and discuss is constituted by the four walls of a rented room, by the stairs of a tenement house, or at most by a poor section of the most artificial and absurd city that men have constructed on the face of the earth: Petersburg. The work of Dostoyevsky has been the first to make us feel the terrible imprisonment of stone and lime, and it is precisely from that that is born in correlation with the exterior signs of urban progress and with the vulgarization of his myths, that narrative epidemic of the postwar period which was called "literature of asphalt." The novels of Dostoyevsky and of Kafka are really, as a critic has said apropos of the writer from Prague, "novels of human solitude," of a solitude which expresses itself materially and spiritually in the one dimension of a brick pavement or an inlaid floor, in the eternal fatality of a trip around one's room, a trip not even cheered up or eased by the familiarity with one's own furniture or with the loving and intimate contemplation of one's own things. Dostoyevsky's and Kafka's characters live in rooms which do not belong to them, anonymous and unadorned, and certainly not very clean: their thought and their manner of existing are nothing but a magnetic ebb and flow set free from their brain, which are reflected and refracted on the four walls which surround and enclose them, condense and concentrate them, exalt and humiliate them. The cosmos of Dostoyevsky's creatures is a monad of bricks and lime, and as you know, monads have no windows at whose sill one can press one's face to enjoy the spectacle of the world and through whose blinds and panes the perfume of the flowers or the light of the sun can penetrate. That's why many of his creatures perceive only shadows and believe that they are the only reality of life, thus renewing the Platonic myth of the cave. But the Platonic cave, natural and primitive, intended to symbolize the errors of logic and the limitation of experience, represents precisely in this the obscurity of the lack of civilization and the darkness of instinct, while the four walls of Dostoyevsky, constructed by will and artifice, a fruit of the practical reasoning which teaches us to protect human existence from the offenses of inclement weather and the elements, mean nothing else than the narrow, inexorable, and perpetual prison of conscience. Civilization, beyond constructing them, has illuminated houses and oil light; the gas burner and the electric light are the generators of a thousand shadows on the smooth porous walls of our grottos of masonry or cement. But if the caves of instinct defy the weather by ignoring it (because their destiny, written as it is on the book of nature and of geological cataclysms, is signed in hours and in dates which are not those conventional ones of the calendars of society and of the clocks of history), the houses of men are subjected instead to ruin and to destruction, and it is in this sense, in that of Nietzsche, that their inhabitants are "decadents." But by a law of fatality and compensation notice how those ruined walls, those walls dusty and full of spiders, arouse in the mind of their extravagant lodgers the sense of the infinite and the eternal, and it is this fatality which a pupil and an interpreter of Dostoyevsky, Leo Shestov, has called "second sight," a light which makes even the opaque transparent.

110

Now Kafka is one who has succeeded in making a similar sense of the eternal live again, that dangerous virtue of reflecting on an infinite series of mirrors which is exclusive of the conscience, in an atmosphere quite different from that in which the creatures of Dostoyevsky act: we are no longer in the capital of the North and in the last century, but in a great city of Central Europe and of our own day; we no longer have anything to do with hungry students or with decadent nobles who live in the great populous agglomerations of Petersburg, but we find ourselves before bank clerks or salesmen from Prague or Vienna, who live in furnished but comfortable rooms, near some good average or moderately rich family. In a word Kafka has transplanted Dostoyevsky's drama of conscience from the barbaric and mystic mould of orthodox Russia into the gracious flower-vase which adorns the window-sill of so many petit bourgeois apartments of our oldest Europe. The particular tragedy of the novels of Kafka is that the catastrophe takes place in almost crepuscular and "intimist" circles, at times even *"gemütlich."* And if the sense of prison emanating from the work and fantasy of Dostoyevsky is a hundred times more universal and grand, that depends not only on the force of the art but also on the fact that beyond the walls and under the foundations of his houses is fermenting all that boiling spring of a spiritual existence as vast as the steppes, of a mystic and uncultivated Muscovite barbarism which multiplies the echo of conscience in the very grottos of a more domineering and savage instinct. It can almost be said that the skepticism and the anti-Europeanism of Dostoyevsky are the amplifiers of a voice which does nothing but repeat the latest and most absurd words of the logic of the Occident. On the contrary, the widest spiritual center within which the vibration of Kafka's word branches forth occupies the narrow limits of a well, of a tradition which is vertical and obscure, that of the Jewish soul, which outside its own rooms and habitations presupposes no human societies vaster than the ghetto. As in Svidrigailov and in Dostoyevsky, the sense of sin forces Kafka to recognize that an eternity thus formed (that of the *dark recess* and of the *spiders*) is the only fatal, possible and just one, but the weight and the importance of the condemnation are precisely limited by the

111

fact that he underlines unconsciously in the cosmic recognition of original sin that principal flaw of a people merely local-minded, which is his world, the Jewish, and of a predominantly bourgeois civilization, which is the modern world and ours. Kafka has forgotten that the sinful fruit of good and of evil has been plucked from the tree of science, and has identified the greatest fault of the moderns with the reduction of the concept of eternity to the sole dimension of time. Dostoyevsky's conception of the eternal, more abstract and I would say almost geometrical, is perhaps the only just and possible one, according to Svidrigailov, because in his famous image he determines the prison of being as a punishment which tends to limit liberty of movement; and that preoccupies him much more than the thought of his duration: man for him is not the "detained" (a temporal criterion), but the "recluse" (a spatial criterion) in the secrets of the universe. And his taskmaster is nothing else but his intelligence.

And it is only on this plane that Kafka's two masterpieces, that is to say, "The Metamorphosis" and *The Trial*, can be understood. The two books begin in the same way: in one just as in the other, the protagonist one fine morning wakes up in his own bed, and notices that something unexpected and extraordinary has happened to him. In the case of Gregor Samsa, the traveling salesman of "The Metamorphosis," just as in the case of Joseph K., the bank clerk of *The Trial*, an unexpected and curious accident suddenly determines another life and another destiny: nay, since the only and supposed preliminary fact of their existence is reduced to the norm of habit and the daily round, we can say without further ado that this new fact determines for the first time their true life and their real destiny. This extraordinary event, which is implanted on the recurring fatality every twenty-four hours of the cessation of sleep, consists in the sudden necessity of wakefulness and of insomnia; and indeed they perceive that it will no longer be permitted them to close an eye until their eyelids yield to the sleep of death or that of nothingness: since in them took place that morning the most tragic and the most surprising of awakenings, that of conscience. In Gregor Samsa such a spiritual catastrophe is expressed in his unforeseen notion of having been converted during the night into a mon-

strous vermin, into an unclean animal; in Joseph K. it is manifested by the unexpected notification made to him by two unknown men who have the air of being two policemen, that he is
under arrest and in police custody for an unknown crime which
he has (or has not) committed. Therefore, all at once, you have
prisoners of a miraculous and terrible event, whose range is
measured in terms of the fact that it canalizes immediately the
existence of its own victims into one logical track and one tight-
packed with consequences, necessities and habits, which in and
of themselves are banal, natural and common. And just as the
protagonist of "The Metamorphosis" must submit to the bare and
crude exigencies of animal and vegetable life, so that of *The
Trial* is inexorably forced to enter into the great conventional
game of judicial customs and of penal procedure. They have
suddenly become two men of the underground: and as such
judged and condemned for eternity.

Gregor Samsa has been transformed into a cockroach
only because the sense of eternity and of sin, the awakening of
conscience, reveals to the man his own bestiality: and because
only to a cockroach can a room, a wall or a bit of furniture seem
infinite. Joseph K. is submitted to a judicial proceeding and is
put under arrest because the man who begins to observe himself
living immediately becomes a man accused; and because the
tribunals of men, dirty and dusty, anonymous and habit-worn,
unjust and absurd, monstrous fruits of the civilization of the four
walls, are one of the circles which most resemble the eternity of
Svidrigailov.

The extensive and lucid artistic intent of Kafka is completely directed toward making it possible for the reader never
to imagine, for example, that a Gregor Samsa has been changed
into a cockroach through an act of magic or enchantment. A
traveling salesman, a man of everyday life, an average citizen
completely given over to comfort and to thrift, immersed up to
his neck in logic and practical reasoning, can be miraculously
and monstrously changed into an impure vermin, but it is not
possible for his soul to be purified or changed through the catharsis of the miracle and of the fabulous: in the days of the fates,
the kinglets could be changed into animals by the treacherous

113

arts of a sorcerer precisely because they retained the hope of a magic wand which would restore them to their original state. But the average citizens and the moderns do not believe in the fates, and for Kafka even the prayers of Solvejg are impotent to remove Troll's tail from Peer Gynt. The metamorphosis of Gregor Samsa and the trial of Joseph K. are irremediable internal catastrophes, tectonic earthquakes which change the structure of a spirit once and for all. This is the sense of Kafka's work, extended to three dimensions to describe without pity the hard prison of our logic, a prison from which has never been heard the echo of a prayer nor the song of a prisoner. The times of the myths are over, and when men discontented with nature wanted to build a city (so goes a common Balkan legend apropos of the foundation of Scutari), the genii every time used to destroy that which had been constructed by day, and in the end the founders understood that it was necessary to placate them by a human sacrifice. Then they walled in alive into a structure the young wife of one of their number: and she lived for months and months in that way, shedding infinite tears and giving milk to her child through the openings of the wall. But the new and modern victims of the four walls, those walled in alive by conscience, are no longer bound by anything to nature and to life, and it is for this reason that they do not know regret.

The other works of Kafka, which can all be collected under the common attribute of minor works, also discuss the same problem, which we might call the squaring of the vicious circle of conscience. But in respect to "The Metamorphosis" and to *The Trial*, they act in an indirect and marginal way, and to continue the image of the circle, I will say that they are limited to the matter of delineating various tangents. Indeed they study the spiritual forces which are centrifugal, peripheral and eccentric, that is to say those that tend toward evasion and liberation, or that seek desperately to resist the gulf of conscience. Some instead are directed toward the describing of states of mind which precede and present the awakening, those which we would call the drowsy state of conscience, when even instinct collaborates unconsciously in its own ruin, and lets itself be seduced by phantasms of the dawn and the last sleep. A typical work of the first sort seems to me to be *Amerika*, which describes the vicissitudes of a rather simple adolescent put into contact with the marvels of mechanics: it is Kafka's least successful book because in spite of the fact that here too the marvelous is limited to the field of possibilities and of conscience, the fantasy of our author is a curious balloon or better a football which is held in check and cannot get poised at its proper height without the ballast of the real and the everyday, understood in their most bourgeois, crude and worn-out sense. Apropos of this book it is worth remembering perhaps, without claiming to give to the observation any allusive value, that when Svidrigailov is about to be killed, to the sentinel-soldier who is interrogating him on his manner of acting, he replies that he is going to America.

A characteristic example of the second current of the minor works seems to me rather *The Castle*, which merits a longer treatment, because it also is a sort of pendant of *The Trial*, if only because here too the family name of the protagonist is designated by a simple K. This time K. is a surveyor who depends on the inhabitants of a mysterious castle, where, without anyone's attempting to hinder him, he will try to enter but always in vain. But in contrast to the protagonist of *Amerika*, in the K. of *The Castle* the ingenuous curiosity of the fabulous, which can be recognized also in the initial and thoroughly literary device of the work, which seems worthy of a detective story (a form which, as is well known, prefers above all other atmospheres that of an ancient and mysterious mannerism) is tempered and I would say almost solidified into a vulgar, common and bourgeois sentiment, which gives to the book its necessary vigor as a drawing, and which is constituted by the thoroughly provincial and *"arriviste"* ambition of K. to enter, to take part in a loftier world and a superior society. But that the artistic proceedings of Kafka tend to make the spark of the fantastic rise from the flint of reality is magnificently attested by a famous fragment from "The Country Doctor," entitled "Bucephalus," the only one which gained strength from an ancient myth, which is that of Alexander's horse, projected in the figure of a lawyer of our time, likewise a slave of an unknown tribunal and the victim of some metamorphosis or other. This continual irresolution on the thread which divides the concrete from the abstract is sufficient to demonstrate, contrary to the opinion of one or two critics of

115

Kafka (who then are incapable besides of even following their own advice), that an author so constituted is not explained either by esthetics or by psychoanalysis, but resolutely and in medieval fashion by all possible symbolic researches and on the suggestive and deceptive plane of allegory, the supreme abstraction which is the only cornice, background and relief possible to the obscure realism of all his proceedings as a narrator; an allegory which, under the form of anxiety about the transcendent, filters through like a sun's ray through the only but very necessary crack which cuts through the compact, sordid and gray wall of Kafka's creation.

Such a creation, I repeat, is conceived in the absolute and in the abstract as a series of corollaries to some one of the more lucid postulates of Dostoyevsky: but often the symbolic and metaphysical precedent of the great Russian is concentrated in literary reminiscences, which result especially from the plain and gray text of the individual works of Kafka. Let the example of "The Metamorphosis" suffice for them all, as its moral and fantastic motif is anticipated by the following words of the protagonist of the "Notes from Underground": "I declare to you solemnly that many times I have wanted to become an insect . . . I swear to you, gentlemen, that too much conscience is a sickness, a real and proper sickness. . . ." But there is a page from *The Idiot* which stands as a sort of *avant-lettre* to its first printing, and it is that in which Ippolit, dying, is obsessed in the delirium of his agony with the vision of Holbein's "Dead Christ": "Looking at such a picture, one perceives nature as an immense, merciless, dumb beast, or more correctly, much more correctly speaking, though it sounds strange, in the form of a huge machine of the most modern construction which, dull and insensible, has meaninglessly clutched, crushed and swallowed up a great and priceless Being, a Being worth all of nature and its laws. . . . The picture expresses and involuntarily suggests to one the conception of a dark, insolent, unreasoning and eternal Power to which everything is subject. . . . I seemed almost to see . . . that blind Power, that deaf Being, obscure and mute. I remember, it seems too, that someone, carrying a candle, showed me an enormous and repugnant spider, seeking to convince me that it was really that dark, deaf and omnipotent Being, and laughing at my disdain . . ." It might almost be said that the last image might almost allude to the very art of Kafka, which with the sole help of a candle, and laughing at our shuddering, makes us descend into the sewers of being, and guides us across the subterranean labyrinths of conscience.

A fatal sense of myth invests and interprets something which is worth more than books, and that is the very soul of Kafka, which is a special soul, one of those which could not have been born before our time, because through monogenesis the fantasy of a great modern writer, Dostoyevsky, has begotten it: men believe that a great literary hero is capable only of having a certain number of newborn children baptized with his name during the epoch of his fame and fortune, and they do not know that his example can become a *norm* and an ideal of life and can generate creatures which resemble him. Now it can be truly said that Kafka is the first living exemplar of the men of the underground, as the autobiographical touch of that very K. may demonstrate, that touch with which he designs two of his principal personages: and I suppose that the critic Groethuysen wanted to suggest to us a similar hypothesis when he spoke these words about him to us: "A lucid spirit, he knew how to give us news of the abandoned world in which he had lived." But the necessities of art and the laws of life have so acted that in the series of those individuals he appears as a particular and complex example: that which in the work of Dostoyevsky is represented by the dramatic and dialectical relation of Raskolnikov and of Porphyr, becomes with him the desperate monologue of a soul, the "voice of one crying in the desert," of a man whose vocal cords are diseased. The futility of his cry for help suffocates every religious breath and extinguishes every possibility of demiurge in Kafka's universe. It was thus that I understood how a creature so constituted would even after death be always alive in the pitying memory of a friend, and how he could not have been born and have lived except in that old section of Prague, where still lives the wandering shade of the fabulous rabbi who constructed the Golem by force of clay and cabala.

Translated by John Glynn Conley.

117

kafka and rex warner

george woodcock

In comparing the symbolism of Kafka and Rex Warner, and in estimating the influence of the elder on the younger writer, we have to bear in mind from the start the essential difference in nature between the symbolism used by the two novelists.

Kafka's symbolism is ambiguous and Protean—with all the clues at our disposal we are never sure what he is aiming to teach or portray, and his symbols can, within wide limits, be interpreted by every reader according to his predilections. The struggle he shows of man against his environment is real, on a physical or a spiritual plane, for everyone who is likely to read his books, and his very vagueness makes it easy for anyone to read his own problems, his own struggle, into the life of K. or Kafka's other central figures.

Warner's symbolism, on the other hand, is simple and direct, applicable within narrow limits, and aiming at the creation of a clear-cut allegory to illustrate certain defined facets of the human struggle.

The accepted interpretation of Kafka's writings, taken largely on the authority of Max Brod, is that they have a strictly religious significance, and are intended, as has been pointed out by B. Rajan, to portray the dualism of the universe which divides "the orders of Nature and of Grace." This may indeed be the meaning which Kafka himself attributed to his allegories, the primary conscious meaning, but Kafka's work is so heavily loaded with subconscious tendencies that we should be unwisely hasty if we took a meaning that seems *prima facie* obvious either to the author or to the reader. In order to gain some idea of the wide applicability of Kafka's writings we should examine the circumstances that influenced him and that gave him the peculiar feeling of isolation from any proximate continent of reality, which we find in all his works.

For, taken in their literal and most simple sense, Kafka's writings, and particularly his type-novel *The Castle*, represent the solitary man struggling to wrest from his environment some kind of reality and security. Some of the aspects from which we can view this simple statement of literal interpretation, and which may assist us in assessing its value, are given in the following paragraphs.

Kafka was a consumptive, who spent much of his life in sanatoria, and whose ill-health continually inhibited his joining in the active life of the world around. People in such circumstances usually feel their difference from other men with great poignancy, and their work is frequently much influenced by it. I was sent recently some poems by a young consumptive, from which one gained a feeling of inescapable loneliness very similar to that one gets from K.'s failure to make any real contacts with the people around him during the life of the village.

Kafka was a Jew, and therefore came of a race with an ingrown feeling of isolation in a hostile world. I have not heard that he experienced any great degree of direct persecution, but even in Jews who have lived normally among their neighbours there will remain a memory of hostility and a feeling of difference based on the racial theories of Jewish orthodoxy. When a race has been isolated and persecuted intermittently for twenty centuries, it is unlikely that any of its members will feel completely at ease even in an apparently friendly environment.

In connection with Kafka's Jewish race we must also

recollect the journey symbolism in his work—the journey to America, the setting of K.'s struggle against the Castle as the penultimate stage of a journey by a vagrant, the departure of the explorer in "The Penal Colony," etc. This symbolism can be paralleled by the continual presence of the journey in the historical traditions of the Jews, the great race of wanderers. The series is long—there are the Bedouin wanderings of Abraham and Isaac, the exodus from Egypt and the long desert journey to the Promised Land, the journeys into exile in Babylon, the dispersal after the Roman sack of Jerusalem, and, last of the series in Kafka's day, the breaking up of the ghettos of Europe and the dispersal of the Jews among the Gentiles as neighbours and fellow-citizens in a—comparatively—liberal world.

To the Jews also, we in the West owe the idea of the invisible and elusive God, to be compared with the elusive Castle which K. can never enter or make contact with, except by indirect means. Moses encountered God as a voice speaking from the cloud, but, as St. Paul, the last of the great Jewish prophets, remarked, "No man hath seen the face of God." This saying, with its undertone of defeat, represents the high point of the Hebrew effort to attain unity with God, which was carried on by the Jewish mystics in the Cabala, to which it is likely that Kafka had access and in which we find the distinction between the orders of justice and of grace mentioned by Mr. Rajan.

That Kafka had strong mystical leanings is obvious. We know that he was influenced by the unorthodox and destructive mystic Kierkegaard, and it is likely that his mysticism was another determinant of his frequent use of the journey symbol. The journey of the soul is a common mystical concept, appearing in ancient religions in the journey of Osiris, in the East in the journey of Tripitaka, in Christianity in the legend of Christ's journey into Egypt, and, among more recent religious writings, expressed crudely by Bunyan in *Pilgrim's Progress* and, more subtly, by St. John of the Cross in *The Dark Night of the Soul.*

The last of the tentative indications I shall give is that Kafka lived most of his life in a subject territory of the old Hapsburg Empire, whose bureaucracy was extensive and notoriously pompous. On a farcical plane the authoritarian structure of the

121

Empire was satirised unmercifully by Jaroslav Hašek in *The Good Soldier Schweik,* and we can see that the evasive, vast and dictatorial assemblage of authorities in *The Castle,* even if it were not meant to represent the bureaucracy of the empire, was at least very much influenced in its form by the fact that Kafka lived under such a regime and probably observed its working and methods with a certain hostile cynicism.

These are suggestions which may help in our study of Kafka. I do not contend that any or even all of them will give a full explanation of what Kafka had to say, but I think that between them they give us a good idea of the reason for his feeling of isolation from reality, or struggle against his environment, and also explain why he expressed these feelings in the form of the dialectical struggle of the wanderer against established authority.

Kafka's work represents, as, indeed, does every serious work of the imagination, an attempt to reach the ultimate reality of the natural world, to grapple with the unknown and, by its conquest, to reach freedom.

In human terms this is represented in the struggle of man against authority, against the domination of cosmic or earthly rulers, and it is this, admittedly limited, aspect of Kafka that appeals to me personally, as expressed in one of K.'s remarks to the villagers regarding their relationship with the Castle.

> Fear of the authorities is born in you here, and is further suggested to you all your lives in the most various ways and from every side, and you yourselves help to strengthen it as much as possible.

K. struggles continually against the authorities in order to gain access to the Castle, in other words to make himself one with authority, the father. That is why, after the last remark, he qualifies it with the words—

> Still, I have no fundamental objection to that; if an authority is good why should it not be feared,

because he himself hopes one day to enter into the Castle, to wield the authority against which he now struggles, and so, he thinks, to become free. While he tries to placate the authorities, he at the same time hates them, and when their representatives, the assistants, come into his power, he treats them with contempt and brutality. His hostility is also expressed in a manner which could be taken as illustrative of an important contention of modern psychology, when he appropriates to himself the mistress of Klamm, who for him represents authority, and thus repeats the classic symbol of defeating the father in the affections of the mother, as a substitute for taking his freedom in defiance of authority.

The final important characteristic of Kafka's work is his confirmed pessimism. K. does not attain the Castle, nor, even in the projected ending of the uncompleted novel, does he gain more than a qualified recognition from the Castle authorities. Interpreted according to our tastes, this can be taken to mean that for men there is no possible unification with God, no fulness of freedom, no fulfilment of the personality. The world of reality and the world of man run along parallel lines—the thought of their meeting is an illusion of mental perspective. It is further significant that, not only does K. not reach the Castle—he does not even know what the Castle really is. In the growing skepticism of this novel one is reminded of the reports of certain Western mystics who have gone along the ways of Eastern mysticism to *samadhi* and return with bleak disillusion to tell that they have found nothing at the end of their spiritual journey.

To return to the comparison of Kafka and Rex Warner. The imputing of influences is a hazardous duty for the critic, and I would say, first of all, that the direct influence of Kafka on Rex Warner seems to me more tenuous than is generally supposed, or than one would assume from the nature of the inaugural essay. There seems to have been some direct influence—we find certain concepts in common—but I do not think we can fairly attribute any more influence in the motivation of Warner's books to Kafka than we can to, say, *Gulliver's Travels*.

What, therefore, seems more profitable is to consider them as parallels rather than to consider Warner as derivative from Kafka. To an extent they use a similar set-up and similar

123

symbols. The conflict between man and his environment is common to both of them, and in one at least of Warner's books the journey symbolism is retained. Warner isolates one of the possible lines of meaning which we get from the consideration of Kafka's books, and develops it along a defined and narrow path. By this I do not mean that Warner took the idea from Kafka. It would be sufficient to suppose that the two writers, living in the same period of history, will have similar problems, and that their solutions will also partake of a certain similarity.

With Warner there is relatively little chance of doubt as to his intentions, and the undertones of interpretation we can read into his work are limited, almost, one feels, deliberately limited by the conscious manipulation of technique to reach disciplined ends in which the conscious intent of the writer will be paramount. There is no transcendentalism in Warner's work, no authentic mysticism, in spite of some of his Marxist critics. All his values take their validity from their application to human relationships. The drama is played entirely on an earthly plane, and there is no chance that any of the characters are gods in disguise.

At the outset we find a similarity between Warner and Kafka, in that both use the village or the country as the base from which the central character sets out to struggle against the opposite, authoritarian influence represented by the castle, the city or the aerodrome. At the same time all the protagonists imagine that what they wish to attain can be reached through the antagonistic influence. K. wishes to enter the castle, the brothers see the city as a way to the Wild Goose, Roy sees the aerodrome as the means to gain power, discipline and, through these, freedom. For, while Kafka's heroes are pursuing ends which bear a number of possible interpretations, those of Warner are clearly pursuing freedom. The Wild Goose is freedom, and Roy in entering the aerodrome hopes to gain freedom from the old ties of his family and Bess, and also the wider freedom which the Air Vice-Marshal promises his followers they will attain through the conquest of power.

In Warner the village and the city-aerodrome can be taken as representative of two opposing ways of life. The village

124

is the life of natural man, the city-aerodrome is the mechanised and regimented life of the modern total state, fundamentally unnatural and grounded on abstractions.

Both the brothers and Roy hope to gain their objective of an extension of life by exchanging the village for its antithesis. Unlike K., who never makes contact with the castle, the brothers reach the city, Roy enters the very heart of the aerodrome, the Air Vice-Marshal's office. Here, in all cases, disillusionment awaits them. City and aerodrome represent, as they realise, the death rather than the attainment of their desires. The Wild Goose, which is the god of the city, is a stuffed one—in the city, moreover, David loses his sex and Rudolph his sight. The Air Vice-Marshal talks of freedom, but the power by which he proposes to attain it turns mercilessly upon the people with whom he has had the most human relationships—a son and two of his late mistresses are the victims of his ruthless struggle to establish his domination. Roy realises that, with all its disorder, the life of the village is more desirable than that of the aerodrome.

> Yet I began to see that this life, in spite of its drunkenness and its inefficiency, was wider and deeper than the activity in which we were constricted by the iron compulsion of the Air Vice-Marshal's ambition. It was a life whose every vagueness concealed a wealth of opportunity, whose uncertainty called for adventure, whose aspects were innumerable and varied as the changes of light and colour throughout the year.

In both *The Wild Goose Chase* and *The Aerodrome* the heroes realise that, not only will the city or the aerodrome fail to bring them the freedom they desire, but that these influences are destroying, in the village, the very roots of humanity from which their freedom must grow.

They commence the struggle against authority. In *The Wild Goose Chase* George becomes the leader of a revolutionary army, Rudolph a revolutionary poet. In *The Aerodrome*, from which are purged the crudities of symbolism one finds in the former book, the Flight Lieutenant preaches a sermon in which he tells the villagers that the aerodrome has only done them harm, while Roy accepts a technical breach of the rules of the aerodrome, for which he is not directly responsible, as a possible means of escaping to a recommencement of his life with Bess.

In the struggle with authority, Warner repeatedly uses symbolism recognised by modern psychology as pertaining to such a conflict. In the final denouement in *The Aerodrome,* Roy discovers that the Air Vice-Marshal is both his and the Flight Lieutenant's father, so that the two men struggling against authority are also sons struggling against a father. The sexual competition with the father also appears in a similar manner to that already noted in Kafka. In *The Wild Goose Chase* George, after he has chased away the king, lives for a time by the underground lake with Marqueta, who was formerly the king's mistress. In *The Aerodrome,* both the Flight Lieutenant and Roy become the lovers of Eustachia, who was formerly the mistress of the Air Vice-Marshal.

In the struggle with authority the heroes win. The city is captured, and the king driven away. The Air Vice-Marshal is killed on the eve of attaining his great ambition, when his plane crashes through the sabotage of the Flight Lieutenant. But the heroes realise that the mere overthrow of tyranny is not the attainment of their real desires. As George stands at the celebration of the capture of the city the dome of the Anserium breaks apart and the Wild Geese fly overhead in a splendid procession. Roy realises that the death of the Air Vice-Marshal and his own subsequent liberation mean only the beginning of the development of his life and relationship with Bess. When dominion is ended, freedom has yet to be made positive.

The Aerodrome shows a significant advance in Warner's sense of social reality because, while in *The Wild Goose Chase* George actually assumes power in the city, Roy makes no attempt to set himself in the place of the dead Air Vice-Marshal, but instead merely uses his liberation to return to the life he really desires. In other words, this is a recognition of the social truth that not the assumption but the destruction of authority—whether in the world or in the mind—is the beginning of freedom. A symbolic anticipation of this conclusion is, indeed, contained in *The Wild Goose Chase,* when Marqueta, the king's former mistress, whom George has appropriated and who can, therefore, be taken to represent the power he has appropriated, withdraws herself from him by committing suicide, and leaves him to return to Joan, who represents the human values symbolised by the village.

The main difference between Kafka and Warner would, if this analysis is reasonable, be that, while both are concerned with man's struggle with authority, Kafka works along a broad way which embraces the cosmic as well as the human relationship and, in this progress whose contact with shadowy powers admits of no tangible result, comes to a pessimistic conclusion in which man attains nothing for which he struggles. Kafka, for all his religious interests and mystic affiliations, is in the end skeptic and defeatist. Warner, on the other hand, proceeding on the narrow and defined way of human relationships, reaches the optimistic conclusion that it is possible for man to attain freedom and to fulfill himself.

> It might be said that we anticipated, both of us, that now at last the circle of sin might be broken, that, with what we knew, we might live to avoid murder and deception.

Restricting himself to the human world, Warner has the faith which Kafka did not reach.

It is for this reason that I feel one at least of Warner's novels, *The Aerodrome,* to be ultimately more satisfying than any of Kafka's. Kafka's work, with its cosmic implications, is unfinished in more than one way, because Kafka never attained a whole view of the vast world of relationships he strove to embrace. Warner attains a completeness and validity of his own precisely because his world of relationships is limited to that of humanity and its proximate, physical environment.

"the metamorphosis"

paul l. landsberg

Recently I have been wondering whether it would actually be any easier, or even possible, to translate the prose of Franz Kafka from its original language than to translate poetry. Not that his prose, like that of certain German romanticists, is poetic; on the contrary it is a pure prose, and nothing more. It is closely related to Stendhal's phraseology, which was influenced by wide reading of law, and to that difficult and dry prose of Kleist's novels.° Kafka loved to draw his terms from the language of the juridical and business world. He liked to borrow from both the terminology of the exact sciences and the most up-to-date daily speech. I may even assert that, except for Kleist's *Michael Kohlhaas* and old Feuerbach's *Remarkable Criminal Trials*,† no one in Germany ever told a story in so classic a style

---

° Jean Cassou alludes to the Kleist-Kafka relationship in his essay "Kleist et le somnambulisme tragique," *Cahiers du Sud*, May-June 1937, pp. 275-281.

† Father of the philosopher and grandfather of the painter, Anselm Ritter von Feuerbach originated the Bavarian penal code and is celebrated for his defence of Kaspar Hauser. His two-volume *Remarkable Criminal Trials,* comprising his case reports to the King of Bavaria, may be considered masterpieces as much for their literary merit as for their psychological penetration.

129

as Kafka. Here I am defining classic writing as an ensemble of stylistic qualities characterized above all by a strictly prosaic prose, and by an extreme objectivity in the recital, into which the narrator and his sentiments are not allowed to intrude even through the tone of the report. This method of telling a story resembles a design in black on white. The absence of sentimental tonal variations is equivalent to the absence of color. Such sobriety is in direct opposition to the musical nature of the majority of German literature's novels and stories, which are in general romantic, abounding in "Stimmung." Kleist and Kafka then are already exceptional for the absence of this lyric element. The atmosphere which pervades their works is less pleasing to the soul, the "Gemüt," but more refreshing to the intellect—the sensation of being suddenly immersed in almost glacial waters.

Clearly, Kafka's unique style corresponds to the paradox of his world. His is a world which aims at reality, and in this sense, Kafka could be called a realist. His world wants very much to be real, to resist human imagination and will, to possess its own character, its own causality, and its own habits like the world in which we live. In its strictness and oppressiveness it differs most radically from the popular romantic fairyland, a poetic world which is virtually obedient to the human soul. However, the mere presence of an undeniable realism in his work does not imply that Kafka's world is our everyday one. It is quite evident that it is not at all our own familiar world. Perhaps the reader will even be inclined to range Kafka with whimsical and fantastic writers. But in truth, the transformation suffered by accustomed reality in Kafka's writing is not simply a diminution. Kafka sides with the opposition to all fairytales and escapist literature. His writing treats the question of change—change of a type foreign to our knowledge of reality. To analyze it, we shall discuss the strange story entitled *Die Verwandlung*—"The Metamorphosis." This story is, in our opinion, completely typical of his art.

The nature of the world, if we accept as real the one in which we live, shows a certain coherence in its habits. We are generally quite confident that a certain train or sequence of phenomena will occur, even though previously we have never thought very deeply about the reasons for this sequence. According to our existing yet in general unconscious acquaintance with these habits, we judge reality by its similarity to past, present, and future events. This spiritual tendency existed in humanity and in the individual even prior to the discovery of laws in their proper sense.* In the story which Kafka tells us, there is a single incident foreign to the habits of our world, one which shocks our assumed knowledge of it. This occurrence is introduced in its entirety without hesitation or timidity, brutally imposed as an undeniable fact from the very first sentence: "As Gregor Samsa awoke one morning from a troubled dream, he found himself changed in his bed to some monstrous kind of vermin." Once this happening is accepted, all the rest of the story develops with a logic, a probability, with what I might even call a banality, characteristic of the most everyday world. The reactions of the outside world, of Gregor's family and of the other people affected by this phenomenon are extremely true-to-life reactions, almost entirely predictable. They are average reactions, the reactions of anyone. And in a like manner, the feelings and actions of that pitiful commercial traveler, Gregor Samsa himself, when he finds himself thus transformed, are in complete accordance with the perfect mediocrity of his character. The stifling atmosphere of the apartment of a middle-class Prague family, the setting of the story, differs not one iota from that of thousands and thousands of other middle-class apartments. We seem to have known Gregor's father forever; his mother is a mother, nothing more. His sister is an entirely typical young girl, and the charwoman is full of the classic horror of her role; that is, for an unimportant personage, she is extremely true to life. In short, everything is constructed so as to influence us to accept the initial incident as equally true. This guise of reality, however, is not strong enough to destroy our rational certitude of its impossibility. Even the existence of consequences so logical and predictable, if we admit

* The regular recurrence of the daily and yearly rhythms, as well as the typical rhythm of the human animal, were facts admitted from experience long before the formulation of any scientific hypotheses on their causes. These certitudes are the result of a vast yet limited experience, perhaps, in one way, the result of its limitation in time and space.

131

their cause, cannot make us forget the absence of an acceptable cause for the cause itself. The conflict which arises in the reader's spirit almost forces him to adhere to the sense of the primary incident, and it is probably only in so adhering that he can approach the mystery hidden under the very clarity of the tale. Let us try in our turn to come a little closer to this mystery.

In the first place, we must note that the terms "reality" and "realism" are deeply misleading. To create exactly true-to-life persons, according to the usage of the world, an author would have to create marionettes. The true-to-life does not coincide with the real, but only with our preconceived idea of it. Life is always breaking its bounds, and no one conforms exactly to his rôle. A realistic description of daily happenings can terminate in fantastic unreality. On the contrary, a poet can give an unlikely if not impossible incident an intense semblance of reality if he surrounds it with the genuine stamp of human life. It is in this way that the metamorphosis of Gregor Samsa finally becomes more real than the banal setting in which it occurs.

According to our custom, each morning on awakening we take up our old selves again, unchanged. However, there is no doubt that our body and all that we are have been transformed a little, even during the short space of our sleep. The most modern psychological science is now discovering the truth of the most ancient superstitions. Conditions during our sleep fix the disposition of our being, which in turn influences the character of each one of our days. In truth, everyone who has learned self-observation well knows that every morning it is by means of a certain and peculiar process that we take up our body and soul again and readjust ourselves to the surrounding world. When we have gone to bed the night before in unfamiliar surroundings, it is with a certain difficulty that we realize this fact as we find ourselves once more in the middle of "reality." ° Each morning we are a little like travelers who are coming back from far away;

° This little experience occurs over and over again in the unstable life of a commercial traveler. It is not by chance that Kafka gave his hero this vocation, which like no other tends to render impossible any continuity in life.

132

each morning we set out once more "in quest of lost time." [*]
I myself believe that in this unconscious and subconscious
negligence of the transformation, however slight, of our selves
and our world during sleep, there is a tendency, a deep rooted
instinct calculated to stabilize our coherence and our identity.
According to the habits of the world, and according to the
laws which science has discovered, it would be quite impossible for us to awake one morning and find ourselves transformed into repulsive insects. But in our customary certainty of
the identity of our being and world in general, there is just
enough of artificiality, enough will, enough fragility so that
Kafka's fiction touches an unacknowledged but anguishing reality, nourished from sources deeper than those of rational reflection and scientific knowledge. This is the only way in which such
an incident could be validly introduced. It is on awakening "from
a troubled dream" that the person in question would discover
himself transformed. He would discover his metamorphosis in the
miscarrying of his daily expectations and the shattering of his
effort to re-achieve customary but unconscious continuity.

The metamorphosis of a civilized man into first a cole-
opteron, perfect example of an instinctive and almost automatic
being, and finally into a simple bit of matter, portrays in its
successive stages man's instinct for death, the desire for a return
to the inorganic of which Freud has shown the power in the
human subconscious.[†] All the desires, all the anxiety with which
this hidden antagonist upsets the instincts of life are thus evoked
by the incident. This nightmare of Gregor Samsa is the expression of a deep and stifled impulse. He can no longer obey his
conscious will. In the same way, the "Sorcerer's Apprentice" is
caught within a dream which he himself has evoked to satisfy
his nocturnal spirit, and instead of escaping, as he had expected,

[*] In Proust's writing, the dominant problem, the very one of
the metamorphosis of the self and its relation with time, identity, and the
various forms of remembrance, is closely linked with the analysis of this
daily return.

[†] S. Freud: *Beyond the Pleasure Principle,* and *Civilization and
its Discontents,* and the study by Paul Federn: "Die Wirklichkeit des Todes-
triebes," *Almanach der Psychoanalyse, 1931.*

133

to a temporary diversion, he is caught in his own trap. He had wanted to flee his intolerable role as a civilized man and a living being, but he had always intended to return at dawn to his daily existence. He was lost through the magic of excessive desire. He went too far. Here again, this was not a misfortune imposed by fate, but a flight that was too perfectly accomplished. It is this satisfaction of pent-up desires that fosters the feeling of culpability which dominates the man who was transformed into a cockroach. He had deserted humanity, and this knowledge fosters his conviction that he must justify himself, and his certainty that he will never be able to do so. In the kingdom of life, the father has right on his side and the son carries in his flesh the rotten apple embedded there by the paternal hand. The culprit instills horror into those who surround him because he calls attention to the universal possibility of the crime. Following an implacable logic, the ignoble death of the culprit and the destruction of his corpse finally intervene as the ultimate deliverance, destroying blame when they destroy the living individual. The return, which could not be halted until it reached the stage of brute matter, close as possible to the unimaginable nothingness, had been achieved. All the world is then relieved, all the world is triumphant, but most of all the fugitive himself. The inevitable struggle between the misfortune of being born and the fault of not wanting to be, the misfortune of being responsible and not wanting to be, has only the saddest solution in Kafka's moral universe.

Our body and our total being are continually in the process of transformation, but we are generally conscious of it only at specified moments. At these times we are brought to the inevitable realization of the anguish of living, the anguish of finding ourselves passengers on a train which we cannot leave and which, infallibly, from change to change, is taking us to the ultimate catastrophe.° Those who see a child grow day by day are generally not aware of it. We are only astonished by his growth when we have not seen him for a certain lapse of time.

° According to Bergson's unforgettable words: "Complete existence is mobility in individuality." (*Les Deux Sources*, p. 337.) Here we were thinking of this deep antithesis which established the great philosopher between the "closed" and the "open."

In the same way, the persons who live constantly with the sick and old are not as aware of the stages of their decrepitude as those who see them only from time to time. But over and above this well-known and perhaps explicable phenomenon, there is yet an oblivion of change in ourselves and our contemporaries which indubitably contains an effort to repress, a subconscious loathing to admit certain things, in the last analysis, a fear of death. There is an agony in change which is the agony of life, of a life eternally pregnant with death. It is this fear which makes us search for and affirm the stable identity of our being through the repetition of our acts, through the constitution of ritual habits. This fear is the secret of a certain bourgeois world, a world where the unchangingness of chattels and ways of life expresses an attempt to deceive the liberating force of life and death. In choosing this very bourgeois world as the setting for his metamorphosis, Kafka frames a revolutionary threat much more disquieting than the usual satire. Imagine the terrible need in such a fundamentally deceitful life. It is manifested in the fear which the metamorphosis of Gregor Samsa awakens in those who surround him, in the ferocious hate which the change irresistibly evokes even in those who previously cherished him and had a thousand reasons for being grateful to this son and exemplary brother. We understand only too well that in essence it is not only a question of defending an honest family against the annoying curiosity of the surrounding world, but also of preserving a world in which these "normal" beings can live free from the fear of possible and universal change and free from the fear of that final, mysterious and unavoidable metamorphosis. This is the true nature of his family's anguish. It is evident at the end of the story. The cockroach dies. The family must get rid of the corpse. The charwoman who had always treated the transformed son as if he were a particle of filth, destroys the remains behind the scenes, to the great relief of the family. Everything returns to order, to the inhuman order in which death is passionately excluded and with it the true life of every person.

The terrible apple which the almost unrecognizing father, himself suddenly transformed by his blue uniform of banking house employee, throws at the back of his poor cock-

135

roach of a son, expresses the foolish and inevitable revolt of the likely against the unlikely, of the uniform against the monstrous, of custom against the exceptional, of triviality against the explicit nightmare, of an artificially sweetened, slowed and comfortably falsified life, the life which forgets death, against a true life which progresses resolutely towards the last catastrophe. Besides the psychological resemblance to reality, there is an impression of a truly metaphysical need for this patriarchal act of hostility against a so degenerated son.[*]

So the metamorphosis, certainly an impossible and unreal incident, is nevertheless charged with a significance which is itself neither arbitrary nor unreal. It is not the caprice of an artist which produces such a symbol. It is the inner force of a poet who sees in this symbol the true mystery hidden deep in the life of everyone.

Personally, when I recall certain almost forgotten moments of my life, I believe that I can intimately understand the sense of Kafka's tale. Once, years ago, very late at night, I was in my native village. I was climbing a stairway which led to a restaurant on the second floor of a house. It was impossible to climb the stair without seeing oneself in several mirrors. It was surprising, and all the more so for Germany, where mirrors in restaurants are much less common than they are in Paris. As I ascended, I could see my image from the rear, in a great mirror. Suddenly I noticed that there was a small round bald spot on my head which had formerly been abundantly covered with hair. All at once this slow metamorphosis, for certainly I had lost my hair little by little, shocked my sense and my conscience. The feeling which overcame me at that instant was not wounded vanity, nor, as a psychoanalyst would have it, a manifestation of the castration complex, but was, without doubt, a mortal anguish, the anguish of living, a fear of its rapidity, of its incessant progress, and, like all fear of life, a fear of its ripe fruit—death. I was convinced that all deep anguish has this ambiguous character which, like the mystery of the Ancients according to Heraclitus, identi-

---

[*] The father as judge and defender of order recurs frequently in Kafka's work. See, for example, the story entitled "The Judgment."

fies itself with Hades and Dionysius. But such an experience with transformation in ourselves would be misunderstood if one did not realize that at the same time the experience shows evidence for personal identity. The surprise that I felt told me that I was changed, and yet that I remained the same. My fear did not want to admit the change; nevertheless in the fear itself there was a certainty of another type of identity. This man who had lost his hair was yet invariably myself. No one will deny this truth in regard to the experience of physical transformation. It is perhaps somewhat more difficult to grasp, but equally undeniable in regard to the moral transformations which we have experienced. At the very moment that we are impressed with a spiritual metamorphosis of the self, we feel a certain stability in our being. So my psychological youth, that ineffable levity which impregnates all feelings, thoughts and acts of the human, had forsaken me. I can establish this evolution as clearly and as quickly as I can establish at any given moment any physical sign of my growing old. But at the moment of my discovery of change, I cannot doubt that this new epoch of life on which I am embarking is nevertheless an epoch of *my* life, that there is a unity, which we shall call provisionally a unity of style, connecting all stages of my life, from my childhood to my old age. It is as if there were a mysterious personal controlling center which, according to a typical rhythm, determined almost prior to life itself, creates a whole series of persons. At a given moment I am myself and yet another. Every physical manifestation sooner or later becomes unfaithful to my person, but my intimate unity emanates from a buried source, the center of my being. I am inclined to believe that true knowledge of this center can be acquired only paradoxically, that it is always inherent in the very experience of transformation. In the same way, all valid hope of immortality must be fostered by this experience, the agony hinging on the decay of physical and moral states, and by the comprehension of our true self, or rather our psychological selves.

Gregor Samsa, this poor man condemned to live his metamorphosis, is morally identical with his former self even as a cockroach. His sweet, timid, and amiable character has not suffered any extraordinary change. Since it is primarily physical,

137

his metamorphosis becomes that much more symbolic. The corporal fact, from the metaphysical point of view, is no more superficial than the psychic fact. The truth of the matter, that we are not only associated with but almost entirely in the power of a corporal existence, is perhaps the most anguishing discovery of our human existence. That this body which is in a certain way "myself" should be subject to all the vicissitudes of a physical world which follows laws apparently having nothing to do with my personal law is an evidence of fatality which not only shocks my pride but wounds my very intimate hope to give at least some sense to my own existence. Our corporeity makes the inhuman world our master. It mocks at our pretended autonomy. The fragility of the identity of our character when a radical physical metamorphosis occurs cruelly shows the fragility of our entire condition. Gregor Samsa as a cockroach, for example, does not believe that he has lost the use of words. He speaks continually, tries to explain and excuse himself, and his arguments seem extremely reasonable to him. But after several minutes he perceives that no one understands him any longer. No one even knows that he is speaking. What he judges to be reasonable language is for the others nothing more than the noise of a disgusting animal. He resembles Kafka's other heroes, refined Talmudists surrounded by corporal beings, superb reasoners in a deaf world.° Around Gregor Samsa an abyss has been opened, isolating him from those who were his equals, who still are but do not realize it. This is the way in which a man who becomes insane suffers the awful experience of separation from other men, a radical separation based on misunderstanding. For him reason is no longer reason. One only reasons falsely for others. He makes no faults of logic, for he follows his own logic.

I am reminded in particular of schizophrenia and an illuminating description of it given by one of those unfortunates

° We are thinking in particular of the hero of *The Trial,* isolated from the world by the metamorphosis symbolized by the mysterious arrest. In an analogous manner, the principal characters of Kleist's works are just as radically separated from the world: Michael Kohlhaas by his fanatical passion for justice, the Prince of Hamburg by the fear of death, Robert Guiskard by the plague.

to Dr. Minkowski: "I am surrounded by a great immobility. Things come before me isolated, each one by itself, evoking nothing. Even certain things which should form memories, evoke a huge chain of thoughts, give me a total picture, remain isolated. They are understood more than proved. It is as if there were pantomimes being played all around me, but I take no part in them. I remain outside." Kafka's haunted universe calls up spiritual states which would in all likelihood have induced a veritable schizophrenia if art had not conquered them. From this point of view, his tale expresses a possibility of ill health that the author lived through. It is the schizophrenics who are often truly and irrevocably transformed into other people, historical personages, into animals or objects. If Gregor Samsa himself had told his story, it would be the sincere confession of a schizophrenic. By creating this main character and telling his story in the third person, Kafka is liberating himself of an obsession. The poet himself is not a schizophrenic, but in creating his story he defends himself against the human and universal possibility of it which permits comprehension of such an illness.

Beings like ourselves who show only physical manifestations, who, themselves incarnated, only understand when they incarnate their thoughts and feelings, are subject to this type of adventure, but are generally not aware of the danger.° Finally, there are even some situations in which the genius or, more simply, the reasoning man finds himself just as isolated among a crowd of his fellow beings, just as incomprehensible, as anguished and as hated as Gregor Samsa. "The Metamorphosis," from the date of its publication, seems to be Kafka's "war book." The transformation into a cockroach can be produced in a thousand ways. To be an exception or in the minority is the original social sin. When in society any group of men characterized by anomalous tastes or racial or social heredity is denounced as "vermin," there will always be one group that from then on will see nothing but the other's rottenness, and another fraction within

° In its true meaning, the word "incarnation" seems to me a little too dualistic to be applied to man's corporeity. I shall take this point up again in the second volume of my anthropology.

139

the scorned group that will think and act as if they had truly been transformed into vermin. Since Kafka was Jewish, he had undoubtedly experienced something of this kind. His recital symbolizes even more validly the situation of a poet of his kind in present society. The fear of those who surround Gregor Samsa is the panicky fear which the presence in a poet's work of the most suppressed secrets will evoke even in a crowd of mediocre people.

Translated by Caroline Muhlenberg.

"amerika" and charles dickens

rudolf vašata

Of all contemporary Czechoslovak writers Franz Kafka enjoys more fame in this country than any other, the only exception being Karel Čapek. Possibly the reason why Kafka is so widely read and discussed is that the allegedly obscure and enigmatic character of his work offers an ideal playground for commentators, and various -isms on the lookout for precursors of well-established literary reputation. Edmund Wilson states in his Dickens study, "The Two Scrooges" in *The Wound and the Bow*, that "people who like to talk about the symbols of Kafka and Mann and Joyce have been discouraged from looking for. anything of the kind in Dickens"; but he leaves it at that, probably not aware that Kafka himself gives him the cue to proceed with this parallel. The Prague novelist writes in his diary: "Dickens' Copperfield—(The Stoker.) [This is the first chapter of *Amerika* published during Kafka's lifetime as a short story.] Nothing but an imitation of Dickens, more still the projected novel. The charming man who radiates happiness, the work of low kind, the mistress in the estate, the dirt houses, etc., but above all the method. My intention was, as I am seeing now, to write a Dickens novel, enriched by the sharper light taken from our time and by the dimmer one emanating from myself. Dickens' riches and recklessly powerful flow, but—because of that—passages of a horrible lack of power where he, tired, but stirs round what he has already achieved. Barbaric the impression of the nonsensical whole, a barbarity which I, however, have avoided owing to my weakness and the lessons my being an epigone has taught me. Heartlessness behind the mannerism of overflowing sentiment. Those logs of crude characterisation which are being artificially driven in at every person and without which Dickens would be unable to go on with his story at all."

We need not take the grotesque misjudgments of some of the features in Dickens' work at their face-value. Much more important is Kafka's frank admission of his indebtedness to Dickens and his awareness of their fundamental disparities brought about by the different times which moulded their work. It is now uncontested that Kafka's three posthumously published novels, *Amerika, The Trial,* and *The Castle,* are his most important achievement. A fact not entirely uncontested but, nevertheless, gaining more and more ground is that *Bleak House* constituted not merely a turning point in Dickens' work but that, starting with this novel, he reached a new stage and far greater heights than in anything he had written before. *Bleak House* was written in 1852–53, the immediately preceding novel being no other than *David Copperfield* (1849–50). *Hard Times* (1854) and *Little Dorrit* (1855–57) were to follow. The similarity between *The Trial* and *Bleak House* is obvious, even for the reader who is ignorant of Kafka's avowed indebtedness to Dickens. The central theme of both novels is the machinery of law crushing everybody and everything which comes under its wheels, the victim realising all its horrors without understanding its mechanism. And it is equally obvious that, in both cases, the legal system and its workings are used merely as a symbol for the society which they are serving. Joseph K., the hero of *The Trial,* is K., the hero of *The Castle.* We owe an immense debt to Kafka's life-long friend, Max Brod, who preserved the three great novels for the world, but his explanations are, unfortunately, misleading and, incidentally, contradicting themselves; Brod states that *The*

142

Trial and *The Castle* stand for the two cabalistic qualities of God —Justice and Grace. The theme of *The Trial* is undoubtedly justice but *The Castle* has nothing to do with the problem of grace. The Land Surveyor K. who comes to the village where the castle stands to carry out a job he was summoned to perform and who is unable to gain admission is not the religious man in search of God's grace but simply man seeking his rightful place in a society whose very system necessarily prevents him from reaching, nay even approaching, his goal. No longer is the legal machinery the symbol of this society, society itself is *The Castle's* subject. And returning to Dickens we find that both *Hard Times* and *Little Dorrit* present the same aspect, the former unmasking the economic foundations of Dickens' England and the latter showing that the alternative to the real and small prison of Marshalsea is only the larger but not less real prison of contemporary society with all its contradictions and shortcomings (*Charles Dickens. The Progress of a Radical,* by T. A. Jackson). And whether you want to argue with Jackson that *David Copperfield* is optimistic or merely melioristic, or not—there is a way out for his hero, just as there is a way out for the hero of *Amerika,* a way barred to both the K.'s of Kafka's other two novels as well as to the decent people in *Bleak House, Hard Times,* and *Little Dorrit. Amerika* is undoubtedly a book with an optimistic outlook much broader than that of *David Copperfield,* and Kafka himself explains that he has made use of the sharper light of his time: whether you accept the solution he offers in *Amerika* as a social Utopia or as a symbol for socialism itself, Kafka was able to and did learn a lesson from his times which, some seventy years earlier, could be foreseen by very few only.

But with pointing to these similarities we have yet failed to offer an explanation: Kafka was a writer of so high a literary stature that nobody could accuse him of simply taking out a leaf of Dickens' book, or, rather, books from Dickens' work. The notion of some literary infatuation must also be discarded by reason of the exceptions Kafka takes to the writings of the English novelist.

Dickens was made to suffer by his father being a lovable but rather dissolute chap, and Kafka was almost obsessed by

143

his father's towering personality. Max Brod quite rightly refutes a psychoanalytical explanation of this phenomenon. There is nothing morbid or extraordinary in the relations between Kafka father and Kafka son; the conflict is only sharpened by the fact that the wealthy self-made man's and merchant's son was to become a great artist. Apart from that, it is the typical conflict of that kind of bourgeois family Kafka came from. In a different sphere and at another stage of social development it was Dickens' conflict with his father. As a young lad he had to work in a blacking factory, a period in his life he was never to forget, and later he had to take up the routine job of a little clerk. Kafka, the son of a well-to-do man, could take his university degree and work in an insurance office but both occupations were not less alien to, and hated by, him than blacking bottles and writing in a drab office had been to Dickens. The fetters of society, the struggle against society had, with both these writers, their roots in the conditions of middle-class family, unhappy though they were in the case of Dickens and rather prosperous in that of Kafka. Father and family stood only as symbols for a society which stifled their highest aspirations. There is, therefore, no sign of that queer mixture of hate and love in their relations to their fathers, which might evoke the interest of psychologists: they loved their fathers all right but they hated them as representatives of a society whose oppression they felt everywhere. Starting out with their personal conflicts they were necessarily led to the social foundations of these conflicts.

The great difference between both writers is, however, not altogether in Kafka's favour as one might be induced to believe from what we said about *David Copperfield* and *Amerika*. *Dickens* lived in a period of great political, social, and economic changes, a period full of evil things against which he was fighting. But it was still a period when industrialization and the whole progress of capitalistic society had a task to fulfill and, above all, he lived in a strong country which represented a leading world power, he was a man *of* the people who could write *for* the people, for readers who belonged to various strata of contemporary society, readers who were capable of giving him a response. Kafka's creative work coincides with the decay and fall of the Austro-Hungarian Monarchy, and this German-writing Jew from Prague had as the only readers of his books a small circle of "the chosen few" who could give him a response only in so far as his work appealed to their individualistically coloured sense of aesthetic values and to their not less varied and changing philosophical or religious moods. Although Kafka wrote in German he knew incomparably more about Czech politics and politicians, about Czech common people than about those of his compatriots who spoke his language. This explains, to a large extent at least, the tremendous difference in form and style between Dickens and Kafka.

Jackson characterises *David Copperfield* (*op. cit.*, p. 123) as follows: "The effect is achieved of a vastly ramified plexus of incidents and characters symbolical of the current human life itself," and he says (*op. cit.*, p. 165): "*Little Dorrit* is, in fact, an allegory—of whose true purport its author was only partly conscious." But even if we agree with the general line Jackson is taking in his book and which is followed up by Wilson in the essay we mentioned above—and there is no reason to disagree—the means of symbolism is handled in quite a different way by the two authors. The uppermost layer of Dickens' novels is a "realistic," if melodramatically tinged and perhaps sometimes even overdone, picture of daily-life events. Beneath this layer which is the only one accessible to most of his readers is a hidden symbolism which stands for a much deeper reality presenting life and society of his time as a whole, quite apart from the incidental realities of the actual story told. The uppermost layer of Kafka's novels is seemingly "unrealistic"—strange and unreal stories, strange and unreal events. Beneath this layer which is likewise the only one accessible to most of his readers is a hidden symbolism which stands for a deep reality presenting life and society of his time as a whole and revealing—just as with Dickens—its secret foundations and the interplay of its various features. The story he is telling derives its true meaning from here and from here only. Form and style are the artist's means to communicate with his public, they are determined by it: we have tried to explain above why Dickens could write as he did and why Kafka had to choose the way he followed. There are similar phenomena in

145

other realms of creative work, more striking perhaps because they can be recognized in men not separated by the distance of time and space as in our case. There is, for instance, the revolutionary poet Blake who had to create his own myth to express his vision of reality (Jack Lindsay: *Perceptives for Poetry*) as compared with the revolutionary and plainly realistic poet Shelley or, to take an example from German literature, the similar case of Hölderlin and Heine.

"the penal colony"

austin warren

The earth is a penal colony, and we are all under sentence of judgment for sin. There was once a very elaborate machine, of scholastic theology, for the pronouncement of sentence, and an elaborate ecclesiastical system for its administration. Now it is in process of disappearance: the Old Commander (God) has died, though there is a legend, which you can believe or not, that He will come again. Meanwhile the "machine" seems antiquated and inhuman to ladies, who are sentimental about criminals, and to the new governor, who is a humanitarian.

The two interlocutors are an old official, still faithful to the inventor of the machine, and an explorer: the former, a survivor from the old theology, a member of the saving remnant of believers in God and sin; the latter is a naturalist, a scientist who shares the humanitarian views of his secularist generation but who, as a social scientist, is capable of intellectual curiosity and a suspension of judgment. When he sees that the old officer is willing to testify to his faith by martyrdom, by taking his own place in the machine (which only a moral-professional law requires), he respects him for loyalty to his code, and "would not have acted differently in his place": Scientist and theologian have in common a respect for law, an adherence to professional duty over personal comfort, and a willingness to see life as it painfully is.

Important is the setting of the machine's draftsman. The first victim suffers under "Honor your Superior," the moral law which he has broken: this is a law appropriate to his caste of servant. For his own use, the old officer adjusts the legend to "Be just." Has he violated this injunction? Not consciously; but a judge of his fellow men should be "just," and no mortal man can be: "none is Good save God": the old officer can be sure that, whatever his intentions, he has been unjust in the sight of Justice.

At the end of the story, the explorer has become converted to the doctrine of the machine: he excludes from his boat those who wish to escape from the penal island. "Converted" is too strong; if really converted, he would stay on the island—at least if the machine still operated. But at least he makes no report to the new commander; and he takes the Prophecy of Return seriously: when the men about him ridicule the inscription, he does not join in their laughter: the Prophecy may be true. Like Pilate, he refuses to judge; he finds no fault in the just manipulators of the machine.

In its tone, the story is a matter-of-fact description of an elaborate method of punishment, no longer believed in by the "enlightened," kept going a little longer by the devotion of an old man who doesn't understand it very well and can't repair it. Narration is from the point of view of, through the eyes of, the explorer, who is shocked by what he sees and yet who, unlike the present management of the penal colony, can understand the possible use of the machine in what is, after all, a penal colony; and who becomes increasingly sympathetic as he sees that the operator of the machine believes in it for himself as well as for others. But it is essential to Kafka's purpose that there shall be no suppression of the difficulties in accepting the gospel of the machine: it is cruel; it makes errors; it is costly to keep up; people have ceased to believe in it; its inventor has died, and it is generally thought ridiculous to credit the pious legend that he will come again. "My ways are not as your ways, neither my thoughts as your thoughts," saith the Lord. Like Kierkegaard and Barth, Kafka, fearful of softening religion, wants to present it in all its rigor, its repellence to the flesh—in its irrationality and inscrutability and uncertainty, too. We must put up with the professional pride and the pedantry of the old officer: religionists are always forgetting ends in absorption with means, taking human (and impious) pride in the details of their theological and ecclesiastical systems. Nothing is simple, nothing unmixed. We never get reality straight, but always (as Irving Babbitt said) through a veil of illusion. If we are determined to be scrupulously positivistic and "accept no illusion," then we shall have to content ourself with no more than statistics: we shan't find reality.

This story differs from Kafka's novels in being pretty persistently and consistently allegorical. Yet it is not an allegory which insists upon its conceptual structure. Full of the detail in which Kafka delighted always, it presents itself as a realistic narrative which might, so far as its structural myth is concerned, appear in the cinema as a Karloff thriller or as a study in psychopathology—specifically sadism. Its powerful effect is indeed produced by its complete absence of fantasy in detail: The story offers, by its method, the sense of a fact which you can interpret as you like, of which you can make what you like: I'm telling you, as a sober scientist, what I saw.

149

"the trial"

alberto spaini

In discussing the very strange work of Franz Kafka, one is apt to get lost in comments and interpretations, each making the text more difficult and incomprehensible, a text which is, however, very clear despite all appearances, provided one relies only on the letter and that natural extension of it, that symbolic echo which is tied to the letter. But if we attempt to take a book by Kafka, *The Trial* for example, or *The Castle* which seems a second version of *The Trial,* as an allegorical work to be interpreted step by step and word by word, very probably every lyric and poetic value will be lost from it.

Among contemporary German writers there is none who can even remotely be compared with Kafka. If we had to trace back the origins of his work, we would probably be very perplexed, since all the associations which come to mind most readily we perceive to be completely superficial and actually foreign to the spirit of Kafka. Max Brod has for some time been occupied with a circle of ideas which can be related to Kafka's, but the broad spirituality which prevails in the plot of some of his novels, such as *Tycho Brahe,* becomes pale and scanty before that one basic thought on which the construction of Kafka's books rests. Nor would it be a matter of evoking memories like Meyrink's *Green Face,* where mystic and magical elements are used like devices in a detective story and are stripped of every intimate value. On the other hand, the mystic literature of the Jewish writer, Martin Buber—to anticipate one or two considerations which we presently will make regarding the Hebraism of Kafka— is frankly religious and transcendental and lacks that mysterious fascination which is truly Kafka's, namely the complete dissimulation of mystic elements within the plot of the novel.

We like Kafka precisely because it is superfluous to interpret him. We like him for his ultra-realistic way of describing things which a good average citizen would call, taking the words from our mouth, "things of the other world." Things of the other world which happen in this, with all the schemes, the causes and the effects of this world. Like Joseph K., the protagonist of *The Trial,* we too feel that we are completely disloyal when we are surprised at what happens to him. Nor is anything understood of the trial against Joseph K., as he likewise understands nothing of it; but we too, just as he, are intimately persuaded that everything is in order and that it is well that it is thus. Nor do we escape the trial even if we do not know why we are on trial or who is the tribunal before which the trial is taking place. That is Kafka's strength: to make us accept as indispensable a whole story which contrasts with the elements of daily life, and yet is woven together solely and exclusively of these elements. Not the story only, but every episode and the connection of the various episodes and the characters and the connections between them and little by little the things which they do and say. Everything is perfectly in place, and everything is incredible. But "in the beginning is the word" and Kafka had the gift of that word which in the center of our life evokes and enchants events of which an instinct or an illumination tells us that they can only be the echo of higher worlds.

If we wished to try our hand at some interpretations, there is one that we might perhaps accept, especially since it offers a means of casting a glance at the way Kafka's narrative art functions, and the interpretation would be materialistic or psychological. What is the trial against Joseph K.? In terms of our knowledge of the duty and the law of men, the trial is not explained. One would have to imagine that it deals with a mysterious secret tribunal, a type of unconsecrated Sacred Wheel, which is inquiring into and judging our private life, those actions of ours which can appear before one tribunal only, that of our conscience. Then, however, the construction of the tribunal as it is depicted in the novel would appear too arbitrary and subtle. Instead things appear quite different if we imagine that Joseph K. has not been accused before a tribunal, but that this is only a symbolic way of expressing another situation; for example this: that K. has been struck by an incurable disease, and that he is awaiting death. Imagine all the first steps of a man in this situation, and the successive states of mind through which he will pass: you find them precisely in K. It is enough to enumerate one or two of them: his obstinacy in not wanting to "confess" (that is to admit to being sick); his idea that if instead of being arrested in his house, in the morning when he was hardly awake, he had been arrested in his office "he would not have let himself be taken by surprise" (that is the attachment to active life, which seems of itself to deny the possibility of death); the fact of not having taken the trial seriously at the outset, of almost not having thought of it, and then, bit by bit, to live entirely in its midst, never to be able to detach himself from it, to have to abandon every activity. . . . This interpretation is very beguiling, not only because it gives to the book a very logical and transparent symbolism, but also because it explains to us the spontaneous mood with which Kafka constructs his tale, thinking constantly of a series of hidden events, which still are not actually uttered, which take place on a parallel plane with those which are set forth. And thus it is that the story is told "with the trial as the key" while in reality all the events, the psychological conditions, the sentences which most successfully give form to the events, are thought of "with sickness as the key." The uninterrupted transposition, executed with a technical and almost mechanical perfection which is amazing, explains to us without doubt Kafka's stylistic secret, and it is not inconsiderable.

But this interpretation is likewise very suggestive for a

third reason which without doubt would bring joy to a psychiatrist: Kafka was actually the victim of an incurable disease, he
really expected death. Was it not natural that in the very delicate
and sensitive poet this dramatic situation should be translated
into a series of nightmares, that sickness should in fact become
for him a trial (an image also suggested even by colloquial language, which describes an incurable as one "condemned")? In
the memory of us all there is an infantile nightmare which makes
it almost worth supposing that even the ideas of responsibility
and of justice are innate in us. Where is the seven-year-old child
who has not awakened some night howling with terror because
he saw the most horrible thing which he had ever met up to
that time or had succeeded in imagining, and which now, being
rocked and consoled, he no longer succeeds in explaining? Then
frequently this nightmare returns, until one day he succeeds in
understanding it: the little dreamer had made a promise, an un-
bounded promise, which surpassed all his strength and which he
never in the world would have been able to keep; but he had
given his word and there was no way to turn back. Nor is it
known what catastrophe followed this broken promise but it was
an inevitable catastrophe, and we ourselves had provoked it,
with a spontaneous act of our will. We would not have been
able to fulfill this act, this promise: but now we had created from
nothing a world (which then was the world of our moral duty)
and we were its prisoners.

The psychologists give a thousand beautiful explanations of the dream, and more than one of them could be very
well adapted also to *The Trial*. What is more natural than this
completely spiritual reaction in a man like Kafka to the nightmare of sickness? The events of the physical world he transposes
into the moral world (or rather uses their scheme to give to his
story a material solidity which augments the mystery and the
mystic fascination of it) and by the repression of physical terror
in the face of evil is derived precisely its sublimation in the work
of art. That is why psychology might perhaps furnish a very
fine and plausible interpretation. But if, instructed by this interpretation, we begin to read Kafka's novel, we find it even more
mysterious; now that we *know* everything, we *understand* much

154

less than before. For this reason we were on our guard against the tendency to "interpret" Kafka. For whatever interpretation be given to this account, one fact remains that doesn't change and that has no need of interpretations. In our dream, the first cosmic and tragic terror is born in us out of the consciousness of a destiny which we have created with our will. Thus in *The Trial* it is not the fate of Joseph K. which is of greatest importance, but the moral conduct which he assumes before this fate. As we read it "with illness as the key," or, in the case of *The Castle,* under the veil of social and political ambition, Kafka's novel appears to us only outwardly as an episode of our struggle against destiny. In substance K. does not fight against destiny, he fights against himself; Kafka has imposed upon himself the superhuman task of making this struggle moral. And there is the point. The struggle against destiny reduces man to an animal level, to that of a blind corpuscle crushed by the imponderable mass which weighs heavily above and beyond us. Man's secret is that of forcing destiny onto a spiritual plane. Man's life must take place exclusively in that world over which man has power: his own spirit. Whatever blow may come upon us from the outside (K.'s arrest) must find us unassailable within our spirituality. "The fact that only one world of the spirit exists, takes hope from us and leaves us certainty": those are words of Kafka in which extreme renunciation is mingled with extreme triumph.

Joseph K., our hero, was not the man most ideally suited to sustain that part in life. And indeed the first reaction to the events of which he will be the victim is one of rebellion. "Someone must have been telling lies about Joseph K., for without having done anything wrong he was arrested one fine morning." That is Kafka's first sentence. His first impulse is to deny having done anything wrong and his first thought is that of being the victim of a false accusation: he succumbs, that is, to destiny; he wants to struggle. And the second from the last chapter (but which can be considered the last, since the end is really an epilogue) closes with this sentence: "This Court makes no claims upon you. It receives you when you come and it relinquishes you when you go." Destiny has completely disarmed; it no longer takes place in the material order of facts, but in the moral activities of man. But this withdrawal from destiny onto a more remote plane, from which it no longer has any power over us, lasts only as long as our capacity to remain firm and enclosed within ourselves survives. Has Joseph K. ever reached it? And if he has reached it, has he known how to preserve it? It seemed to him that the shame of it would probably outlive him, so Joseph K. dies without that halo of glory which for a moment or two we believed we saw shining again behind his head; he did not know how, finally and completely, to renounce hope and he did not attain certainty. He dies "like a dog."

In the struggle against destiny therefore he conquers destiny, but the man remains inferior in respect to his duty to create an indestructible moral universe. Joseph K. did not raise himself above the animal level, and even less prepared to meet the serious task which awaits him is the protagonist of *The Castle*. Kafka did not succeed in conceiving an optimistic affirmative situation with his plot (apparently so monotonous); his every attempt toward liberation ended fatally in a tragic catastrophe. Some have chosen to see in this spiritual torture of Kafka a reflection of his Jewish psychology, so frequently gloomy and pessimistic (Weininger, Michelstaedter). It is not so much the search for God which characterizes the Hebraism of Kafka, as Enrico Rocca has noted a cabalistic structure beneath the plot of *The Trial*, or to perceive some relationship between his so painfully realistic symbolism and that of chassidic literature. Is Kafka's dialectical despair Hebraic? But then all philosophy and all the modern world are Hebraic: from the time when we renounced hope in a God who intervenes by his grace to save us, certainly our Jehovah has re-acquired some of the ineluctable characteristics which He of the Old Testament had; his strength is no longer infinite, but it is exactly limited by the strength of our spirit. He hasn't one gram more power than we are able to give him.

Joseph K., when he reaches the threshold of knowledge, in the chapter about the Cathedral, does not dare to ask either the priest or God for help. Suddenly the priest also identifies himself as a member of the court. Consolation, grace thus become impossible. Once again K. is driven within himself. Only

156

his shame will live after him. Here, at this extreme limit, the inexorability of Ancient Law and of modern idealism become equivalent. But it is a coincidence which has been recorded because Hebraism is in style, or precisely because Kafka was Jewish.

But the last word on Kafka seems to us rather what has been said by Groethuysen: "The not-I is before the I." *The Trial* is, to be content with the ugly expression, the poem of the not-I; it is a miraculous effort to understand and to encompass within precise words the not-I, so that we can recognize the limits which separate our personality from the world, and we can prohibit the world from passing across them. The way of speaking which all of Kafka's characters have, from Joseph K. down to the humble Frau Grubach, from the priest who offers his mercy in vain to the guard who has grown fat eating the prisoners' breakfasts, is that of people who are obsessed with one idea, with one idea whatever its type, and must circumscribe it, very exactly. K.'s style creaks under this ferocious task of enclosing all mysteries in everyday words; no shade must remain outside his formulas, all the more besetting since they are of every day. Thus it is with a man's life: "Was help at hand? Were there some arguments in his favor that had been overlooked? Of course there must be. Logic is doubtless unshakable, but it cannot withstand a man who wants to go on living." It is this irresistible logic, a release of vitality, which is behind Kafka's style and truly gives strength to those mannerisms of his, so extremely plain, smooth and phlegmatic; it is the desperate phlegm of the man who knows how to be lost if he loses his calm only for a moment.

Hence the morbid fascination of Kafka's novel. The image of the catastrophe hangs above the whole tale; the most everyday and insignificant events, under this spectral light, become strangely plastic, acquire the unreal reality which is a characteristic of nightmares. But all this would perhaps have disappeared in the great night which encompassed the still very young author without the balance of his language which is poised on ample and airy planes indispensable in supporting such disagreeable burdens. The philosophical undertaking, the symbolic

157

flooring, the romantic and sometimes decadent nature of the visions, the realistic construction of the tale—all passive things in the work of Kafka—are sustained without effort by the style, which, transfiguring these disparate elements, constitutes the originality of his work.

Translated by John Glynn Conley.

Three unnamed drawings by Kafka

"the trial" and the theology of crisis

john kelly

"The whole form of the world lies under the curse of God."
                                                    —KARL BARTH

An eschatological novel—an allegory of man's relations
with God in terms of a Calvinistic theology—is unique in our
time, or in any time; and Kafka's production of such a work in a
style palatable to an unspecialized group of readers is the climax
of his bizarre explorations into the fate of man. *The Trial* sets
forth in the form of an elaborate parable the basic principles of a
modern system of theology, erected on the startling teachings of
the Danish philosopher and psychologist of religion, Sören Kierkegaard. Kierkegaard's opinions were so antipathetic to the ordinary philosophic and religious atmosphere of the nineteenth century that the recognition he has received in the writings of the
"Existenz" philosophers and the exponents of the so-called
Theology of Crisis amounts to a resurrection. This body of
thought, probably the most interesting intellectual product of the
War, is associated with the name of its most forceful and uncompromising exponent, the greatest living Protestant theologian,
Karl Barth. Critics have noted in a very sketchy manner the

159

influence of Kierkegaard upon Kafka; but his close affinity with the thought of Karl Barth has been overlooked. This is understandable because of the absence of any formal association between the two disciples of Kierkegaard; for though they were working at the same time under the Dane's influence, they were quite unaware of each other. A comparison of Kafka's religious views with those of Barth is a distinctly more fruitful approach to him than the customary attitude, that he is to be treated as a remarkable psychological case, or a social oddity. For Kafka, as it happens, is a fairly conventional subject for psychoanalysis. His situation displays quite familiar fixtures; father-complex, sexual inadequacy, Jewish alienness, social timidity, physical weakness, unsympathetic environment, aesthetic sensitivity, and all the rest of a picture that is by now very commonplace in literary criticism. So it is necessary to take with distinct reservations Mr. Philip Rahv's dictum: "In the final analysis, his myth of the Law is nothing more than the idealized impasse of his own experience." A final analysis is not always achieved by reference to psychological conditioning factors, however attractive this method, with its lowered scholastic requirements, may have become to modern critics. Kafka as problem child, Kafka as Jew, is not the clue to the allegory in this novel; it is to be found only in Kafka as theologian, Kafka as fellow of Calvin, Kierkegaard, Karl Barth, and other adventurers in the hard dogmas of a "crucial" theology. Kafka's tale of the bank clerk, Joseph K., unexpectedly arrested in his lodgings by a mysterious, dubious, and absurd "authority," which hounds him through many adventures to an awful execution, is in all its parts a parable of guilt and forgiveness, of sacrifice and salvation. The chief importance of *The Trial* does not derive from any insight it may afford us into the psychological composition of a consumptive Jew in Prague, but rather from its revelation of the power these eschatological elements still exert over the mind of man, even today, when the peculiar arbitrariness of Calvinistic thought renders it, in the general opinion, practically unworthy of civilized discussion. The power, and almost horrifying splendor of the neo-Calvinistic school of thought, may be glimpsed by the layman, untrained in theological technique, by means of Kafka's allegory.

160

Even less fruitful than the psychological approach to Kafka is Mr. Winkler's: "The dilemma is conceived of as being known to us only at the ethical level; that is, it emerges as the general problem of the individual's relation to society, and any attempt at a solution must involve an attempt to come to terms with, and find a place in, the social organism." Whatever this strange statement may mean (it has suggestions which might be useful with regard to *Amerika* or *The Castle*), none of its terms have the slightest relevance to *The Trial*, which, ignoring social problems, plunges directly into the tangled morass of Calvinistic conceptions regarding man's relationship with an Absolute God. All such attitudes produce around *The Trial* a critical atmosphere such as might exist with regard to Bunyan's *Pilgrim's Progress* if it chanced that that allegory should be read by persons who, without any knowledge of Christianity, were considering it simply as a story.

THE FALLEN STATE OF MAN

Karl Barth's celebrated *Commentary on the Epistle to the Romans*, the keystone of his thought, is contemporaneous with Kafka's *Trial*. Strongly influenced by Kierkegaard as was Kafka at this time also, it expounds with technical clarity all the ideas which are perceived through a glass darkly in Kafka's own book. Conceived in the milieu of the War, and in an atmosphere of defeat, Barth's theology is characterized by a sweeping rejection of man and all his works: "Over against man's confidence and belief in himself there has been written, in huge proportions and with the utmost clearness a *mene, mene, tekel.*" This is the theme of Barth's social consciousness, and Kafka, when he wrote the allegory, had reached very much the same conclusions. Barth repeatedly attacks the idealism and humanism active in nineteenth- and twentieth-century Protestantism, its consequent absorption in social problems, and simpering endeavor "to supply society with an ecclesiastical cupola or wing." He disparages philosophy, science, art, aesthetics, and any performance in which he detects anthropomorphic premises. To him the attempted synthesis of Christianity and the philosophy of Plotinus,

161

suggested by Troeltsch as the "way out" for religion, is as absurd as it is irreligious. That Plotinianism which Dean Inge takes for the honey of Hymettus to Christianity is to Barth just a sugary decoration on the tower of Babel—a particularly vicious example of the oversimplification inherent in all religious "solutions." "Simple to us is neither Paul's Romans, nor the present situation in theology, nor the present world situation, nor man's situation in general toward God—Hard and complicated is man's life today in every direction." Such a position defines accurately the nature of Kafka's own "pessimism" (which Max Brod naïvely supposes did not exist, because Kafka was occasionally gay, and bore suffering heroically!)—a pessimism which is only partial; which is a gloomy, but not a cynical feeling about man's fate; which recognizes the hardness of his lot, but in that very hardness finds a basis for positive affirmations, for a belief that there is a *hard*, a "crucial" solution.

Barth and Kafka search for the key to salvation in terms of the events on the road to Damascus, and in the experience of the Jewish prophets. St. Paul's conversion remains the chief clue to the action of God; Calvin and Kierkegaard are, for the crucial theologians, the foremost expounders of this action. Barth totally rejects *human* activity as a way to God. Any assistance in the quest for the Absolute, alleged to be found in philosophy and art, is a complete delusion, for there is no way from man to God; there is only a way from God to man. The theology of crisis knows no "flight of the alone to the alone," no "satisfaction for the yearning soul in finding the Infinite." In the true Church, according to Barth, all cultural values are nil in terms of the Absolute.

On God and his fulfilling "Amen" the Church hopes. She cannot be on hand at the building of a tower of Babel whose summit shall reach toward Heaven. She hopes in God for men, but not *in men,* not even in pious men, and not in the least that man with the help of God will finally build and complete that tower. She neither believes in the divinity of the human spirit, nor in that of nature, and much less still in the alleged synthesis produced between the two. Quite simply she

162

takes death too seriously but that "humanity" can be anything else to her than hope in the resurrection of the dead. She awaits her Redeemer's word, "Lo, I make all things new." With this, the eschatological preconception, she encounters society. Not in depreciation of the work of culture, but in the highest valuation of it, for she sees the goal of all the work of culture. Not out of pessimism, but from overwhelming hope. Not as a "spoil-sport," but knowing that Art and Science, Business and Politics, Technique and Education are really a game ["ein Spiel, ein ernstes Spiel, aber ein Spiel"], that is to say, a picturesque and ultimately pointless performance that has its meaning not in its achievable purposes but in what it means in itself, which would perhaps be played better and more realistically were it better understood as such. . . . The Church renders society no service, if for fear of disturbing herself and making herself disliked, she makes this preconception invalid, if she brings not to expression the comfort and warning of eternity. Society is waiting just for this service. [*Die Theologie und die Kirche*]

Kafka likewise encounters society with an eschatological preconception, which is certainly as strange to conventional literary and artistic attitudes as the theology of Barth and Kirkegaard is to liberal Protestantism. It explains the absence, very rare in modern authors, of artistic references and decor. Eliot, Mann, Proust, and the others all make elaborate use of the artistic experience of man, when they unfold their thoughts. But in Barthian speculation, there is nothing but contempt for persons who find God in Nature, in their own hearts, in a sublime poem, in a quartet by Beethoven, in a Wagnerian opera, and the like. To professional esthetes, who are prone to call such raptures "religious," the philosophy of Kafka must seem very alien, indeed. Possibly it is for this reason that it is chiefly Kafka's style which has been imitated. His content has made very little impression. It might be wondered at that Kafka has chosen to deal with such profound and intricate matters in such a highly humorous manner. It is partially because of his extraordinary command of humorous expression (he shows every sign of being the greatest humorist since Swift), and partially because of certain suggestions found in Kierkegaard. That extremely melancholy Dane, for some reason, called himself a humorist. In his "Postscript," he calls irony "the incognito of the ethical," and humor, "the incognito of the religious"—and again, "in the last resort Christianity is humour. Humour diverts the attention a little from the prime qualification, God." And so on, in a rather obscure and surprising vein. The humorous qualities of Kierkegaard are certainly anything but obvious, if they exist at all; but Kafka's humor is his outstanding characteristic. He has preserved with remarkable skill the complete incognito of his eschatological subject until the very conclusion of *The Trial.* Thus he becomes a religious humorist in Kierkegaard's sense, as well as a literary humorist in the manner of Swift.

Among humanitarian and idealistic thinkers, the fallen state of man is usually considered, when its existence is recognized at all, to be the result of his failure to realize his inherent possibilities, or the "wickedness" or "inhumanity" of certain individuals or groups. Barth, on the other hand, asserts that man's state "is a perplexity felt by man simply by virtue of his being a man, and has nothing to do with his being moral or immoral, spiritual or worldly, godly or ungodly." And again, "man from the viewpoint of the good is powerless." Kafka, as is well known, was deeply and peculiarly involved in a quest for "the good," and for "the right way of life." "Men want to hear a word they can rely on and live by," observes Barth. Neither Barth nor Kafka was able to find a right way of life in any of the recognized ethical systems they found about them, whether religious or philosophic. Barth considered every ethical system to be either the product of cynical determinism, or of enthusiastic ideology. "Human ethics are impossible to both, for one removes responsibility and freedom, the other guilt and entanglement." Kafka bestows these four qualities upon his hero in abundance; they dominate the hard solution at which the allegory arrives. Joseph K. is entirely free, entirely responsible, wholly guilty, hopelessly entangled. His only escape is the way of "crisis."

The "crisis" is Kierkegaard's most striking concept. From him Barth and Kafka develop it elaborately, starting from his premise: "Finitum non capax infiniti—There is an infinite difference between time and eternity; God is in heaven, man on earth." God is transcendent and absolute—*ganz anders*. Religious experience, therefore, can be grounded only in a direct speech from God to man. Any quest for Him on the part of man is pointless, for there is no way up to Him. He reveals Himself to man or He does not. All ideas of God's immanence, from Wordsworth's crude pantheism to the refined raptures of Plotinus, are ruthlessly set aside. "God cannot be known by his active presence in the world, but is regarded as hidden, so that what God is is not revealed" (Emil Brunner). God speaks and commands; man hears and obeys—or turns away from the command to his own destruction. This revelation of God is the crisis in the man's life —the turning point of his existence, the beginning of a struggle, in which he can be saved only by making the right turn, in the right way.

"God's command is the categorical imperative of absolute urgency, of absolute stringency. He who is claimed by God knows nothing of 'Still we have time' (the evolutionary view); of 'Not-yet' (growing perfectibility); of 'gradually, or more or less' (the metaphysical view); or a 'Not-now' (the moralist's view). It is a 'No-longer!'" (Karl Barth). This is the Barthian view of Kierkegaard's great "Either-Or"—the starting point of the neo-Calvinist's Vita Nuova. After this crisis, all that has existed before in the life of the "claimed" man must be discarded. "There is absolutely no continuity between the natural life and the new one, and in consequence a complete breach with the natural human development takes place. . . . One can no longer seek God, by falling back on the past and one's true self" (Kierkegaard). "No moment is not a turning-point in the drama, in which every victory or defeat, standing or falling, living or dying, is indicated, a Jacob's flight in which man is necessarily wounded in the thigh, if the matter is to go on—every moment with the character of once-for-allness and non-repetition. Entirely to asso-

165

ciate with God truly in this relation is claiming the stake, the risk of man's existence at every moment" (Karl Barth). All this is a perfect commentary on the career of Joseph K. from the moment of his arrest, and on the struggle which the mysterious command forces upon him.

THE MORAL LAW

Does Joseph K. accept his "trial"? The Barthian theology teaches that every man at the time of crisis is free to take another turn, free to reject the struggle at any point. At first, Joseph K., quite rationally, contemplates some resistance to this unauthorized arrest:

> Who could these men be? What were they talking about? What authority could they represent? K. lived in a country with a legal constitution, there was universal peace, all the laws were in force; who dared seize him in his own dwelling? He had always been inclined to take things easily, to believe in the worst only when the worst happened, to take no care for the morrow even when the outlook was threatening. *But that struck him as not being the right policy here . . . his very first glance* at the man Franz had decided him for the time being not to give away any advantage that he might possess over these people . . . if this was a comedy he would insist on playing it to the end [italics mine].

From that moment of decision, Joseph K., entirely by his own manipulation, remains in the grip of the Law. Bit by bit, the continuity of his life is broken down, and all his reliances, habits, and safeguards cease to operate. More and more completely he becomes absorbed in the processes of the Law, in discovering how it works, and in its relationship to him and his "case." "Here are my identification papers." "What are your identification papers to us?" sneer the minions of the Law. So begins the Jacob-fight to the death.

What is the Law? What must a man do to be saved?

Kafka works out his hero's problem by basing his allegory on the prophetic writings of the Old Testament, and on Calvin's Pauline Christianity, absorbed through Kierkegaard. The most bewildering problem which confronts Joseph K. after his arrest is that of his "guilt." In the court offices, K. encounters some other "claimed" men. "They did not stand quite erect, their backs remained bowed, their knees bent, they stood like street beggars. K. waited for the Law-Court Attendant, who kept slightly behind him, and said: 'How humbled they must be!' 'Yes,' said the Law-Court Attendant, 'these are accused men, all of them are accused of guilt.' 'Indeed!' said K. 'Then they're colleagues of mine.'" Thus sarcastically, humorously, tentatively, K. fumbles with the notion of his own "guilt" for a time; but, in the end, he is so convinced of it that he wills his own destruction in expiation. He evolves into a Pauline Christian. "And I lived sometime without the Law. But when the commandment came, sin revived, and I died. And the commandment that was ordained to life, the same was found to be unto death to me" (Epistle to the Romans).

But he becomes still more, a Calvinist; for the Law of Wrath by which K. is bound is elaborately discussed by Calvin in his *Institutes*.

> Let us examine what sort of righteousness can be found in men during the whole course of their lives. Let us divide them into four classes. For either they are destitute of the knowledge of God and immersed in idolatry. . . . [Joseph K. is clearly in this first class, so we halt in it.] In the first of these classes judged according to their natural characters, from the crown of the head to the sole of the foot there will not be found a single spark of goodness; unless we mean to charge the Scripture with falsehood. . . . But if any among them show that integrity in their conduct which among men has some appearance of sanctity, yet since we know that God regards not external splendour, we must penetrate to the secret springs of these virtues, whatever they may be, or rather the images of virtues, if we wish them to avail anything to justification. . . . The observation of Augustine is strictly

true—that all who are strangers to the religion of the one true God, however they may be esteemed worthy of admiration for their reputed virtue, not only merit no reward, but are rather deserving of punishment, because they contaminate the pure gifts of God with the pollution of their own hearts.

This elaborate and terrifying view, discreetly laid to rest for some centuries by liberal Protestants, has been revived with great emphasis by the Barthian theologians; and Kafka is again on their side, by way of Kierkegaard. "Guilt and transitoriness are the characteristics of even our best deeds. Just here, we can do nothing else than confess: 'Surely what we do is to no profit, even in the best life.' And it is just the converted man who can say that." (Karl Barth.)

It is characteristic of the thinking of the time that the problem of guilt and forgiveness has been pushed into the background and seems to disappear more and more. . . . There are even today, a great many people who understand that man needs salvation, but there are very few who are convinced that he needs forgiveness and redemption. . . . Sin is understood as imperfection, sensuality, worldliness—but not as guilt. . . . Man can do nothing to remove guilt. . . . No continuity of action, no accomplishment of works can create anew the broken connection. [Emil Brunner.]

This, in short, is the lesson which Kafka teaches in his allegory. Every experience of Joseph K. demonstrates the futility of human endeavor to remove this primordial "Guilt."

Such is the framework of the hero's struggle: to establish a connection with the higher authority, to understand his guilt, to be freed from it, if possible. This is an enterprise which is foredoomed to failure by the terms of this theology, in so far as the hero attempts it by his own efforts. Even when he has come so far as to accept his guilt, we find him still hatching schemes to free himself from it. Only at the end has he reached the full realization of the futility of this conduct. His first defense is the naïve one that he is ignorant of the Law. "'I don't know this Law,' said K. 'All the worse for you,' replied the warder. 'And it probably exists nowhere but in your own head,' said K. . . . 'You'll come up against it yet.' Franz interrupted: 'See, Willem, he admits that he doesn't know the Law and yet he claims he's innocent.'" Eventually K. acquires the services of an advocate to assist him with the Law. In the advocate's milieu he encounters the cheapest sort of graft; but the advocate is a fairly good Calvinist. In passages which achieve unparalleled heights of humor, the nature of the court and its judgments are discussed. "The advocate was always working away at the first plea, but it had never reached a conclusion, which at the next visit turned out to be an advantage, since the last few days would have been very inauspicious for handing it in, a fact which no one could have foreseen." The reasons for all this shuffling on the part of the advocate are alleged to derive from the peculiar character of the court. Actually the ultimate character of the court is as hidden from all the advocates and officials connected with it as it is from Joseph K., himself:

> . . . the legal records of the case, and above all the actual charge-sheets, were inaccessible to the accused and his counsel, consequently one did not know in general, or at least did not know with any precision, what charges to meet in the first plea; accordingly it could only be by pure chance that it contained really relevant matter. . . . In such circumstances the Defence was naturally in a very ticklish and difficult position. Yet that, too, was intentional. For the Defence was not actually countenanced by the Law, but only tolerated, and there were differences of opinion even on that point, whether the Law could be interpreted to admit such tolerance at all . . . the whole onus of the Defence must be laid on the accused himself.

It soon becomes clear that all this legal defense is the sheerest quackery, and that only the most menial officials of the court can be approached at all. A case in its higher stages cannot be followed by anyone, not even the accused himself. Yet far from displaying any rebelliousness or dissatisfaction with a court of this

169

shifty and arbitrary character, the advocates and the officials regard it as a paragon of unerring justice. In this they follow Calvin who observes (in a chapter attractively entitled, "The destined destruction of the reprobate procured by themselves"):

> We, who know that all men are liable to so many charges at the Divine tribunal, that of a thousand questions they would be unable to give a satisfactory answer to one, confess that the reprobate suffer nothing but what is consistent with the most righteous judgment of God. Though we cannot comprehend the reason of this, let us be content with some degree of ignorance where the wisdom of God soars into its own sublimity.

In a conversation with the court painter, the question of Joseph K.'s innocence is discussed, without much consolation for the unfortunate defendant.

> "Are you innocent?" he asked. "Yes," said K. . . . "That's the main thing," said the painter. He was not to be moved by argument, yet in spite of his decisiveness it was not clear whether he spoke out of conviction or out of mere indifference. K. wanted first to be sure of this, so he said: "You know the Court much better than I do, I feel certain, I don't know much more about it than what I've heard from all sorts and conditions of people. But they all agree on one thing, that charges are never made frivolously, and that the Court, once it has brought a charge against someone, is firmly convinced of the guilt of the accused and can be dislodged from that conviction only with the greatest difficulty." "The greatest difficulty?" cried the painter, flinging one hand in the air. "Never in any case can the Court be dislodged from that conviction. . . ."

For the Court, he explains, while not impervious to proof in general, is distinctly impervious to any "proof which one brings before the Court." Acquittals are, of course, entirely possible, he adds; but

The final decisions of the Court are never recorded, even the judges can't get hold of them, consequently we have only legendary accounts of ancient cases. These legends certainly provide instances of acquittal; actually the majority of them are about acquittals, they can be believed, but they cannot be proved. . . . I myself have painted several pictures founded on such legends.

Thus the allegory is provided with a hierarchy of saints, of persons who are supposed to have won through this trial to something like acquittal. The painter's attitude towards Joseph K. does not indicate that he numbers him among these elect.

Meanwhile K.'s break with his old existence becomes as complete as the Barthian theology requires. His old social, business, and sexual lives slip away from him. Despite his contempt for the milieu of the Court, his thoughts turn more and more to the "final result of the case." He neglects his work at the bank as much as he can, and becomes increasingly indifferent to the other persons in his lodging house, who have interested him for one reason or another at the outset of the trial. He even becomes cautious and patient. Women cease to concern him. His regular mistress of whom he has been quite proud drops out of his life fairly early in the proceedings. Promiscuity naturally continues for a while, for the most part with the advocate's strange servant, Leni. She is a sort of Thaïs of the scullery, to whom "accused men" are particularly appealing. "She makes up to all of them, loves them all, and is apparently loved in return," observes the Advocate.

If you have the right eye for these things, you can see that accused men are often attractive. It's a remarkable phenomenon, almost a natural law. . . . It can't be a sense of guilt that makes them attractive,—for—it behooves me to say this as an advocate at least—they aren't all guilty, and it can't be the justice of the penance laid on them that makes them attractive in anticipation, for they aren't all going to be punished, so it must be the mere charge preferred against them that in some way enhances their attraction.

171

This is, of course, the old "eternal feminine" indispensable in any Germanic work; but in K.'s behavior there ·is a close suggestion of Calvinism. It is his exclusive devotion to the progress of his trial which induces him to give up Leni. Calvin declares that continence is a peculiar gift of God, bestowed upon a few, who have been "called," and notes that Christ himself has mentioned "a certain class of men, who have made themselves eunuchs for the kingdom of Heaven's sake,—that is, that they might be more at liberty to devote their attention to the affairs of the Kingdom of Heaven." K.'s abandonment of sex is a strong hint that his trial is nearing its climax.

GOD'S ELECTION

"Joseph K." A priest's voice rings through the Cathedral. K. has been decoyed there by the customarily confused methods of the Court. He goes under the assumption that he is to show the Cathedral to an Italian client of the bank; but the Court has by now taken control of the external forces surrounding him, and subverted every element in his normal existence. Hearing his name called out through the darkening and empty Cathedral, "K. started and stared at the ground before him. For a moment he was still free, he could continue on his way and vanish through one of the small dark wooden doors that faced him at no great distance. It would simply indicate that he had not understood the call, or that he had understood it and did not care." This insistence on K.'s freedom of choice throughout the allegory is absolutely essential to the theological concepts with which he is working. Even at the end of the shattering colloquy with the priest which ensues, and during which the imminence of his fate becomes apparent, K. is told: "The Court makes no claims upon you. It receives you when you come and it relinquishes you when you go." Man is always free to make his choice, to hear and obey the word, or to turn away.

The parable and exegesis which occupy this section of the novel is probably the most important statement of Kafka's theological views. The actual story of the parable is clear enough. A man comes from the country and seeks admission to the Law;

he is stopped at the gate by a keeper and told he cannot enter "at this moment." The man sits down by the gate to await permission to enter. He waits all his life. Near the end he perceives a "radiance that streams immortally from the door of the Law." Whereupon, all the experience of his life condenses into one question which he puts to the doorkeeper.

> "What do you want to know now?" asks the doorkeeper, "you are insatiable." "Everyone strives to attain the Law," answers the man, "how does it come about, then, that in all these years no one has come seeking admittance but me?" The doorkeeper perceives that the man is at the end of his strength and that his hearing is failing, so he bellows in his ear: "No one but you could gain admittance through this door, since this door was intended only for you. I am now going to shut it."

The exegesis of the parable which the priest offers is highly confusing to K., which is natural enough, for it reveals the paradoxical character of the Kierkegaardian theology in a satiric manner. The priest points to two important statements in the parable, the first that the doorkeeper cannot admit the man at the moment, the second, that the door was intended only for the man. Here the doorkeeper is speaking in the character of the church of Calvin, with its emphasis on man's eternal election by God, but his inability to procure it by any activity of his own, and the final uncertainty as to whether he is really elected and saved. Even Calvin is rather timid on this important point:

> The discussion of predestination—a subject of itself rather intricate—is made very perplexed and therefore dangerous by human curiosity, which no barriers can restrain from wandering into forbidden labyrinths, and soaring beyond its sphere, as if to leave none of the divine secrets unscrutinized or unexplored. As we see multitudes everywhere guilty of this arrogance and presumption, and among them some who are not censurable in other respects, it is proper to admonish them of the bounds of their duty on this subject. First,

173

then, let them remember that when they inquire into predestination they penetrate the utmost recesses of Divine wisdom, where the careless and confident intruder will obtain no satisfaction to his curiosity, but will enter into a labyrinth from which he will find no way to depart . . . to those whom he devotes to condemnation, the gates of life are closed by a just and irreprehensible, but incomprehensible judgment.

Thus Calvin scares away the inquirer, very much as the priest puts off Joseph K.

The second statement, that the door was intended only for the man, brings one face to face with the great riddle of Kafka's novel. Is Joseph K. saved or damned? At the beginning of his discourse with the priest, K. is still in a hopeful frame of mind. "I am going to get more help," he announces. "There are several possibilities I haven't explored yet." The priest naturally disapproves of this attitude. " 'Can't you see anything at all?' It was an angry cry, but at the same time sounded like the involuntary shriek of one who sees another fall and is startled out of himself." But in the ensuing discourse, the tremendous complexity of his position is brought home to Joseph K. Rational truth he discovers is useless to him. "It is not necessary to accept everything as true, one must only accept it as necessary," says the priest. "A melancholy conclusion," replies K.

It is possible to treat the final, brutal dispatch of K. as really a "melancholy conclusion," representing his damnation; but the preponderance of evidence derived from inspecting the theological background indicates that this execution represents in reality his salvation. Calvin gives some valuable hints on this problem:

The declaration of Christ that many are called and few chosen, is very improperly understood, for there will be no ambiguity in it, if we remember what must be clear from the foregoing observations, that there are two kinds of calling. For there is a universal call, by which God, in the external preaching of the word, invites all, indiscriminately to come to him, *even those*

to whom he intends it as a savour of death, and an oc-
casion of heavier condemnation. There is also a special call, with which he, for the most part, favours only
believers when, by the inward illumination of his
Spirit, he causes the word preached to sink into their
hearts.

Which of these calls has been given to K.? At first glance it might
seem that he was one of the outstanding victims of the Calvinistic
God's brutal sport, one called in the "savour of death." This seems
to be the opinion of the priest and the court officials. But there is
more to be said for K.'s position by Calvin and the Barthians.
Calvin says further: "Now the elect are not gathered into the fold
of Christ by calling, immediately from their birth nor all at the
same time. . . . Before they are gathered to that chief shepherd,
they go astray, scattered in the common wilderness, and differing
in no respect from others, except in being protected by the special mercy of God from rushing down the precipice of eternal
death." There are many more grounds for assigning K. to this
fortunate class. Luther, for instance, says that there are no perceptible signs by which the senses can discern the work of grace.
Karl Heim, of the Barthian theology, elaborates this: "The divine
accent that falls upon the Yea does not depend upon an enhanced
feeling of happiness, nor upon the strength of the religious emotions—nor upon the visionary irruptions from another realm,
which could be established in William James' sense, nor upon any
attestable sign whatever, by which the affirmation could be em-
pirically given preference over the denial." Barth holds, moreover, that faith, itself, "is never given, never ready, never secured;
seen from psychology, it is ever and ever anew the leap into the
unknown, into the dark, into empty air."

So far there is at least a negative case to be made out
in favor of Joseph K.'s salvation; and the signs that he is a man
about to undergo a frightful doom may be read in an entirely
different light. The doom may be really his salvation, his peculiar
call from the Absolute. This view is made certain, when the nature of his death is inspected. In his death Joseph K. makes what
is considered by Kierkegaard the greatest gesture toward salva-

175

tion it is within the power of man to make. This gesture is the famous "teleological suspension of the ethical." This principle appears to be not too well understood, as may be gathered from Mr. R. O. C. Winkler in *Scrutiny*, who makes an egregious error with regard to it: "The most obvious of temptations that offer themselves is a discussion of Kafka's philosophy. The Kierkegaardian system of belief that was responsible for much of the form and content of Kafka's novels is sufficiently remote from contemporary English habits of thought for an account of it to give an appearance of throwing light on the novelist's apparent obscurities. . . . For whether or not we care to admit from a doctrinal point of view the possibility of a teleological suspension of the ethical, there can be no doubt that something of this kind is assumed whenever one asserts the universality of a work of art." This passage is not much more confused than most contemporary English criticism, being notable only in that it crams more errors into less space than is usual. In the first place, the principle of the teleological suspension of the ethical has no more to do with art, universal or otherwise, than Boyle's Law of Gases, or Gresham's Axiom that "bad money drives out good." Secondly, there is no question of our admitting it or not admitting it, for it is primarily a descriptive phrase for that conduct which results from our acceptance of a spiritual prompting, to disobey the established ethical standards of our personal or social lives, as a direct command from God, taking precedence over these ethical standards. The great type of this sort of behavior is Abraham's sacrifice of Isaac in obedience to Jehovah's command. An account of the Kierkegaardian system, moreover, *does* throw light on Kafka's obscurities, which are much more than merely "apparent." (By *apparent*, Mr. Winkler must have meant *obvious*, unless he contends that the novelist's difficulties can be resolved without reference to Kierkegaard. In any case, he has given a clear demonstration of just how remote Kierkegaard is from contemporary "English habits of thought.")

Kierkegaard scandalized Copenhagen by the elaborate manner in which he broke off his engagement to be married. He announced that this was the offering of all that was dearest to him to God, whereby he hoped to experience the double action of infinity, the paradoxical character of God's love, that by giving up all he should receive all. The real reasons for this performance were probably considerably less exalted; but, in any case, he regarded it as a case of the teleological suspension of the ethical, and considered it his greatest bid for salvation. At the end of the allegory, Joseph K. is in the same position. In this case, the offering is an even more striking one, his own life.

A great change has come over Joseph K. since his interview with the priest. He has abandoned all attempts to escape from the jurisdiction of the Court, and is in a mood to go forth joyfully and meet its sentence. He accepts his guilt and responsibility; he longs for escape from the Barthian "entanglement," and he hopes for forgiveness. His executioners arrive to lead him away; he is expecting them. He had hoped that the final scene would be more elegant; but these executioners are two coarse, fat creatures, as shabby and unsavory as all the other officials of the Court. As he marches along the street between these two, the appearance of a policeman offers him a last chance of escape; but he rejects it and delivers a final judgment upon himself. "Am I to leave this world as a man who shies away from all conclusions? Are people to say of me after I am gone that at the beginning of my case I wanted it to finish, and at the end of it wanted it to begin again? I don't want that to be said." With such finality does he now will his own sacrifice that he hustles his executioners along, and does all he can to assist them in their unsavory job.

The final scene is even conceived in an atmosphere of ritual: the ceremonial attitude of the executioners, the questions of precedence that arise between them, the pains taken to find a suitable sacrificial stone. Kafka introduces a very novel element here, possibly to reveal his whole purpose. For the first time a personal and singular term is used to designate the authority pursuing him, instead of a reference to the Court in general. "He could not completely rise to the occasion, he could not relieve the officials of all their tasks; the responsibility for this last failure of his lay with *him* who had not left him the remnant of strength necessary for the deed." It is further suggested that Joseph K., having at last abandoned his entire will and personality to "him," is brought face to face with God, his Judge, and his potential

177

Saviour, as was Abraham at the moment of his great sacrifice. "His glance fell on the top storey of the house adjoining the quarry. With a flicker as of a light going up, the casements of a window there suddenly flew open; a human figure, faint and insubstantial at that distance and that height, leaned abruptly far forward and stretched both arms still farther. Who was it?" Hope and shame are the last feelings of Joseph K., as the knife is plunged into his bosom. The Barthians say that sin, while so awful, is only known when it is forgiven. This is the source of Joseph K.'s final, overwhelming shame. But adds Barth: "In God ... forgiveness and penalty." Joseph K. has reached the only solution possible for man's perplexity, the violent and hard solution, prescribed by the theology of crisis, the complete surrender of one's self to the will and punishment of God. The Absolute has come to Joseph K.; it has come, as usual on its own terms, thwarting all his efforts to uncover its secrets, and careless of all his values, destroying his life, but offering its own peculiar salvation.

In all modern literature, Kafka's performance probably most deserves the term, Dantesque; not for his scope, or varied technical power (actually he is very limited), but for the pitch of his profundity and the strength of his intellectual background. *The Trial* is as firmly grounded in the rigid and elaborate theology of crisis, as was *The Divine Comedy* in the Scholastic theology and philosophy; and Kafka adheres as faithfully to his intellectual standards as does Dante. Most modern writers either do not adhere faithfully to any standards of this sort, or the standards to which they do adhere are relatively shallow. In the former class might be placed novelists such as Proust, Joyce, Thomas Mann, and their followers; in the latter, mostly poets, Yeats and Eliot, representing the real poets, and the vast horde of poetasters. These three novelists are probably all greater than Kafka; they are much larger figures. But they do not invade the realm in which Kafka is supreme, the world of man's doubt and perplexity. Kafka realized that in religious writings were to be found the most careful analyses of man's reflections on his ultimate fate. He proceeded to master the content of religious teaching, and did not employ it as mere decor in his writings. In fact, religion does not appear at all on the surface of his work. His

178

overwhelming seriousness as compared with almost any other modern writer is emphasized most by this fact. Yeats and Eliot, for instance, have distinctly religious elements, and exhibit a great amount of what might seem at first sight to be Barthian "perplexity." But both are chiefly concerned because the Kingdom of God is not on this earth. Yeats' religion is merely an attractive compound of whimsy and theological quackery. Eliot's performance is no more religious than a troop of nuns crossing the stage in an opera; his perplexity is the perplexity of a ballerina Queen of Swans, alarmed at the approach of the Huntsmen.

Poetry, says I. A. Richards, will save us. In one way or another, most modern writers accept this view, or exhibit pretensions implying that they do, or that their work is somehow part of the historical program by which man's salvation is to be accomplished. Kafka, Barth, and Kierkegaard are far removed from this nonsense. Their "pessimism" derives chiefly from their profound conviction that man can in no way save himself.

"blumfeld, an elderly bachelor"

lienhard bergel

Blumfeld, the "elderly bachelor," is only in appearance the hero of this story; its real hero is the routine which, in various forms, dominates the world. Blumfeld himself is only part of an experiment which an unknown power makes with all of us in a world which consists largely of mechanical routine. This power is curious to see how we will react to given conditions. The routine of the world has two aspects: one manifests itself in the so-called "laws of nature," the other in the repetitive regularity of everyday life, without which man could not exist. We would therefore misunderstand the story if we were to see in the deadening routine which rules Blumfeld's life the result of specific historical developments, an outgrowth of modern mechanization. We should not attribute to the poet the intention of criticizing man for permitting such degrading conditions to come about. In any historical situation, under any social system, Blumfeld would have to face the same problem which he meets as the employee of a modern factory. For Kafka the world would always be a factory, even if machines had never been invented, because its distinguishing feature is mechanical routine, even without machines. This routine has not been introduced into the world by the will or the negligence of man; if the world were not an eternal repetition of the same, it would not be the world. This is why life appears to Kafka as a prison. A prisoner differs from a free man in that he has to subject himself to an unchangeable routine and finally becomes part of it. Therefore the story of Blumfeld is not the psychological study of a man who happens to be fond of routine. Neither Blumfeld nor anybody else could have made this routine superfluous by being more ingenious, more flexible, more spontaneous: whichever way he turned, he would run against the prison bars. The problem is therefore not whether to accept routine—one has no choice, if one wants to exist—but *how* to accept it.

Blumfeld not only does not revolt against routine, he recognizes nothing but routine. He is like the mouse in the "Little Fable," who runs into a world which becomes more narrow with every step he takes. Blumfeld adds more bars to his prison; he builds himself a prison within a prison. Thus he takes his daily work so seriously that his hypertrophied sense of duty makes him ridiculous and becomes a constant source of irritation to himself and others. Like the salesman in the story "The Married Couple," he is so completely absorbed in his work that everything else escapes his notice. He thinks himself secure, in his reliance on the routine outside of him, the "laws of nature," and in the good conscience which the meticulously executed routine in his work affords him. Blumfeld is an exception among Kafka's characters in that he has a good conscience and feels secure and satisfied.

But he is not completely happy. He does not sleep well, mysterious knocks disturb his rest, "as if someone demanded entrance." His routine does not satisfy him completely. He likes to edify himself by looking at pictures of grandiose events which are beyond his circle of experience. And from time to time he feels a vague desire to own a dog to keep him company. But he immediately represses this thought, for it would mean not only a change in his routine, but a complete revolution. Routine would not be routine, if it were not absolutely impersonal. He who has made of routine his god must become a rigid egoist. Routine and affection for other beings are incompatible. So he decides for his routine, and against the dog.

182

And now this machine-like existence is upset by a mysterious event. The world which is beyond that of routine proceeds to attack with stronger weapons. To the appearance of the celluloid balls, which are driven by an unknown power, Blumfeld reacts in the only way possible to him. He tries to overcome the non-routine by routine. Routine means rules, mechanical rules, applicable always and everywhere. So he looks for the rules underlying the motions of the balls. But this is the irritating element in his search for the routine of the balls: apparently they are subject to the ordinary "laws of nature," yet the moment Blumfeld believes he has identified this law it fails to apply. One can trace back the routine of these motions a short distance, but then suddenly they are devoid of system and routine. The world of routine leads into a world of non-routine. The isolated movements of these balls are mechanical, yet their total behavior is that of a living, almost human being. Blumfeld is completely baffled by this "unruly" behavior of the balls. For the flash of a moment, it dawns on him that they might come from a world now unknown to him: "Too bad that Blumfeld is no longer a small child, then these two balls would have been a pleasant surprise, whereas now all this makes a rather unpleasant impression. Or perhaps it is not entirely worthless, to live for himself as a lonely bachelor of whom no one takes notice; someone, it does not matter who, has broken through his loneliness and sent him these two funny balls."

But these fleeting glimpses into the world of non-routine pass quickly. He refuses to admit that anything exists which is more than mere routine. He is willing to make the one concession that his experience is "unusual," surely an understatement, considering the behavior of the balls. By calling his experience "unusual," however, he fits it into the world of the "usual." The "unusual" is still related to the "usual," though negatively, and there is still hope left that on closer scrutiny it may become "usual." The balls themselves, for the moment at least, strengthen him in this belief, for they observe certain mechanical rules, and triumphantly he proclaims this as their "weakness." In their non-mechanical behavior, too, they follow certain habits. For instance, they always try to keep behind his back.

183

These "weaknesses" of theirs he decides to exploit by crushing them. With supreme irony, the poet makes Blumfeld conceive a strategy against the balls which he can carry out without even interrupting his normal routine: he will simply go to bed. To encourage himself beforehand, he quotes to himself some of the "rules" of nature which are here applicable, and he is almost "cheerful." Only when the stratagem fails, because the balls do not observe their "routine," does he break out with bitter complaints: this is "unjust," "unfair." If the world is run by routine, it should always keep the routine, without exception.

This invasion by the "non-routine" produces other curious effects upon him. Not only has it shaken his confidence in the omnipotence of "rules," it has also widened those minute cracks in the shell of his routine through which he had peeped earlier into the world of non-routine: his wish to have a dog returns. And when he reaches down from his bed to push a carpet under it in order to soften the noise of the jumping balls, he feels "as if he had a little dog for whom he wants to make a soft bed." It is as if it had been necessary for the world of non-routine, in its first meeting with Blumfeld, to disguise itself in the mechanical forms familiar to him. When he hears the balls for the first time behind the closed door, he is reminded of the sound of a dog pawing.

After the shell has once been cracked, the routine disturbed, the beneficial effects continue. The ugly child of his cleaning woman, whom he formerly avoided, is no longer repulsive to him: "After all, he is a child, in this clumsy head there are children's thoughts; if one were to talk to him gently and ask him something, he would probably answer with a clear voice, innocently and politely." But it is not easy to break through the shell completely. The danger of hypocrisy is inherent in this incipient metanoia. By making the boy a present of the balls he can obey his original impulse of doing something for the child and at the same time get rid of these annoying things. Thus the circle would be completed and the balls have been cheated of the accomplishment of their mission. The invasion into the world of routine would have been repulsed by an apparent yielding to it. Such is the intricacy of the relationship between the two worlds.

184

The story of Blumfeld is a fragment only in the sense that the action is incomplete. It has sufficient unity, however, if we consider not Blumfeld but routine as its hero. While in the first part routine struggles against non-routine, in the second part those who have not yet yielded to routine struggle against its encroachments. Now the other side of the problem of routine is shown: is routine inevitable, is it "just"? We cannot change the routine of the physical world and the restrictions it imposes on us; but is routine necessary in the conduct of our life? Blumfeld had considered it "unjust" that the balls did not behave according to routine; the young office boys consider it unjust to be forced by Blumfeld to follow a routine. In the running battle between Blumfeld and his apprentices, the routine of everyday life, whose strict observance had made of him an unpleasant and ridiculous person, is shown in a new light. We cannot unreservedly side with the office boys against Blumfeld, because the work which must be done would be impossible if Blumfeld did not insist on a routine. The fault is not with the boys, the fault is not with Blumfeld, it is a fault of life itself, which makes routine unavoidable. Even if the boys were more willing to work, that alone would not suffice to excuse them from routine. It is the rule of life that one must do what routine demands, sacrificing what one is eager to do, if it has not been assigned to one, even though it may be useful work of no personal advantage. This is the meaning of the grotesque struggle for the broom between the office boys and the old servant whose duty it is to sweep the office. Kafka is aware, however, that routine, though necessary and justified, blights their lives. Outside the office they are lively and cheerful: "They go arm in arm and seem to tell one another important things which, however, have only a forbidden relation to the work in the office. The closer they come to the office door, the more slowly they walk." After he has entered the office, the boy "seems to be very tired and rubs his eyes; after he has hung his coat on the hook, he uses the opportunity to lean a little against the wall; outside on the street he was lively, but being near his work makes him tired." Routine is the curse of man's life, but it is inescapable. At the end of the story, "The Married Couple," Kafka says: "Ah, there are so many unsuccessful busi-

185

ness trips and one must go on carrying the burden." But it can be made a little lighter if one does not always attend to "business," by admitting the miracle into the life of routine. In this story the traveling salesman says of the wife devoted to her husband: "Whatever one might say: she could work miracles. What we had destroyed, she repaired." Because this way out is at least vaguely indicated in the story about Blumfeld, because, in contrast to many others of his stories, Kafka admits in this the possibility of mutual helpfulness and companionship, it deserves more attention than it has yet received.

For its artistic perfection, too, this story deserves particular notice. It does not belong among the stories which might be called "directly mythical," such as "The Great Wall of China," for instance, or "The Hunter Gracchus," in which mythical or fantastic events carry the meaning directly, but it is among the large group in which the mythical assumes the form of everyday life. Such "indirectly mythical" stories allow a full play of irony not possible in the purely mythical stories, though the open lyricism which often breaks through in the directly mythical stories is absent. Characteristic of the "indirectly mythical" stories is the combination of a most precise rational construction of events with their concrete visualization. The behavior of the balls is given in the minutest detail, each detail fitting either their physical or their human aspect: "their low jumps, which are gauged to each other"; "each step is followed almost without intermission by the bouncing of balls; they keep pace with him." When one of the balls jumps up on the bed before joining his companion under the bed, Blumfeld sourly observes: "The ball probably wanted to look around up there, and was not pleased." Blumfeld's annoyance with the balls translates itself into expressive gestures: "with his legs spread apart, he drives them into the corner"; "involuntarily he kicks back at them before turning around"; "he drags his slippers on the floor, he takes irregular steps" to chase them away.

With the exception of the opening sentences, the story is told in the *"style indirecte libre,"* that is, not from the point of view of the story teller, but of the person acting and experiencing

186

in the story, yet at the same time it is told in the third person. This creates a double perspective: the reader identifies himself with Blumfeld, but at the same time he looks at the events objectively; it is as if he were looking at the world with his own eyes and with Blumfeld's simultaneously. The esthetic effect of this objectivized subjectivity is that the torturing experiences of Blumfeld are doubly excruciating. Blumfeld does not want his housekeeper to see the balls: "And during this whole time Blumfeld must stay in bed; he dares not move unless he wants to drag the balls behind him; he must let the coffee get cool, though he likes to drink it as hot as possible; he cannot do anything but stare at the lowered window curtain behind which day dawns gloomily."

Sometimes this double perspective widens into a triple view: to that of the hero and the reader is added the perspective of the author. The poet assumes here a double function. Not only does he tell the story objectively and invite the reader to take his place, but to this impartial function he adds that of a commentator. It is as if the objectivized *monologue intérieur* were spoken by three voices, by Blumfeld, by Kafka the reporter and by Kafka the interpreter. These are the decisive moments of the story, they contain the key to it. Such a passage is the following: "Too bad that he is no longer a small child, then these balls would be a pleasant surprise to him." In the last sentence of the story, Kafka inserts one word spoken by him and not by Blumfeld or the office boys and thus he reveals the ambivalence of routine: "Always and without any tact they try to insist on their real or *imagined* rights." This restraint, this casual way of revealing the most decisive things, is typical of Kafka. Just as for Kafka the world of everyday shows its real meaning only to him who calmly and carefully observes its most minute and apparently insignificant details, so the world of Kafka's poetic invention reveals itself only to him who is willing to weigh its every word.

187

the homeless stranger

max brod

Kafka's novel, *The Castle*, is a compendium of the world; in it the exhaustive presentation of the behavior of a certain type of human being towards the world is made with the utmost exactitude and finesse, and inasmuch as every human being senses an element of this type in himself—just as he discovers in himself a Faust, a Don Quixote or a Julien Sorel as a component part of his "I"—Kafka's *Castle* becomes, in spite of the individuality of the character depicted, a book of self-recognition for everyone.

Kafka's hero, whom in autobiographical fashion he designates simply as "K.," goes his solitary way through life. Thus it is the loneliness-component in us which causes this novel to assume supernatural dimensions, dimensions that stand forth with shocking clarity. Withal it remains a very definite nuance of loneliness, one we continue to know deep inside ourselves, one that rises to the surface in quiet hours. For, after all, the hero is very much a man of good will, who neither seeks loneliness nor is proud of it. On the contrary—it is wished upon him; for as far as his wishes are concerned he would like nothing bet-

189

ter than to be an active member of society, to fall into line and to cooperate in a conventional manner; he seeks a useful profession, wants to marry and to found a family.

But all that fails. Ever more definitely does one realize that the cold layer of isolation enveloping K. is by no means accidental, that it is likewise not accidental that the villagers among whom K. has insisted on abiding shun him and that in his search for human contact he meets the one peasant family that all the rest have ostracized.

However, the riddle of K.'s inability to feel at home anywhere remains unsolved. He is a stranger, and happens to come to a village where strangers are looked upon with suspicion. No more is said; yet one soon feels that this mood of almost universal "strangeness" is made concrete in one very specific case. "No one can be anyone's comrade." One can, in fact, go even a step further and add: This is the particular feeling of the Jew who would like to set root in strange surroundings, who strives with all the power of his soul to come closer to the strangers by becoming completely like them, and who never succeeds in achieving the fusion.

The word "Jew" does not appear in the book. Nor does it appear in any other novel or short story of Kafka's. (Against that, it does appear in his diaries, whence many threads lead over to his fiction.) Yet you detect almost tangibly that in *The Castle* Kafka has set forth the great and tragic presentation of assimilation and of its futility, that from his Jewish soul he has said more in this simple tale about the universal situation of Jewry than can be gleaned from a hundred scientific treatises.

Nevertheless, while the specific Jewish interpretation goes hand in hand with the universal human one, the one never eclipses the other or disturbs it in the slightest degree. The universal (religious) interpretation I have attempted to set forth in my epilogue to *The Castle*.

a note on "the castle"

denis saurat

This Prague Jew is the greatest German writer since Nietzsche, the only writer of our time who can stand beside Proust. Kafka has fully expressed the modern mentality in its German mood.

First, he is a great German. *The Castle*, which I place far above the rest of his work, is an allegory: but not one word in the tale gives a clue to the meaning. Not a hint of philosophy comes through: merely a series of incomprehensible events, related in a style of absolute simplicity and convincingness. The mind of the reader is at once aroused by the absurdity of the story, and builds up a dream which develops parallel to the unfolding of the tale.

This is a perfect triumph of German art. For a German who is perfectly understood is a German deflated: his ultimate meaning is commonplace, trivial, or puerile. Thus Goethe, or Wagner: when you get at the final meaning of *Faust*, or of *Parsifal*, it is nothing but a platitude: you must reclaim land and feed the people; you must not waste your time with girls if you want to succeed in life. Sickening. But then you have missed the

191

real meaning by looking for the *final* meaning. For a German, the real meaning is somewhere in the process of development of the work of art, not in the result obtained. Whereas with a Frenchman, like Proust or Racine, you get the maximum meaning when you understand him fully; with a German you reach the maximum somewhere on the way, and are let down at the end: the urge in *Faust* carries you on; the rhythm in *Parsifal* astounds you. Therefore a true artist, if he be a German, draws a veil over his meaning and casts his spell on you by his manner; your journey leads nowhere, but you have the great pleasure of the journey.

Kafka has done this marvelously; and his destiny or his temperament, served him well: his masterpiece is left unfinished, so that we are left on the brink of an abyss, and full of wonderment. It would have been better for *Faust,* or *Parsifal* or *Zarathustra* to have been left unfinished.

Thus Kafka is a great German, Jew though he be. Then he is a great modern. More ruthlessly than even Proust himself, he has torn off the soul everything which is not pure immediate sensation. He has torn off the dirty romantic gown and also "divorced old barren Reason from his bed."

Classicism and romanticism are equally anathema to the modern. Only what we do feel, at the moment when we feel it, counts; and we are not to base on that either the romantic or the classic dreams. But through the chaos of incoherent and maddening sensations, runs the need of a God incessantly searched for, but who recedes farther and farther the more efforts we make to get to him.

K. has received a letter asking him to call for instructions at the Castle; but then no one knows who sent that letter. He tries to get to the Castle and clear up the matter. In vain. He is soon made to realize that communications between his inn and the castle are practically impossible. Some of the officials come to the village, but as a rule only their servants can even be seen. The women move about in a dream: they aspire to be the officials' mistresses, and are given honor by their own men only inasmuch as they are the officials' mistresses. One or two messages come to K. But they are mistakes, and perhaps even lies. K.

192

takes as a mistress one of the officials' girls; but the affair goes wrong and K. then gets friendly with another girl who has committed the monstrous crime of refusing one of the officials. Mistake follows mistake; and in the end we see just a bare possibility of K. having an interview with a secretary who has nothing to do with K.'s business at all.

Thus the soul is at first full of assurance that God has called. But the first rush ends in nothing. Religious orthodoxy is a sort of bureaucracy which allows no soul to get through to God. Nature seems to have held communion with God, but it is thereafter found that Nature is only a prostitute for the pleasure of menials. Intellect is no good: it is merely an incompetent administration. Feeling is no good: it is mere promiscuity, the filthy trade of barmaids off duty. But if K. cannot get to the count, yet he may work for him; if he cannot work for him, he may yet get permission to live and die in that strange village, where the inhabitants hold some sort of degrading but intimate relationship with their Lord.

It seemed as though Proust had expressed the very minimum of hope, below which hope exists no more. But Kafka descends lower, much lower still, and yet there is still a glimmer of hope where he is, darkness is not yet absolute.

the castle of despair

daniel-rops

Franz Kafka is one of the most astounding examples
(together with Proust, and, in another way, Joyce) of an artist
who creates his work out of that which essentially destroys both
the artist and the work. It is not an exaggeration to say that in
our age a great many works of art are no more than the records of
these acts of destruction. Kafka was rooted deeply enough in the
human drama, and his art in its formidable lucidity was great
enough to fashion a portrait, a likeness, of this being so irre-
trievably shattered. A Kafka goes infinitely further in this direction than a Proust whose meaning remains almost exclusively
psychological, or a Joyce who tried to explain everything in terms
of myths and verbal magic. By the very anguish that engulfed
him, an anguish metaphysical in the true sense of the word,
Kafka was one of the truest and most dramatic witnesses of modern man and his struggle with nothingness.

   The Castle is without question Kafka's most important
book. Important, first, because of its length, which is so unusual
in its author; his shorter works might lead one to think that one
of the main elements of their perfection lay in their brevity; it is

195

now clear that this highly personal art can adapt itself to the difficulties of plot development, and far from wearying the attention of the reader constantly spurs it on. This book is unfinished, but, in a sense, neither more nor less so than all of Kafka's works, which we know he regarded as provisional and incomplete. It is unimportant that the adventure of the Land Surveyor intent on making contact with the Castle should have a few extra scenes. It is not by the succession of episodes that Kafka commands and holds our attention; we might even say that from the moment we enter his world everything (including ourselves) finds itself set in a strange fixity, wherein doubtless lies the profound explanation of the amazing metaphysical tension that prevails there.

But the importance of *The Castle* depends less on these purely exterior conditions than on the internal elements we find there which are fully significant to Kafkan art and thought. Of all Kafka's books this is the one which best realizes what seems to have been his most unerring aim: to achieve the mysterious, the secret, the esoteric without yielding to the fantastic. From this standpoint the book is purer (in the sense that we speak of pure poetry or of matter being chemically pure) than the majority of his works.

In "The Metamorphosis" there was an arbitrary hypothesis: that a man could be changed into a monstrous cockroach; in *The Castle* there is nothing like that; the plot is completely banal. The myth springs from nothing. It has no need of startling phenomena. It is natural and at the same time charged with terrible significance. It could be said that the deepest mystery is obtained by pushing realism to extremes. All the details are simple and commonplace; yet the writer subjects them to a transmutation which makes them seem to compete with each other in enveloping us with some weighty secret. Nowhere in his work has Kafka been so close to that ideal he set for his art: "dazzled blindness before the truth."

In *The Castle* we recognize the two dominant themes of Kafkan thought, both used with extraordinary persuasive force. The actual plot behind these two hundred and fifty pages of writing can be reduced to very little: It is concerned merely with a man's efforts to make contact with an inaccessible castle and its inhabitants. This castle, which may have been suggested to the author's imagination by the Rhadschin at Prague, is defined in a contradictory way. Depending on the point of view, it is "only a wretched-looking town, a huddle of village houses"; or else "a place of renown and certainties; its bell when it rings proclaims the accomplishment of those things the heart dimly longs for." It is evidently, then, the symbol of those inaccessible realities toward which man gropes without ever being able to reach. For in the character of K. the author is concerned with man in general; the very name used to describe him is significant—the Land Surveyor—the man who measures everything.

Through this outline, then, appear the two fundamental themes found throughout Kafka's work. One is concerned with a suprahuman justice, strictly incomprehensible, even absurd, that condemns a human being to think of himself as always—to use the excellent expression of Groethuysen—"indicted though free." Carried to less extreme than in *The Trial*, this theme is nonetheless sustained from the beginning to the end of *The Castle* with a whole paraphernalia of trials, judgments to give and verdicts to accept. It is perhaps even given a new direction here: one episode (where Sordini would like to make a person do evil in order to attain the good) seems to indicate that Kafka, following Kierkegaard, admitted the complete incompatibility of this suprahuman justice with human morality. The surveyor may work in vain, he will not *deserve* to be introduced to the castle. This entrance is a gift, an act of grace; let only those to whom the powers that be grant their favors for nothing aspire to it.

And it is the certainty of the futility of all effort that makes Kafka's view of man's position so depressing. This is the second essential theme in his work: that of an entirely unacceptable state which is nonetheless completely accepted. The incomprehensible events that weave the hours of this life, mysteriously shorten the days, reverse the times of rest and work, continually upset logic, are indeed only symptoms of this intolerable situation in which everyone endures life nevertheless. Many writers today take for their theme the impossibility of modern man's resolving the antagonism between conscience and external forces. Malraux's *Man's Fate* is one such testimony. But literary work usually springs from the actual impact between man and the obstacle he beats himself against. Kafka, in my estimation, is the only one who has placed his work not at the point of conflict itself, but beyond, right in the forbidden zone. He does not seek to resolve the contradiction, he accepts it. His work actually thrives on it. He writes, in spite of appearances, more the novel of inaccessible forces that ignore man than the novel of man seeking to conquer them.

Such an art, which tries with such superhuman force to grasp the intangible, meets with a basic difficulty, the difficulty of the mystics, the difficulty that Rimbaud faced: how to make comprehensible to men of flesh and blood that which by its very nature goes beyond life. For Kafka's symbols are not formulated, nor are they even the most important thing. Actually he becomes more and more wary of symbols. But the more we uncover his thought the more we desire to understand the meaning of the symbolism, surmising that it corresponds to something irreplaceable in our consciousness. But at the same time the symbol recedes and we are unable to grasp it completely. The law, finding the law, yet never being able completely to understand the law. Kafka's world is a universe of absurdity through which the human intelligence is groping, and in the end can lead only to despair. Art which should elucidate this despair is only the most futile of interpreters since it can end in nothing but uncertainties. The endless search for certainties in life as in death only led Franz Kafka to the brink of nothingness. It is as a perfectly natural conclusion to this "spiritual quest" (as Rimbaud would have said) that his order to destroy all his works must be understood. Such an art may seem to *us* to borrow grandeur from the force that is really destroying it; to the artist it is only a failure by comparison with what he wanted to accomplish.

Nevertheless we must not consider the aesthetic side alone if we are to understand what it is in this literature of Kafka that causes us (we must admit) such a surprising uneasiness. It is not only because he takes us into a fourth dimension that he fascinates us. We have the feeling that he touches us in a part of our being where we like to keep our secret connivances. This

Prague Jew, nourished on the Talmud, haunted by the search for and despair of the law, later deeply influenced by the philosophy of the famous Dane, Sören Kierkegaard, gives us, should we say, one of the most moving and most apt symbols of modern man at the mercy of God and at the same time ignorant of Him. Let us see how.

His entire work is dominated by the theme of judgment, sentence and acquittal. In Franz Kafka's universe every man has to undergo judgment and is liable to punishment because of the simple fact that he lives and must die. But can we at least make this judgment favorable to us? Is acquittal possible? Kafka's despair replies in *The Trial*:

"The Judges of the lowest grade haven't the power to grant a final acquittal, that power is reserved for the highest Court of all, which is quite inaccessible to you, to me, and to all of us. What the prospects are up there we do not know and, I may say in passing, do not even want to know. The great privilege, then, of absolving from guilt our Judges do not possess, but they do have the right to take the burden of the charge off your shoulders. That is to say, when you are acquitted in this fashion the charge is lifted from your shoulders for the time being, but it continues to hover above you and can, as soon as an order comes from on high, be laid upon you again . . . In definitive acquittal the documents relating to the case are completely annulled, they simply vanish from sight, not only the charge but also the records of the case and even the acquittal are destroyed, everything is destroyed. That's not the case with ostensible acquittal. The documents remain as they were, except that the affidavit is added to them and a record of the acquittal and the grounds for granting it. The whole dossier continues to circulate . . . A detached observer might sometimes fancy that the whole case had been forgotten, the documents lost, and the acquittal made absolute. No one really acquainted with the Court could think such a thing. No document is ever lost, the Court never forgets anything."

199

Such then is man's fate which none can escape. Each one of us is imprisoned in himself, subject to a responsibility which he may pretend to forget, but which others, Another, will not forget for him. And so over the whole of Kafka's universe hangs an atmosphere of horror, related to the one we are familiar with in a Rimbaud, a Strindberg, a Novalis, a Hölderlin, and also in painters like Civetta, Breughel the Elder, Van der Goes, Hïeronymus Bosch, and in some pictures of Dürer.° Actually others have had a clear vision of this unremitting captivity of mankind. Where Kafka is more original is in the reply he gives to this dramatic questioning.

Some people have tried to reply to this question by a denial: deny man's fate, go beyond it. This is what the surrealists have done, following Rimbaud and Lautréamont (but by infinitely more rudimentary methods). To escape mankind or reality is a way of evading oneself. Since the pressure of a soulless world has weighed more heavily on modern man a large number of these attempts at evasion have appeared in our literature, some of them rather over-simplified. There is nothing of that in Kafka. This man dominated by a passion for the absolute is really a spiritual son of Kierkegaard who accepts man's fate even to the limit of his worst agony, and from his suffering draws the basic element of his greatness.

At the same time nothing could be more mistaken, as some interpreters have suggested, than to regard Franz Kafka as a sort of lucid madman who would extract from his madness a magnificent orchestration, a kind of a crystalline symbolism. If this were so then the only rational people would be those who go through life without bothering to look for a meaning, and who, without knowing it, are imprisoned in the revolting hard skin of their routines and complicities like the grotesque cockroach of "The Metamorphosis." No, Kafka was not mad; but his enquiries took place in a region where men are usually not willing to enter, doubtless out of fear they might find themselves there for good.

To understand the judgment we need to know the law. But can one know the law? Kafka answers this question in

° Picabia, among our contemporaries, is in this line.

each of his books, we might even say in the least of his fragments. He replies in the negative. Whether he speaks to us of the Castle, the symbol of inaccessible realities which man in spite of all his efforts can never reach; whether he analyses the emptiness of all knowledge in "Investigations of a Dog," the reply will always be the same. Man does not know the law, he is incapable of understanding the word. He will beat himself against his own reflection and against the mirror that shows it to him. He is a prisoner; if he sees clearly, like the hero in "The Metamorphosis," he suffers more on that account, but conscious of it or not, he is always imprisoned. On the other hand if he wishes to try to escape from himself, this can only be done by the premeditated destruction of all that makes his existence real—like the terrifying protagonist of "The Burrow," a horrible creature, a kind of mole, who decides to leave the earth of mankind and bury himself in a deep burrow, living there no longer like a being really alive but like a grub, in a series of petty routines, minor details, and a whole disgusting collection of bestial habits.

Kafka's conclusion is that man is a prisoner who cannot escape his fate. He is so acutely conscious of it that his life is to a certain extent inhibited by it. This fatalism is expressed very well in "The Next Village." It is precisely this fatalism that he accepts. Since there is no way out, and since the mind cannot even penetrate the meaning of this ridiculous balance of forces that holds us prisoner, there is nothing to do but to yield, to bow the head and be resigned to it.

"Don't be so obstinate; we must admit that there is no defence against this justice. So admit it at the first occasion, it is only later that you will be able to try to escape from yourself, only afterwards; and even then you will only succeed if someone comes to your help."

Be reconciled then; but to whom?

It is impossible not to respond to the mysterious sort of appeal which re-echoes in the numerous phrases analogous to those we have just read. Beyond doubt there is in Franz Kafka a sense of waiting—the waiting for a mediator, for an infinite, superhuman power who can give men the answers to the dread questions of life. It could be described as an almost sacramental waiting. The man of Kafka's world is "indicted though free." It is an intolerable condition. He aspires to a judgment, to a formulated law that would allow him to know exactly where he stands. Kafka's characters are in a way *beyond good and evil* because for them everything is reduced to an attempt at clairvoyance that does not allow them to put the problem in the way it should be put. Judgment, that is, the affirmation of good and evil, is a respite, the most sensitive of respites. Beyond a certain boundary there is evil, there is the abyss, the night without end and the existence without peace.

In this world, entirely dominated by the highest themes proposed to man, what is there lacking that keeps one from feeling completely held by it? Upon reflection, it seems to me to lack a sense of responsibility. It is a world of absurdity, and we can only think of it as such. But if we can accept without understanding the *how*, we have an instinctive need to know the *why*. This man always threatened by punishment, and whose efforts are always futile, is like a vapid reflection of the Christians' sinner. But the religious teaching of good and evil, of sin and forgiveness gives a deeper meaning to life. Kierkegaard, Pascal, starting from similar observations, sink roots much deeper into the mystery of existence. We might say that Kafka's world bears witness to that "wretchedness of man without God" or rather "without the possibility of grace." But even so man is still quite laden with promises —with even more promises than Kafka believed possible. And Max Brod was right when he wrote of his friend in the novel in which he affectionately recalls him: "His writings bring to men who wander through the night the presentiment of higher and irreplaceable good toward which they are groping. . . ."

Translated by Muriel Kittel.

the three novels

r. o. c. winkler

The Kierkegaardian system of belief that was responsible for much of the form and content of Kafka's novels is sufficiently remote from contemporary English habits of thought for an account of it to give an appearance of throwing light on the novelist's apparent obscurities. And it does seem as though the Danish philosopher's conception of a religious way of life transcending human codes and sanctions was peculiarly profitable in stimulating Kafka's approach to his own material. For whether or not we care to admit from a doctrinal point of view the possibilities of a teleological suspension of the ethical, there can be no doubt that something of this kind is assumed whenever one asserts the universality of art. The explicit moral concern of any given artist (and most have something of the sort) may be his source of strength, but what will make his work of lasting significance will be his insight into the sensible and mental reactions of the human being to everyday experience and into the problems that arise therefrom. Whether or not, therefore, Kafka was proselytizing on Kierkegaard's behalf isn't relevant to the literary-critical evaluation. Our concern is with his success in recreating

203

from a sympathetic and consistent standpoint the complexity of the individual problem in its wider and profounder implications. I think it can be shown that he does this with an insight as penetrating as that of any other novelist of our time.

The Castle was Kafka's last and greatest achievement in the novel form, and any estimate of his significance as a novelist is bound to start from a consideration of this apotheosis of his method. Here the trends of interest that appear rather diversely in the earlier novels are fused to give an account of the whole range of human experience in what seemed to Kafka its most significant implications. The ultimate concern is religious. In Kafka's view there is a way of life for any individual that is the right one, and which is divinely sanctioned. So much is perhaps admitted by most of our moral novelists; but to Kafka this fact itself constitutes a problem of tremendous difficulty, because he believes the dichotomy between the divine and the human, the religious and the ethical, to be absolute. Thus, though it is imperative for us to attempt to follow the true way, it is impossible for us to succeed in doing so. This is the fundamental dilemma that Kafka believes to lie at the basis of all human effort. He gives some insight into its nature in "Investigations of a Dog," where the dog-world corresponds roughly to human society and we as humans bear something of the same relationship to the hero as the Castle officials bear to K. in *The Castle*. The solution of the Dog's problem is perfectly plain to us, yet we can see that the Dog is constitutionally incapable of ever realizing the solution.

This fundamental problem, however, doesn't present itself to the human mind in naked simplicity. It isn't the Puritan problem of justifying one's behavior in the eyes of God alone. The dilemma is conceived of as becoming known to us only at the ethical level; that is, it emerges as a general problem of the individual's relation to society, and any attempt at a solution must involve an attempt to come to terms with, and find a place in, the social organism. We are told, and it is probably true, that Kafka felt this problem with peculiar acuteness in virtue of his racial isolation as a Jew and his general isolation as a consumptive; but it is important to realize that this only made more keenly felt a difficulty that is implicit in any attempt at social organization, and one that has manifested itself particularly in recent years as a result of the centrifugal tendencies of modern civilization. In *"He," Notes from the Year 1920*, Kafka writes: "He was once part of a monumental group. Round some elevated figure or other in the centre were ranged in carefully thought-out order symbolical images of the military caste, the arts, the sciences, the handicrafts. He was one of those many figures. Now the group is long since dispersed, or at least he has left it and makes his way through life alone. He no longer has even his old vocation, indeed he has forgotten what he once represented. Probably it is this very forgetting that gives rise to a certain melancholy, uncertainty, unrest, a certain longing for vanished ages, darkening the present. And yet this longing is an essential element in human effort, perhaps indeed human effort itself."

One has only to run one's mind over the more significant literature of Kafka's generation, from *St. Mawr* and *The Waste Land* to *Ulysses* and *Manhattan Transfer* to realize how prominent a part this view of modern European civilization has played in determining the artist's attitude to his material. Preoccupation with this problem—the problem presented by the corruption, not of the individual as such, but of the inter-human relationships that give him significance as a member of civilized society—recurs throughout Kafka's work, and is realized most effectively in his short story, "The Hunger-Artist." Its most positive aspects are persistent throughout *The Castle*, where the hero's whole efforts are directed immediately toward an attempt to establish himself in a home and a job, and to become a member of the village community—to come to terms, in fact, with society.

Kafka's particularization of the teleological problem doesn't stop at the social level, however. Just as the attempt to follow the religious way of life is seen as a social problem, so the social problem is in its turn seen as one that appears in terms of individual human relationships. The complexity of relationship that exists between the individual and the undiscoverable way of life emerges as the complexity of the relationships between the hero and the other characters in Kafka's novels. In this his method isn't essentially different from that of most other novelists; the

205

difference lies in that, in his treatment of interhuman relationships, Kafka's concern is between their more general implications, their significance for the social, and ultimately for the religious, problem, and the framework and properties of the novels are constructed with this consideration in mind. But just for this reason he is scrupulously careful in presenting even the minutest detail relating to any given situation, so that the complexity never becomes confusion, and the nature and extent of the subtlety and delicacy of the network of relationships are always exactly determined at any given point. His language maintains an almost scientific lucidity, and there is almost a complete absence of explicit figures of speech in his prose. His eye is always on the object, noting carefully details like a change of tone in a person's voice, whether a person is sitting or standing, and even what he is wearing—all such points are noted with a view toward objectifying the exact relationship between two people. Explicit comment is rarely offered by the author; the implications of every detail are allowed to speak for themselves in creating the atmospheric tension that arises as soon as two people enter into one another's sphere of consciousness, and the detailed precision with which the shifts and changes in that tension are traced invests them with a constant sense of apocalyptic significance; so that sudden shifts into the physical are quite in keeping with the whole effect:

> For a moment K. thought that all of them, Schwarzer, the peasants, the landlord and the landlady, were going to fall on him in a body, and to escape at least the first shock of this assault he crawled right underneath the blanket. (*The Castle.*)

The effect of this passage is to crystallize the whole emotional atmosphere when it is discovered that K. has no right in the village and has lied about it into the bargain, and the explicit physical action of crawling underneath the blanket (obviously useless as a protective measure), serves to epitomize K.'s emotional reaction to this atmosphere.

The basis of Kafka's method thus lies in the creation of a complex and continually changing dramatic situation subsisting mainly in the relation between the hero and the other characters. Where the prose is not concerned with defining some element in an interhuman relationship, either external or introspective, but with describing the hero's situation purely objectively, it frequently becomes itself dramatic in movement.

> "So ging er wieder vorwärts, aber es war ein langer Weg. Die Strasse nämlich, diese Hauptstrasse des Dorfes, führte nicht zum Schlossberg, sie führte nur nahe heran, dann aber, wie absichtlich, bog sie ab, und wenn sie sich auch vom Schloss nich entfernte, so kamm sie ihm doch auch nicht näher." (*Das Schloss.*)

The effect of the prose here is to produce the sense of physical effort appropriate to the situation. The short phrases and the jerky movement of the sentence suggests the feeling of frustrated effort that K. experienced, striving to get nearer the Castle, but repeatedly being prevented. The end of the sentence gives us a closer view of the process; the movement forward "sie führte nur nähe heran," the pause "dann aber," the moment of suspense, hanging on the tortuous syllables of "wie absichtlich," then the sudden recoil, like a spring snapping back into place—"bog sie ab," then the ensuing sense of disappointment and disillusion, embodied in the flat phrasing, "so kamm sie ihm doch auch nicht näher." One is reminded of the similar passage in Donne's third "Satyre" in more ways than one.

It is necessary to insist on this fusion of the mental and the physical in Kafka's works for two reasons. In the first place, it is the basis of his allegorical method. The whole of his hero's experience, whether spiritual, mental, emotional or physical, is regarded as absolutely continuous, and the distinctions that for the sake of exposition I have drawn between the religious, the social and the individual levels simply do not exist in the actual writing. The objectification of emotional experience into physical that I have noted emerges in the large as a concrete visualization of the individual's sense of the wider issues of existence in terms of the institutions and officials that characterize his novels and stories. Secondly, it is this preoccupation with the concrete and

207

the physical that forces itself first on the reader's attention, and the remoter implications of the hopeless struggle are realized only over a wide area; the stress, that is, is on the struggle and not on the hopelessness, and the preoccupation with this struggle in the most immediate sense engages the reader's emotional energies, directs and disciplines them, and offers him a positive interest amid what would in abstraction be described as a philosophy of pessimism.

Those standards by which *The Castle* is appraised must also be referred to in finding the two earlier novels of less importance. In *The Trial,* which in point of time came between *Amerika* and *The Castle,* the religious considerations which are the implicit ultimate in the later novel predominate, and it is the dichotomy between the actual true way and our conception of the true way that is insisted on, with the result that the unity and the continuity of method isn't here present. In *Amerika,* this preoccupation with teleological considerations doesn't intrude at the expense of more immediate interests, not because, as in *The Castle,* it has been completely assimilated to those interests, but simply because religious considerations haven't yet become so pressing to the author. Although the novel has the same purposive air of endless pilgrimage about it, the purposiveness is not insisted upon, and the light-hearted symbolization of spiritual salvation in the incomplete last chapter is entirely in keeping with the implicit general assumption that "it will all come right in the end"—an assumption that allows the whole question to be a less constant concern. The disruptive effect of *The Trial* is thus avoided, as the general organization at the more immediate levels —what I have for convenience called the social and personal levels—is complete. With this source of emotional pressure much diminished, the whole texture of the novel is much looser and the effects less concentrated, though the method is the same.

The hero, Karl, is expelled from his habitual environment for a venial sexual offense, and makes his acquaintance with a new order of things, first on the liner in which he leaves Europe, and then in America itself. On the liner we find that same highly organized, incomprehensible hierarchy of officials that appears in the later novels, and it serves much the same function of objectifying the individual's sense of human society, both locally and generally, as a complex organization the nature of whose bonds he can scarcely comprehend. Kafka gives his account in terms of an encounter between Karl and the captain and officers of the ship, and he uses to the full his powers of expressing the interaction of human personality in order to achieve his effect. American civilization later plays a similar function in the hero's life, and Kafka makes clear that full participation in community life is something to which there is no golden road. As in *The Castle,* his attempts to achieve this meet with the more *real* success the less ambitious they become. Hobnobbing with social organization at its most sophisticated proves a complete failure; as soon as its assistance is required in quite a trivial matter in the process of living, it lets him down completely. Then Karl becomes one of the timeserving bell-hops of the social organism with which we are all familiar (Kafka, of course, makes him a real bell-hop in a big hotel), and seems to have achieved some real success in establishing himself in a satisfactory way of life; but when the crucial moment comes, his second position proves of little more value than the first. So he sinks lower and lower in society, coming closer and closer to grips with the realities of the problem that arises from being a member of a complex civilization, until finally ("finally" in a purely relative sense; since the novel is not only incomplete but endless, there can be no finality) he is submitted to all sorts of indignities at the hands of the mistress of a ruffianly tramp, and at last approaches some degree of the awareness of his problem which is the asymptote to success of solution. The technique is less accomplished than that of *The Castle* because of the sense of unrealized possibilities that indicates the author's incomplete grasp of his material; yet the achievement is comparable, and in a final estimate, it would probably have to be ranked as Kafka's second greatest work.

"the burrow"

lienhard bergel

The central theme of this story is the relationship between mind and reality, between the effort of man to construct a
rational world, a "burrow," which is entirely his own creation,
and the outside world which is dominated by irrationality. Before
this world full of whims and surprises, which is inaccessible to
calculation, man feels helpless; as a protection against it he begins
to build his burrow, in which he wants to be the undisputed
master, free from any foreign interference. Thus the burrow becomes a pure construction of the mind, a substitute for reality. It
is man's desire for metaphysical security which drives him to
build his burrow. He knows it would be futile to search for any
transcendental entity which would give this security, or to expect
any mystical illumination; he can only rely on his own mind. The
burrow is built with his own brow: "With my brow I ran against
the earth, day and night, a thousand times; I was happy when I
had beaten it bloody, for this was proof that the wall had begun
to become firm." The burrow is the symbol of a solipsistic world
which is superior to reality, because it is rational, which is perfect
and completely identical with its creator: ". . . my fortress which

211

cannot belong to anyone else and which is so much mine, that here I could receive the fatal wound from my enemy with calm, for here my blood will be absorbed in my own soil and will not be lost."

The building of a really secure burrow depends on two parts of the construction: the entrance, its point of contact with the outside world, and the central chamber, the "inner fortress," the last place of refuge in an emergency, the strategically placed nucleus which controls the system of tunnels. The world which the mind builds for itself and out of itself must have the functional perfection of a crystal or an atom; otherwise it would not withstand the pressure from without. Devising the "perfect" burrow with a perfectly located and perfectly constructed "inner fortress" becomes an obsession. In the search for such a burrow the tragic aspects of the competition between the human ratio and reality soon become apparent, for to be perfect, the burrow should be completely autarchic, and this is impossible. In spite of all efforts at autarchy, existence in the burrow depends on the outside world, which is the source of food and air. A perfectly safe inner fortress would be possible only under one condition: if it were surrounded by empty space. But this complete separation from reality can never be obtained; there always remains "a small fundament which unfortunately cannot be detached from the earth." Because this last separation can never be achieved, the burrow will always remain insecure.

The awareness of this imperfection is a constant source of uneasiness which sometimes grows into a panic. Nevertheless, life in the burrow is not always unhappy. Here one enjoys at least a temporary feeling of security and power. The mind revels in the contemplation of its own creations. This absorption in itself sometimes reaches the intensity of an orgy; it is a kind of metaphysical intoxication, which is described with all symptoms of voluptuousness. "For a while it is a certain consolation to have all chambers and tunnels free, to see how in the inner fortress the supplies of meat grow, which send far to the outermost tunnels the mixture of their many odors, each of which delights me, and which I can distinguish exactly, even from a distance. Then, once in a while, come especially peaceful times, in which I move my

212

sleeping places slowly, gradually from the outer circles to the center; then I plunge deeper and deeper into the odors, until I cannot resist any longer; one night I hurl myself on the inner fortress, devour the supplies ravenously and fill myself with the best I have until I am in a complete stupor. . . . I could almost suffocate in my own supplies, sometimes I can protect myself from their pressure only by greedily devouring them."

The temptation of such auto-intoxication is always present, even when the burrow is threatened with destruction by another animal: "I quickly taste the meat and nibble at it, I think alternately of the strange animal . . . and then again that, as long as I still have this opportunity, I should feast and revel in my supplies."

Though the master of the burrow constantly strives to make himself independent of the outside world, it still exerts a fascination over him. From time to time he leaves the peace of his subterranean hiding place and exchanges the security of his "domestic life" for the unpredictable "possibilities" of reality. He admits that "once in a while an excursion is necessary," and he approaches the exit "with a feeling of solemnity." But the decision to leave the burrow is not easy: "why should one engage in such a gamble with high stakes? Are there any rational reasons for it? No, there are no rational reasons for such a step." The contact with irrational reality is possible only at the momentary sacrifice of the speculating and anticipating ratio. The place of the ratio has to be taken by will. With a wild thrust forward he finally rushes out of the protection of the burrow. But once he is outside, reality comes into its own rights. Now "he feels in his body new energies for which there was, so to speak, no room in the burrow." Reality momentarily loses its terror; there arises the possibility of an existence outside the burrow. He even dimly realizes that this form of life is the higher one: "Here success is more rare than in the burrow, but the results are in every respect to be considered more valuable." Thus the conflict between introversion and extroversion appears solved, but only temporarily. The attractiveness of the uncontrolled life outside soon begins to fade, the new freedom appears "senseless." "I am tired of this life in the open spaces, it seems to me that here I cannot learn anything more,

213

not now and not later." If he returns into the burrow, it is not because he is still afraid of reality, as he was at the time when he began to build his refuge. He has proved to himself that he can live outside: "I am not hunting, like a tramp, out of irresponsibility or despair, but with purpose and calm." It is the sense of a higher duty which calls him back to his burrow. It appears to him a more important task to comprehend existence than simply to live it; man is called upon to master the metaphysical problem with his own mind. The burrow has become more than a place of refuge, and the cares he experiences in it go beyond the merely "technical" problem of making it safe. "Do the cares ever cease in it? These are other cares, more proud, more significant, cares which have often been repressed, but they are probably just as consuming as the cares brought about by the life outside. If I had built the burrow only for my protection, my exertions would not have been in vain, but the proportion between the immense work done and the actual security obtained . . . would not be favorable."—"I have returned for your sake, tunnels and chambers of my burrow, and particularly for the sake of the problems you pose, inner fortress; delaying my return to you for a long time was a mistake." Introversion is in itself justified and necessary.

These brief contacts with reality, though they did not lead to a more stable and permanent relationship with it, were not wholly vain. The experiences in the upper world have sharpened his eye; in comparison to them the creations of his own mind now appear dreamlike and shadowy. "I have now received the distinction, so to speak, of seeing the ghosts of the night not only in the helplessness and blind confidence of sleep, but I can now meet them simultaneously in reality with calm judgment, fully awake. . . . In this respect . . . these excursions are an absolute necessity."

Thus the relationship with reality remains ambivalent; no definite choice has been made between introversion and extroversion nor have the two been reconciled. Reality has not been conquered by being lived nor has it been fully replaced by a completely solipsistic construction; man has not become the demiurge of his own world. The inadequacy of this solution soon takes revenge. The world of reality whose threats, until now, it

214

was possible to hold in check, proceeds to a new and powerful attack. The whole burrow is endangered by an animal which tunnels its way closer and closer to the center. And again man, relying only on his rational power, proves to be helpless before reality. Formerly the abstract operations of his mind had been concerned with plans for a perfect burrow and he had failed; now he is straining himself to calculate theoretically the movements of the enemy, and again he fails. The doubts about the sufficiency of the burrow, which were never absent but had always been repressed, now become certainty: the burrow will be destroyed, reality will assert its superiority. Ironically enough the only place which affords comparative safety is the weakest spot in the system, the entrance, the point nearest the world outside. The escape into reality under the threat of reality, the yielding to the foe as a way of conquering him, had from the beginning appeared as a possible rescue: there was the plan, never executed, of building a tunnel through which one could reach the outside directly, instead of using the complicated system of tunnels. The helplessness before the enemy now turns into self-accusations; the builder of the burrow pronounces judgment on himself. He is ready to cope with the enemy "independent of all theories," he is tired of all "discoveries" made through systematic calculations: "I have reached the point where I no longer want any logical certainty." The burrow is no longer a task or an ideal. The peace in it becomes oppressing, "mute and empty." He questions even his motives for building it; he no longer prides himself on being called upon to answer the "problems" posed by it. He is forced to recognize that his own comfort, the wish to avoid the risks and responsibilities, the "gamble" of the upper world, led him into building it: "arrangements for a peaceful life were always given preference." His proud metaphysical constructions reveal themselves as irresponsible and playful dreams, which distracted him from his duty to prepare for the coming attack of reality which has now overtaken him. The protection of the burrow has been deceptive; rather than making him more secure, it has weakened his ability to resist. "Particularly because I am the owner of this sensitive structure, I am really defenseless against any serious attack. The comfort of its possession has spoiled me,

215

the sensitivity of the burrow has made me sensitive too." There is a final irony which destroys his faith in constructing a "burrow" for himself: the animal which he assumes to be at work undermining his fortress, may not even work in his direction, it may not even know of the existence of his burrow; the danger reveals itself not as an objective threat, but as the projection of his bad conscience for having constantly recoiled from reality. His obsessive fear of it cannot be justified by the nature of reality itself; it is a nightmare he has himself created. There were some early indications that the construction of the burrow was superfluous. Whenever he was near the entrance and listened to the noises of the world above, nowhere could he discern any vestige of interest of the world in him, either friendly or hostile; the world above ignored him. He took himself much too seriously in believing that the world was even in the slightest concerned with harming him; it pursues its own course and disregards little animals and their burrows. The burrow is not a superior creation, but a product of fear and lassitude. Reality wins the duel, not because it is more powerful or more brutal but because it represents the higher value.

○   ○   ○

This analysis of the story conflicts with the brief indications of an interpretation given by Max Brod in the notes to the fifth volume of Kafka's *Collected Works*. Brod, always anxious to claim for his friend "healthy" convictions and satisfying solutions, shrinks from the implications of self-condemnation contained in this story, particularly because it is one of Kafka's last writings. According to Brod "the poet . . . raised the veil a little and indicated that the 'burrow' meant more than safety, it meant a home and a fundament for life acquired by honest work—that which the Land Surveyor K. in *The Castle* tried in vain to obtain." Kafka loses nothing of his greatness as an artist if no edifying sentiments can be extracted from his work. We are grateful to him that his sincerity prevented him from providing sham solutions, that he did not become a yogi, a mystic or a tasteful reinterpreter of traditional dogma. The function of the artist is not to "solve problems" but to feel them and to express symbolically the emotional atmosphere in which they are experienced. Kafka's stories are prose poems, not dissertations or allegories.

The richness of the symbolic world of "The Burrow" has not been exhausted by this analysis. The story is in itself a "burrow" of the most complicated construction, with an ingenious system of coordinated and intertwining tunnels. The purpose of this essay was limited to locating the "inner fortress," whence the whole structure can be overlooked.

In the tightly knit coherence of its symbols the story reveals a basic trait of Kafka's art. It is a perfect illustration of that which T. S. Eliot calls the function of the "objective correlative," "a set of objects, a situation, a chain of events" which serve as the framework for the emotional content. Amado Alonso, in his book on Pablo Neruda, probably independent of Eliot, makes similar observations: "The emotions search for, select and adapt external objective structures, which on their part serve as favorable resonators. The poetic meaning of these constructions is the emotion itself which constructed them; but the constructions preserve also in themselves a rational order, a rational meaning, although they cannot be in any way identified with the poetic meaning." The basic emotion crystallizes around such an "objective correlative," in this case the life of a burrowing animal, and uses it as its conductor. The situations suggested by the objective correlative, perhaps not all foreseen in the original conception, serve to develop the basic theme in more and more detail. What rhyme and word association accomplish in poetry in the traditional sense of the word, is here accomplished by the "objective correlative." The danger inherent in this procedure is that in order to preserve the coherence of the substructure, elements may be introduced which are devoid of symbolical meaning (a French critic called them *"des chevilles"*), or that the situation suggested by the substructure does not reach full symbolical significance, but congeals into intellectual allegory. It is the uniqueness of Kafka's art that the most subtly constructed details of the "objective correlative" only enhance the lyrical intensity.

It goes beyond the scope of this essay to follow the threads which connect "The Burrow" with the other writings of Kafka and to establish its position in the whole of his work. A

217

few indications may here suffice. The ideal of "complete detachment from the earth" suggests "The Hunger-Artist." The attempt of the animal to create rationally a "perfect" burrow, and particularly its efforts to combat the approaching danger by minute calculations, has some similarity with Blumfeld's struggle against the balls; both stories deal with the clash between rationality and irrationality.

Another investigation might contrast this story with the "burrow" theme in Kafka's contemporaries, with Stefan George's "Algabal" and with the dramatic poetry of the young Hofmannsthal, particularly "The Emperor and the Witch" and "The Mine of Falun." Such a comparison would demonstrate even more clearly the power of artistic concentration which was Kafka's own.

the diaries and letters

ernst weiss

The diaries and letters of Kafka are of burning interest to his friends and important even to those who have not read a line of Kafka. They are important to the psychologist, to the philosopher and even to the psychiatrist. Perhaps more than by Kafka's other works the reader will be moved and touched by the richness and depth of insight to be found in these confessions, and this in spite of their narrow horizon, which Kafka at one point compares to a pit. Here, over and over again, is the settling of accounts with himself, the trial against himself: alternating between the supreme joy of the artist, the joy of creating, and the ultimate wretchedness, because passive, of a man infinitely gifted whose fate was nevertheless dominated by a star of ill omen.

In order to come a little closer, even if only from the outside, to the enigma of this great, miserable man, we perhaps should see him first as a citizen of Old Austria. Like Grillparzer, a strong young man suffers from the weakness and the paralyzing indolence of his senile fatherland. Like Grillparzer he is tied to a city which he dislikes, to a strictly regulated, hierarchic "official" position which he dislikes but holds on to with self-sacrifice; like Grillparzer he loves and is not rejected. On the contrary, he is loved too much, and yet he cannot grasp the fruit beside his lips; so that love becomes empty and devoid of fulfillment.

Resemblances are to be found to another great Old Austrian, Adalbert Stifter, whose novelette *The Descendants* Kafka loved. Stifter, too, condemns the "Bachelor"; both, in a world now obsolete, overestimate the positive value of marriage "for the common well-being" and the ethical value of having children. Stifter wasted away from the same lack of ideals that starved Kafka: the ideal of a nation—an ersatz ideal, to be sure, but nevertheless one which today inspires nearly all parts of the inhabited globe and moves men to their very depths—this ideal of an idolized, even deified, nation was not accessible, in the super- but not international Old Austria with its many languages, to either a Grillparzer or a Stifter or a Kafka.

This "bottomless" feeling Kafka expresses magnificently in his diary: "It is not indolence, bad intentions, clumsiness . . . which cause me to fail in everything: home life, friendship, marital life, profession, literature; it is rather the lack of 'soil, air and natural necessity.' To create these is my task. . . ." And at the end of the same passage: "I have not been led into life by the—it is true—now heavily sinking hand of Christianity like Kierkegaard, nor have I, like the Zionists, snatched the last corner of the disappearing prayer shawl of the Jews. I am an end or a beginning. . . . It is a mandate. It is in my nature that I can only take over a mandate which nobody has given me. It is in this paradox, always and only in this paradox, that I can live. But I believe this to be true for everybody; for living, we die." He is fully aware of his wonderful gifts; this is what he means when he speaks of a mandate. A real flame burned within him. But was he a beginning or is he an end? We are still too close to him to decide.

Looking at his choice of material, at the uncanny atmosphere of his works, one can see in him a descendant of E. T. A. Hoffmann. Like Hoffmann he believes that justice and reason exist, but not in our grotesquely tragic world; hence there must be at work a counter-principle, a "counter-God," as I call it; and

220

Hoffmann's world is dominated by the more or less successful struggle of good archangels against evil demons, accompanied by a vigorous and moving music. But Hoffmann was a good musician; there is hardly an echo of music in Kafka's works. Kafka is too religious and too much an artist to paint the world as something hopelessly dull, as only ruins where an endless battle of good against evil is being fought. He searches more deeply and is led to the pit. In the passage quoted above he speaks of the Tower of Babel which has become a pit. About the Tower one finds a noisy, trivial, motley throng; in the pit it is oppressively hot, in the distance one hears the rushing waters; the one thing that can be clearly distinguished is the beating and trembling of the lonely heart, the accusation of the isolated "I." This is Kafka's basic experience, and the castle is indeed nothing but the wall. Nobody can come near to the masters of the "castle," nor even to their servants, and hardly even to the bootblacks of these servants; and yet everything depends on the invisible great power. But why does this infinitely great, this infinitely pure power (Kafka believes in it, and that belief makes him a religious, magic poet) conceal itself from the honestly searching Land Surveyor, the individual, that is, who wants to mark the boundaries between "here" and "there"? There are only two answers. Either the master does *not* exist—the servants are the masters, he is always traveling abroad so that he need never give an account of himself—or the pitiful little "I" is unworthy, as a homeless stranger, to approach from the outside the innermost circles: he is guilty, he is condemned without knowing it. (These circles of nearness to God correspond to neo-Platonic ideas.)

Kafka chose the second solution; this was his greatness but also his destruction. With Hoffmann, with Dostoyevsky, man, the Land Surveyor, who has the strength to see God with his own eyes, cannot reach Him, because he is too worldly, too sensuous and covetously voluptuous. But if the poor sinner is this no longer, even if he only earnestly desires to be this no longer, as did Faust the great arch-dilettante of sin, then there is revealed to him, if not God in His full glory, yet a faint gleam of hope, a foreboding of peace. All this never penetrates into Kafka's her-

221

metically sealed pit, it never climbs over the Chinese wall, it never bores itself into the complicated maze of tunnels dug by over-cautious and greedy rodents. Kafka is alone. He is lonely. He is loved, he has wonderful friends, a nice family, a charming, pure, kind woman who wants to belong to him but to whom for ten years he has offered nothing but hopes and phantoms; but nothing has access to him. Does he not know it? He does, and this is his tragic guilt: "Everything is fantasy," he writes, "my family, my office, my friends, my street—all fantasy, that which is distant and that which is near—even my sweetheart. The nearest truth, though, is only the fact that you press your head against the walls of a cell without windows or doors." In "The Penal Colony" an offender is tortured with a most refined cruelty. In *The Trial* a poor devil is persecuted in a most cunning fashion, the persecution always being justified by an appearance of a Mephistophelian right. One is always condemned but neither justice nor pardon is ever administered. If at least he were a bloodstained criminal like the one in *Crime and Punishment* or *Elixirs of the Devil!* But the punishment is there, the crime is not. For in order to commit a crime one needs a certain passion which is a complete acceptance of life. This acceptance is not given to the poet so helplessly exiled into his "I." "How much do I need solitude and how much does every conversation defile me," he writes to his best friend.

We are dealing with a mind of the first order. It is true when he says of himself: "I possess a strong hammer," but just as true when he adds: "but I cannot use it for its handle is afire." At another point he sits in judgment upon himself even more cruelly: "He eats the droppings from his own table," so terribly does Kafka mirror himself within the walls of his pit, "thus he manages to stuff himself fuller than the others for a little while, but soon he forgets how to eat from the table; thus in time even the droppings cease to fall." But why does he not break his fetters? Is this gigantic mind not strong and cold and great enough to conjure up the devil, to throw the inkpot at his head and to set a new "scripture"? Rightly Kafka speaks of his art: "Writing as a form of prayer." But in order to translate this energy into action, to exercise this power, he should possess cour-

222

age. He should revolt against the devil, instead of hiding from him there where the world is deepest and darkest. It is strange and, decades before, it was a prophetic sign of our times, that millions of the most civilized or at least technically civilized peoples have completely lost the taste for "liberty," that even this chosen, virile mind should not even miss freedom. Nowhere does one discern the revolt of Promethean characters against the stupid workings of stupid nature, of blind fate; nowhere the healthy, foolhardy rebellion of the "I" against the "must." He does not want freedom. That is, he wants no balance between the unlimited longings of the over-passionate "I" and the claims of society as a whole—much less does he want mercy. Only the punishment he accepts, and that without discussion. "He who cannot master life needs one hand to ward off his despair over his fate; but with the other hand he can note down what he sees among the ruins, for he sees different things and more than the others . . . for indeed chronologically he is dead and the 'real survivor.' . . . My good luck was this: that punishment came, and that I bade it welcome in such an open, happy and convincing way, which must have touched the gods. Even this comparison of the gods almost moved me to tears."

Certainly, most certainly! This magic genius perceived more and different things than others, his glance was deeper, more divine and more infernal than that of others. But what did he see at the bottom of everything? Only himself. Time by-passed him. At least in all these powerful confessions not a suggestion is to be found, not a hint that events of his time had made him doubt, that his friends or a beloved woman had ever made him swerve from his path, or that he had lost his way and found it again. Nothing of that at all: nothing but this dark genius, face to face with his guilt. What the noble muse of music was to the good-natured, drink- and music-loving Hoffmann, his own guilt was to the ascetic, reserved, internally burning Kafka. But what guilt? It is not an immoderate craving for the concrete pleasures of the world, nor for the property of others. Envy and jealousy are foreign to him. Never is the mandate, which he wanted to seek, either named or recognized. It conceals itself, it plays hide-and-seek behind trees or rocks, laughing mockingly at the honest

223

Faustian searcher. It is a petty mandate, something like an old, sullen, ironical Old-Austrian bureaucrat, who teasingly plays with the weak petitioner, protracts his petition for years and to his very death makes a fool of him. Kafka, however, is humble, but not a fool. He is lucid. In his aphorisms we find unmistakably the enormous precision, the concreteness of his vision. In this gift to convert thoughts into something of flesh and blood, and at the same time to make the visible world spiritually transparent and symbolic, Kafka stands comparison with the greatest authors of modern times; we have to agree with him when he says of himself, at an early date: "When I write down any sentence at random . . . it is absolutely right." It seems that something within him must have whispered to him all the time not to develop himself but to destroy himself, not to draw closer to but to renounce his own self. Once he writes: "What is my excuse for not having written so far today? None whatever especially since I am feeling all right. Ceaselessly I hear a voice in my ears: 'I wish you would come, O invisible judgment!' " Truly he is sitting in the narrowest, most isolated room, somewhere in the pit, facing an unofficial jury, an invisible court of justice, and nobody can save this defendant without plaintiff, nobody can save Kafka from himself. How he would like to take flight! A few moving passages in his confessions (the same applies to his larger works) prove how such a man as he was, always wants to be near a friend, to confide in him and give him presents and joy! Thus it is that he is helpful, full of tender and thoughtful kindness, when, stricken with tuberculosis and subject to frightful nightmares, he still thinks of sending food packages or good butter to his friends, or gives them the better bed beside the stove in winter time, contenting himself with an unheated room. How are these contradictions to be solved? A man endowed with gifts to speak to an immense audience, to make it happy and to elevate it, imprisoned in the most bitter solitary confinement. A man so wise, so serenely profound, who weighs the whole world, who wished to survey and could survey known as well as unknown lands and who, in spite of this, says of himself: "Only the senseless things gained admittance." Perhaps a strange passage in his diary will take us a little closer to the center of his inner contradictions, fathomless

224

in their full tragedy. It is the passage relating how he called on Rudolf Steiner, the miracle worker, and described to him his accursed, hopeless situation. Here he speaks also of his "states of clairvoyance." But what follows is not the answer of the miracle worker, nor his advice or warning, but a detailed description of how Steiner blew his nose, "with his handkerchief reaching deep into his nose, one finger in each nostril." Thus an "I" comes to a man from whom he expects a miracle; to him Kafka lays bare— as he later did his withered chest to the lung specialist—that which he has hidden from everyone else; from him he expects help, advice and consolation. A different "I," however, completely dissociated from the first, sits maliciously in the corner and captures forever in an unforgettably sharp and precise manner, the minor mannerism of the miracle worker. I must admit, the impression remains. Perhaps in years to come someone will discover in Kafka's grandiose experiments (which he never would have dared attempt without the atmosphere of goodness and love created by his friends Max Brod, Oskar Baum and Felix Weltsch), perhaps some one will discover in his works—insoluble riddles full of great significance—the creation of a man who from the very beginning had to fight against insanity. And this with success, with real success. For even though he died, trowel and hammer in his hands, during the building of his temple or his jail, he died of the wound in his chest and not of the one in his mind. He defeated and triumphed over insanity; with every day of his unthinkably difficult life he made room for light against darkness. Perhaps in this sense his works will become to later generations the symbol of a true "survivor" of our time.

Translated by Annelore Stern.

escape from father

frederick j. hoffman

"My writing was about you, in it I only poured out the grief I could not sigh at your breast. It was a purposely drawn-out parting from you, except that you had forced it on me, while I determined its direction." Thus does Franz Kafka underscore the significance for him of his life-long struggle with his father. A struggle for recognition it was, fraught with misunderstanding, anxiety, scorn, and willfully and willingly accepted pain. The temptation is strong to give it the sole credit for all of the peculiarities of Kafka's writings. The formula is ready at hand. Nowhere in twentieth-century letters is there a better case for the Freudian. Yet Kafka's biography, when examined closely, does not permit of such glib interpretations. His is a spirit which conceals an almost terrifying complexity of cross-purposes beneath an apparently simple exterior.

Consider the Kafka environment. It is not at all unusual. His father was a successful wholesale merchant in Prague. Franz, born in 1883, was the only one of three sons who had survived birth. The distance between him and the youngest of his three sisters was six years. He was, therefore, a lonely child,

227

whose interests were fairly well controlled from the start by the overruling and dominating interests and convictions of his father. Almost from the beginning, Franz's will and purpose failed to suit the pattern his father had naturally assumed all persons under his direct control would follow. Kafka's responsibility seemed therefore to involve the surrender of his uniqueness of personality to the will and wish of his father. Kafka recognizes that such submission makes simple the task of bringing up the child:

> In my experience, both school and home strove to obliterate individuality. This simplified the work of bringing up the child, while also simplifying life for the child, though of course he first had to taste the anguish caused by repression. . . . [My parents] did not acknowledge my individuality, but since I felt it—being very sensitive about it, and always on guard—I necessarily recognized in this attitude their disapproval of me. But if they condemned an avowed idiosyncrasy, how much worse were to be considered those idiosyncrasies which I kept hidden, because I myself found some wrong in them?

Kafka's father was an excellent representative of the successful middle class. Because his life had proved its worth by the rewards it heaped upon him and because he was not inclined in any way to recognize any other type of life, he regarded it as the only kind of experience which a sane man would wish to have. Such an example might well have converted a son less inclined to question all models of behavior; for Kafka it was above all a living and ever-present proof of his own incapability. Once having decided upon the fundamental estrangement of the two personalities, Kafka constructed in his imagination a strict division between the two points of view. The world of his father—the world to which his father belonged, and in which he had scored his successes—was both inaccessible and frightening to the son. In whatever experience he had or wished to have, the domination of that world over his individuality was strongly felt. At one time he had thought of collecting all his writings under the title

228

The Attempt to Escape from Father. Kafka saw in his father the model of an authority which ought not be questioned—which *can* not be questioned, without serious damage to the questioner. It is not a matter of reasonable action; all independent decision, whether made with good reason or not, will be implicitly or explicitly punished. Authority often overrules the question of human dignity; at no time does it permit the subject to escape without some scar, in memory of the unequal conflict.

It is this implicit resignation to the will of the father, this constant reference to the example of parental tyranny, to which Max Brod often points in his biography of Kafka. Kafka, says Brod, overestimated his father's power over him, and this overestimate prevented him from claiming any independent validity for his own talents. Thus his independent action, which he must inevitably take—since he was both by temperament and talent widely separated from his father's life—carried with it as a consequence a sense of guilt. Kafka's life, then, is an ever-shifting law-court scene, in which the son is always the defendant, the father both the prosecutor and the judge. In the course of this lifelong trial, the weight of argument brought forth by the defendant is intelligible and intelligent, a rational persuasion, grounded upon the principle of sufficient and good reason. The judgment and accusation, on the other hand, are frequently mysterious and vague. One is not always sure, either, that this accusation comes from the prosecutor. It appears at times to come from the defendant—a psychological ventriloquism which is essentially a self-accusation. Two important points stand out from the mass of court proceedings: the deeply certain and authoritative pronouncement of the judge, which must be accepted, though it is not entirely understood; and the vacillating querulousness of the defendant, as though he did not entirely trust the reasonableness of his own argument.

In "The Letter to My Father" (fortunately preserved by Kafka's mother, who in her family wisdom withheld it from the father's scrutiny) Kafka allows his father a "rebuttal." After some one hundred or so pages of careful explanation and penetrating criticism of the prosecutor-judge, the defendant breaks

229

down, and allows him to cancel out, in a single, brief statement, the dignity and ostensible reasonableness of the defense:

> While I openly blame you for everything, meaning just what I say, you are outdoing yourself in "cleverness" and "filial affection" by explaining why I am not to blame either. Of course here you succeed only apparently (that is all you want anyway) and between the lines it turns out that, in spite of all the talk about personality and essential nature and contradiction and helplessness, I was really the aggressor, while you acted only in self-defence. The results of your insincerity so far ought to be enough for you, as you have proved three things: first, that you are innocent; secondly, that I am to blame; and thirdly, that you are ready, out of pure magnanimity, not only to forgive me, but, what is more as well as less, to prove and to believe that I am innocent too, although this is contrary to fact. . . . I admit that we are fighting each other, but there are two kinds of fight. There is the knightly battle, where equal opponents are pitted against each other, each for himself, each loses for himself or wins for himself. And there is the struggle of vermin, which not only stings, but at the same time preserves itself by sucking the other's blood. Such is the professional soldier, and such are you. You are not fit for life, but in order to live in comfort, without worry or self-reproach, you prove that I have taken away your fitness for life and put it all into my pocket.

In the short story, "The Judgment," this ambiguity and guilt-relationship are again explained. George Bendemann, a young businessman, has all but taken over his father's business and made a great success of it. He has also decided upon marriage, and he finds it difficult to break the news of his plans. The father, now weakened by age, has reluctantly depended upon George for the management of his business. From his bed, George's father upbraids him for taking manifest advantage of him. " 'I am still much the stronger,' " he cries. " 'How long you hesitated before becoming mature. . . . Now you know what was going on outside yourself. Before you only knew about yourself.

230

You really were an innocent child, but in reality, diabolical!—
Listen: I now condemn you to death by drowning.'" Dazed by
the fearful sentence, George rushes out of his father's room, into
the street, and leaps from the bridge, crying, "'Dear parents! Yes,
I have always loved you.'"

There is something pitifully helpless and hopeless in
the powerful hold which Kafka's reference to his father has over
the conclusions of his tales. So strong is his sense of debasement
and of self-criticism that occasional glimpses of success on his
own part almost inevitably bring about a disastrous and sudden
collapse of self-assurance. He forswore the temptation to take up
a writer's career and became a Doctor of Laws in 1906. He was
engaged, apparently with some success, in a semi-state office in
Prague. In 1912 he met a young woman from Berlin, "Fräulein
B"; he became engaged to her in April of 1914, broke off the
engagement in July of that year, was again engaged to her in
1916, and finally ended their relationship in 1917, pleading his
illness as an excuse. To some critics, this illness appears to have
been brought about deliberately. In August, 1916, in a letter to
Max Brod, Kafka sums up the advantages and disadvantages of
married life. Alone, he will be free to concentrate upon his work,
without any trivial cares or distractions. His powers will be available for his own uses. Married, he will be forced to dissipate his
strength, all of it expended in the support of the "Blutkreislauf
des menschlichen Lebens." * What he has accomplished, says
Kafka, has always followed from his "having been alone," independent of conventional responsibilities. Kafka himself had suggested to Brod that his illness was psychically caused, a release
from the obligation of marriage.† It is in the important "Letter
to My Father" that he shows the relationship—real or imagined,
it apparently does not matter—between the "Verlobungskrise"
and his father's hold upon him. The need for his father's approval
has qualified his every decision, and in many cases has rendered
it impotent.

* Max Brod, *Franz Kafka: Eine Biographie*, 186.

† "'Er stellt sie als psychisch dar, gleichsam Rettung vor der
Heirat.'" *Ibid.*, 199.

231

The most important obstacle to marriage is the already ineradicable conviction that, in order to preserve and especially to guide a family, all the qualities I see in you are necessary—and I mean all of them, the good and the bad, just the way they are organically united in you: strength, coupled with a tendency to ridicule the other fellow, health and a certain recklessness, speaking ability combined with aloofness, self-confidence and dissatisfaction with everyone else, sophistication and tyranny, knowledge of people and a distrust of most of them. . . . Of all these qualities I had comparatively few, almost none, in fact. And yet what right had I to risk marriage, seeing, as I did, that you yourself had a hard struggle during your married life, that you even failed toward your children. . . .

However, I did not ask this question; I only lived it, from childhood on. The problem of marriage was not the starting point of my self-probings anyway; I had always questioned myself over every trifle; in every trifle you convinced me, by your example and by the way you brought me up, as I have tried to describe it, of my incapability. And what was true, and justified you in all trifling matters, would of course be insurmountably true for the Highest, that is, marriage.

One genuine source of unity there was between Kafka and his parents—their Judaism. Yet even here the relationship was not steadfast or assuring. His father, it seemed to him, accepted the religion in terms of his adjustment to "a certain Jewish social class." Hence the performance and fulfillment of his religious obligations, though punctual within their limits, was casual and perfunctory. Franz was bored with the whole thing. When, later in his life, he became intensely interested in Jewish thought and religion, it was to the excellent learning and impressive sobriety of his mother's family that he felt indebted. The memory of his father simply hindered Kafka's complete acceptance; ". . . my new interest bore your curse." Though Kafka was in a sense reviving the Judaism of his family in his own study and devotion, this effort did not bring them closer together. His

232

father seemed to turn away from the Jewish theology. This, says Kafka, could only mean that ". . . you realized subconsciously the weakness of your own Judaism and of my Jewish upbringing, that you wanted in no wise to be reminded of it, and received all reminders with open hatred."

It is impossible to determine accurately the extent to which this ambiguous relationship managed to affect Kafka's writing. It is far too easy to offer a simple psychological explanation—all the easier because such an explanation accounts for everything in his life and in his writings. "Any psychoanalyst," warns Klaus Mann, "could define Kafka's religious pathos—his humble and yet mistrustful fear of God—as the productive 'sublimation' of an obvious 'father complex.'" So far as an artist's aesthetic conscience and consciousness are affected by his personal experiences, the father-son relationship, it must be admitted, is responsible for much of the peculiarity of style and point of view which is Kafka's contribution to the world of letters. Indeed, this relationship takes many forms in Kafka's writings. In all cases where the masculine and feminine wills are in conflict over a moral issue, the masculine will overrules the feminine, and the circumstance of the hero does not permit him to question or effectively to contravene that will. The feminine will and being play an important role in the progress of Kafka's heroes—but this role stops far short of the doorway to understanding, sympathy, or ultimate salvation. Kafka will not accept the easy way of feminine sympathy—because this way is endlessly qualified by the power of the paternal-masculine. The role of women is secondary—and the female can only alleviate pain or torture, not remove it. Many of the painful situations in Kafka's stories arise from a misunderstanding and a lack of good will. The hero-victim *knows* the reasons for his innocence, has evidence of it (usually, however, no witnesses); but the guilt is supported by an overwhelming and desperate weight of circumstantial evidence. The hero, therefore, though innocent (or just, or right), may be implicitly guilty of being innocent! Against this paradox, feminine sympathy avails little; it can offer only petty subterfuge, for essentially its presence is trivial and unimportant.

Kafka found it all but impossible to understand his

233

father, partly because his sense of guilt prevented such understanding. To him, the *authority* invested in the father image was *beyond* understanding. Thus his perplexity and disillusionment was both *incredible* and *poignant*. For his father did not act reasonably; and yet his unreasonableness did not make it possible for Kafka to renounce him altogether, or to accept him unequivocally. Authority is always incomprehensible, says Kafka; one cannot reduce it to reasonable terms, compromise with it, or dismiss it with easy ridicule. There is no reasonable way of justifying one's father's way to his son. " 'It's impossible to defend oneself where there is no good will,' " Karl Rossman tells himself after his interview with the Head Waiter of the Hotel Occidental has reached an impasse, and his circumstantial guilt is so rigidly fixed that he appears actually guilty.* This sense of a complete collapse of reason in the face of irrational or mysterious circumstance sometimes assumes horrible forms. In the story "Metamorphosis," Gregor Samsa, a successful salesman who has been supporting his family, one day awakes and finds himself changed into an enormous bug. "Lying on his plate-like, solid back and raising his head a bit, he saw his arched, brown belly divided by bowed corrugations, on top of which the blanket was about to slip down, since it could not hold by itself. His many legs—lamentably thin as compared with their usual size—were dangling helplessly before his eyes."

It is not a hideous dream. He has emerged from sleep into a world horrified and made furious by the change. The simple construction of his former world has collapsed. He has become an object of loathing. This shame and debasement which Gregor feels has in a sense been willed by him—this sudden collapse of the order of his everyday surroundings. For Gregor's father the metamorphosis is a demonstration of his son's malice. On one occasion the father, infuriated by the turn of events, begins to throw apples at him. One of these apples is imbedded in Gregor's back, causing a wound which he suffers for more than a month. This wound "seemed to recall, even to his father, that Gregor was a member of the family, despite his present sad and

* Kafka, *Amerika*, 188.

234

loathsome shape, whom they could not treat as an enemy. Family duty demanded that they swallow their repulsion and tolerate him—tolerate him, and nothing more." °

Just as Gregor had somehow *willed* the metamorphosis —it is *his* crime and responsibility—so he must will to die, to remove the shame which it has caused his family. He must, in other words, remove himself from the consciousness of his family, in atonement for having thought and willed independently of it. Gregor refuses, therefore, to take any food, and as a consequence the family is released from the responsibility of his loathsome presence. The metamorphosis is thus a symbol of man's willful denial of authority. That this authority is absurd, or unreasonable, does not alter the circumstances or reduce the guilt.

Kafka's failure to manage the father-son relationship has important implications for his eventual decision regarding the God-man relationship: incomprehensible demands for duty and obedience in the face of absurdity which is all too obvious to a person accustomed to the "reasonableness" of things. Only once did he suggest a plan or order which might accommodate incongruous moral and psychological ideas. *Amerika,* his first attempt at a sustained work of art, closes with the description of an immense spectacle—the "Nature Theatre of Oklahoma." Karl first learns of this project when he reads a placard announcing a recruiting for service in it. " 'If you think of your future you are one of us! Everyone is welcome! If you want to be an artist, join our company! Our Theatre can find employment for everyone, a place for everyone!' " Karl is amazed and incredulous: "Everyone, that meant Karl too. . . . He was entitled to apply for a job of which he need not be ashamed, which, on the contrary, was a matter of public advertisement." † More than that, Karl finds that everything promised is true. He is taken on as a student engineer, not because he is at all qualified for that profession, but because he had at one time *wanted* to become an engineer! The fact that he

° Cf. Harry Slochower's suggestive comment: "We have here the reversal of Abraham's sacrifice of Isaac." "Franz Kafka—Pre-Fascist Exile," in *A Franz Kafka Miscellany*, 9.

† Kafka, *Amerika*, 272-73. Written in 1913.

235

has no identification papers on his person does not seem to matter. His willingness and his desire are passport enough. This gigantic social project is the product of wish-fulfillment and a lively imagination—Kafka had never visited America—through which he saw the new world happily providing what his own world had denied him. He would flee from his father and from the perplexing ambiguities of his personal world to the refuge of a world fantastically designed for the unified and happy praise of God.° This is an exception to Kafka's usual conception of man's struggle for religious and ethical security. Its very superficiality points to the fact that it is a single moment of release from the weight of his ordinary cares and the uncertainty of his search.

His writing, then, shaped itself in accordance with the difficulty in and dread of the father-son relationship. Briefly, the circumstance is as follows. Kafka felt an essential difference between his father and himself—a difference in temperament and in talents. But he did not throw aside his family because of this difference. His father's strength and the strength of authority which was related to it prevented him from adopting any simple expedient, such as revolt or departure from the family circle. He allowed the authority of his father to act as a judge of everything with which he was subsequently concerned. When his decisions were arrived at through some independence of judgment, they were qualified and circumscribed by a feeling of guilt, which made them half-hearted and ambiguous. A sense of utter helplessness, mixed with rage and hatred, came over him. It seemed that he should accept what to him seemed unreasonable, almost unintelligible. Hence his struggle for peace is characterized by an ambivalence of protest and submission—a protest against the unreasonableness, often absurdity, of authority, a submission to its inevitability and its power. Here we have qualities which when appraised logically cancel each other out—absurdity, unreasonableness, attractiveness, love and hatred, fear and suspicion. The effects are gruesomely comic, as in "Metamorphosis";

° See "Die Welt als ein Schauspiel zum Preise Gottes!" Herbert Tauber, *Franz Kafka: Eine Deutung Seiner Werke*, 57.

236

or wearisomely hopeless, as in *The Trial;* or exasperating, as in *The Castle.* Inevitably, however, the art of Kafka is employed in describing the tortuous pilgrimage of a soul beset with doubt and skepticism to some spiritual refuge, which is never reached. The search always ends in an irrational confusion, in which all rational laws are suspended; it often ends in the death of the hero.°

°   °   °

Concerning this important and enduring fact of Kafka's life—his ambiguous relationship with his father, and the sense of guilt which it brought with it—Max Brod has had this to say:

> . . . it seems impossible to deny the applicability to Kafka's case of Freud's theories of the subconscious. And yet this interpretation seems too facile. For one thing Franz Kafka himself was thoroughly familiar with these theories and never regarded them as anything more than a very approximate, rough picture of things. He found that they did not do justice to details or, what is more, to the essence of the conflict.

Brod's reaction to the fact that Kafka's life lends itself easily to psychoanalytic investigation is curiously ambiguous. He admits the opportunity for psychoanalysis, but insists that psychoanalysis can never search deeply enough for essential causes, which in his estimation are much more important than any psychological interpretation can make them. It was inevitable (or at least quite likely) that Kafka should read Freud, for their homes were but a short distance from each other, and for a time at least they were almost neighbors. Slochower suggests that both the economic and the moral conditions of twentieth-century Austria were ready soil for "psychoanalysis and mystic doctrines." There is no question about Kafka's knowledge of psychoanalysis, or its peculiar pertinence to his case. Were this a psychoanalytic study of biography, it might be a simple matter for one to argue the case conclusively, drawing for evidence upon Kafka's own admissions—in

---

° His own death Kafka called a return to the father, a day of great forgiveness. " 'Mein Leben ist das Zögern vor der Geburt.' " Quoted by Tauber, *Franz Kafka,* 218, 219.

his notebooks, his letters, and elsewhere.° But such an easy treatment of a complex life and of its literary product might well cause serious omissions of interpretation; it would certainly not fully agree with more than one half of Kafka's own thinking about the matter, and would deny the relevance or importance of Kafka's own statements about psychoanalysis. Kafka's *life* may be a simple, open and shut case for a psychoanalytic biography; his *art* is far too complex, much too richly rewarding in several areas of aesthetic and intellectual contemplation, to be dismissed as an imperfect sublimation or an "anxiety neurosis."

What might Freud have said about Kafka's life? Hostility toward the father stems from a boy's love of his mother, his intense desire to "return to her," a desire which is constantly interfered with by the father, who bars the way and himself enjoys the love which the child believes belongs to him. The hatred for the father is repressed, for several reasons, one of which is of course the father's strength and authority, another the fact that this hatred is not unmixed with a sense of duty, even at times a certain tenderness toward the father. The father is, therefore, the first important barrier to the child's free path to instinctual gratification.†

In 1909 Freud published "The Analysis of a Phobia in a Five-Year-Old Boy." ‡ In this essay, and in a subsequent study of anxiety, he demonstrates the ambivalence of a child's

° Cf. Brod ". . . it must be admitted that Kafka himself, in stating that he had, not explicitly, or 'in ordinary thinking,' formulated his attitude toward his father's superiority, but had 'experienced it from childhood on,' seems to confirm the psychoanalytic point of view. So do his remarks on his father's 'methods of training'—amplified in numerous diary entries dealing with his 'miscarried education'; and his letters on pedagogy, based on Swift's thesis that 'children should be brought up outside of the family, not by their parents.'" See also "Aus Zwei Briefen Kafkas über Kinderenziehung," in Brod, *Franz Kafka,* 261-68.

† The mother herself sets up barriers too—such as are necessary for the education of the infant, to make him gradually independent of her. But the father's presence and his deliberate pre-emption of what the child blindly regards as his prerogative, is the most powerful of all barriers, and the most likely to lead to hatred and ultimately to anxiety.

‡ See *Collected Papers of Sigmund Freud,* III, 149-289.

238

attitude toward his father: "He finds himself in the jealous and hostile oedipus attitude to his father, whom, however, in so far as his mother does not enter the picture as the cause of dissension, he loves devotedly. Thus we have a conflict springing from ambivalence—a firmly founded love and a not less justified hatred, both directed to the same person." * The effect of this withdrawal of the mother's attention is twofold: first, the union with the mother, originally the only source of the child's sense of identity, is rudely shattered for long periods of time; secondly, the child's sense of importance (for importance is purely biological in infancy) is given a severe shock. His instinctive reaction is to strike blindly at the source of this discomfiture. When that move does not succeed, the child is forced into a none too strategic retreat. The "enemy" has aroused a number of as yet unformed emotions: respect, hatred, anger, disappointment— which, when combined with the child's natural love for his father (as a convenient "sex object"), cause a serious enough disruption of his simple life, and are his earliest introduction to the painful complexity of experience awaiting him in future life.

The *measure* of this disappointment, as well as of its effect upon the child's nature, is the strength of control with which the father orders and regulates his son's new-found relationship with his mother. Since the father's severity and "family zeal" can only be interpreted as a strong barrier to the child's gratification of his desires, the latter may very well, as he grows older and finds this barrier interfering in other ways as well, adopt a relatively strong and sometimes enduring resentment toward its source. In some cases, perhaps especially those in which the doctrine of obedience and the effect of painful and senseless discipline apparently dominate the child's growing awareness of his outside world, the mother also becomes a prisoner of the father's will. This is not to say that the mother actually *is* suffering from the father's rule (she may very well submit to it gladly, out of respect or love); rather, the child *assumes* or believes that his mother shares his imprisonment, since of course she is as anx-

* Sigmund Freud, *The Problem of Anxiety* (New York, 1936), 38.

ious as he is to satisfy his wishes. Hence, the father becomes a tyrant; his authority is unquestioned; occasional relaxations of it are eagerly awaited and gratefully received. Protests against it on grounds of reason or justice only aggravate the wound; for reasonable protest does not avail against the tyranny.

Further, the child, after he has matured, and recognizes independently a superficial difference between justifiable and unjustifiable commands of his father's will, may consider some of them absurd. If the will of the father resembles that of a tyrant, the absurdity of his command and the child's recognition of that absurdity have as little effect upon authority as natural erosion has upon the shape or substance of a rock. Solutions to this intolerable situation are many: complete severance of the family ties, suicide, murder. But each of these presumes a strong will on the part of the son, a determination that "this wrong will be shattered." If his will is weak—if it has been all but drawn within the orbit of the father's will—the solution is so unsatisfactory that it can scarcely be *called* a solution. The child may very well spend his life in an endless search for independent decision; each such effort may fall stillborn from his mind or spirit. He cannot renounce his father, he cannot accept him. Each attempt to renounce him will be hindered by the desire (for the sake of peace) to accept him. Every resolve to accept him will (because of the implicit absurdity or unreasonableness of the tyranny) reawaken in him the desire to renounce him. All of this, of course, varies with each specific family situation.

The extension of this early father-son relationship—the "oedipus reaction"—affects the quality and intensity of the child's acceptance of moral and social restrictions. Actually, Freud says, the development of a conscience, the super-ego, replaces the oedipus relationship: "During the course of its growth, the super-ego also takes over the influence of those persons who have been concerned in the child's upbringing, and whom it has regarded as ideal models. Normally the super-ego is constantly becoming more and more remote from the original parents, becoming, as it were, more impersonal." * Thus the super-ego develops out of the

* *New Introductory Lectures on Psychoanalysis*, 92.

parental situation, using such objects or images as are readily available in the child's heritage or surroundings—the school, the church, the community—and, of course, acting as an inner deterrent both upon the id and the ego.

Psychoanalysis might thus have explained Kafka's affairs, and should certainly have had little difficulty adjusting each of his writings to that explanation. Kafka's ambivalent attitude toward his father, and the power which his father apparently had over him, affected the development of conscience, or super-ego, in his personality. Kafka's God, therefore, bore strange but undoubted resemblance to the writer's father. His was a personal God, but one with whom any intimacy or understanding was extremely difficult of attainment, almost impossible. The tyranny of this God made his every step hesitant, recalled to him the egregious presumption of any moment of self-confidence, and made unthinkable the prospect of a mutual trust or obligation. The strange conclusion of that morbid tale, "The Penal Colony," suggests ominously that the ingenious torture machine is after all just, and that any reformist notions which might have made salvation easy or sins readily forgiven, will eventually be overruled. Most of Kafka's shorter stories deal symbolically with the strange figure of the father and his family position. *The Trial, The Castle*, and "The Penal Colony" treat of the father-position transformed into the image of an inaccessible and incomprehensible God, the whimsical God of the Book of Job, or the stern and demanding God of Kierkegaard's *Fear and Trembling*.

The biographical sources of Kafka's art lend themselves readily to a psychoanalytic exposition. This he himself admitted, though he condemned the explanation as "too facile." The ultimate progress of his art goes beyond the limits of psychoanalysis. It is an aesthetic statement of an irrational ethics—an ethics and religion which are beyond reason, or which demand a suspension of reason to be comprehended. Such a position cannot employ a single scheme; it is not bound or limited by the requisites of any school of psychology or philosophy. Kafka shares with many others, European and American, the distrust of simple rationalism and Hegelian dialectic. Avoiding the confidence and optimism of late nineteenth-century scientists, these men denied

241

that science and its eighteenth-century partner, rational religion, had satisfactorily answered the questions and resolved the paradoxes of the God-man relationship. Such a negativistic attitude is characteristic of all periods of transition; for a transition is peculiarly empty of the confidence of traditionalism and does not enjoy the cynicism of a nihilistic position. Kafka thus looked to Kierkegaard for example, though not for encouragement.

It is possible that Freud would have had more to say to Kafka had the latter lived long enough to see his discussion of Judaism in *Moses and Monotheism*. As it was, Kafka rejected psychoanalysis at the threshold of the analyst's laboratory. The confidence of psychoanalysis in its therapeutic procedures did not impress him. The tendency to locate all spiritual and emotional depression within the area of mental and nervous diseases suggested to him that psychoanalysis was evading its essential responsibility. Simply to bring the *source* of a neurosis to the surface, to subject the irrational to conscious scrutiny does not, he said in effect, alter the situation or improve it.

> Try to understand it by calling it a disease. It is one of the many symptoms of disease which psychoanalysis claims to have uncovered. I do not call it disease, and I consider the therapeutic part of psychoanalysis a helpless error. All these so-called diseases, pitiful as they look, are beliefs, the attempts of a human being in distress to cast his anchor in some mother-soil; thus what psychoanalysis finds to be the primary source of religions is none other than the source of individual "disease." Today, to be sure, there is no religious unity, the sects are numberless and mostly confined to individuals, or perhaps that is only how it seems to any eye entangled in the present. But such anchorings which find real soil . . . are performed in his being, and afterwards continue to form his being (his body too) further in that direction. Who can hope for cure here? °

Psychoanalysis has had some important things to say

° Franz Kafka, "Meditations," in *A Franz Kafka Miscellany*, 70.

about religion and the religious impulse. But, in Kafka's estimation, it is nonsense to regard a religious belief as merely a submission to the "impersonal father image" or a successfully religious person as using religion merely as an escape from a personal neurosis. Freud's interpretation of religion as an illusion on a grand scale might have received an answer from Kafka similar to the following: It is true that a religious belief can be called an illusion, if by illusion you mean a belief which receives no immediate—or even ultimate—justification in fact, no miracle which in some startling way adjusts the supernatural to a man-made causality. More than that, Kafka objects to the psychoanalytic treatment of beliefs as diseases, as though a laboratory or official pronouncement—this is contrary to reason, it is not reasonable or polite or in the best taste to subscribe to it—were to exorcise the paradoxes of faith in God. Freud described religion as one aspect of culture, as a large-scale sublimation, to which man contributes his fears and troubles, a kind of reservoir of unnatural shock. The gods, therefore, man-made as they are, are used as a means of comforting man against the terrors of nature, and as a spiritual (or illusory) refuge from the sufferings which an exacting communal culture has made possible. Freud wishes us to get rid of these illusions, since they are wish-fulfillments, barring the way to an honest appraisal of man's weaknesses. The task of psychoanalysis is to shift the control from God to human society, to admit "honestly the purely human origin of all cultural laws and institutions." The result, he says, will be a healthy and courageous view of the world as it is, a moderate control of pleasure, a discreet government of pain. The shock of reality should not lead to illusion or to a large-scale theological schema, but to an intelligent mastery of the situation, through knowledge or conscious awareness. For, at bottom, Freud believes firmly in the dictum that "Knowledge is Power," that a conscious awareness of biological and psychological mechanisms will lead to a sensible appraisal of them and adjustment to them. Such a readjustment will eliminate the unfortunate, neurotic detours which the human mind has had to take in the realm of the spirit. "The true believer," says Freud, "is in a high degree protected against the danger of certain neurotic afflictions; by accepting the universal neurosis he is spared the task of forming a personal neurosis." *

*   *   *

Kafka's reaction to Freud's view of religion should be fairly clear. What Freud regarded as an aberration, a misconstruction or distortion of the process of sublimation, Kafka insisted upon calling a reality. There are three ways in which God may be constructed or called into the human consciousness. There is the reasonable God, who by a happy chance bore himself with the deportment of an enlightened gentleman, who gave a metaphysical guarantee to all who would purchase his clock-universe. In the face of catastrophes not listed in the rule-books, this God might be absolved from the responsibility, but each such absolution weakened in his polite constituency the respect accorded him.†

The second God-construction is a mythical figure, in whom the qualities of tenderness, mercy, kindness, and commiseration are essential as a means of protection against the harsh realities of human existence. This is in part what Freud calls the illusion whose future disappearance he hopefully predicts. Such a God may not be a reasonable being, but his lack of reasonableness is a prerequisite to his service to the community of men. Prayer to him and worship of him are both signs of the illusion as an operating principle in theology. He bears the burden of human sin and of physical and geological disturbance. He is a gigantic complaint department; and, though the complaints are

---

* *The Future of an Illusion*, 76, 77. This book was written in 1927, and Kafka could not therefore have read it. However, it is closely related with the general intention and purpose of psychoanalytic therapy, and Kafka had long before his death in 1924 inferred its conclusions from others of Freud's writings.

† The only opposition to such a God which might have in any way pleased the gentlemen of the Enlightenment is satire, such as we find in Voltaire's *Candide*. Kafka regarded satire—especially as directed against ethics or metaphysics—as a low form of humor. Kierkegaard, of course, used it as a weapon against his contemporaries. But to satirize the ways of God was unthinkable, in the opinions of both Kierkegaard and Kafka.

244

not always heeded and the wishes not always immediately granted, there is something in having made the complaint or expressed the wish. Both Freud and Kafka would like to see such a vision of God dissipated and destroyed: Freud because it interferes with the immense reconstruction project which science has undertaken for some two centuries or so; Kafka, because it is a deliberate and puerile denial of the reality of an actual God, whose ways are neither temperate nor comprehensible.

Thus, the third God-construction, the God of Kierkegaard and Kafka. Far from denying responsibility for evil in the world, for accidents in an otherwise perfect world, this God is indifferent to the querulousness of complainants against them. Far from acting as a tribune of easy justice or as a means of comforting refuge, he remains starkly cruel, cruelly whimsical, inaccessible to the yardstick of sufficient reason. His manner fluctuates incomprehensibly from good to evil to good, not because he is aware of any ethical dichotomy but because he is beyond all systems of ethical appraisal. Man's worship of the first God is a pastime, of the second a flight from reality, of the third an unreasonable and unreasoning acceptance. In the words of Pascal, whom Kafka studied with interest, man's finiteness of body and intellect limits his chances of either measuring or controlling the infinite:

> We sail within a vast sphere, ever drifting in uncertainty, driven from end to end. When we think to attach ourselves to any point and to fasten to it, it wavers and leaves us; and if we follow it, it eludes our grasp, slips past us, and vanishes forever. Nothing stays for us. This is our natural condition, and yet most contrary to our inclination; we burn with desire to find solid ground and an ultimate sure foundation whereon to build a tower reaching to the Infinite. But our whole groundwork cracks, and the earth opens to abysses.*

* Blaise Pascal, *Pensées* (New York, 1941), 25. Kafka rejected the notion of a Christian intermediary, the persuasive conclusion of Pascal's argument. Cf. Kafka, *The Trial*, 198-99; Tauber, *Franz Kafka*, 216-17.

The majority of Kafka's writings describe man's relationship to such a God, personalized, an anthropomorphic judge to whom rational appeals are of no consequence, because he is not aware of, or is indifferent to, man's rational schemes for achieving salvation. This is why the Book of Job, the story of Abraham and Isaac, and the legend of Prometheus interested him profoundly. More specifically, he became attracted to the story of Abraham as a key to his philosophy, through reading Kierkegaard's *Fear and Trembling*. That we may avoid certain pitfalls of easy interpretation, we ought to keep all of this in mind if we are to appraise correctly Kafka's literary work.

Kafka's style is, above all, realistic. The details are starkly clear. Unlike Joyce and the expressionists, who attempted in one way or another to pay fealty to sensory disintegration and to the irrationality of unconscious habits, Kafka presents situations clearly and within easy range of the immediate understanding. "If the expressionists converted natural events into magic," says Slochower, "Kafka attempted to show the magic within the simple course of events." Kafka regarded Flaubert as an arbiter of style; he too sought a clear approximation to the reality of the event he was describing. But this clarity, though painstakingly achieved, is illusory. Within the range of the reader's attention—it is almost as though a reader's attention were limited by the quality of his sense-perceptions—the facts are unmistakable, concretely realized, and plausible. Beyond the reach of this attention—at the point where the reader is called upon to fit a succession of events within a time, space, or thought sequence—obscurity sets in and the reader is forced to readjust his position, or to regard the book as a whole as absurd. It is only then that one realizes that it is not intended as representation, but as allegory and symbol.* Thus, the realism of details is designed to demonstrate that man's actions, considered singly, are

* More strictly as *symbol*. For, as Brod points out, allegory suggests a careful correspondence between abstract and concrete truth, whereas symbol allows for an endless process of interpretation and provides for shifts in meaning consistent with the nature of Kafka's quest: ". . . Sache der Spannkraft, die den Einzelfall ins Grenzenlose ausstrahlen läszt. . . ." Brod, *Franz Kafka*, 236-37.

comprehensible and plausible. The larger obscurity of plot and development is designed to show that man's actions in the aggregate, especially if man is engaged in a spiritual quest, are incomprehensible and strike one immediately as puzzling or absurd.

Far more suitable to the nature of Kafka's thinking is the use of irony, or ironic comedy. For, in the eyes of Kafka's God, the strivings of man are pitiful and grotesque. More than that, he is indifferent to' them, and they acquire their grotesqueness from man's own despairing observation of them. Man's earnest striving for a successful rapport with God leaves him breathless, and his efforts, considered from the perspective of the immediate future, are stupid. They are laughable. But laughter directed against oneself is likely soon after to lead to a meditative silence. It is as though an earnest endeavor or striving were suddenly to appear grotesque, as though the floor beneath the worshiper were suddenly to disappear, or the board into which the carpenter is pounding his nails were to be snatched away. The measure of such irony is not the slapstick nature of any given situation, but the seriousness with which one has initially regarded the purport of events leading up to it. Max Brod describes one of many readings with which Kafka entertained his friends. "All of us laughed loudly [at one of Kafka's comical passages]. But we were soon silent. This was no laughter to which men were accustomed. Only angels would dare to laugh thus. . . ." This was a new kind of laughter which Kafka's humor provoked, a laughter near to the sober insight into final truths, a "metaphysical laughter." The crudity of many of Kafka's comical situations, reminding one as they do of circus clowning or vaudeville slapstick, is designed to point to the despairing conscientiousness of a man as he pursues his paltry way toward success, or God, or the evening dinner. "For though his humor persistently reminds us of the knockabout comedian and the circus," says Edwin Muir, "it is founded on the most grave and exact reasoning. Its originality lies in its union with the deepest seriousness. K.'s predicaments [the reference is to the hero of *The Castle*] are absurd, but they are also desperate."

The concept of absurdity is earnest of Kafka's religious usage of literary irony and humor. It was Kierkegaard who first

247

pointed out the significance of this concept for theology. We are accustomed to regard a thing as absurd when it violates good sense or reason, and in a sense therefore to dismiss it as either stupid, incredible, or dangerous. Kierkegaard uses the idea of the *absurd* as a qualitative judgment upon the ways of God to man. If we are to keep faith in him, we must wrench the idea of the absurd from its rational context, and, while recognizing an act or whim or wish of God as absurd, resign ourselves to it as another of the things which are beyond man's understanding. Thus resignation to something one cannot comprehend is tantamount to accepting it in an act of faith. This is the clue to the faith of Abraham. The relationship of God to man is essentially paradoxical, when measured by human reason. But when qualified by man's mature acceptance of God's will, paradox no longer exists. Paradox, then, is a characteristic of man's search for faith. As David Swenson puts it, ". . . it is his *reason* as concrete expression for what he initially *is*, in contradistinction to what he strives in faith to *become*. Hence there exists indeed no paradox for faith in its perfection, but for the human individual who is in process of becoming, the paradoxical cannot be avoided without arbitrarily limiting the spiritual process." [*]

There is a superficial resemblance between this notion of the absurd, and Freud's discussion of "secondary elaboration" in the dream work. The dreamer, upon awakening, considers some aspects of his dream absurd and unthinkable, and he qualifies his acceptance of them by saying, "Well, it's only a dream after all." [†] The analyst, of course, asks his patient not to regard these dream elements as absurd; on the contrary, he requests that they be considered as important parts of a successful analysis. Both for Freud and for Kierkegaard, therefore, man is asked to accept what appears to be contrary to good safe principle. But the resemblance breaks off at this point: the patient is requested to consider the absurd seriously because such an attitude will lead to the discovery of its cause, which he can thenceforth reject as absurd. Kierkegaard asks his reader to

[*] David F. Swenson, *Something about Kierkegaard*, 145.
[†] See *supra*, p. 41.

248

recognize the absurd so that he may eventually accept it as index to a higher truth.

Such an acceptance causes man great, almost intolerable, anxiety or dread. His ordinary, rational supports are removed from him. The order of his life—such order as his society gives him or forces upon him—becomes meaningless. His reason tells him that such or such a thing is absurd; his groping, fumbling, almost helpless search for faith causes untold anxiety of body and spirit. This idea of anxiety (*Angst*) is explained by Freud as the result of a sudden interruption of instinctual gratification. The anxiety neurosis is a protective device used by the ego to ward off danger which might come as the result of need for repression. "Anxiety is the reaction to a situation of danger; and it is circumvented by the ego's doing something to avoid the situation of retreat from it." ° Again, psychoanalysis treats the situation as a "disease problem"; a cure will eliminate not only the problem but the anxiety accompanying it. Kierkegaard regards dread, or anxiety, as a necessary emotional constituent of the search for faith. Here too is the lesson of Kafka's writings. Man's way to God is plagued by uncertainty and insecurity. His persistence in the face of absurdity and the experience of dread is by way of becoming an act of faith (*Glaubensakt*). We note that Gregor Samsa suffers debasement and shame in his metamorphosis, which is part of his self-release from the society he knows and understands, the society in which he has assumed a position of dignity. This release involves the acceptance of a horrible external appearance; and the first portion of "Metamorphosis" depicts the dread which this appearance causes him. Joseph K., in *The Trial*, resists almost to the end, the demand to give himself up to the horror and strangeness of a mysterious judgment. In the end, however, he goes without much protest. He assents to the pathos and paradox of his death at the hands of two minions of the Court:

> Logic is doubtless unshakable, but it cannot withstand a man who wants to go on living. Where was the Judge whom he had never seen? Where was the High

° *The Problem of Anxiety*, 85-86.

Court, to which he had never penetrated? He raised his hands and spread out all his fingers.

But the hands of one of the partners were already at K.'s throat, while the other thrust the knife into his heart and turned it there twice. With failing eyes K. could still see the two of them, cheek leaning against cheek, immediately before his face, watching the final act. "Like a dog!" he said; it was as if he meant the shame of it to outlive him. [*]

Perhaps this interpretation of anxiety in the face of strange and disagreeable surroundings is best demonstrated in another passage of *The Trial*. Joseph K. has come to the Interrogation Chamber on a day when there are no inquiries taking place. He becomes oppressed by the stifling atmosphere and feels faint. The female servant tells him not to worry; such an occurrence is not at all out of the ordinary. The air, " 'Well, on a day when there's a great number of clients to be attended to, and that's almost every day, it's hardly breathable.' " K. must remember also, she says, that " 'all sorts of washings are hung up to dry.' " She assures him that " 'in the end one gets quite used to it.' " K. is himself so overcome by his spell of dizziness, and by the shame of appearing weak before these people, that he cannot answer her.[†] The two symptoms of anxiety are here demonstrated: a physical repulsion, caused by the unattractiveness of the strange surroundings, and the agony of shame that he should have appeared weak within them. This experience is repeated in K.'s interview with Tintorelli, the portrait painter to whom he has come for advice about his case. The two incidents suggest both the dread felt in the presence of an overpowering circumstance—dizziness is a normal physical reaction to an insupportable circumstance—and the shame felt because of the decline of self-respect and superficial dignity.

The great difference of opinion which Kafka had with psychoanalysis in the matter of religion and ethics can be demonstrated in no better way than by reference to the story of Abra-

[*] Kafka, *The Trial*, 228.
[†] *Ibid.*, 84.

250

ham's trial. Considered from the point of view of social ethics, Abraham's intention must be thought of as murderous. With this conclusion Kierkegaard would certainly have agreed. For to slay one's son, if one does not have faith in God's decree—absurd as that decree may appear—is actually to commit murder. It has no spiritual justification and has therefore to be judged in a secular court. The psychoanalyst would dwell upon the absurdity of the notion and would consider Abraham's religious justification of it as an enormous and dangerous illusion. He would probably have committed Abraham to an asylum, as a dangerous incurable, and would be justified in so doing, in terms of his scientific evaluation of motives and behavior.* Kafka played whimsically with the theme.† He studied Kierkegaard's book carefully during the time when he was composing *The Castle*. In this novel he develops Kierkegaard's thesis most fully in the story of the Barnabas family. Amalia has angrily refused to accept an order from Sortini, which she regards as absurd and loathsome. As a consequence, quite without any deliberate action on the part of Sortini, who has probably forgotten the incident altogether, Amalia and her family lose their position in the Village, are looked down upon, and Amalia is forced to take upon herself the burden of caring for her prematurely aged parents. Amalia's act of refusal is right and reasonable, so K. tells her. That is in accordance with rational standards. Amalia, however, eventually senses the truth that her act was a defiance of the demands of faith—demands which are loathsome, incredible, and repulsive. Kafka is attempting to say here, and elsewhere, that one cannot judge the demands of one's God in terms of rational being. It is in the accept-

---

* American treatment of this theme is to be found in Sherwood Anderson's story "Godliness," in *Winesburg, Ohio*, 55-87. Jesse Bentley tries to offer up his son David as a sacrifice to God, but David escapes. Bentley fails because his faith is anchored in material wishes, and he expects the sacrifice to be rewarded. See especially *ibid.*, 86-87.

† See Kafka to Robert Klopstock, in *A Franz Kafka Miscellany*, 73-74. See also Franz Kafka, "Fragment: Four Sagas Tell About Prometheus," in *Transition*, XXIII (1935), 25, where he discusses four possible versions of the Prometheus story.

ance of the irrational that one transcends rational ethics and enters into a hitherto inexplicable relationship with God.

°   °   °

Man is somehow suspended between nothingness and infinity. He can measure neither by means of his reason. His experience of infinity leaves him breathless and incredulous. Within this experience, as a result of it, he appears pathetically comic, and the cream of reason turns sour with the acid of irony. Man is, according to Kierkegaard, established upon both an eternal and a finite basis. If he wishes to grasp his relationship with God, he will have to accept the fantastic nature of his reality and forego the pleasures of finite understanding. God manifests himself in strange ways. The trivial may be important, the important trivial. For Kierkegaard, and for Kafka, existence is both comical and pathetic: pathetic because the striving is endless, comical because it is a deliberate distortion and debasement of self. From man's finite point of view, the infinite is incommensurable. Only in the moment of insight (*Innerlichkeit*) can he see the relationship to the eternal, when in this moment of painful comprehension he gains a consciousness of the impotence and pettiness of external reality and when, through these means, the eternal becomes comprehensible.° His restless search for this understanding and his numerous hesitations and half-glimpses by the way give rise to the variety of ironic, paradoxical, ambiguous, and comic situations which fill Kafka's pages.

In one sense, Kafka's God is the "father image" multiplied and amplified, his every eccentricity and tyranny exaggerated to give his operations a wider scope. In that sense, Freud might explain, the father-relationship had failed to disappear under the influence of external, social pressures, and it remained to haunt the religious struggles of Kafka's later years. In another, very superficial sense, Kafka's bewilderment and obscurity are simply a picture of the general disintegration of tradition of the age. This, according to Edwin Berry Burgum, is at least one of Kafka's meanings. The inconsistencies of the modern personality, says Burgum, "were locked in permanent contradiction within

° Cf. Tauber, *Franz Kafka*, 143.

[Kafka] himself." Such an interpretation might account for the desperate cry of the country doctor, in the story by that name, who falls victim to the merciless ingratitude of a faithless age:

> Naked, exposed to the cold of this unfortunate age, with a terrestrial carriage and supernatural horses, I go wandering on and on, old man that I am. My coat drags behind the carriage; I cannot get hold of it and none of these vacillating blackguards of patients will lift a little finger. Betrayed! Betrayed! once is enough; I was wrong to obey the night bell. . . . It can never be undone.

But the great import of Kafka's writings is not that the age has itself collapsed into a riot of broken traditions, leading to an anarchy of spirit; rather the relationship to God—and correspondingly the resolution of all dilemmas—is and always has been that of a finite person to an infinite God. It is a singular and personal relationship, in which no external organization or system can aid more than superficially. The superintendent of the Village thus answers K.'s question about a Control Authority in the Castle: "Only a total stranger could ask a question like yours. Is there a Control Authority? There are only control authorities. Frankly it isn't their function to hunt out errors in the vulgar sense, for errors don't happen, as in your case, who can say finally it's an error?" *

The nature of the Castle is understood only imperfectly by those in the Village. Documents and papers are piled recklessly in corners and on tables. The officials work hard and long but with a certain eccentric irregularity. The roads leading from the Castle to the Village are known only vaguely, and the officials pass over these roads with distressing irregularity. " 'Now one of them is in fashion, and most carriages go by that, now it's another and everything drives pell-mell there. And what governs this change of fashion has never yet been found out.' " † The officials themselves alter in appearance. Klamm, for example, the

* Franz Kafka, *The Castle,* 85.
† *Ibid.,* 278.

253

official whom K. is anxious to see, has one appearance when he comes into the Village, another when leaving it, "'. . . after having his beer he looks different from what he does before it, when he's awake he's different from when he's asleep, when he's alone he's different from when he talks to people.'" * These alterations of appearance and eccentricities of behavior simply underline the absurdity of attempting to grasp the nature of God through the reason. K., in his restless and erring search for this satisfaction, employs a variety of means, but—because he is at the time limited in his insight—he neglects such important matters as answering Momus' questionnaire and listening to the official Buergel, whose droning commentary on Castle affairs puts him to sleep. At one time Brod asked Kafka if he could promise any hope in such a position. The answer was: "'Much hope for God —infinite hope—but none for ourselves.'" † Besides this vagueness of God's nature as man imperfectly views him, the actions of God's will often strike man as repulsive, loathsome, or obscene. Such is Joseph K.'s reaction, for example, when he sees the female servant carried off for the pleasure of one of the Court officials. So long as man's faith is lacking, the peculiar ways of God cause a loathing and are therefore not justifiable in human terms. Once the eternal "Yea" of faith is given, God's ways appear no longer to be peculiar or unpleasant.

The God-man relationship is achieved by an act of faith which goes beyond reason and accepts what would arouse only scorn in the reasonable man. By a recognition of his impotence and a willing suspension of his rational judgment and scorn, man achieves a knowledge of divine authority. In *The Trial* and *The Castle*, the heroes (who are in many ways identical) travel the long path toward that knowledge, achieving it only imperfectly, but finding glimpses of it and at least sensing its majesty and omnipotence. Abraham, the model for Kierkegaard and Kafka, had achieved this insight by a remarkable stroke of strategic submission.

The journey to God is difficult and sorrowful. Kafka's

* *Ibid.*, 228.
† Brod, *Franz Kafka*, 95.

254

heroes employ all means within their power. Each one falls short of the necessary act of faith. It is not wise, for example, to attempt bludgeoning one's way, for that method implies a self-confidence and a scorn for the eternal. Such is at times the attitude of K., hero of *The Castle*, for he is much too self-confident and regards the struggle too often as a game of wits in which cleverness and shrewdness may win. It is especially improper to employ earthly standards or bourgeois ethics as a means of gaining spiritual ends.* Thus Joseph K. all but destroys his case by lecturing to his inquisitor over the injustice of his arrest. The inquisitor listens with great interest to K.'s accusations, but ultimately he loses confidence in this method of handling his case; and a scream from one of the female servants brings the proceedings to an end. Reformists are treated with negligence and boredom. Tintorelli, who has for years painted the portraits of the judges, suggests that the court is not interested in those of their defendants who wish to reform the state of the court. " 'Almost every accused man,' " he says, " 'even quite ordinary people among them, discovered from the earliest stages a passion for suggesting reforms which often wasted time and energy that could have been better employed in other directions. The only sensible thing was to adapt oneself to existing conditions.' " †

    The idea of religious reform, of an enlightened religion designed to take out of God's hands the responsibility of punishing man for his evildoing, is criticized by Kafka in the story "The Penal Colony." The old commander—who, in his multiple role of judge, soldier, builder, chemist, and draftsman, must be regarded as a portrayal of God—has apparently lost his hold over the colony, and the explorer from a foreign land has successfully induced the commander's sole remaining follower to give up the inhumane tortures which were the practice of the earlier government. The torture machine which the old commander had designed is ingenius and cruel. According to the original code, the

* In this connection see the suggestion of Burgum, "The Bankruptcy of Faith."

† Kafka, *The Trial*, 153.

condemned man is an indifferent matter; he has no right of appeal, nor does he know the precise nature of his sentence (note the parallels with Kafka's other stories). This code has now been completely overruled by the introduction of a humane ethics. But on the stone which covers the grave of the dead commander, there is an inscription, "in quite small letters," which reads: "Here lies the old Commander. His adherents, who may no longer bear a name, have dug this grave for him and erected this stone. There exists a prophecy to the effect that, after a certain number of years the commander will rise from the dead and lead them out of this house to the reconquest of the colony. Believe and wait!" *

The story thus presents the human code of morality, characterized as it is by reform and a progressively scientific attitude toward immorality. Superficially the triumph lies with this code; actually the story points to Kafka's eventual preoccupation with the futility of man's attempt to circumvent or even to understand divine justice and wrath.

No stratagem, reasonable or unreasonable, avails in the struggle against the verdict (as in *The Trial*) or for the blessing (as in *The Castle*) of a super-rational power. The path to the God-relationship is uncertain and insecure, and thus the ordinary means at one's disposal—the use of lawyers, advocates, friends of the judges, the "feminine consciousness"—all fall far short of achieving their mark. In his exhaustive and brilliant series of caricatures of worldly professions—so startlingly clear and often so comical that critics have repeatedly considered *The Trial* as a satire of court procedures—Kafka is simply picturing the modern disintegrative approach to salvation through scientific and legal methods. We cannot eliminate from our consciousness the evil of the world simply by setting up courts or professions. The evil is essentially a "misunderstanding" of a law which cannot be grasped by human understanding, or reinterpreted in the interests of humanitarianism. Evil cannot be legislated out of the human soul; nor can it be "cured" by a physician or analyst.

* Franz Kafka, "The Penal Colony." Cf. Kierkegaard's remarks about the clergymen of his time, *Fear and Trembling*, 34-37.

Grace cannot be reached through the intercession of sympathetic intermediaries.*

The only way left is the way taken by Abraham—the noncommittal acceptance of a decree which from all standards but those ascribed to a wrathful and incomprehensible God is bewildering and absurd. Such a way demands of the individual gruesome sacrifices of his mind and spirit, and suggests to some critics at least a masochistic surrender to bodily and spiritual torture. It is true that Kafka admits that a belief is often a disease, when judged by modern medical and therapeutic standards. Kafka felt that an act of faith was so much more profound than bodily well being or social adjustment, that it *appeared* to be a serious disruption of ordinary health of body and spirit. Hence it is that he frequently portrays his heroes in an act of spiritual discovery or search under unhealthful and sometimes horrifying circumstances. It is as though disgust with or scorn for the body were a prerequisite for such a discovery. Health, physical love, while not loathsome, are superficial and disillusioning. Only once does a hero of Kafka have an actual love affair—under circumstances not exactly pleasant or agreeable, and for an end quite beyond itself.† In his notebook Kafka once made the statement:

* Kafka's philosophy does not imply an advocacy of fascism, or passively prepare the way for it, as Burgum has suggested. He regards fascist methods as fully inappropriate as other means. The shift from humanitarianism to totalitarian cruelty does not bring man any nearer salvation. All such methods are earthborn and ineffectual in the face of the one great spiritual—and, by definition, psychological—problem, the personal relationship of each individual to his personal God. The prototype of this relationship is the family relationship, more specifically as outlined in Kafka's "Letter to My Father." For a suggestion regarding the futility of expecting the proletariat to stamp out evil, see the story, "An Old Page," in *A Franz Kafka Miscellany*, 67-69. For Kafka's opinions of the fascist solution, see "Jackals and Arabs," in *New Directions, 1942*, 408-412.

† K. and Frieda spend the night together on the floor of the Herrenhof. Sexual intercourse is only another of K.'s devices for achieving his ultimate end. It fails because K. mistakenly assumes that he can approach nearer the castle by lying with one of the women who have been favored by Klamm, an official of the castle. But there is as wide a difference between physical love and spiritual love (not, of course, to be confused with a Platonic love of Ideas) as there is between other earthly affairs and their divine counterpart.

"Coitus is a punishment inflicted upon two who find too much happiness in being with each other." * Disgust with the body is connected with yearning for death; death is the closest approximation to infinity available to the ordinary mortal. This idea is more than adequately presented in one of Kafka's shorter stories, "The Hunter Gracchus." Gracchus has fallen from a cliff and hurtled to his death below. On the funeral journey, however, the steersman has made a turn in the wrong direction. " 'Thus I, who would live in my own mountains, journey after my death through all the countries of the world.' " This thwarting of the death wish has resulted in an uncomfortable and absurd condition. " '. . . I slipped into my shroud like a girl into her wedding dress. Then the misfortune happened . . . I am here. More than that I do not know. More than that I cannot do. My bark has no rudder, it travels with the wind that blows in the nethermost regions of death.' " † The first sign of an awakening consciousness of God is the wish to die. At times this death wish takes the form of a suicidal flight from a sense of guilt—as in "The Judgment." But usually it is the end of the journey toward salvation, as in *The Trial, The Castle,* and "Metamorphosis." ‡

The writings of Franz Kafka are undoubtedly a reflection of modern disintegration, as both Slochower and Burgum have pointed out. They are an aesthetic expression of disgust, a gesture of hopelessness in the face of growing confusion and bureaucratic chaos. In that sense they are a spiritual *Little Man, What Now?* By other standards of measurement, biographic and psychoanalytic, they are persistent demonstrations of an anxiety neurosis—a constant flight from anticipated affective danger. Such criticism points to Kafka's relationship with his father—a relationship which, it is said, prevented permanently the normal and successful transition from father image to social and moral con-

* "Der Coitus als Bestrafung des Glücks des Beisammenseins." Tauber, *Franz Kafka,* 212.

† Franz Kafka, "The Hunter Gracchus," in *Yisröel: The First Jewish Omnibus,* ed. Joseph Leftwich (London, 1933), 457, 458-59.

‡ Kafka differs from Kierkegaard in a number of ways here. Kierkegaard insists that the "knight of faith" remain within the world and be of the world, enjoying it as no common mortal can.

258

science. There is much supporting evidence for such an interpretation. But Kafka rejected it because of its easy confidence
that a mere recognition of an emotional disturbance initiates an
effective cure of the disease. In his refusal to accept beliefs as
simply disease or illusion, Kafka separated himself from his
psychoanalytic interpreters. Ultimately his contribution to the
thought of our time is the conviction that a belief begins with
emotional disturbance, and proceeds to an act of faith by virtue
of its acceptance of bodily and spiritual torture and horror. The
act of faith culminates in the recognition of God's ways as incomprehensible, absurd, capricious, but just. The attitude which
precedes this final acceptance, and which explains much that is
mysterious in Kafka's writing, is summed up in the words of
Max Brod: "Er hadert nicht mit Gott, nur mit sich selbst." *

* Brod, *Franz Kafka*, 165.

social awareness

rudolf fuchs

For many years one often heard it said that just as the real reason for Kafka's death was his inability to find a way out, so there was no way into Kafka's writings. Now suddenly he is being subjected to the most varied interpretations, such as few writers have undergone. A social interpretation has, however, not yet been tried. There are many passages in Max Brod's biography of Franz Kafka which might serve as a basis for such an attempt, but they are lost in a plethora of other interpretations. Brod learned of Kafka's deep interest in social questions only after the death of his friend, partly from his posthumous diaries. Yet this subtle and fascinating biography is remarkable for its gaps. The four years of World War I are barely touched upon. It throws no light on Kafka's reactions to this time of horror. We learn nothing about what the Russian Revolution meant to him. It is unthinkable that such a keen observer and wide-awake and sensitive person as Kafka should not have paid it the slightest notice. But in spite of all this incompleteness, this biography warrants the following conclusion: Kafka was not granted the opportunity of realizing himself, of finding himself as he so fervently wished.

261

And who can say he might not have been able to develop his magnificent gifts in a society in which a poet is not dependent on his father's pocketbook and not forced to exhaust his energy earning his livelihood in an occupation to which he is utterly indifferent?

Kafka was an employee of the State Institute of Workers Accident Insurance. In surroundings in which accident, disability and old age insurance was still regarded as the answer to the problem of the worker, Kafka said: "The insurance business is like the religion of primitive tribes who think they can avert misfortune by means of various kinds of manipulations." Brod reports the following: "Kafka's social conscience was deeply disturbed when he saw the mutilations workers suffered because of inadequate safety measures. 'How modest these people are!' he said to me with wide-open eyes. 'They come to us and plead! Instead of storming the building and smashing everything to bits, they come to us and plead!' "

Brod quotes the preliminary outline of a reform plan which Kafka had conceived. Among its principles we find the following: "The field of economic activity is a matter of conscience and of faith in one's fellow beings." Passages like these testify how strongly Kafka felt drawn toward socialism. These and similar passages and aphorisms, such as the following: "The worries that weigh down the privileged, serving them as an excuse toward the oppressed, are worries precisely about the maintenance of the privileged position," clearly indicate a social consciousness quite evident in Kafka's novels and short stories. Here a vast field of research is open.

Max Brod distinguishes two kinds of misfortune: "ignoble, that is, avoidable, misfortune" and "noble, unavoidable, metaphysical misfortune which has its roots in the civilization of created man and in his finiteness." According to Brod this second kind of misfortune cannot be explained by social, "rational and economic" factors. Brod terms the whole the "double-track system" of life. He addresses to man the philosophical demand that as an individual and as a member of a collective he do justice to both these factors. I believe that normally the distinction between avoidable and unavoidable misfortune suffices completely.

262

I think that avoidable rather than unavoidable misfortune deserves to be called noble. Why should one be in love with misfortune and call it noble simply because one cannot get at it, as for instance at a malicious disease? In regard to the sorrow of life from which Kafka suffered, he did not believe in "damnation," but tried by rational means to obtain clarity regarding the roots of evil. Brod himself supplies his readers with the proof for this. According to his theory of the "double-track system" of life, heavenly and earthly sorrows, he gives the following formulation of Kafka's fate: "Certainly life would have been hard for Kafka even in an ideal social order; the incurable misfortune which had its roots in a metaphysical and romantic sorrow would have weighed upon him even more heavily. But then he would have found in himself the corresponding counter forces. However this may be, because of the present still primitive state of our society's organization, he foundered on obstacles which were removable (I call them 'ignoble' in another connection), and the great struggle on the metaphysical level was therefore never fought on the right ground."

For well-founded reasons we cannot accept Brod's principle of the "double-track system." But there is no doubt that it finds some basis in Kafka's work, not so much in the writings which he intended for publication, but more especially in his fragmentary writings published after his death. That which is in them parable, fable, legend, I do not consider in the least metaphysical; though they contain elements which, if not metaphysical, are occult. The beginning of the novel *Amerika*, for instance, is marvelously realistic in the now famous chapter "The Stoker," published as an independent story. Gradually this novel expands into occult spheres. The young hero is joined by two ghostly figures: Delamarche and Robinson, who have all the attributes of occult phenomena. I am bold enough to say that particularly these elements, which also occur in the other novels, Kafka somehow felt to be impure, and he hoped to treat them later in a different manner. His was a titanic struggle for the pure observation of reality and its adequate expression, a battle against the improper domination of impertinent dreams, a battle of creative imagination against whimsical fancy. This battle was

263

made particularly difficult because Kafka conducted it without the necessary equipment of empirical and rational methods. How strong the attraction of the occult was at that time can be seen from Thomas Mann's essay "An Experience in the Occult" (published in 1924, the year of Kafka's death) describing his experiences with the medium Willy S. "May lightning strike me," he declared solemnly, "if I lie." He admitted that his experience belonged to "suprasensual realms," but added: "I only want to see the handkerchief rise up into the red light before my eyes. For the sight has got into my blood somehow, I cannot forget it. I should like once more to crane my neck, and with the nerves of my digestive apparatus all on edge with the fantasticality of it, once more, just once, see the impossible come to pass." A short time later it was reported in the newspapers that the medium Willy S. had been exposed as a faker.

The occult was a disease of Kafka's time. Expressionism showed symptoms of it and the weaknesses of surrealism are caused by it. Kafka fought against it. He would have overcome it marvelously. All his books are full of this certainty. But not enough time was given him. He died too early.

hope and absurdity

albert camus

The whole of Kafka's art consists in compelling the
reader to re-read him. His denouements, or their absence, suggest
explanations, but explanations which are not clearly revealed and
which require, in order to appear well founded, that the story be
re-read from a new angle. Sometimes, there is a double possibility
of interpretation—whence the necessity of two readings. This is
what the author was seeking. But it would be wrong to want to
interpret everything in detail in Kafka. A symbol is always in the
realm of the general, and, however exact its translation, an artist
can only restore movement to it: there is no word-for-word correspondence. Besides, nothing is more difficult to understand than a
symbolic work. A symbol always goes beyond him who would
use it and makes him say in fact more than he is conscious of expressing. In this respect, the surest means of laying hold of it is
not to provoke it, to take up the work in no deliberate spirit, and
not to look for its secret currents. For Kafka, in particular, it is
fair to consent to his game, to approach the drama by its appearance and the novel by its form.

At first sight, and for a detached reader, these are disquieting adventures which carry off trembling and stubborn characters in pursuit of problems which they never formulate. In *The Trial* Joseph K. is accused. But he does not know of what. Doubtless, he is bent on defending himself, but he does not know why. The lawyers find his case difficult. Meanwhile, he does not neglect to make love, to eat and read his newspaper. Then he is judged. But the courtroom is very somber. He understands very little of what is happening. He supposes only that he is condemned, but he scarcely asks himself to what he is condemned. Sometimes he doubts his condemnation as well, and continues to live. A long time afterward, two well-dressed and polite gentlemen seek him out and invite him to follow them. With the greatest courtesy, they lead him to a desperate-looking suburb, prop him up against a boulder, and thrust the knife into his heart. Before dying, the condemned man says only: "Like a dog."

Clearly then, it is difficult to speak of symbols in a work whose most perceptible quality is precisely its naturalness. But the natural is a difficult category to understand. There are works in which the events seem natural to the reader. But there are others (rarer, it is true) in which the character accepts what happens as natural. By a singular but evident paradox, the more extraordinary the adventures of the character the more perceptible will be the naturalness of the narrative: this is proportional to the separation that can be felt between the strangeness of a man's life and the implicity with which he accepts it. This, it seems, is the naturalness of Kafka. Precisely thus, we perceive what *The Trial* means. People have spoken of an image of the condition of man. To be sure. But it is at once more simple and more complicated. I mean that the meaning of the novel is more particular and personal to Kafka. To a certain degree, it is he who speaks, if it is we whom he confesses. He lives and he is condemned. He learns this in the first pages of the novel which he is living in the world and if he tries to remedy this, he does so nevertheless without surprise. He will never be astonished enough at his own lack of astonishment. It is by these contradictions that one recognizes the first signs of the absurd work. The mind projects its spiritual tragedy into the concrete. And it can do this only by means of a perpetual paradox which gives to colors the powers of expressing the void and to our daily actions the power to translate eternal ambitions.

Likewise, *The Castle* is perhaps an actual theology, but it is above everything else the individual adventure of a soul in search of grace, of a man who asks of the objects of this world their kingly secret and of women the signs of the god slumbering in them. "The Metamorphosis," in its turn, certainly displays the horrible imagery of an ethics of lucidity. But it is also the product of that incalculable astonishment that man experiences in perceiving the creature he is capable of becoming without effort. It is in this fundamental ambiguity that the secret of Kafka resides. This perpetual counterbalancing of the natural with the extraordinary, the individual with the universal, the tragic with the banal, absurdity with logic, are found through all his work and give it at once its resonance and its meaning. These are the paradoxes that must be enumerated, the contradictions that must be intensified, in order to understand the absurd work.

A symbol, in fact, presupposes two levels, two worlds of ideas and sensations, and a dictionary of the correspondence between the one and the other. It is this lexicon that is the most difficult to establish. But to be aware of the two worlds in contact is already to be on the road to discovering their secret relations. In Kafka these two roads are those of daily life, on the one hand, and supernatural anxiety, on the other.° We seem to be present here at an inexhaustible elaboration of Nietzsche's saying: "The great problems are in the street."

There is in man's condition—it is the commonplace of all literatures—a fundamental absurdity as well as an implacable grandeur. The two coincide, as is natural. Both are represented, we repeat, in the ridiculous divorce which separates our spiritual intemperances from the perishable joys of the body. The absurdity is that the soul transcends its body so immeasurably. Whoever wishes to delineate this absurdity will have to give it life in this

---

° The works of Kafka can just as legitimately be interpreted in the sense of social criticism (for example, in *The Trial*). Probably, moreover, there is no forced choice: both interpretations are valid. In terms of the absurd, we have seen, the revolt against men is directed *also* to God: the great revolutions are always metaphysical.

267

play of parallel contrasts. It is thus that Kafka expresses tragedy by the banal, and the absurd by logic.

An actor lends more force to a tragic character in proportion as he keeps himself from exaggerating. If he is restrained, the horror that he will excite will be enormous. In this respect Greek tragedy has much to teach us. In a tragic work, fate is always perceived better under the visage of logic and the natural. The fate of Oedipus is announced in advance. It is supernaturally decided that he will commit murder and incest. The whole effort of the drama is to show the logical system which, from deduction to deduction, proceeds to bring about the misfortune of the hero. The simple announcement of this unusual fate is scarcely horrible, because it lacks verisimilitude. But if the necessity is demonstrated to us in the framework of daily life, society, state, familiar emotion, then the horror is consecrated. In this revolt which shakes the man and makes him say: "That is not possible," there is already the desperate certainty that "that" can be.

This is the whole secret of Greek tragedy, at least in one of its aspects. For there is another aspect which, by an inverse method, would permit us to understand Kafka better. The human heart has an unpleasant tendency to call fate only that which crushes it. But happiness also, in its fashion, is without reason, since it is inevitable. Modern man, however, attributes to himself the merit of it, when he does not disown it. There would be much to say, on the contrary, about the privileged destinies of Greek tragedy and the favorites of legend who, like Ulysses, in the midst of the worst adventures are rescued from themselves. It was not so easy to find the way back to Ithaca.

What must be remembered in every case is this secret complicity which, in tragedy, unites the logical to the banal. That is why Samsa, the hero of "The Metamorphosis," is a commercial traveller. That is why the only thing which disturbs him in the extraordinary adventure which reduces him to a bug is that his boss will be displeased by his absence. The legs and antennae of an insect grow from him, his spine arches, white spots appear on his belly, and—I will not say that it does not astonish him, the effect would be missed—but it causes in him a "faint vexation." The whole art of Kafka is in this nuance. In his central work, *The*

Castle, the details of daily life are what appear in the foreground and yet in this strange novel where nothing is concluded and everything begins again, it is the essential adventure of a soul in quest of grace which is represented. This translation of the problem into action, this coincidence of the general and the particular —one recognizes them in the little artifices appropriate to every great creator. In *The Trial,* the hero could be named Schmidt or Franz Kafka. But his name is Joseph K. It is not Kafka and yet it is he. It is a central European. He is like everybody. But he is also the entity K. who poses the X of this fleshly equation.

Also, if Kafka wishes to express the absurd, he makes use of coherence. There is the well-known story of the crazy man who was fishing in a bath-tub; a doctor who had his own ideas on psychiatric treatment asked him "If they were biting," and got the answer: "Of course not, fool, this is only a bath-tub." This story is a bit baroque. But it makes very clear how the effect of absurdity is bound up with an excess of logic. Kafka's world is truly an unspeakable universe in which man allows himself the torturing luxury of fishing in a bath-tub, knowing he will draw nothing out of it.

Here then I recognize a work absurd in its principles. With regard to *The Trial,* for example, I can say that the success is total. The flesh triumphs. Nothing is lacking to this, neither the unexpressed revolt (it is that which writes), nor lucid and mute despair (it is that which creates), nor the astonishing liberty of gesture which the characters breathe up to their final death.

However, this world is not as closed as it appears to be. Into this universe without progress, Kafka is going to introduce hope in a peculiar form. In this respect, *The Trial* and *The Castle* do not move in the same direction. They complete one another. The imperceptible progression that can be disclosed from one to the other represents an enormous conquest in the order of escape. *The Trial* poses a problem which *The Castle,* to a certain extent, solves. The first describes, with a method almost scientific and without drawing a conclusion. The second, to a certain extent, explains. *The Trial* diagnoses and *The Castle* imagines a treatment. But the remedy proposed does not heal. It only makes the sickness re-enter normal life. It helps us accept it. In a certain sense (let us think of Kierkegaard), it makes us cherish the sickness. The surveyor K. cannot imagine another care than that which devours him. Those about him fall in love with this void and this suffering that has no name, as if suffering enclosed here a privileged fate. "How I need you," says Frieda to K. "How abandoned I feel, since I have known you, when you are not beside me." This subtle remedy which makes us love what crushes us, and gives birth to hope in a world without issue, this brusque "leap" by which everything becomes changed—this is the secret of the existential revolution and of *The Castle* itself.

Few works are more rigorous, in their pace, than *The Castle*. K. is named surveyor of the castle and he arrives in the village. But from village to castle, it is impossible to communicate. For hundreds of pages K. will persist stubbornly at seeking his way, will try all steps, ruses, shifts, will never get tired, and with a disconcerting faith, will wish to recover the function that has been conferred upon him. Each chapter is a checkmate. And also a new beginning. This is not in the spirit of logic, but of mere continuation. The extent of this persistence constitutes the tragic aspect of the work. When K. telephones the castle, he hears confused and jumbled voices, vague laughs, far-off appeals. These suffice to nourish his hope, like the occasional signs that appear in the summer sky, or those promises of the evening which give us reason for living. Here we find the secret of melancholy peculiar to Kafka. The same, in fact, that one breathes in the work of Proust or in the landscape of Plotinus: the nostalgia for paradise lost. "I become very melancholy," says Olga, "when Barnabas tells me in the morning that he is going to the Castle; this journey which will be probably useless, this day probably lost, this hope probably vain." "Probably"—on this nuance Kafka stakes his entire work. But it is all of no use, here the search for the eternal is meticulous. And these inspired automata who are the characters of Kafka give us the very image of what we would be if deprived of our diversions ° and surrendered completely to the humiliations of the divine.

° In *The Castle,* it seems clear that the "diversions," in the sense of Pascal, are represented by the assistants, who "turn" K. from his care. If Frieda ends by becoming the mistress of one of these assistants, it is because she prefers appearance to reality, everyday life to the sharing of dread.

In *The Castle* this submission to daily life becomes an ethics. The great hope of K. is to get the castle to adopt him. Being unable to reach this end alone, his whole effort is to merit this grace by becoming an inhabitant of the village, by losing this character of an alien which everybody makes him feel. What he wishes is a profession, a home, a normal and healthy human life. He is worn out with his madness. He wishes to be reasonable. He wishes to get rid of the peculiar curse which makes him a stranger in the village. In this regard, the episode with Frieda is significant. If he makes a mistress of this woman who knows one of the functionaries of the castle, it is because of his past. He draws from her something which transcends his past—at the same time he is aware of what makes her forever unworthy of the castle. One thinks here of Kierkegaard's singular love for Regina Olsen. With certain men, the fire of eternity which devours them is large enough to burn the heart even of those around them. The fatal error of giving to God what is not God's is also the subject of this episode of *The Castle*. But for Kafka, it seems that this is not an error. It is a doctrine and a "leap." There is nothing which is not God's.

More significant still is the fact that the surveyor detaches himself from Frieda in order to approach the sisters of Barnabas. For the family of Barnabas is the only one in the village which is completely abandoned by the castle and the village itself. Amalia, the eldest sister, has rejected the shameful proposition made her by one of the functionaries of the castle. The immoral curse which followed this has forever rejected her from the love of God. To be incapable of sacrificing one's honor for God is to become unworthy of His grace. Here is a theme familiar in existential philosophy: truth contrary to morality. Here, matters go further. For the road taken by Kafka's hero, from Frieda to the sisters of Barnabas, is the very road which leads from trusting love to the deification of the absurd. Here again, Kafka's thought rejoins Kierkegaard. It is not surprising that the "narrative of Barnabas" is placed at the end of the book. The final attempt of the surveyor is to find God through what denies Him, to recognize Him, not according to the categories of goodness and beauty, but behind the empty and hideous faces of His indifference, His injustice and His hatred.

271

The stranger who asks the castle to adopt him is, at the end of his voyage, a little more exiled since, this time, it is to himself that he is unfaithful and because he abandons morality, logic, and the truths of the mind, in order that he may try to enter, rich only in his mad hope, the desert of divine grace.

The word hope is not ridiculous here. On the contrary, the more tragic the condition narrated by Kafka, the more austere and provoking becomes this hope. The more *The Trial* is truly absurd, the more the exalted "leap" of *The Castle* appears moving and illicit. We find here in its pure state the paradox of existential thought such as Kierkegaard, for example, expresses it: "One must strike dead earthly hope, it is only then that one is saved by true hope"; which can be translated: "One must have written *The Trial* to understand *The Castle*."

Most of those who have spoken of Kafka have, in fact, defined his work as a despairing cry in which no recourse is left to man. But this needs to be revised. There is hope and hope. The optimistic work of M. Henri Bordeaux seems to me singularly discouraging, because it permits nothing to hearts which are a little difficult. The thought of Malraux, on the contrary, always remains a tonic. But in the two cases, it is not a question of the same hope and the same despair. I see only that the absurd work itself can lead to the unfaithfulness which I wish to avoid. The work which was only a narrow repetition of a sterile condition, a clairvoyant exaltation of the perishable, becomes here a cradle of illusions. It explains, it gives a form to hope. The creator can no longer separate himself from it. It is not the tragic game that it ought to be. It gives a meaning to the life of the author.

It is singular, in any case, that works of an inspiration so kindred as those of Kafka, Kierkegaard, or Shestov, those, in short, of existential novelists and philosophers, turned completely towards the Absurd and its consequences, come out at the end with this immense cry of hope.

They embrace the God who devours them. It is through humility that hope is introduced. For the absurdity of this existence assures them a little more of supernatural reality. If the path of this life ends with God, there is, then, a way out. And the perseverance, the stubbornness with which Kierkegaard,

Shestov, and the heroes of Kafka repeat their journeys are a singular guarantee of the exalting power of this certainty.°

Kafka denies his god moral grandeur, evidence, goodness, coherence, but only in order to throw himself more completely into his arms. The Absurd is recognized, accepted, man resigns himself to it and from that moment we know that he is no longer absurd. Within the limits of man's condition, what greater hope than that which permits one to escape this condition? I see it once again: existential thought in this respect, and contrary to the common opinion, is shaped by an enormous hope —the very same which, with primitive Christianity and the annunciation of good tidings, raised the ancient world. But in this leap which characterizes all existential thought, in this stubbornness, in this surveying of a divinity without surface—how can one fail to see the mark of a lucidity being given up. One wishes only that it be pride which abdicates in order to be saved. This renunciation would be fruitful. But this fruitfulness would not change that other. The moral value of lucidity is not diminished in my eyes by pronouncing it as sterile as all pride. For a truth, too, by its very definition, is sterile. Everything evident is sterile. In a world where everything is given and nothing is explained, the fruitfulness of a value or of a metaphysic is a notion empty of meaning.

In any case, it is clear here under what tradition of thought the work of Kafka is inscribed. It would be intelligent, in fact, to consider as rigorous the progress which leads from *The Trial* to *The Castle*. Joseph K. and the surveyor K. are only the two poles which attract Kafka.†

I shall speak like him and say that his work is probably not absurd. But that does not prevent us from seeing its grandeur and its universality. These qualities derive from his ability to represent with so much abundance the daily passage from hope to distress and from desperate wisdom to voluntary blindness. His

° The only character without hope in *The Castle* is Amalia. It is to her that the surveyor is most violently opposed.

† On the two aspects of Kafka's thought, compare "The Penal Colony": "The guilt (i.e., of man) is never in doubt"; and a fragment of *The Castle*: "The guilt of the surveyor K. . . . is difficult to establish."

273

work is universal (a truly absurd work is not universal), in proportion as it represents the touching face of man fleeing humanity, extracting from his contradictions reasons to believe, reasons to hope from his fecund despair, and giving the name of life to his terrifying apprenticeship to death. It is universal because its inspiration is religious. As in all religions, man is delivered here from the weight of his own life. But if I know that, if I can also admire it, I also know that I am not seeking what is universal but what is true. It is possible that the two do not coincide.

This point of view will be better understood if I say that really disheartening thought is defined by opposite criteria, and that the tragic work could be that which, with all future hope exiled, describes the life of a happy man. The more exalting life is, the more absurd is the idea of losing it. Here, perhaps, is the secret of that superb aridity that one breathes in the work of Nietzsche. Within this order of ideas, Nietzsche appears to be the only artist who has drawn the extreme consequences of an esthetic of the Absurd, since his final message resides in a sterile and conquering lucidity, in an obstinate negation of every supernatural consolation.

The preceding will have sufficed, however, to reveal the capital importance of Kafka's work within the framework of this essay. We are transported here to the confines of human thought. Giving to the word its full meaning, we can say that everything in this work is essential. In any case, it proposes the problem of the absurd in its entirety. If we wish to connect these conclusions with our initial remarks, the basis of the form, the secret meaning of *The Castle,* of the natural art with which it develops, the passionate and proud search of K., the appearance of daily life in which it unfolds—we shall understand what its greatness can be. For if nostalgia is the mark of the human, no one, perhaps, has given so much flesh and relief to these phantasms of regret. But we shall grasp at the same time what is the singular greatness required by the absurd work, which is perhaps not found here. If the characteristic of art is to attach the general to the particular, the perishable eternity of a drop of water to the play of its lights, it is truer still to appreciate the greatness of the absurd writer by the separation which he is able

274

to introduce between these two worlds. His secret is to know how to find the exact point where they meet, in their greatest disproportion.

And to tell the truth, the pure in heart can see everywhere this geometrical point of intersection between man and the inhuman. If Faust and Don Quixote are outstanding creations of art, it is because of the unmeasured greatness they show us with their earthly hands. A moment always comes, however, when the mind denies the truths that its hands can touch. A moment comes when the creation is no longer taken as tragic: it is taken only as serious. Man then busies himself with hope. But this is not his business. His business is to turn away from subterfuge. Now, it is this which I find at the end of the vehement trial which Kafka brings against the whole universe. His incredible verdict is this hideous and overwhelming world in which the mice themselves get entangled in hope.°

Translated by William Barrett.

° What is proposed in the foregoing is obviously an interpretation of Kafka's work. It is just to add that nothing prevents our considering it, apart from every interpretation, from the purely esthetic angle. For example, B. Groethuysen in his remarkable preface to *The Trial* limits himself, with more wisdom than we, to following in it only the sorrowful imaginations of what he calls, in a striking phrase, a wakened sleeper. It is the fate, and perhaps the greatness, of this work to offer us everything and to confirm nothing.

kierkegaard and kafka

jean wahl

I. The impossibility of communicating the paradox probably exists, but this impossibility does not show itself as such, for Abraham himself does not understand the paradox. However, he need not understand it nor is he supposed to, therefore he need not interpret it for himself, but he may try to interpret it for others. In this sense, that which is general is also not unequivocal; in the case of Iphigenia, for instance, the oracle is never unequivocal.

II. Is there repose in the general? Equivocation of the general. The general is sometimes understood as repose, but usually as the "general" to-and-fro between the particular and the general. Only repose is really general, but it is also the final goal.

III. It appears as if the to-and-fro between the general and the particular were taking place on the real stage, while existence in general were registered only on the backdrop.

IV. The transitory world does not suffice for Abraham's solicitousness; he therefore decides to emigrate with it into eternity. But, perhaps because the exit or the entrance gates are too narrow, he cannot get the moving van through. The fault for this he ascribes to the feebleness of his voice in giving orders. This is the torture of his life.

V. The intellectual poverty of Abraham and the clumsiness resulting from this poverty are advantages, for they make it easier for him to concentrate or rather they are in themselves concentration, but this way he misses the advantage found in applying the power of concentration.

VI. Abraham is the victim of the following deception: he cannot bear the monotony of this world. But, as everyone knows, the world is extremely varied, a fact which one can verify easily by taking a handful of world and examining it closely. The complaint about the monotony of the world is therefore really a complaint that one has not blended oneself thoroughly enough with the variety of the world.

VII. His argumentation is accompanied by a magic spell. From an argumentation one can escape into the world of magic, from a magic spell into the world of logic, but both together oppress, because then they have become something else, living magic or a not destructive, but constructive, destruction of the world.

VIII. He is too brilliant, with his brilliant intelligence he rides over the earth as if he were in a magic carriage, even there where there are no roads. This way his humble request to follow [Christ] becomes tyrannical, and his honest conviction to be "on the way" becomes presumptuous.
—FRANZ KAFKA, *"Meditations," Collected Works*, VI, pp. 235-237.

Commentary:
I. It could serve as a motto for Kierkegaard's work that he wants to indicate the transcendental. It is a formidable undertaking to interpret the transcendental. For he who is in constant relation with the transcendental does not conceive it as such in its non-

communicable and paradoxical character; and he is not supposed to understand it. Nevertheless, he is supposed to interpret it to others; or at least he can interpret it, and since he is able to, he is obliged to do it. Kafka says that there exists an ambiguity in the individual who has no need to understand but is authorized to interpret. He explains to others that which he himself does not understand.° In the same way the doorkeeper in *The Trial* does not know the incommunicable of the interior: "He never tells anything whatsoever about the interior."

Compare the following passage from "The New Attorney": "No one can ever lead the way to India. Even in Alexander's time, the gates to India were beyond reach, but their direction was indicated by the King's sword. Today these gates have been moved somewhere else, farther away and higher up; no one indicates the direction."

I & II. Let us not forget that the general is not less ambiguous. The general is the to-and-fro between the individual person and the general, but at the same time it is essentially and definitely repose. Moreover it suffices to reflect on the pagan oracles to perceive the ambiguity of the general.

I, II & III. These remarks of Kafka about Kierkegaard lead to other reflections: Kafka observes an analogy between what he calls the ambiguity of the general and what he would probably call the ambiguity of the individual. But this analogy seems superficial; strictly speaking there is no ambiguity of the individual. The fact that Abraham himself does not experience the incommunicability, but must nevertheless interpret it to others, does not imply any ambiguity.†

° Kafka, without referring to Kierkegaard, writes in a passage of the *Meditations* which has some similarity with Kierkegaard: "[the inner commandment to welcome eternity] delights and frightens without reason; but the former much more rarely than the latter. It cannot be communicated because it cannot be understood, and for the same reason it wants to be communicated."

† The German word *deuten* is in itself ambiguous: it may mean "to point out" or "to interpret."

One can go even further and ask whether Abraham actually does not experience for himself the incommunicability. Kierkegaard seems to mean the exact opposite of what Kafka thinks he means.

Concerning the general which, according to Kafka, is the "equivocation," does this mean that the ambiguity of the oracle is caused by the ambiguity of the general? This is not established.

The other possibility is that the general might be ambiguous because sometimes it is the general, sometimes the relation between the individual and the general. It is difficult to give an exact interpretation of this remark by Kafka and to find its relation to Kierkegaard's views on the general. (The general means integration into the community, exercising a function in it, a family. Flaubert, of whom Kafka was so fond, called this the common route.) The same applies to Kafka's idea that the general is supposed to be in the stage wings, and the to-and-fro between the general and the individual person on the stage itself. What he apparently wants to express is that the general in its absolute form—the repose in the general—is an ideal which can never be attained. In our realm, which is the realm of appearance, something individual always remains. We therefore discover two incommunicable spheres in the world of Kafka: the incommunicable of the particular, and the incommunicable of the general. For Kierkegaard on the other hand, only the particular is incommunicable, while the general is communicable (which is the social and moral order). For Kafka the general becomes an unattainable ideal and a mysterious driving force.*

VII. Kierkegaard has unusual gifts as a logician and as an enchanter. This in itself is very remarkable. But what is even more remarkable is the fact that at the same time he knows how to destroy logic and enchantment. He is constructive in the act of

* The difficulties of this passage are partly caused by an error in the French translation used by Wahl. In II and III the translator confused the individual as an adjective (in contrast to the general) with the individual as a noun: *das Einzelne* with *der Einzelne*. Kafka meant the adjective; the French translator rendered it as the noun. (*Translator's note.*)

destruction itself. His is a constructive destruction. He constructs in the third realm (to use Ibsen's term); this realm is situated beyond that of logic and enchantment where both are merged into one another.

IV. I wish that this third realm could be identical with the first, Kierkegaard thinks. I wish that I could retrieve the whole reality in the eternal—myself—and all my possessions.

If Kierkegaard did not retrieve it, he believed it was because he did not long for it passionately enough (cf. his voice, which is not able to give orders forcefully enough).

No, answers Kafka, it is because the gates of this world or of that leading to the eternal are too narrow. Only persons can pass through them, not possessions, not things.

VI. But must one not be satisfied with the transitory world? Is it necessary to search for the real "elsewhere"? Is it not enough to find it in this world? Kierkegaard complains about the monotony of our reality, of the earthly reality. This is because some remnants of the esthetic, in Kierkegaard's sense of the word, can still be found in him. But he who is not a mere amateur of reality, he who takes part in the variety of reality, who "blends himself" with it—does he need an "elsewhere"?

This idea can be compared with no. 98 of the "Reflections": "The conception of the infinite breadth and variety of the cosmos is the result of a mixture of laborious creation and free auto-analysis, carried to the extreme."

V & VIII. Kafka finally directs our attention to two traits of Abraham (but is Abraham not Kierkegaard himself? one might ask). First his intellectual poverty, and the clumsiness of his movements caused by this poverty; this poverty makes concentration possible, but—here we find another paradox—it destroys part of the advantages resulting from this concentration. Then, and this seems to be in contradiction with what just has been said, an excessive richness of the intellect.

VIII. Kierkegaard indicates to us the transcendental, the region

281

without roads. But how does he know that there are no roads? He is obliged to rely upon authority, an authority to which he listens, and which he takes upon himself. From then on, instead of humbly begging his brethren to follow Christ, he assumes *nolens volens* the part of a tyrannical and presumptuous guide. Kierkegaard has some resemblance to the doorkeeper of *The Trial*, who inclines toward vanity and arrogance. "There are holes in the character of the doorkeeper."

Kafka thus draws a portrait of Kierkegaard in which not all details harmonize: quickness and slowness; lack of participation in the world, which explains his longing for another world; a cautious penuriousness which wants to find in the other world the values of this one; a kind of intellectual poverty which explains the concentration and at the same time the difficulty in applying this concentration, but also an intellectual richness which makes possible the combination of enchantment (Kierkegaard as the poet of the religious) with dialectics (Kierkegaard as the dialectician of the religious) and at the same time their destruction (in a negative theology which opens the way for that which Kierkegaard calls the repetition, which is something positive), finally a kind of tyranny and presumptuousness which are a result of this richness.

But Kafka does not say: Kierkegaard. He repeatedly speaks of Abraham. We know that the first book of Kierkegaard's with which he became acquainted was *Fear and Trembling*. This is why he saw Kierkegaard in the image of Abraham. Here and there, however, Kafka thinks of himself rather than of Abraham and of Kierkegaard. Brod observes that Kafka had at first written not "the intellectual poverty" but "my intellectual poverty."

Besides the criticism which Kafka offers, an observation can be made on the double difficulty of Kierkegaard's work— a difficulty which is due to his mode of expression, which should direct attention not to the author but to the meaning; and a difficulty in the nature of the work, for its author should not be fully conscious of what he brings to the consciousness of others.

Another not less important observation can be made on the dual weakness of this work; it is based on the assumption

282

that the world is monotonous but that it is nevertheless possible to transfer into another world the possessions of this world.

Should we believe that Kafka is led to oppose to the Christian conception of the world a conception which redirects our attention to this world? (Brod says: a Jewish conception; one could also say: a Nietzschean or naturalistic conception.)

This would lead to the question of Kafka's attitude toward Kierkegaard. Here we are confronted with two positions: one believes in a close affinity between Kafka and Kierkegaard, and another—the position taken by Max Brod—does not deny this affinity, but rather sees in him an opponent of Kierkegaard. According to Brod, Kafka, as far as his personal life was concerned, was very close to Kierkegaard; both were exceptions and both were lonely. But Kafka's hope and his will are entirely different from those of Kierkegaard, as Miss Hélène Zybelberg observes, whose interpretation is on this point similar to that of Brod. Kafka the lonely man would like to have a place where he can rest his head. In other words, he wants to return from the religious stage where he finds himself by nature, to the ethical stage.

Now the question arises whether the ethical stage as he conceives it, belongs to the first ethics (to use Kierkegaard's terminology), the ethics preceding religion, or to the second ethics, that which one reaches after having passed through the religious stage, a transfigured ethics.

Or is it not more correct to say that Kafka erects opposite the Christian faith of Kierkegaard the will to have faith in this world, to accept this world, not in an irreligious manner, but in a way which remains religious outside of any specific religion? His problem and even his nature are very similar to those of Kierkegaard. But the solution he vaguely perceives is probably quite different.

KAFKA'S READING OF KIERKEGAARD

"Kierkegaard is a star shining over a region almost inaccessible to me; I am glad that you will read him, I know only *Fear and Trembling*." (Letter to Oskar Baum—Kafka: *Collected Works*, VI, p. 270)

283

"Today I received Kierkegaard's *Book of the Judge*. As I thought, his case is very similar to mine in spite of essential differences, anyway he is on the same side of the world as I. He confirms me like a friend." (August 21, 1913—*ibid.*, VI, p. 98)

In 1917 Kafka studied Kierkegaard.

KAFKA'S ENGAGEMENT AND KIERKEGAARD'S ENGAGEMENT

"I am sketching the following letter to the father (of my fiancée) which I shall send off tomorrow, if I have the strength to do it:

" 'And now compare me with your daughter, with this healthy, cheerful, unaffected, robust girl. No matter how often I have repeated it to her in more than five hundred letters, and no matter how often she has assured me with her 'No'—an answer which she has not supported sufficiently well—nevertheless the truth remains that she must become unhappy with me, as far as I can foresee. Not only because of the conditions in which I am living, but especially because of my real nature. I am an ingrowing, taciturn, unsociable, dissatisfied person, but I cannot call this a misfortune for myself, for it is only the reflection of my goal.'" (August 21, 1913, following the above remark on Kierkegaard—*ibid.*, VI, p. 99)

"I loved a woman who loved me also, but I had to leave her." (*ibid.*, VI, p. 161)

"I would make you unhappy by writing to you." (Brod, p. 172)

"Forget as quickly as possible the ghost that I am, and live as cheerfully and undisturbed as before." (Brod, p. 173)

"I need much solitude. All I have accomplished was possible only through solitude." (Brod, p. 174)

"I shall gradually recover, she will marry." (Brod, p. 175)

"What I shall suffer, what she will suffer cannot be compared with what we should suffer together." (*ibid.*)

So he is "diabolical," in all innocence.

Compare the engagement in the story, "The Judg-

284

ment," and in general the part of women in "The Metamorphosis," "The Judgment" and "A Country Doctor."

One could also compare the importance of Kierkegaard's father with that of Kafka's father (cf. the part of the father in "The Judgment"). Finally sentences like this—"I shall never grow to become a man; from a child I shall immediately change into a white-haired old man" (Brod, p. 51)—are completely in the spirit of Kierkegaard.

But one should not overlook certain ideas of Kafka foreign to Kierkegaard. For instance: "I am incapable of bearing life alone, this is not an incapacity to live, on the contrary, it is even improbable that I know how to live together with someone else, but I am completely incapable of bearing alone the stress of my own life, the attacks of time and approaching age, the vague impetus of the desire to write, insomnia, the threatening insanity." (Brod, p. 174)

The work of both Kierkegaard and Kafka is based on the idea of misunderstanding, of the *qui pro quo*, of error. "Whatever one may do, it is never right." The comprehension of the doorkeeper in *The Trial* is an understanding which misunderstands.

Finally the Jewish problem cannot be separated from this. Should a Western Jew marry if he has not reached clarity on the basic issues? (Brod, p. 204)

THE DUTY IMPOSED UPON HIM

"It is not laziness, lack of good will or lack of skill—even though they contribute slightly to it, because 'the vermin' is born out of nothingness—which make me fail in everything or do not even make me fail completely: family life, friendship, marriage, profession, literature, but it is a lack of foundations, of air, of a compelling commandment. It is my task to obtain these, not in order that I may catch up with that which I had neglected, for one task is as good as any other. It is even the most fundamental task or at least its reflection, it is as if a person who is climbing in a high altitude suddenly stepped into the light of the distant sun. It is also not an exceptional task, for it

285

has been assigned often enough before. But I am not sure whether it has ever been assigned with such dimensions. As far as I know, I do not have any of the qualities required for life, only the common human weakness. With this weakness—in this respect it is an enormous strength—I took resolutely upon me the negative elements of my epoch, which I have not the right to combat but have the right, so to speak, to represent. I do not share by inheritance any of the few positive elements of my time nor any of the negative elements in their extreme position where they are on the verge of turning positive. I was not, like Kierkegaard, introduced into life by the tired hand of Christianity and I did not, like the Zionists, catch the last corner of the disappearing prayer shawl of the Jews. I am either an end or a beginning." (Kafka: *Collected Works*, VI, p. 158)

THE MEANING OF LIFE AND THE STRENGTH OF FAITH

The following passages will illustrate more fully Kafka's tendency to oppose Kierkegaard's transcendental mysticism with an immanent mysticism which, however, does not give up faith in the "indestructible."

"How much more oppressive than the most unshakable conviction of our present sinful condition is even the most feeble conviction of the future, eternal justification of our temporality. Only the strength in bearing this second conviction which in its pure form fully embraces the first one, is the measure of faith." (*Collected Works*, VI, p. 214)

"One cannot say that we are lacking in faith. The simple fact in itself that we live is inexhaustible in its value of faith.

"Should one consider this a value of faith? It is impossible not to live.

"It is just this 'it is impossible' which constitutes the mad strength of faith; it expresses itself in this negative form." (*ibid.*, p. 217)

"To have faith means to liberate the indestructible in

oneself, or more correctly, to liberate oneself, or more correctly, to be indestructible, or even more correctly, to live." (*ibid.*, p. 226)

"The Messiah will come as soon as the most unrestrained individualism in matters of faith is possible; when no one will destroy this possibility, when no one will tolerate such a destruction; in short when the graves will open. This is perhaps also the Christian teaching as it is shown in the concrete demonstration of the example which is to be followed as well as in the symbolical demonstration of the resurrection of the Mediator in each person." (*ibid.*, p. 226)

"What is oppressive in the conception of the eternal is this: the justification, incomprehensible to us, which time must receive before eternity, and, resulting from this, the justification of ourselves such as we are." (*ibid.*, p. 232)

In Max Brod's biography of Kafka there are passages in which one can observe a tendency to establish a kinship between Kafka and Kierkegaard and the theology of crisis. (Brod, pp. 65, 214-216, 222) In another passage, however, Brod inclines to diminish the opposition between God and Man: God must submit to the same moral laws as Man. (Brod, pp. 225-226) And finally in a third passage Brod seems to discern in Kafka a kind of naturalism—or shall we say Nietzscheism. (Brod, pp. 209, 241) °

Brod says: "Kafka as a person and as a writer is abstruse only on the surface. He to whom Kafka appears abstruse and of a bizarre attraction has not understood him, or is perhaps only in the first stage of understanding him." (p. 68)

Brod's explanation is perhaps not entirely satisfactory. Kafka's work may be bizarre, because he perceived unusual things; this is certainly true; but perhaps in contrast to many

° This indicates that Brod's interpretation is somewhat indefinite. One has to make reservations on certain points where Brod does not clearly distinguish between his own opinions and those of Kafka. Nevertheless, the book is rich in documents and very moving.

other creators, Kafka detests his own creations, or more exactly, he detests the world which imposes itself upon him and of which he knows that he, for his part, can impose it upon his readers. He tries to rid himself of this world which he describes with such accuracy and such visionary power, but which he himself hates: "I have hundreds of thousands of false sentiments, horrible sentiments—the true ones do not come to light—or if so, only in fragments and very feebly. . . . We are nihilistic ideas arising in God's mind. . . . No, we are only one of his bad moods, one of his spleeny days." (Brod, p. 95)

Should we assume that this applies also to the relation between Kafka himself and his creations? What he left to us are certain aspects of the somber side of life, aspects which attracted him, but which he himself considered detestable and of which he tried to rid himself.

Brod asked, "So there might be hope beyond our own world?" Kafka answered with a smile: "Much hope—for God—infinitely much hope; only not for us." (Brod, p. 95)

"Not for us" is one of Kafka's fundamental ideas.

But Kafka did not always limit himself to this transcendent view of a religious world beyond reach. "The specific form of Kafka's religion was a religion of life fully lived, of meaningful and useful work which absorbs the whole of life, of integration into a national community." (ibid., p. 118)

What, then, was the rôle assigned to Kafka in this world? It could only be this: to express what he was able to express—the horrible and senseless aspects of life. This was undoubtedly the task given him, the mandate especially created for him, certainly not by the Lord directly, but by one of his subordinate intermediaries. He was called upon to work in the shadow at the projection of his shades and his apparitions, he himself being an apparition. This was his justification.[*]

[*] We therefore do not follow Brod when he writes: "He wrote these horrors against his will." But our explanation still oversimplifies, in spite of being so complicated. One should compare the following: "God's wild rage against the human family" (Brod, p. 190) or Kafka's prayer: "Have pity with me, I am a sinner in every corner of my existence" (Brod, p. 191).

After a conversation with Kafka in 1918, Brod noted down the following: "His confidence that pure intentions and honest work are never senseless, that nothing really good can ever be lost . . ." (Brod, p. 207)

Therefore, and here we agree with Brod, the numerous characters of lonely and unmarried people in Kafka's work are only the wrong side, the reversed reflection of his ideal.° "Everywhere there are courts in session and executions are being carried out everywhere. Horrible metamorphoses are taking place." But one should not be mistaken: If Kafka wrote an Inferno, this was for him justified by the idea of a Paradiso: "It does not disprove the presentiment of a final liberation, if on the next day imprisonment still remains unchanged or even if it is made more severe or even if there is an explicit declaration that the imprisonment will never end. All this may rather be a necessary condition for the final liberation. . . . He is of the opinion that one should only once step over on the side of the good and then one would be saved, without consideration of the past, and even without consideration of the future." (Brod, p. 226)

Brod retracts what had been said before—"The salvation is never for us"—and writes: "The deliverance is also for us." †

° The metamorphoses are only symbols of transmutation; the horrors symbolize compensatory transmutations. The same act which transforms Gregor Samsa into the dead roach transforms his sister into "a beautiful young girl with a youthful well-shaped body." And is this idea of compensation not also to be found in the piece "A Dream"?—"While he plunged into this unfathomable abyss with his head still raised, up there his name is speedily engraved with great flourishes upon the stone." His death is his immortality. Here, as in Shakespeare, everything, even the horrible, and particularly the horrible, is transformed into something strangely beautiful.

† The hero never despairs, even if there is only the slightest hope left, and we can see in the "Report to an Academy" whither a senseless hope can lead. It can lead to the fulfillment of the most absurd pledge. (One could say of the person who writes this report that he is a disciple of Shestov in the body of Maldoror.)

Olga speaks words of hope to Barnabas, "There are obstacles and disappointments, there are problems; but this only means—and we knew this before—that one must struggle for the smallest trifles rather than give up, and this is another reason why one should be proud and not dejected." (*The Castle*, p. 180)

289

The redemption will also be for us if we keep our faith in the indestructible, although we cannot say anything about this indestructible. If we keep up our courage in spite of the horrors which Kafka showed us, if we always think: tomorrow I shall be freed; then we shall be purified; then the unjust punishment will turn into justice and purification. Today more than ever we are ready for such a conviction. There will be a catharsis through our fear for ourselves and through our pity for ourselves. There will be something indestructible which will be the result only of our indestructible faith in the indestructible.

The vision of the Inferno cannot prevail against the assurance of a Paradiso. From then on the suffocating atmosphere of the labyrinth will be dissipated. In this world without an exit we have dug an exit. As is said in *The Trial*, however unshakable the logic may be, it cannot resist him who wants to live. This will to live was lacking in the hero of *The Trial*. It was lacking in Kafka as far as he is identical with this hero, but Kafka shows us how to obtain this will.° We shall find this liberation for which Kafka always longed. At last we are in the open air.

Translated by Lienhard Bergel.

° Brod quotes from Kafka's note books: "When you seem to be completely exhausted, there still comes a new strength to you, and this means that you are alive."—"A heavy downpour. Offer yourself to the rain, let its iron spray pierce you, swim in the water which wants to carry you away, but nevertheless stay and wait there, upright, for the sun, streaming in suddenly and immensely."

the oak and the rock

john urzidil

"Neither from the old oak nor from the rock do you come."

—HOMER

Kafka has always surprised me by his utter lack of cognizance of nature, its facts, phenomena and processes. No landscape appears in his works, and even if he tries to sketch one, it is, as in "Description of a Struggle," nothing but dream scenery. There are fragmentary reminiscences of some Prague street corners. The scenic background of *Amerika* is a compound of imagination and transcribed second-hand information. Its last chapter—"The Nature Theatre of Oklahoma"—offers Kafka's only valid description of natural scenery. Sometimes he mentions meadow flowers but they lack every characteristic mark and are only metaphorical specimens. His animals, be they monkeys, dogs, jackals, moles, horses or mice, are only anthropomorphic symbols, chosen because the use of elementary prototypes enables him to give a more impressive description of human events, tempers and peculiarities.

It is the realm of the soul and the spirit exclusively that matters to him. Hence Kafka's stories are not stories, his novels are not novels; they are purely spiritual architectures.

291

Their builder could not avoid using at least some tangible material. But he very seldom did so and then only with the utmost abstraction.

Lack of intimacy with nature and fragmentarism are correlative, as a rule. To be sure, every masterpiece of the highest standard appears to be perpetually in the making and is therefore, in a certain sense, always fragmentary. Its completion, if any, is only superficial, provisional and seeming. Kafka's three novels, *The Trial, The Castle* and *Amerika,* are fragments. But it is the same with almost all his shorter stories, except those in which a sort of aphoristic conciseness saved him from fragmentarism. The root and the reason of this fragmentarism is Kafka's highly developed intellectualism and his solely anthropocentric viewpoints. They imply his remoteness from nature. He cannot find any consolation in "oak and rock." The spirit of contradiction pursues him like a demon, adheres to the totality as well as to the details of his work, to the totality as well as to the details of his life. The fragmentarist Michelangelo lacked intimacy with nature, too, and he was also highly anthropocentric. On the other hand Leonardo da Vinci enjoyed closer contact with nature; so his work was less fragmentary, although he was an intellectual as well as an anthropocentric. To take a modern example, Marcel Proust, in describing entangled mental problems, still succeeded time and again in rendering the beauty and vitality of nature. Like Leonardo da Vinci, who was attracted by grotesque faces and loved to draw horrid grimaces, Kafka showed considerable interest in the description of nauseous objects and the invention or portrayal of sadistic happenings ("The Penal Colony"). However, the attempt to overcome nausea and aversion, which is a result of religious sublimation, is unsuccessful ("The Metamorphosis"). Franz Werfel, in his poem "Jesus and the Path of the Carrions" glorifies the overcoming of aversion as the highest symbol of all-embracing redemption. So does that Buddhistic epigram about the mendicant friar who receives his charity bread from a leper.

"And as he threw to him the bite
There fell a finger in the dish."

292

The friar, nonetheless, eats the morsel

"and while he ate and afterwards
no nausea did to him occur."

The epigram concludes with the remarkable and quite humanistic revelation:

"But who took this upon himself
Is citizen of all the world."

Kafka struggled sincerely for this highest degree of Franciscan humility and self-denial. But nature and the recognition of its equilibrium remained unattainable. Perceiving man and mankind in their purely abstract essence, he had to look at life from a disconnected viewpoint. The attempts to face life in spite of this are dependent upon the possession of a religious ethos which waves of skepticism denied.

Kafka's life and work are identical phenomena. Fulfillment of life and work is found in its preparation. No sooner does it take shape than it is over. Such a conception may originate from a feeling of fear but it may equally be the last conclusion of wisdom. Whatever happens is subject to innumerable viewpoints and produces its opposite at the same time. A trivial and seemingly logical perception of life considers it natural that something black cannot, rationally, simultaneously be white. Nevertheless, a writer whose descriptions of world and man proceed from such categorizations offers an embellished and not a sincere picture. Kafka, on the contrary, feels that every *esse* becomes problematical and conflicting since something black might be white at the same time; that everything displays all conceivable colors at once, and that the portrayal of these contradictory values creates the only true and genuinely symbolical literary work. A so-called unambiguous character remains Kafka's private as well as his poetical daydream. His failure to make this daydream a living reality results from his incapacity to enter into nature, to give himself away to "oak and rock."

His own soul, as well as the soul of his creatures, is so concerned with its own, has so much to discover in itself and to

293

compare with other souls, that it can never reach "the oak and the rock." It is the soul that offers always new objects of contemplation which are never ending. However, as Goethe said, "each new object, carefully looked upon, creates in us a new organ of contemplation," and every such organ produces new aims, and so on. Unattainability ("An Imperial Message," "The Great Wall of China") is the real secret of all human existence, of our relation to God and of our despair. Comfort is to be found, perhaps, only in the fact that unattainability is to be encountered everywhere and in everything. Thus, man, by virtue of his meditative mind, fails in his practical obligations. The Land Surveyor in *The Castle* wants to do a certain job but he is distracted by innumerable other happenings, his initiative is criss-crossed by steadily increasing hindrances and so his life passes by before he ever reaches the castle. Human life is to Kafka nothing but a road of obstacles. Inhibitive forces interfere with all endeavors. This is the subject of *The Castle,* of *Amerika* and of *The Trial,* a novel very comparable to the "Circumlocution Office" described by Charles Dickens in the tenth chapter of *Little Dorrit.* There, too, honest efforts are frustrated by endlessly entangled red tape produced by institutions devoid of all humaneness and existing only for their own sakes.

In *The Castle* and *The Trial,* there is a kind of cosmic bureaucracy of fate administered by fabulous authorities. "Whether there are control authorities? . . . There is nothing else but control authorities. . . . Official decisions are shy like young maidens. . . . Thus, people are working on their own confusion. . . . To make it easy and to avoid unnecessary talking, our officials do accept bribes but, as a matter of fact, you can get nowhere with it." In *Amerika,* too, the adventurous story of the young Prague lad consists of the struggle with labyrinthine institutions and with the most delicate, impenetrable and cheating webs of a world in which everything just established immediately renders itself dubious again. No sooner does something show a distinct and definite character than it restricts itself again by adding a "but" or a "however" and thus changes its countenance.

Not only mankind but, consequently, all of its institutions as well bear a double or even a multiple face. Now since man remains the measure and man changes himself continuously, becoming great or little, short- or far-sighted, there may be giants who appear microscopic and there may be pygmies who look like giants. Only a life devoted incessantly to constructing and reinforcing walls of safety and security ("The Burrow") is fit to resist such nightmares. But even so, one cannot succeed. Not even Kafka's Poseidon is actually familiar with all of his waters and oceans for he has to spend all of his time managing them.

The Land Surveyor in *The Castle*, a character made of humbleness and obstinacy, fails because he wants to make compromises and because he cannot afford to devote himself uncompromisingly to the castle. The necessity of giving himself away is suggested to him over and over again by the villagers. He, however, wants to dwell in the village as well as in the castle. He wants to be at home in this as well as in the other world, in other words, in matter as well as in spirit. None of these attempts, naturally, leads to any success. Similar ordeals are set forth in "Investigations of a Dog": "Why do I not do as the others—live in harmony with my people, in silence, and accept whatever disturbs the harmony, ignoring it as a small error in the great account, always keeping in mind the things that bind us happily together, not those that drive us again and again, although by sheer force, out of our social circle?" Obviously, such a self-accusation points not only to individual and personal problems but to the Jewish problem as well. The same applies to "The Burrow" and, of course, to *The Castle*. ("No one is keeping you here, but still this is not yet expulsion.") You do not come from "oak and rock." The Greek sees; the Jew listens (Hans Kohn: *The Idea of Nationalism*): "Hearken, Israel!" The problematical position of the Jew lies in the abstractness of his relation to God, which is being complicated, simultaneously, by the idea of mutual interdependence. The Lord is the geometrical point of all human emotions and, reciprocally, human life, in all of its particulars and in its totality, is the geometrical point of the Lord. There is no room for intimacy with nature. The modern Jewish problem is, moreover, accentuated by Jewish landlessness. Thus the Jew depends utterly on listening, and to listen means the most abstract kind of perception, as the tune or the sound is but the abstract result of the mutual relation between motion and matter. (Reading is but a transcribed listening.) The reality of "the oak and the rock" as well as the reality of man and his internal and external attitudes exist for Kafka in only two forms: as symbol and as adjustment (*Zurechtlegung*).

As symbol: the noblest teachers of mankind used the parable, the metaphor, the symbol because the simple value of words could not suffice to express their ideas. "Whatever happens is a symbol, and in expressing itself completely, it points, at the same time, to something higher" (Goethe). Nothing is merely what it is and how it is. It is the privilege of poetry to recognize and interpret the symbolical meaning. If, however, in attempting to answer such an extraordinary demand, the poet lacks the power of giving himself away to the factual and to the manifest, if he is unable to compose himself by amalgamating with nature, if he does not repose in the tranquillity and integrity of nature, then his own soul becomes to him only a source of unrest. He is surrounded by a chaotic multitude of everchanging symbols but none of them offers him the comfort of synthesis. He traces out things and their means like a confidential agent, he follows their clues for a while only to leave them and hunt after new ones, he comes and goes, he is here and there. Kafka demonstrates the symbolical character of every happening by showing that all human life is subject to guidance by unknown powers. This is the case not only in his three chief works but in his numerous shorter pieces. Whatever takes place is not only just an event. It points further. Who could explain what it really means? Behind the thing lies the mystery. A writer who would speak out and say, "Mind you, I can reveal it. The mystery is thus and so," would be but a naïve figure. Things are not so simple, although we desire nothing more than that they and ourselves should possess that simplicity.

As adjustment: every contemplation proceeds as an adjustment. Without these adjustments that are changing with each subject and object, the world would be inconceivable, disintegrated and chaotical. Principles, orders and forms not contained in the world *a priori*, but brought into it by human thoughts and assigned to it by us, are merely adjustments. The shape of things is not owned by the things themselves but is produced by man. Thus, daily, he becomes creator of the world. By adjusting he conceives. The objectivity and adequacy of its adjustments make the great mind. The very isolated, solely subjective and egoistically focused adjustment makes the madman. The adjustment is the interpretation of the symbolical contents of things. The adjustment is at the same time the breathing-spell of skepticism, beginning with the most primitive physical law up to the cognition: "There is a God in us; if he stirs then we glow." No less is *Paradise Lost* an adjustment than Mill's *System of Logic*. Kafka's entire work is nothing but an inexhaustible sequence of adjustments, each of them intended to overcome the immanent contradictions of existence. This intention in itself means obviously that the goal cannot be reached (just as it is with Kierkegaard). For if the contradiction could be resolved it would not be a real contradiction but only a seeming one. It would be blasphemous to suppose that Kafka was concerned with only seeming contradictions or that he did not recognize them as such immediately. The ethos lies in the fact that efforts are made to overcome contradictions although one is conscious of their insolvability. This is the problem of faith, the moral problem *kat exochen*, and from this point of view too, Kafka presents himself as an ethical and religious mind of the highest order. The great moral act of man is his decision to make an attempt. The strength to continue rests upon faith alone and the outcome remains utterly uncertain and incalculable in reality. It is the *decision* that matters, not some instinctive performance made in a kind of trance. The great risk, of which Abraham the Patriarch's attitude (Sören Kierkegaard, *Fear and Trembling*) remains the eternal example, is avoided through indecision by Kafka's man from the country ("Before the Law"), and consequently he misses the Law.

A poet whose personal meditations abound in self-accusations does not treat mankind with the correction rod of a preceptor. He knows too much about man being lost in the world. He has penetrated too deeply into his own weaknesses. He has suffered too much from the demonism of propensities. To such a poet, the political or historical "Yes" or "No" is but an exhibit of

297

the infinite and inevitable human sorrow and harm. Therefore, he does not consider it particularly subject to his judgment. He will avoid actual or political allusions. He will write non-historically and only the mythos by which history is absorbed and generalized may occasionally influence his writings.

Kafka is aware of the Talmudic wisdom according to which the good one makes his bad impulse the Lord's vehicle; but he knows, too, that such an act demands two presuppositions of grace: goodness and ability to decide. "Woe to that man by whom the offence cometh!" However the premise, "it must needs be that offences come," does not permit evasion of responsibility. These are the labyrinths in which man misses God and God misses man. It remains a metaphysical question whether the Lord of Grace may rightfully demand from man the decision to make an effort; but within the staggering world of insecurity this decision affords the only support which man may grant to himself.

Within a world of insecurity, there are no unimportant and secondary matters. If there were, then there would exist a basis for a distinctive classification and the way of acting would be settled. In a literary mirroring of a world of insecurity nothing, not even the slightest act, passes unnoticed. The seemingly casual and insignificant may be deemed worthy of a close-up, the mundane trivialities may be found to be something significantly noteworthy. All things and appearances are marked by special and variable proportions which make them odd, deformed, grotesque but, at the same time, new and interesting. Thus, Kafka may talk about a casual fact, about an incidental occurrence as if it were something never heard of, and he becomes an explorer of trifles, a researcher of the spiritual microcosm. This searching for minutiae produces the impressive and almost scientific gradualness of his writing.

Consideration of all this leads one to feel how wonderful it would be to come from "the oak and the rock," simply to exist and to lead a well disposed family life with the unsophisticated joys of home. In this way, one may avoid the bad luck of the bachelor ("*Das Unglück des Junggesellen*") who suddenly stands there "with a body and a head and, therefore, with

298

a forehead, too, to strike it with his hand." Kafka intended to write "A Story of a Simple Man with Regular Habits." It never was written. If he had written it, it would probably have turned out to be the story of an exceedingly complex creature with amazingly peculiar qualities. Personally, he found himself in the position of Odysseus of whom we are told in Plato's "Politeia" that dwelling in Hades he desired nothing more ardently than to lead "the life of a simple private person."

The very problem of the conscious man is the everlasting conflict between his tendency to isolate himself and his desire to be like the rest. No less, this is the conflict of Jewry within this world, and it remains likewise insolvable. Neither the ego nor the object can solve it. Jewry is only a group example of an otherwise individual problem of mind. Whatever Kafka wrote is, therefore, as much Jewish as it is generally human. Thus, it ought to be granted to Max Brod to interpret Kafka utterly from the Jewish point of view whereas others may consider Kafka's Judaism only as a ferment of his work and may take him as an analyst of the human soul in general. The narrow interpretation is no less right than the broad one. This, too, makes Kafka an outstanding author.

To Kafka Judaism was only the personification of his religiousness in general. His simple phrase, "Writing as a form of prayer," may be considered the key to his works. The quality of his religiousness is shown by the following sentences: "Man can not live without an abiding faith in something indestructible in himself, even though this indestructible element as well as this faith may remain forever obscure to him. This obscurity finds its expression in belief in a personal God." The power of this God manifests itself mostly in the unpretentious and the small, in the unnoted and the despised. Everywhere and suddenly man may be summoned before God's tribunal. In Kafka's continual discussions between the self-accusing defendant and the divine, for instance in *The Trial,* there certainly is a kind of modern Job-like attitude. He does not cease to quarrel with God who, at the same time, appears to be ultimately vindicated by this quarreling. This is the substance of almost all Kafka's works. It is most obvious in *The Castle* where the introspection of the hero is most profound

299

while he vainly struggles to attain admittance to the castle and has to follow an endless, complicated road abounding in bizarre sinuosities and in innumerable internal and external impediments.

True, the Jew as a stranger, and the loneliness of a Jew, are expressed not only by the hero of *The Castle*, but also in Kafka's various animal stories, as for instance, in "The Giant Mole," in "Josephine the Singer," in "Jackals and Arabs" or even in "The Metamorphosis"; but the example of the Jew, being the most obvious and perfect case, suggested itself to the author as a symbol of the general strangeness and loneliness of man. He presents us with the innumerable means, cautious experiments, deliberate undertakings man has to invent and the fabulous habitations, underground canals and labyrinthine zigzags to overcome the Babel-like confusion, the incommensurability of phenomena, the askew contrapositions of life, the lack of mutual understanding. He shows us how man struggles for regions which lie beyond his life and which cannot be reached by his soul. These, however, are religious problems in general and cannot with reason be confined behind the walls of a solely Jewish attitude, notwithstanding the fact that it is this attitude which gave Kafka his standard of judgment and the principal material for his most impressive symbols together with certain formidable Talmudic weapons of his style. In this respect he reminds us of Spinoza who also drew from Jewish sources both deliberately and unconsciously and who likewise achieved a far-reaching general effect.

There are religious roots to Kafka's transcendental and tragic irony, too, and to his sense of humor which explores the peculiar and the grotesque. This irony and this humor result from his deep sympathy with the creature which always and in every individual case offers some peculiarity and which, consequently, always falls to the mercy of a problematic fate. Kafka's sense of humor, therefore, is but the demoniacal glittering of his melancholy. Somebody performs something which apparently is quite commonplace. Under the X-rays of the discerning, however, it is bizarre because that person had been unconscious of the real symbolical significance of his action. It is just this esteem for the importance of the scope of haphazard fortuity where Kafka's religiousness manifests itself. He always discovers the hidden relationship that is active between the smallest and the greatest facts and phenomena. Just why are human beings so inevitably bizarre? Because an abyss gapes between the divine and the human worlds; their mutual relations bridge unfathomable empty spaces and can be grasped but by irony.

Nowhere, perhaps, did Kafka approach the coveted simplification as much as in his novel *Amerika*. There he displays his deepest connection with nature. His invention of a romantic America corresponds amazingly to the real one. His vision of this country proves to be surprisingly perfect. So is his superb description of the newcomer's difficulties. If he had ever actually visited America he could not have offered a more competent picture. It was Goethe who once stated that there exists something like an "exact fancy." This kind of fancy made *Amerika* possible. The atmosphere of the port of New York never has been rendered so thrillingly as in the first chapter of this novel ("The Stoker"). The troublesome life of an elevator operator working at a provincial American hotel is described in a striking and convincing manner. There is to be found in Kafka's novel a true characterization of American habits and qualities, even though this America shows a symbolical face, and the whole plot develops within spiritual scenery. Kafka believes in "the signs and miracles still existing particularly in America." He certainly is right in so doing. For if, according to Franz Werfel, childhood represents the genius age of man, then America still lives at the genius age of a nation abounding in signs and wonders. Over the highways of America Kafka observes that tremendous radiation which stupefies the traveler often enough in reality, "an overwhelming light diffused, carried away and eagerly returned again and again by the multitude of objects, a luminosity which seems as corporeal to the beguiled eye as if, over this road, an all-covering pane of glass were smashed incessantly with all possible force."

Kafka was not yet forty-one when he died. However, "our task is co-extensive with our life" which becomes the more sublime the more unattainable its goals and the more painful and hopeless its struggles for decision.

the tragedy of faithlessness

hans joachim schoeps

What it is to be so overwhelmed by a mythical awe, by the remembrance of a thing past, that the shadow of God in his absence overpowers and destroys man—without grace, without forgiveness, without purpose—can be seen in the poet Franz Kafka, prophet of the message of salvation, which in this time of transition has been reversed into a message of damnation. Franz Kafka who came from a German-Jewish family in Prague which had abandoned its faith, was neither a philosophical nor a theological thinker, but a poet, in whose works mythical concepts, dream fantasies, were precipitated; this fact will determine the method of our further presentation. We shall call "mythical" a mode of thinking whose content is not determined concretely and directly, but which is veiled and without application to practical reality. Here is recalled the essence of things gone by, that which has sunk into the past and which can no longer reach the daylight of the present, but remains in the timeless twilight of intuition. Mythical thinking as the remembrance of something forgotten in the shadow of vague recollections is the form which shapes the whole of Kafka's works. The center of all of them is the inex-

303

haustible phenomenon of having forgotten, a forgetting that forgets itself; that which has been forgotten can no longer be named, a meaningful motivation seems no longer possible, what remains is only an oppressive vague recollection of having forgotten. The following passage from one of his stories in *The Great Wall of China* is revealing: "I can well understand the hesitations of my generation; it is not really hesitating, it is the forgetting of a dream dreamt thousands of nights ago and forgotten a thousand times." But that the thing forgotten can no longer be recalled, that only its shadow remains in the consciousness like a dark threat, this depresses man, for it causes him to be concerned about his present condition. "And it is just this forgetting which produces a certain sadness, uncertainty, unrest, a certain longing for times past, which beclouds the present. And yet this longing is an important element of the life impulse or perhaps this impulse itself."

This then is the tragic position of him who is still bound to revelation even if he no longer can seize upon it. It is not pure, utterly inconceivable nothingness, but a something forgotten and vanished, which man cannot recall, but cannot renounce either. Hence the perhaps hopeless search for a meaning, this longing for the fullness of meaning which the past once possessed and which was joined to the presence of God—this longing begins to dominate the impulse of life or perhaps becomes this very impulse itself. All his life Franz Kafka remained in negativity, in the state of not-possessing and not-knowing, but invisible forces drove him like a hunted animal to search for God and for the lost Law of God. "The chase passes through me and tears me to pieces—but somewhere rescue is waiting, and the chasers lead me there." (Diary of March 9, 1922).

Franz Kafka was a Jew; inherited faith become mythical drove him to search unceasingly for the Law; for this is the nature of the catastrophe, that God's Law has lost the world and that now the world is drifting along in emptiness, that man who has lost the consciousness of being created has also lost all traits of individuality and in the impersonal anonymity becomes faceless, a thing, an object. In Kafka's world of symbols there appears such a ghostlike creature, called Odradek, which means, according to the Slavonic components of this word, something like

304

"escaped from the Law." We learn of this thing-creature Odradek, which symbolizes man's having become a thing, the "I" having become an "it," that it had assumed the senseless form of a reel of thread and had become an automatically running mechanism. Half alive and half dead, it hesitates in the balance. The question where does Odradek live is answered by: Residence indefinite. But the continuation of this passage is revealing: "One is tempted to believe that this monstrosity formerly possessed a purposeful shape . . ." in other words Odradek in former times had been something else. But immediately following this it is said that no evidence of this can be found. This is the situation; nothing more specific can be said about the "why" and "wherefore" of the human condition. Odradek=Odradek. Everything else is uncertain. And it is even uncertain whether Odradek is alive and therefore shares the characteristic of all life—death; for "everything that dies has had before some kind of activity, and has consumed itself in it; but this does not apply to Odradek." Nothing remains therefore but doubts and possibilities which are nothing more than possibilities. Nothing is certain; only this, that the possibilities oppress like a nightmare. The only certainty is uncertainty. The title of this sketch is uncannily revealing: "The Anxieties of the [Heavenly] Father."

Nevertheless this situation of no longer being a person does not signify neutrality; man continues to search and he divines that the goal of his search is his lost personality. One of the strangest observations about Kafka's novels is this, that on closer inspection no figure in them possesses the character of a person in the sense of genuine individuality; their faces are always borrowed faces, acquired in the course of their existence. In Kafka's novels the people hurry past one another without ever really recognizing each other, always hurrying toward the assumed or real goal, though yet without ever reaching it. In the two great novels *The Castle* and *The Trial*, which had to remain incomplete because of the impossibility of attaining the goal, this goal is always the same; the recovery of lost salvation. Only the directions are opposite in the two cases. In *The Castle*, K. (symbol for man in general) in his despair at having lost God and himself tries to take heaven by storm. From the unknown

305

distance the man K. has set out to reach the "castle," an edifice apparently perceptible but actually completely mysterious, being terrestrial and celestial at the same time. But K. is not desirous of entering the castle itself, he merely wants to become a member of the village community which owes fealty to the castle and is happy in the banality of everyday life. But at the end he finds himself further away from the castle than at the beginning. Heaven remains closed to him and its instructions completely unintelligible. Of the messages issuing from the castle it is said: "The reflections to which they give occasion are endless, and where one happens to stop is only determined by chance, therefore the meaning arrived at is accidental." But an anxious unrest which cannot be stilled again drives K. out of all certainties and hiding to renew the assault, to try new ruses, though continued failures have absolutely convinced him that entrance is impossible and no will-power can ever force it. But in the course of the story the reader vaguely surmises: the ultimate reason for K.'s failure is perhaps only this, that he cannot have faith and commits the error of trying to force Grace upon himself. For he lacked one thing during all his struggles, during all his life: the pious conviction, the hopeful confidence that what the castle would give him would be that which he considered good for him —that which eternity finds good. Therefore, because of his impatience, the castle refuses to receive him during his life. When he finally breaks down, K. gains the painful insight: "He who searches, finds not; he who does not search, is found."

If, in *The Castle,* man fails to obtain the lost Law and with it the possession of Grace, the procedure is the opposite in the parallel novel *The Trial:* here the Law sets out to search for man; Heaven tries K., the man. K. himself is not aware of any guilt; nevertheless real messengers from an imaginary court appear and threaten him in his security. For man is always in the position of defendant. And precisely because K. does not realize this or at least does not wish to recognize this situation, his guilt increases, grows to immeasurable proportions and finally requires his execution in punishment. To the end K. is guilty, since in his thinking he never takes leave of the ethical and legal concepts, and since he remains upright to the last moment because no evidence of any specific wrongdoing can be produced. But it is through his conviction of being right that he puts himself in the wrong with the (celestial) court and, without knowing why, himself brings about the final punishment by pronouncing judgment on himself, again unwittingly. This is the religious meaning of the novel *The Trial:* the real significance of the trial is the mythical progress in the objectivization of the guilt, but this process remains below the level of consciousness. The metaphysical implication of the unknown but real guilt is this, that the awareness of sinfulness is lacking. If K. had been able to recognize his guilt he would have arrived at an overwhelming feeling of the sinfulness of existence and so have been saved in the eyes of Heaven, for then the opportunity for repentance would have offered itself. This way, however, he is beyond good and evil, not because he wants to be there (here Nietzsche's position has become more radical, more terrifying), but because he is no longer capable of recognizing the distinction between good and evil which has its foundation in revealed Law. What remains is only the fear of having missed the real purpose of life, of having become guilty in a way which is beyond all imaginable guilt, because what it means here is the total guilt of a misconducted life which can only be atoned for by its own destruction, so that the trial undertaken for unknown reasons in the prosecution of unknown wrongdoings calls unequivocally for capital punishment.

With this we have reached the extreme limits of the possible situations of man: nihilism has dissolved religious faith into mythical feeling. No more meaning is recognized in life, the Law is forgotten, earthly objects have made themselves independent, man floats in emptiness, Heaven is removed from Earth. Nevertheless man does not cease to search for the Law and to assault Heaven. But even if he vainly tries to abandon his efforts, he is tortured by feelings of anxiety and guilt. Man is not delivered from his duality, even though his destination and the Law have been lost. But he can neither recognize nor forget it. This is the tragic situation of man today, for whom God is dead, if, detached from the faith and the tradition of the past, he wants to obtain God's revelation by means of *his* knowledge and *his* understanding of the world.

307

Therefore the crisis of transition, the religious despair of modern man, who, detached from tradition, asks the question of revelation, must be sharpened in Franz Kafka some degrees beyond the normal. Because for a Jew who by his nature is intended for the Law, it is a most frightful discovery that in our times the Law has lost the world. Hence Jewish faith in the tragic position must remain directed toward recovering the lost Law. The world lost by the Law is different, more heavily fraught with disaster than the world of the Christian in which God once appeared corporeally, and in which the reflected glow of the epiphany can never be totally extinguished. Knowledge of the Law of Revelation and the fear of God make it possible to carry out the Law and to sanctify life; without these the Jewish world finally fell into the tragic situation; that is, the existential question led it to the edge of the abyss. But a world which has lost the Law must desperately search for it, because only through the Law can be recalled the order of creation in which true life is rooted. But the Law has become unintelligible, the entrance definitely forbidden.

The Trial contains a legend which expresses in symbolic form the situation of modern man before the Law:

> Before the Law stands a door-keeper on guard. To this door-keeper there comes a man from the country who begs for admittance to the Law. But the door-keeper says that he cannot admit the man at the moment. The man, on reflection, asks if he will be allowed, then, to enter later. "It is possible," answers the door-keeper, "but not at this moment." Since the door leading into the Law stands open as usual and the door-keeper steps to one side, the man bends down to peer through the entrance. When the door-keeper sees that, he laughs and says: "If you are so strongly tempted, try to get in without my permission. But note that I am powerful. And I am only the lowest door-keeper. From hall to hall keepers stand at every door, one more powerful than the other. Even the third of these has an aspect that even I cannot bear to look at." These are difficulties which the man from the country

308

has not expected to meet, the Law, he thinks, should be accessible to every man and at all times, but when he looks more closely at the door-keeper in his furred robe, with his huge pointed nose and long, thin, Tartar beard, he decides that he had better wait until he gets permission to enter. The door-keeper gives him a stool and lets him sit down at the side of the door. There he sits waiting for days and years. He makes many attempts to be allowed in and wearies the door-keeper with his importunity. The door-keeper often engages him in brief conversation, asking him about his home and about other matters, but the questions are put quite impersonally, as great men put questions, and always conclude with the statement that the man cannot be allowed to enter yet. The man, who has equipped himself with many things for his journey, parts with all he has, however valuable, in the hope of bribing the door-keeper. The door-keeper accepts it all, saying, however, as he takes each gift: "I take this only to keep you from feeling that you have left something undone." During all these long years the man watches the door-keeper almost incessantly. He forgets about the other door-keepers, and this one seems to him the only barrier between himself and the Law. In the first years he curses his evil fate aloud; later, as he grows old, he only mutters to himself. He grows childish, and since in his prolonged watch he has learned to know even the fleas in the door-keeper's fur collar, he begs the very fleas to help him and to persuade the door-keeper to change his mind. Finally his eyes grow dim and he does not know whether the world is really darkening around him or whether his eyes are only deceiving him. But in the darkness he can now perceive a radiance that streams immortally from the door of the Law. Now his life is drawing to a close. Before he dies, all that he has experienced during the whole time of his sojourn condenses in his mind into one question, which he has never yet put to the door-keeper. He beckons the door-keeper, since he can no longer raise his stiffening body. The door-keeper has to bend far down to hear him, for the

309

difference in size between them has increased very much to the man's disadvantage. "What do you want to know now?" asks the door-keeper, "you are insatiable." "Everyone strives to attain the Law," answers the man, "how does it come about, then, that in all these years no one has come seeking admittance but me?" The door-keeper perceives that the man is at the end of his strength and that his hearing is failing, so he bellows in his ear: "No one but you could gain admittance through this door, since this door was intended only for you. I am now going to shut it!" *

This story, which has the awe-inspiring power of a mythical legend, reveals modern man's existence without the Law. Man—even though he may have the humility and simplicity of the "man from the country"—can no longer reach the Law which is supposed to be "accessible always and to everyone." But this does not exhaust the tragic possibilities inherent in the tragic situation, it is not even the decisive factor. Not only can man obtain no understanding of the Law as a supernatural revelation, but the message from Heaven does not even reach the ear of man. Not only the road from Earth to Heaven, but the road from Heaven to Earth is too long to be traveled. This tragic experience finds its poetic expression in the legend "The Imperial Message." Characteristically Kafkian, it combines symbolism with hard reality:

> The emperor—it is said—has sent to you individually, to his wretched subject, to the infinitesimal shadow that has fled into the remotest distance before the imperial sun, it is to you that the emperor has sent a message from his death-bed. He had the messenger kneel down by his bed and whispered the message into his ear; he considered it so very important that he had the

* In the context of the novel this legend has the significance of a hieratic text. A priest tells it to K. in the Cathedral at the moment when he enters the decisive phase of his crisis with the Court. In order to emphasize the significance of this text, it is followed by a conversation more than three times as long as the story itself about the various possibilities of explaining and interpreting it.

messenger repeat it into his ear. By nodding his head he confirmed the correctness of what was said. And in the presence of all the witnesses of his death—all the intervening walls are broken down and the great ones of the empire stand in a circle on the outer staircases that ascend tall and wide—in the presence of all these he dispatched the messenger. The messenger set forth immediately; a powerful, tireless man; stretching out now this arm, now the other one, he clears a path through the multitude; if he encounters any opposition he points to his breast which bears the sign of the sun; and he makes his way easily, like nobody else. But the multitude is so great, there is no end to their dwellings. If a clear field were to open up before him, how he would fly, and soon you would hear the magnificent pounding of his fists upon your door. But instead of that, how needlessly he exerts himself; he is still forcing his way through the chambers of the innermost palace; he will never overcome them; and if he did, nothing would be gained; he would have to fight his way down the staircases; and if he succeeded in this, nothing would be gained; he would have the courtyards to cross; and after the courtyards the second surrounding palace, and again staircases and courtyards; and again a palace; and so on for thousands of years; and if he should finally plunge through the outermost gate—but that could never, never be—the capital would lie before him, the center of the world, piled high with its sediment. No one can get through this, particularly with a message from the dead. But you sit at your window and dream about it when evening comes. (*Translated by Rosa M. Beuscher*)

This little story contains the tragic experience of a whole life. It is decisive for the situation of man that he still dreams of the arrival of the heavenly message. It is true that an infinite distance separates Earth from Heaven, and man's prayers even if he were still able to pray, seem to reach it no longer. Nevertheless, in the face of the closed heaven, man adheres to his feeling that the word from above is the redeeming truth. In con-

311

trast to the Nietzsche disciples, Martin Heidegger and Ernest Jünger, K. cannot draw their conclusions from the hopelessness of the distance, namely to rely solely upon himself and to overcome his persistent feelings of anxiety and guilt by establishing on his own authority a new destiny and a new salvation for man. Kafka stands on his rights toward the closed Heaven, he insists on having a place—although forgotten—in the unknown sequence of generations bound to one another according to unknown laws before the unknown God. Thanks to his insistence upon a tradition underlying his claims, even though ignorant of its laws, and in spite of the solitude and uncertainty of his situation, something like a consoling vision of the destiny of man dawns upon him. "He does not live for the sake of his personal life; he does not think for the sake of his personal thoughts. It seems to him that he lives and thinks under the compulsion of a family, which, it is true, is itself superabundant in life and thought, but for which he constitutes, in obedience to some law unknown to him, a formal necessity. Because of this unknown family and this unknown law he cannot be exempted."

This, however, remains certain; that to live in such an irremediable situation is sheer desperation. Kafka's whole life has been one of despair. But this situation of concentrated despair approaches so closely the divine paradox that a mere gesture from beyond can change everything. Only for this reason can man endure his unrelieved wretchedness. For here, beside the irony which endures the finite for the sake of the infinite—this is why Kafka is a master of irony—lies that tremendous power of messianic hope, which, the flimsier its foundation, the more vigorously it arises. And only in an existence of complete despair is this "insane" messianic hope, as Kafka calls it, possible; a hope which in Kafka's private life was, in spite of all misery and suffering, a real power. In all the literature of the world no document better testifies to the strength of hope and messianic expectation than these words of the poet Franz Kafka about the mythos of faith in the tragic situation: "A first sign of nascent knowledge is the desire for death. This life seems unendurable, any other unattainable. One is no longer ashamed of wishing to die; one prays to be conducted from the old cell that one hates into a new one that one has yet to hate. There is in this a vestige of faith that during the change the Master may chance to walk along the corridor, contemplate the prisoner, and say: 'You must not lock up this one again. He is come to me.' "

Translated by Lienhard Bergel.

the bankruptcy of faith

edwin berry burgum

We speak sometimes of our own writers of the "lost generation" of the twenties. But such terms are relative. American writers were by no means so lost at that time as their contemporaries in defeated Germany, and the importance of Kafka is that he was without question the most lost of them all. The fact that he was born of Jewish middle-class parents in Prague when it was under Austrian domination only emphasized an alienation and insecurity which had become typical of the middle class generally. Culturally, moreover, Kafka was a German. He lived in Germany and wrote in the German language. And, though his writing was mostly done before the First World War, his attempt to escape a dominating father left him afraid of the responsibilities of freedom in a way symbolic of the later passage of German society from the tyranny of the Empire to the Weimar Republic. His own deep-seated despondency, which had not yet routed traditional obsessions of blind faith and vague hope, lay bare the perplexities of mind and the vacillations of conduct typical of German life generally under the Weimar Republic. His own diseased personality symbolized the disease at the heart of

315

German society. The progress of his personal deterioration paralleled the degeneration of the society that produced him. And his own life ended as abruptly and prematurely as that of the young republic, though he died of tuberculosis some years before Hitler set himself up as the brutal father-symbol of the German people. Whether the work of so disordered a talent will live at all or only for a select audience may be disputable. But its historic importance can hardly be denied. Kafka's novels cut through the distracting irrelevancies of superficial realism and afford a direct participation in the degeneration of personality of the petty bourgeoisie which began under Bismarck and was completed under Hitler. They present this degeneration even more vividly to the foreign reader than *The Magic Mountain* does, because Kafka is incapable of any reasoned judgment upon his material. He takes us into the personality structure itself, remaining unconscious of its nature since he shares it, and unconscious of its concealment in ordinary men beneath the conventions of social intercourse because of his own abnormality.

This interpretation of Kafka has received curious confirmation in the kind of praise lavished upon him by the small group of his admirers that existed in Germany and repeated by its even smaller American counterpart. They have extolled him not for the reasons which I have put forward here, but for those which would have appealed alike to his own attitude and those of the Weimar Republic. They have given an almost hypnotic attention to his perverse and mystical religious faith. In that conflict which kept him morose and helpless between a belief in God he could not renounce and a skepticism he could not deny, they have condoned the skepticism out of veneration for the faith. They have not seen that this dubious faith is psychological evidence of the dissolution of the reasoning process itself. Kafka was incapable of the common sense of everyday life, so obscure and contradictory had become the springs of personal conduct in him. Like Kierkegaard, his favorite philosopher, he represents the breakdown of mysticism itself, both as a discipline and a philosophy. In the light of the great religious mystics of history, to emphasize Kafka's religious mysticism can only mean to share his own incapacity for reasoned judgment.

Only Max Brod, the wisest among his admirers and the closest to him, has suggested the possibility of a non-mystical approach to his work. Brod has published—apparently out of sheer sense of duty to the facts, since he does not relate it to his own exposition of Kafka's mysticism—considerable evidence that his personality verged upon the psychopathic. We may anticipate that sooner or later psychiatrists will discover that his novels are as rewarding an object of investigation as those of Dostoyevsky. The types of abnormal personality are not as varied as in the pre-revolutionary Russian writer. But the presentation of the particular type of which Kafka was himself an example is even more rich and detailed within its limits since he became progressively more alien from formal attitudes as his short life ran its course. But a novel is presumably something more than the book of devotions for a degenerate mysticism or a case history in psychiatry. It is also a communication to some sort of general public. I shall therefore limit my interest in the theological and psychiatric aspects of Kafka's work to their bearing upon his novels as an expression of certain patterns of living in our own era and as the satisfaction of the esthetic needs of a limited contemporary audience.

Since Kafka's last stories are almost exclusively devoted to his hallucinations, they may be used to clarify the orientation I am seeking. I take for this purpose the most extremely subjective of them all, "The Burrow." In this short story, which has a beginning but no end, the hero conceives that he is being pursued by what must be vaguely called enemies. But there is nothing vague about the defenses with which he surrounds himself. He first digs a tunnel into the earth in which he hides like a mole. He conceals the entrance with foliage, and for a time feels safe from pursuit. But it seems wise to make safety doubly sure by digging many branches to his tunnel. Thus he will be able to elude the enemy at numerous points by circling around behind him. Next, in case through some accident he should not be able to do so, he decides to make an exit at the other end. But no sooner has he completed this escape into the upper world than he realizes with dismay that he has also created another possible source of attack. Enemies may now enter at both ends and leave him caught at the middle. He becomes so frightened that he leaves his tunnel altogether. But above ground, even though he hides in the bushes, he feels unprotected on every side; he lacks the tangible comfort of both walls and darkness. So he returns, determined at least to protect his valuables (which remain as abstract as his enemies) by building a special vault for them. His labor is baffled by the sandy soil. But he manages to beat the wall firm by desperate blows of his head; and he is delighted to discover that the blood flowing from his wounds actually welds the sand into a cement. His satisfaction is immediately interrupted, however, by the faint sound of digging elsewhere. The disconcerting suspicion crosses his mind that his enemies may have turned his own plan against him, and started digging parallel tunnels so that they may break through almost anywhere at the strategic moment. Though he listens intently and in every part of his maze, he cannot define the direction of the sound. He tries to close his ears to see whether it is a figment of his imagination. But he is too excited to make a fair test. In a crisis when his enemies may fall upon him at any moment, he flings himself the more hysterically into action. His only hope is to make the maze more labyrinthine. When the story breaks off, his frenzied digging is no longer guided by a plan and is already beginning to be baffled by fatigue.

That Kafka's anxieties have passed the norm and approached the psychotic in "The Burrow" is obvious. But there are curious proofs from the story that they have not yet reached the extreme and passed out of control. The first is a bit of symbolic action which shows that they are being kept in check by the sense of security he obtained from his disease. The image of blood from the hero's head which firmly cements the walls of his storage place for his valuables reveals Kafka's attitude toward his tuberculosis. Brod has quoted him as expressing relief that it obligated his breaking his engagement which had dragged on for five years. This passage makes it clear that his later hemorrhages afforded a more active protection of his spiritual values in general. The weakness of physical prostration by taking the burden from will and consciousness expiated his sense of guilt; and at the same time by diminishing his material values as a person

318

seemed to reduce the liability to attack from without. The progress of his bodily disease, in other words, retarded the progress of his mental disease. The second evidence is the communicability of the story as a whole. Kafka has used no eccentric imagery or autistic language, but the simplest, everyday diction. A child could understand the story as readily as an adult. Perhaps its lack of overtone, its lack of the irony I have allowed to creep into my summary, is pathetic evidence of his surviving will to remain sane, of his direct reaching out to an audience he is willing to assume is receptive, is certainly not "enemies." Indeed, the suggestion in the story, weak though it is, that the sounds may be imaginary is a literal measure of the degree of sanity remaining; while the complete absence of humor testifies to the desperateness of his situation. But at the same time his capacity to write is not only an unconscious appeal for help; it is also a temporary source of security; it is the part of himself most adequately under control. And paradoxically since his obsessions have become more simple as they grow more extreme, his stylistic expression of them can give him the satisfaction of becoming more simple too. The simple casualness of the style, its frank colloquial air, is somehow not inappropriate to the abnormality of content. A complete psychiatric investigation of Kafka would certainly shed light on that *terra incognita*, the nature of the creative talent in more normal persons.

But my problem here is rather with his audience. Presumably Kafka would not have developed as a writer and have eventually written "The Burrow" if he had not sensed a similar agony in the society around him. The presence of a Kafka cult proves that he was not mistaken. The existence of the story, as lucid as a parable from the Bible, must be taken as an alarming measure of the amount of similar anxiety in the Weimar Republic. If an investigation could be made, I think it would be discovered that a large percentage of Kafka's admirers (excluding of course many critics whose attitude must be in part one of professional interest) share his disorders of personality. In the problem of the relation of literature to its audience, therefore, I believe that Kafka is important evidence as to the meaning of "esthetic distortion," "literary idealism," the difference, in short,

319

between life and art. In the broadest sense, psychologically, we are permitted to conclude that art brings into the open the latent tendencies of society, whatever they may be. From this point of view, the Kafka cult would not necessarily be composed of persons as abnormal as he, but rather of those who possess similar tendencies which different life experiences may be holding in check or which are in progress of formation and doubtless will be formed more rapidly as a consequence of their admiration. I cannot imagine any other readers accepting Kafka without qualification. These alone will respond to his appeal to aid him by entering the confraternity of the doomed. For the time being, for them as for him, the very lucidity of "The Burrow" may be consoling. But in the end content passes out of esthetic control, the story breaks off; art ultimately fails in its attempt to control life.

With more normal readers the reaction, I think, must be more complex. We live in a period of unusual instability, and the average reader will not wish to add through his fiction to the amount of real anxiety circumstances are forcing upon him. He will reject "The Burrow" as repulsive, and probably decide the rest of Kafka is also a waste of time. A certain few may find a sadistic enjoyment in a story which seems to present anxieties they are free from. I find my own recollection of the story alternating between a recovery of its disturbing effect upon first reading and a protective recoil into humor; to take it as funny is to alienate one's self from contamination. The future will probably take it in similar fashion as a literary curiosity, though only a minority of readers will be interested at all. When we live in a society which permits us to accept its content without a sense of personal threat, it will appear too monotonous to sustain interest. Its concern with only one character, its unvaried repetition of the same motive, will cause its rejection for esthetic reasons. But from this point of view also, Kafka retains his importance for the esthetician, since this story illustrates the wide variation of reaction the same story may arouse in different readers.

One puts aside these later defects of personality in Kafka, and turns with relief to the esthetic defects of his earliest work. Here the shortcomings are of a sort to testify to the initial possibility of normalcy in him. As a youth, Kafka seems to have had his share of our wholesome human desire to meet the world on its own terms, to act and to survive, indeed, to bring, however grotesquely, order out of conflict. He was scarcely more eccentric than the average petty bourgeois youth, anxious to get ahead and dominate other people. As a writer also he responded to the prevalent and I believe desirable practice of leaving whatever intellectual conclusion his novel was reaching to be implied symbolically from the action. But, although these are his aims in *Amerika*, he did not succeed in writing a gracious or even a comprehensible novel. *Amerika* consists of a series of episodes, each clear in itself, but culminating in a fragment the incomprehensibility of which emphatically registers his inability to solve his problem in terms of plot or symbolic meaning. Even though the ultimate failure so graphically presented in "The Burrow" may be latent here, and the immediate failure is evidence of his apprenticeship in his craft, most of the blame at this time must be put, I believe, on the inadequacy of the social background, of which Kafka was painfully conscious. The structural defects of the book are Kafka's record of the bankruptcy of what we sometimes call "the American way."

As though convinced of the validity of Spengler's thesis in *The Decline of the West* that the European situation was hopeless, Kafka sought to embrace Spengler's opinion that the future of European culture might lie in the United States. He goes in imagination to the country in which bourgeois attitudes have been least checked by aristocratic precedents, in which pragmatic philosophy has endeavored to relate the ideal to the actual without the least sullying of its purity. In contrast to all his later work *Amerika* presupposes an acceptance of the validity of the objective world, with the concomitant belief that one's ideals must be written into actuality by sweat and blood. Its hero, Karl Rossman, is the only one among his writings to whom Kafka gave a name. The others are unnamed or generalized into "K." And he is the only one who is conscious of a certain security in his physical strength. Whatever timidity he possesses may have been due to Kafka's latent masochism, but it is also normal to the inexperience of the adolescent. And it is concealed by a conscious acceptance of aggression as normal in human relationships. In short,

321

Karl accepts the philosophy and psychology of rugged individualism. But like Mr. Hoover or Mr. Westbrook Pegler, he fears the combined aggression of the working class, since he conceives of the individual worker as a selfish illiterate brute and his labor union as the organization of racketeering to devour society. At the same time Karl is alarmed and disgusted to find that men of wealth live in a false security. He refuses to avail himself of their friendly offers to work not merely because he has an adolescent desire to make his way by his own will, but because he cannot trust men who are so obtuse to their real dangers. The millionaire whose palatial home outside New York he visits sits chatting in his vast drawing room indifferent to the drafts that blow through it because workmen employed to build a new wing have struck, leaving walls as open to invasion as the entrance to what was later to be the burrow. This attitude may already be a neurotic one, but it has a valid objective basis if one is an industrialist who continues to believe in rugged individualism. In other words, it anticipates the psychology of fascism. It is interesting to note that Karl ceases to worry on another occasion. He has been alarmed at the riotous street meetings of a political candidate; but he calms down when informed that all these disorders mean nothing since the outcome has already been arranged by powerful interests behind the scenes. He does not inquire as to who or what they are; that they are powerful enough to dominate is sufficient for him.

Yet Kafka remains fundamentally an individualist. Stated in political terms, his dilemma was that he could not become a fascist. Not its cruelty but its apparent denial of individualism prevented. In his concluding chapter he sought a solution in which the actuality of free competition might lie at peace with the spiritual presence of cooperation. Ruthless competition clearly has bred an unsatisfactory anarchy. The problem was to find some machinery to bring the spiritual and the material together without corrupting their essentially contradictory character: to provide that competition become spiritually cooperative and that the ideal chasten the practical like a catalyst without bureaucratic loss of its own integrity. But when one examines the final story of the "Nature Theater of Oklahoma" (as when one tries to give content to "the American way"), no tangible program for action can be found. It is impossible to determine whether the mechanism is to be governmental activity or the emergence of some private organization. Whichever it is, the improvement is clearly to be made gradually; the new organization is presumably a model which either will be imitated elsewhere or will gradually and painlessly absorb the functions of other organizations into itself. The title of the new theater suggests that Kafka is giving the naturalistic basis of pragmatism a trial, that he is testing the spiritual possibilities latent in the world of actuality. But the most confident deduction one can make from this ambiguous and fragmentary allegory is that any such approach to the problem is likely to be hypocritical, whether consciously or not. To take the project in the best light, it is probably a well-intentioned hoax. Its instigators, whoever they are (for we never get to the real motivating power in Kafka) are impelled by the delusion that the material and the spiritual can be brought together. Certainly when Karl and his friends, wearied by the hazards of competition in the East, go, like the latterday pioneers of the New Deal into the West where handbills (such as the Joads had naively accepted) promise employment to all with the initiative to come, they find nothing adequately prepared. To be sure (like the promise of a Second Front in the recent war) a dramatic spectacle is being acted at the entrance. But one has positively to fight his way beyond the captivating static beauty of this tableau into the amphitheater behind, where everything is still chaotic. Clerks take down Karl's name, though his qualifications seem uncertain. Not only does nobody know what sort of pageant will be enacted on the cluttered race course; the reader feels an uneasy suspicion that the whole venture, the very project of a theater, is being put into the terms not of life but of some fictive and therefore practically useless if not spiritually delusory allegory of life instead. He is tempted to conclude that to believe the material world can have a spiritual aspect, to imagine that competition can be in any way allied with cooperation is a fallacy. Nor does he know whether it is wisdom on the part of the many that had kept them indifferent to the handbills; or whether the

323

few, like Karl, who have the initiative to venture, are not themselves under the enchantment of "the American way."

Now I take it that within the limited social outlook available to Kafka all this is impressively sane comment. In *Amerika* Kafka's tendencies to abnormality have only freed him from the easy fallacious rationalizations which leave more normal individuals of prosperous bourgeois family in the realm of illusion. American readers will at first sight find Kafka's picture of American life amusingly inaccurate. He is as absurdly uninformed about the surface facts as he is incapable of the surface rationalizations. He knows America only as it is presented in our tabloid newspapers, in which the contradiction between the ideal and the actual glares from every column but is denied to exist on the editorial page. At one and the same time they present our country as the haven of the downtrodden, the land of opportunity, the hope of the future; and as the battlefield of anarchic individualism, of murder and racketeering, of Anglo-Saxon dominance, and the devil's right to the hindmost. The tabloids cut through the veil of distortion which the respectability of other papers draws over this living contradiction between our ideals of democracy and their too frequent violation in our practice. There is, of course, another side to the story, but one does not get it from this quarter, in these simon-pure reflections of petty bourgeois hysteria and inconsistency, the validity of which Kafka could recognize from his foreign land.

When he turned back to the European society he knew directly, however, Kafka became convinced that his observation in *Amerika* was superficial. Men might appear to live in a state of brutal personal competition. Go deeper into their actions, and they are found to be the puppets of a hidden authority. A different kind of Nature Theater, so to speak, is actually in operation. It is only men's trust in it that is delusive. They do not realize that they are helpless under the authority of the evil that controls the material world. So now it is not their competition but their apathy that impresses Kafka: their ignorance of their own dilemma, their indifference to the difficulties of their fellow men. Kafka anticipates the picture of the "little man" that was to become established in German fiction as one of the types of the

324

Weimar Republic, restless, impotent, insignificant. If he treats him without the usual contempt, but as a tragic figure, it is that he saw in the story of his helplessness the bankruptcy of his own optimism in *Amerika*.

In *The Trial*, the hero, "K.," a clerk, trusted and expecting promotion for his fidelity, is served in his roominghouse with a warrant for an unnamed crime by two policemen. The officers themselves do not know nor care what the crime is, since their function is only to issue warrants for court appearance. Under such circumstances, the normal man, knowing himself innocent, would go about his business, confident that the mistake will readily be cleared up. K., on the contrary, in his humility and desire to cooperate with the civil authority, must drop his business, assume the preoccupied air of the guilty man, and take over the function of pushing his case through to a decision. His uncle secures the aid of an important lawyer who assures him to his surprise that all legal cases are actually settled out of court by influence or bribery. When neither works for him within a reasonable length of time, he invades the judicial offices where he makes a nuisance of himself since nobody has heard of his case. In due time he begins to grow desperate not only because his quest remains futile, but because he begins to feel that some sinister authority has been ever-watchful and is becoming annoyed at this anxiety for the speedy triumph of justice. Perhaps this intangible authority may be outraged that so insignificant a man should inflame its own guilty conscience. So K., who has been hypnotized by trust, gradually becomes hypnotized by fear. Finally, two other policemen show up, take K. to the edge of town, hand him a knife to slit his throat with, and when he demurs, thrust it home themselves.

The Trial has several layers of symbolic meaning, the most superficial of which I have just presented. It is an exposure of the evils of bureaucracy from the point of view of the common assumptions of democracy. Even though Kafka's experience of a decaying bureaucracy was that of the moribund Austrian Empire, it will apply equally well to the bureaucracy, struggling to be born, of the Weimar Republic. The reader takes it first of all as a trenchant satire upon the delays of justice, the red tape by which

325

the average man may well feel himself strangled in the modern democratic state and its characteristic business corporations, and which the inefficiency of the Weimar Republic merely pushed to the extreme of a tragic burlesque. It emphasizes the sadistic self-importance of some petty officials, the callous indifference of others, until the average citizen appears to get either no attention or abuse for having expected it. But at the same time that the action clarifies this contradiction between our bureaucratic structure and our ideals of democratic equality and individualism, it does not permit us to assume that any evil capitalists are to blame. Though bureaucracy surely defeats the natural aspirations of the common man, there is no assurance that it does anybody good. The fault is in the system, in the fact that life must be organized at all on a practical level. It would perhaps be appealing to conclude that the policemen who finally kill K. have been authorized to do so by Nietzsche's supermen. But made sadistic by the system, they may have been acting at their own impulse or in obedience to an authorized or unauthorized command anywhere along the line.

A second level of meaning is perceptible if we take the action as symbolic of the change in the German personality structure as a result of the functioning of bureaucracy under the Weimar Republic. The Republic, it must be remembered, arose after the collapse of an Empire which had functioned fairly efficiently within the surviving forms of feudalism. To defeat in the First World War therefore was added the insecurity caused by a graft in government less disguised and more reckless than under the Empire, accompanied by an unsettling confusion of novel ideas and policies. Faltering experiments in social reform and magniloquent pretense of progress alternated with the unexpected fall of the iron fist of police repression. But the little man with his feudal background humbly took the blame for his unhappiness upon himself, believing that only his insignificance prevented his recognizing the remote organizational wisdom that must exist at the top. Indeed, behind apparent inefficiency he felt the abject need for, and could sense the rising anger of, some new external authority that at whatever cost would remove the spiritual burden and the practical uselessness of the new freedom

326

of the Weimar Republic. From this point of view, K.'s murder symbolizes the final ascendancy of fascism, with its delusive promise of a security beyond good and evil. Psychiatrically, K. was waiting to be slain, going out of his way to get somebody else to remove the burden of seeking the just and the guilt of ambition and the mirage of freedom which had grown so disturbing that the security of individual annihilation drew him like a magnet, only he must, with the pathetic submission of the Bismarck tradition, receive even death as a grant from above. K.'s death is thus also this strange novelist's prophecy of the fictive life beyond either pride or humility of the Nazi automaton in which the human spirit has been slain. Here, I believe, the value of the novel for most readers is to be found. It affords us the most complete and subtle delineation of the petty bourgeois German temperament, in which feudal attitudes of obedience were translated into the needs of a belated capitalism under Bismarck; then were confused by the ineffectual democracy of the Weimar Republic; became suspicious of their own dawning self-reliance, and when this self-reliance seemed of no profit either to the individual or to society invited its slaughter and replacement by an even more excessive obedience and submission under Hitler than feudalism had imposed.

But it is a third level of meaning which gives Kafka's own intention in *The Trial*. He used the book to reject his toying with the possibilities of a naturalistic theology in *Amerika*, and to state his conviction that whatever is not spirit is evil. His hero's tragedy is that he repeats Kafka's error in *Amerika*, by seeking to root the spiritual in the material when he acts to promote justice. Governments and corporations, being materialistic, the powers of evil that control the practical world, are naturally aroused by the threat of virtue. Other ordinary citizens who accept the conditions of the material world—that it knows neither good nor evil —and act automatically without idealism or insight, are not molested. One best survives in proportion as he can live as the passive unconscious automaton of the powers of evil, in proportion indeed as he can remain completely in the realm of fantasy as far as our notions of democracy and progress are concerned. K. made the mistake of acting in daily life upon principles which

327

are real in the spiritual world but must remain a fantasy in the material. Thus he violated the nature of the material world, aroused the powers of evil that control it, and promoted its revenge in his own death. The theme was fortunately such as to permit *The Trial* to become the only one of Kafka's writings in satisfactory esthetic form. The finality of its conclusion, moreover, is of an order superior to that in other novels with a fatalistic philosophy such as Thomas Hardy's. For there is no emotional ambiguity. The horror and the relief of dying cancel into a state of tranquillity. The book has fulfilled its own laws of inevitability, and we are done with it.

But though *The Trial* adequately explains the source of Kafka's mysticism, it is concerned with only the negative aspect of it and does not illuminate its essentially paradoxical nature. His observation of life had become so cynical that no other escape was possible than the rejection altogether of the importance of the material world. Yet he was so involved in that world that he must reject it both verbally and emotionally in its own terms. His mysticism had the same flavor as well as the same origin as Tertullian's despair at the corruption of the Roman Empire. He too was forced to believe what the evidence of his senses had convinced him was absurd. Indeed his paradox was the more glaring. In the fourth century Tertullian's axiom was less "absurd" because his era, though disillusioned, had inherited a disposition partial to a mystical view of the world, to which his dogma gave the assent of a man by temper skeptical. But Kafka, living in an industrialized world which had not secured order and happiness at the price of its loss of faith, was overtaken by a bitterness so harsh that he could not let it rise into consciousness. He was forced to bury it beneath the level of emotive expression, to reduce it to a matter of no importance, to grope for belief in spite of its being absurd. He was, in short, compelled to embrace a mysticism which, unlike previous types, subdued the body neither in the oriental fashion by inducing hysteria nor in western fashion by chaining it to will under the authority of abstract logic. His must be a mysticism which justified the paralysis of will and the shrinking back from sensation, by setting up a complete dichotomy between the spiritual and the material life. Against his back-

328

ground of scientific rationalism, to believe the absurd might be eccentric and psychopathic. But for the time being it seemed to make the facts of his experience endurable. He might escape schizophrenia by assuming it to be the normal state of the human personality.

But the absurdity of the paradox has now to be directly faced. Experience was forcing Kafka further into his labyrinth. If *The Trial* had to be written because the optimism lurking in the conclusion of *Amerika* had proved unfounded, *The Castle* had to be written because life was scarcely possible if one accepted only the approach of *The Trial*. Personal salvation demanded that the skeptical view of the world give way to its description through the eyes of faith. The materialistic aspect of man and human institutions, valid and hopeless on its level, sent Kafka hurrying into the burrow of faith. Only faith was not really an escape since somehow the spiritual existed side by side with the material, every person having only this curious relation to every other person that they alike were split into these two aspects essentially unrelated. The new explanation was only a new dilemma. If by definition of humanity itself, the flesh is unescapable, the spiritual must appear to function through the forms of the material. *The Castle*, therefore, is only Kafka's exaggeration of K.'s mistake in *The Trial* (from the theological point of view). The quest for God is certainly more comprehensive than the desire for human justice and the theological dilemma consequently more august. But psychologically the new situation was less difficult. One knew that the good, unlike the evil, was incapable of revenge. The very fact that one's search was to find out if it really existed to man's perception made life indeed the safer; action banished the misgiving that action might be useless. The average man doubtless did not need to pursue the castle because he was reconciled to the contradictions that life had thrust upon him. He had become resigned to a chaos he did not understand, whether he found it within himself or in the outside world. But I think Kafka was right in assuming that this was a view of the situation from the outside; or, at all events, that if it was the true situation, it could not last. Look inside any common individual and he does not have the impulse to act for the good such

329

as led to downfall in *The Trial*. But, certainly, we may imagine Kafka arguing, if the impulse for the good is completely divorced from the practical, if it is nothing but man's quest for the disembodied perfection of God, there can be no revenge from the sources of evil. What he did not see was that he has made life ultimately useless and boresome.

It escaped him because his talent as a novelist was a distraction from the dilemmas of his mysticism. The fascination of the immediate creative task postponed his consciousness of ultimate implacable despair. It reduced the traditional dilemma of mystic communication: that mysticism posits the impossibility of communication at all. If he had lived in the middle ages, he would have repeated the thin allegorizing which was the best the medieval writer could achieve in human characterization. But the very skepticism of his age, by obligating the sort of novel in which the human personality must be first presented in all its immediate richness and inconsistency, enabled him to postpone recognition of the fact that *The Castle* was bound to remain another unfinished work. Kafka indeed sensed the inconsistencies in our personalities more keenly than most writers; for they were locked in permanent contradiction within himself. The new interest, furthermore, in the introspective novel with its apparent indifference to the external world of material values must have normalized for him the malady of his personality, by affording him an appearance of escape from the level of *The Trial*, satisfactory for the time being. He could as a novelist thus take for the spiritual, as contrasted with the materialistic, the working of our unconscious as contrasted with our ordinary habit of living on the conscious surface of experience. By abandoning the consciousness under the joint auspices of the new technique of fiction and his developing psychosis, he could delude himself into believing that the presentation of the world as transformed by his own unconscious was the world of spiritual reality. Doubtless the process was chiefly unconscious. But the result of the process was that for the time being the hostility of the actual lost its actuality, became transformed into the cold distance of the objective world as it appears in dreams, as, to the dreamer, it is the actuality hovering on the fringe of consciousness that is the dream. In the dream for the time being appears to lie the reality, and to Kafka's satisfaction if it did not possess the full-blown perfection that faith could hardly require this side the grave, it was at least harmless and impersonal.

Kafka has only transferred his doubts into a realm where they may be handled without emotional disturbance. The locus of *The Castle* is an isolated village high in the mountains. The atmosphere is that of the feudal pre-Bismarckian world, remote and ambiguous. The castle is even higher up, most of the time hidden in the mist and storm of the mountain top, and inaccessible because of the state of the roads. But in the village also the snow cuts off easy communication and reduces clarity of vision. Winter drives people indoors so that the scene (unlike that of *The Trial*) is never populous. When one breaks through the drifts to reach the peasant's door, it is opened as though suspicion of the stranger were confused with dislike of the cold. Even within the inn, though men crouch resentfully, they are half hidden by the shadows. The author appears to have been as much affected by the cold as his characters are. For he describes all this as though himself experiencing the same partial anesthesia. We scarcely realize, so extreme has the numbness of our sense become, that we are back in the competitive world of *Amerika*. The conviction in *The Trial* of implacable doom has disappeared. But the fact that everybody works for the castle, even though the spiritual must take this inconsistently materialistic form, guarantees to men non-competitive qualities also. Kafka's theology has succeeded in enriching his presentation of men and their social relationships. They are at last in his novels fully human, to the imagination of the normal reader, in that they now show what impresses us as being a realistic complexity. They are both aggressive and considerate, both selfish and unselfish. The reader follows their conversation or the description of their actions with the same lively interest in the immediate situation which is certainly the essential characteristic of life itself, and the presence of which in this novel of Kafka's is the secret of its esthetic worth. But the esthetic satisfaction of the narrative has another ingredient in that this liveliness is entirely visual and verbal. The story has the coldness of the Grecian urn, the remoteness of the silent moving picture. Whatever happens we accept without any emotional involvement of our own. If our own emotions could be aroused, the book's flavor would become ironic as we read on. For it turns out that this flash of action and conflicting motive is a chaos. Men seem to act from impulse and their attempt to understand their action only leads into a maze of speculation. By implication, *The Castle* is a parody on the introspective novel, the elusiveness of our so-called "stream of consciousness."

In this benumbed world of Kafka's, though the act is always clear, its meaning and justification remain forever doubtful, and acts, therefore, cannot have coherence, when taken together. Now that life is presented in both its spiritual and material aspects, it becomes a bedlam of concrete particularities that lead nowhere. If we go within the single act to discover its motives, the act disintegrates. But it is the same when we pass from act to act. They fail to integrate into a pattern unless the perpetual repetition of Sisyphus' toil can be so described. The reader, for instance, gets the impression that K. comes to the village bearing a definite letter employing him as a land surveyor of the castle. But as the book progresses, one begins to doubt whether K. received such a letter or only came with the hunch that a job was vacant or thinking he could bluff his way. Nor do the castle officials succeed in clearing away the uncertainties. Possibly a letter had been sent some years ago, but they are positive that there has not been a valid recent communication and no such official is needed. Yet K., on his side, may well feel that a higher official (if he could reach him) may be better informed; the only guarantee that the bustling official he meets really acts for the castle is his appearance of self-assurance. Even this cannot be trusted, since if one got to know him better (as K. did Amalia's brother) the arrogance might only hide his own inner doubts. For Amalia's brother, though he poses as a messenger of the castle, has no assurance that he is accepted as such on the hill. He can only try, becoming in human eyes a hypocrite, in the hope that the castle may reward him for his good intention by a sign that never comes. And since his good intention is often disproved by some human frailty, he lives in perpetual doubt of his deserving the reward he seeks. All this is clear as ecclesiastical symbolism. The existence of the spiritual itself has been reduced to the suspicious dimensions of an intuition within one's own obviously insufficient ego. The individual intuition of the divine has only the verification that other equally fallible persons seem to share it. For, if there is no inspired Bible that Kafka can trust, it goes without saying that he is not aware of the possible existence of an inspired religious institution. The castle is obviously a criticism of the organizational hierarchy in the Roman Catholic Church culminating in the inaccessible recesses of the Vatican. But since Kafka begins by positing the absolute separation of spiritual and material, the book is a broader criticism also of the notion of spiritual hierarchy among men. It is primarily the Jewish-Protestant-mystical tradition that is failing him. Its belief that the inner light, the indwelling of grace, is the only assurance of the possession of divine authority is what paradoxically he can no longer either believe or disbelieve. He cannot reject it because it seems tied up in his own personality and that of other men with the restraining influence of conscience, a reversion from the cruel deed, a reaction against pride into humility. But the evidence is against it.

Equally devastating is the book's implied attack upon the pragmatic philosophy which is the ultimate lay application of this Protestant tradition. The book acknowledges the validity of the act as clearly as it makes a parody of the "will to believe." Always the act is there; what is wanting is any test of its "working." From this point of view *The Castle* comes near to being a refutation of James' *Varieties of Religious Experience*. He gets close to shattering pragmatism by bringing into the open its explicit metaphysics, and showing that it rests on the absurd foundation that, despite our inner doubts, we believe because others act as though they do, and belief, thus secured, seems to do us good. Kafka's own mysticism is, in fact, merely an emphasis upon this assumption which the pragmatist makes only to neglect. The pragmatist has been able to neglect it because he has been distracted by the exhilaration of wallowing among particularities which seem to add up to progress. But the misery and poverty of modern life, Kafka saw, have reduced the exhilaration, indeed

333

have transformed it for most persons into despair. At this point he seems to have become aware that the pursuit through the medium of philosophy of this assumption that the good is what works (when what works is so evidently the evil) lands the thinker in the theory of the useful make-believe, the philosophy of As-If. Though inclined to the same conclusion, Kafka hesitates to accept it. He recoils altogether from formal philosophy into that variant of functioning pragmatism which is the writing of novels and that peculiarity of its theory which accepts without a protest lack of coherent pattern in both our emotional and intellectual life. Pragmatically the only certainty in *The Castle* is the efficacy of public opinion. Faith has become a superstition in a world where nothing else but public opinion would seem to work, even though it works to the disaster of the well-intentioned. For, as though to prove he had not forgotten *The Trial*, Kafka introduces one coherent episode: the fall of Amalia's family. They are socially ostracized and reduced to beggary for a number of reasons (for nothing is simple in Kafka), but essentially, I believe, because Amalia's father believed in progress, has tried to improve the fire department, and therefore had sought to relate the spiritual to the material aspects of life. His spiritual urge became corrupted into personal pride and ambition, and the revenge of the public upon his pride was the restoration of the hopeless chasm between the two facets of the human personality.

How hopeless it was Kafka seems now to have realized. Once more, as though fatigued by the useless repetition of the same motions, the book breaks off in mid-course, leaving K. as far as ever from the castle, which still stands upon its mountain top, sometimes visible to our senses through the mist. But we remain ignorant whether its material appearance justifies our assumption of spiritual power within. Perhaps, as Kafka suggested in a later story, our vision of God is as perverse and inaccurate as would be a dog's assumption of ideal qualities in its master. Kafka had lost his struggle to attain religious faith. The later stories like "The Burrow" ignore it. Fantasy and hallucination now are the last resort of a man who never had faith in humanity and could never secure a faith in God. His had been the symbolic prototype of the German personality. But he was forced to

334

wander into death and madness alone. For Hitler had not yet offered the fantasy of a fantasy in his confraternity of the doomed, who for the time being were able to distort their doom into the hallucination of a glory. We who are more happily situated than Kafka can draw from his novels the desolate pleasure that there too we should have gone if we had been unable to believe in the potentialities of democracy and the common man.

faith and vocation

d. s. savage

I

Present critical opinion of Kafka would seem to be divided between the view that he was a religious genius and a consummate artist, and the contrary view that his personality was psychopathic and his work a continuous case-book of his neurotic obsessions. It seems to me useless to discuss the symbolism of Kafka until one has made up one's mind which of these two views contains the more truth. Kafka is in any case patently a "problem" figure, and for any understanding of his method of work it is necessary first to arrive at some understanding of the total pattern which is given us in his work as a whole. It is to this end that the present essay is written.

It may be convenient to begin with a glance at one of the representatives of the second point of view—the psychopathological. Mr. Edwin Berry Burgum gives forceful expression to the opinion that Kafka is significant chiefly as a symptom of social decadence. From the beginning Mr. Burgum is determined to place Kafka in his social perspectives and to interpret him in their light. It is significant that throughout his essay he depends greatly

337

upon a criterion of "normality." Had Kafka been more "normal" (or been born in more "normal" circumstances?) he would, presumably, have come to satisfactory terms with life and would have found no necessity for the tortuous and torturing process of self-analysis of which his writing is an expression. And Mr. Burgum, considering Kafka's later writings, concludes:

> Fantasy and hallucination now are the last resort of a man who never had faith in humanity and could never secure a faith in God. His had been the symbolic prototype of the German personality. But he was forced to wander into death and madness alone. For Hitler had not yet offered the fantasy of a fantasy in his confraternity of the doomed, who for the time being were able to distort their doom into the hallucination of a glory. We who are more happily situated than Kafka can draw from his novels the desolate pleasure that there too we should have gone if we had been unable to believe in the potentialities of democracy and the common man.

This final phrase should be enough to reveal the level at which Mr. Burgum makes his approach. But this is altogether too facile a judgment. Whether we like it or not, Kafka was certainly preoccupied with pressing problems to which the proffered solution of a "belief in democracy and the common man" is entirely impertinent. And yet, on the other hand, there are features about Kafka's work which make it impossible for me, at least, to accept the valuation placed upon him by his admirers: by Mr. Muir, for example, when, comparing *The Castle* with *The Pilgrim's Progress*, he writes:

> If anyone wanted to estimate how immensely more difficult it is for a religious genius to see his way in an age of scepticism than in an age of faith, a comparison of *The Pilgrim's Progress* with *The Castle* might give him a fair measure of it. Yet hardly a fair measure, perhaps. For Bunyan's mind was primitive compared with the best minds of his age, and Kafka's is more subtly sceptical than the most sceptical of our own. Its

338

scepticism, however, is grounded on a final faith, and this is what must make his novels appear paradoxical, perhaps even incomprehensible, to some contemporary readers. His scepticism is not an attitude or a habit; it is a weapon for testing his faith and his doubt alike, and for discarding from them what is inessential.°

If one is able to accept that view of Kafka—the view that he was a religious genius who has something meaningful to contribute to our knowledge of spiritual reality—then we may be able to accept Mr. Muir's further statement that

> What he sets out to do is to find out something about those [unknown, heavenly] powers, and the astonishing thing is that he appears to succeed. While following the adventures of his heroes we seem to be discovering—almost without being fully aware of it—various things about those entities which we have never divined before, and could never perhaps have divined by ourselves. We are led in through circle after circle of a newly found spiritual domain, where everything is strange and yet real, and where we recognize objects without being able to give them a name . . . his allegory is not a mere recapitulation or recreation; it does not run on lines already laid down; it is a pushing forward of the mind into unknown places; and so the things he describes seem to be actual new creations which had never existed before. They are like palpable additions to the intellectual world, and ones which cannot be comprehended at a single glance, for there is meaning behind meaning, form behind form, in them all.

The difficulty with which such a presentation of Kafka faces us is the insuperable one that Kafka leaves us with no solution at all to the problems which he has been exploring. The issues are certainly raised, but no conclusion is come to. The writings themselves trail off into uncertainty, uncompleted. Bafflement and frustration reign. The Trial, as a trial, gets nowhere,

° Introductory Note to *The Castle.*

339

and K. is assassinated out of hand; the Castle is never reached, and its few messages remain always of dubious authenticity. Nor do the later stories induce in us a belief that Kafka had reached the goal which he had set himself. And we can hardly be such simpletons as to suppose that in fact Kafka had set himself no goal. The conclusion to which we may well be led is that Kafka was certainly a "case," though not so obvious a one as Mr. Burgum thinks: and that he was as well a fine artist and a penetrating intellect—within the limitations of the circle drawn around him by his determining obsessions.

II

Whatever we may think of the character of Kafka's vision of life, it is surely impossible to ignore the very obvious psychopathic foundation of his work, its obsessive character, its narrow limits and its reiteration of certain inescapable themes. It is clear that Kafka's work possessed for him a primarily therapeutic function, although this is in no way to denigrate the artistry with which he was sometimes able to present his picture of life. It was the medium through which he exteriorized his dilemmas and thus to a certain extent obtained a control over them. It is, at any rate, clear that he was not writing for the amusement or edification of a public (not only the form of his work, but the reluctance with which he permitted publication in his lifetime, and his posthumous instructions for the destroying of his MSS support this.)

Kafka himself, in a long, hundred-page "Letter to My Father," written in 1919, attempted, according to Max Brod, "to classify his entire literary work under the general heading of 'attempt at flight from his father.' "

> 'You were the subject of my books,' he writes. 'In them I poured out the sorrows that I could not pour out on your breast. My writing has been a purposely drawn-out parting from you. But though this parting was forced by you, its direction was determined by me.'

This seems like an oversimplification on Kafka's part, and yet there can be no doubt that the shadow of his successful, aggressive, powerful parent had an inhibiting and introverting effect upon his timid and sensitive son which no would-be explorer of Kafka's mind can afford to minimize. "You are unfit for life," he makes his father say to him, in this long letter, "but to make things more comfortable and easy for yourself, and to spare yourself any self-reproach, you prove that I have robbed you of all your fitness for life and put it in my pocket." The manner in which his relationship with his father had "unfitted him for life" is shown in the same letter where Kafka speaks of his unavailing attempt to get married.

> The most important obstacle to my marriage is the ineradicable conviction that the support and conduct of a family require everything that I have recognized in you, the good and the bad together, as you organically combine them: strength and arrogance; health and a certain immoderation; eloquence and unwillingness to listen; self-confidence and contempt for the abilities of others; power over men and an inclination to tyranny; knowledge of people and mistrust towards most. Not to mention such unmixed virtues as diligence, endurance, presence of mind, fearlessness. Such are your qualities—mine by comparison seem next to nothing. Could I, thus equipped, venture into wedlock, when I saw that even you had to struggle hard in your marriage and were positively deficient in your relations with your children? Of course I did not ask myself this question so explicitly; otherwise my common sense would have shown me men quite different from you (Uncle R., for instance), who had married and at least not collapsed under the strain—a considerable accomplishment, that would have been plenty for me. But I did not ask this question, I *experienced* it from childhood on. I examined myself not only in reference to marriage, but in my relation to every other trifling matter. Everywhere you convinced me of my incapacity, both by your example and by your training (as I have attempted to describe it). And what was true in connection with trifles could

341

not help but apply to the greatest step of all: marriage.

It seems beyond question clear that Kafka's emotional nature was frustrated and suppressed, and personal relationships made excruciatingly difficult for him, by the overwhelming effect his father's personality had upon him as a child. In the same letter he writes:

> My courage, decision, confidence, joy in a thing did not endure if you were opposed to it, or if your opposition could even be surmised; and I surmised it in almost everything I did. . . . In your presence I developed a halting, stuttering speech—you are an excellent speaker as long as you are speaking of the things that interest you—but even my halting speech was too much for you, and ultimately I stopped talking altogether, at first for spite, and then because I could neither talk nor think in your presence. And since you were my actual teacher, this affected everything in my life.

Like many individuals, whose emotional life has been similarly negated, Kafka imagined that his difficulties could be overcome by self-investigation and the laborious, protracted and conscientious analysis of relationships—of which this long letter to his father (which surely is destined to take its place in the Kafka opus) is typical. But where the growth of emotional life has been suppressed, there is little help in rational analyses of the process of suppression. Nevertheless in many cases this is the only instrument left in the hands of the emotionally-inhibited, and indeed an intense, conscientious introspection may be one of the consequences of a deep emotional frustration, resembling the prisoner's minute and prolonged exploration of his prison cell. The effect upon Kafka was to isolate him, to cut him off from relationships with other persons, and to set him at a ceaseless unravelling of his own actions and motives.

What was the "direction" of Kafka's parting from his father, of which he speaks? It would seem that throughout his life Kafka's desire was for a normality which he was unable to attain.

342

According to Max Brod, who knew him perhaps better than any-one, and who deliberately compares his situation to that of the poet, Heinrich von Kleist—

> Kafka's highest ideal is nowhere better expressed than in Kleist's longing words: 'To cultivate a field, to plant a tree, to beget a child.'

This brings us at once to the primary orientation dis-coverable within Kafka's work. In this connection, Max Brod has, in another place, the following remarks to make about the action of *The Castle:*

> K. sought a connection with the Grace of the Godhead when he sought to root himself in the village at the foot of the Castle: he fought for an occupation, a post in a certain sphere of life; by his choice of a calling and by marriage he wanted to gain inner stability, wanted as a 'stranger'—that is from an isolated position and as one different from everybody else—to wrest for himself the thing which fell into the ordinary man's lap as if of itself, without his striving for it particularly or thinking about it. Decisive for this interpretation of mine is the deep emotion with which Franz Kafka once referred me to the anecdote which Flaubert's niece mentions in her introduction to his correspond-ence. The passage runs: 'May not Flaubert have re-gretted even in his last years that he had not chosen an ordinary vocation? I could almost credit it when I think of the touching words which once burst from his lips when we were returning home along the Seine; we had been visiting one of my friends, and had found her in the midst of her brood of lovely children. "They're in the right of it" (*Ils sont dans le vrai*), he said, meaning the honest family life of those people.'

And Mr. Muir, as if in confirmation of this, states Kafka's problem as follows:

> The problem with which all Kafka's work is concerned is a moral and spiritual one. It is a twofold problem:

343

that of finding one's true vocation, one's true place, whatever it may be, in the community; and that of acting in accordance with the will of heavenly powers. But though it has those two aspects it was in his eyes a single problem; for a man's true place in the community is finally determined, not by secular, but by divine, law, and only when, by apparent chance or deliberate effort, a man finds himself in his divinely appointed place, can he live as he should. Many people slip into their place without being aware of it; others are painfully conscious of the difficulty, the evident impossibility, of finding any place at all; and nobody has been more clearly and deeply conscious of it, I think, than Kafka.

Now, so far as the question of "vocation" is concerned, it is important to recognize that one can, in this life, roughly speaking, pursue one of two courses. The first is, to adapt oneself to the life, domestic, social, national, and so on, that goes on around one and within one, to accept its values of possession, domination and survival, to integrate oneself into its pattern, accepting its self-assured validity and entering into the conventional relationships with which it provides one. This was the pattern of life pursued by Kafka's father, whose example, however, had a positively inhibiting effect upon his son. The other course is to reject that life, perceiving its makeshift, blind, conventional character, in order to live according to standards received from a relating of one's ideas and actions to some principle of being which is ultimate and absolute, and therefore truly authoritative.* In either case one may be given a pattern of conduct, one will be given at least the possibility of consistency, integrality and power. But Kafka's dilemma took shape from his repudiation of the first course and his inability to take the plunge into the second. This dilemma in fact is central to his work. Kafka's own irresolution, guilt-sense, timidity, over-conscientiousness, etc., derived from his vacillation between the two spheres of being designated respec-

* This is to state the position as it appears from outside. But, in truth, spiritual life can have nothing of "authority" about it, since authority is a matter of externals, and the spiritual life is an inward existence.

344

tively as "earth" and "heaven." As he himself put it, in one of his aphorisms:

> He is a free and secure citizen of the world, for he is fettered to a chain which is long enough to give him the freedom of all earthly space, and yet only so long that nothing can drag him past the frontiers of the world. But simultaneously he is a free and secure citizen of Heaven as well, for he is also fettered by a similarly designed heavenly chain. So that if he heads, say, for the earth, his heavenly collar throttles him, and if he heads for Heaven, his earthly one does the same. And yet all the possibilities are his, and he feels it; more, he actually refuses to account for the deadlock by an error in the original fettering.

It can be seen from this how Kafka was torn between two irreconcilable needs or longings. He desired a place in the community, which was granted to everybody else (seemingly) without their having to struggle for divine recognition. To be like them, if that was his desire, he had only to accept life as it came to him, and trouble no more about a divine sanction for it than anybody else—his father, for instance—whose attitude toward ultimates was passive. But he was psychologically incapable of this passivity, and incorrigible passion for "rightness" made him struggle to obtain a divine sanction for his earthly existence. Such a sanction could not be forthcoming. From this point of view it might be said that K.'s error, in *The Castle*, was in not proceeding at once to the Castle and taking it, as it were, by storm. Instead of doing so, however, he "obstinately insists to the point of exhaustion on regulating his life on earth in accordance with instructions from the Castle, although he is forcibly and even brutally rebuffed by every Castle functionary." (Max Brod.)

It is useless to speak in terms of "belief in the potentialities of democracy and the common man" to anyone who has progressed so far in disillusion as Kafka had done. It is equally useless to make a criterion of "normality." These things operate on a certain level of social validity, but beyond that level they are seen, as Kafka saw them, to lack any satisfactory justification.

345

Kafka may be regarded as a psychopathological "case," in that his abnormality made him incapable of accepting the half-truths and compromises which are embodied in human conduct on the average, social level, but it must also be recognized that this abnormality caused him to gain a valid insight into the hallucinatory nature of the social contract. The answer to such an appeal to social values is to be found in certain of Kafka's fables, which are as valid in their application to life on a certain level in the Republican America of the 'forties as they are to the life of the Republican Germany of the 'twenties—in particular, "The Great Wall of China" and "The City Coat of Arms," the point of each of which is that the once purposeful human social system is carried on when all its original meaning has left it. ". . . To this must be added that the second or third generation had already recognized the senselessness of building a heaven-reaching tower; but by that time everybody was too deeply involved to leave the city." (It is true that Kafka more than suggests that the original meaning may have been an illusion anyhow.)

Unable, then, to accept and make do with the compromises which help most people to come to terms with their lives, Kafka was left with the only possible alternative of committing himself completely to the divine will. But this he could not do, as he explains in his aphorism concerning the two chains. His attitude toward the world leads only to confusion owing to his obsessive insistence on regulating earthly life in accordance with the divine laws (which are undiscoverable). But his attitude toward the divine leads also to a stalemate because he will not accept it for its own sake, turning away, if need be, from the world; but insists upon narrowing it down to fit within the confines of earthly existence, attempting to bring the infinite down into the service of the finite under the pretense of making the finite serve the infinite. This leads only to stultification and the cancelling out of each realm by the other. In fact, Kafka's writings give us no clue to the real nature of the spiritual world, and to suppose that they do so is to become the victim of Kafka's own confusions. They merely delineate the world of his own confused wanderings, of which all we know in it as spiritual life is the incommensurability of the divine with the human. The action of

346

The Castle, as of *The Trial*, takes place neither in the actual nor in the spiritual world, but in the void between, where the distorted shadows and images of each lie thrown together in complete confusion.

> There is a goal, but no way; what we call the way is only wavering.

III

The dilemma, then, which a study of Kafka's writings reveals as central to his existence, is the dilemma of faith. To the "normal," average sensual man who is able to remain immersed in the conventions of his social and biological existence, the issue of faith does not arise with any pressing urgency. It arises as a conscious and urgent question for those who have *lost* their faith in the rightness of so-called "normal" mundane actuality—

> 'No one can say that we are wanting in faith. The mere fact of our living is itself inexhaustible in its proof of faith.'
> 'You call that a proof of faith? But one simply cannot live.'
> 'In that very "simply cannot" lies the insane power of faith; in that denial it embodies itself.'

Franz Kafka, one might very well say, was in the predicament of a man who had lost this fundamental, unconscious faith in the rightness of things (a loss which is a necessary prelude to a religious conversion, an assertion of faith at a higher level) but who was incapable of making the leap toward that higher level in which lay his only hope of salvation and personal reintegration. Instead, he oriented his life toward a stubborn, blind and pathetic attempt at reintegration upon the lower level, an attempt which was inevitably foredoomed to failure. Max Brod, again, who speaks of *The Castle* as Kafka's *Faust*, remarks of this:

> Certainly K. is a Faust in deliberately modest, even needy trappings, and with the essential modification

347

that he is driven on not by a longing for the final goals of humanity, but by a need for the most primitive requisites of life, the need to be rooted in a home and a calling, and to become a member of a community. At the first glance this difference seems very great, but becomes considerably less so when one recognizes that for Kafka those primitive goals have religious significance, and are simply the right life, the right way (Tao).

The leap of faith, however, it is commonly recognized by religious thinkers, requires a renunciation of a concern for this world and its affairs. It is necessary to "hate" the world, to turn wholly to the eternal realm and to center one's life and hopes *within* that realm, even if this should mean the enmity of the world and worldly disgrace—which as a matter of fact it usually does. Kafka could not conceive this; but that he was not altogether unaware of the nature of the act of faith is shown by his close familiarity with Kierkegaard's *Fear and Trembling,* a work which, according to Brod (and significantly) Kafka "loved much, read often, and profoundly commented on in many letters."

The act of faith, however, is not an intellectual act. It is a whole direction of the will, involving the abrogation of the intellect, and it is indissolubly associated with the noumenal realities of personality and love—which, indeed, are unable to manifest themselves on the level of unconscious, natural existence and require the act of faith to bring them into being. It is interesting to note, therefore, that in Kafka's work, just as there is no evidence of faith, so also there is none of personality or love. Kafka's is the abstract, colourless world of the nerves and the intellect.

I have already stated that K.'s mistake (given the symbols "village" and "castle") was in not proceeding at once to the Castle, leaving the village to take care of itself. But, in truth, in the terms of the problem which he had set himself, and given the nature of his peculiar demands upon existence, every move which K. could make was bound to be the wrong one. The very opposition between "village" and "Castle" is a product of those demands, and Kafka's symbolism is valid only as a statement of his own curious predicament. Kafka's statement of the problem of the relation between the human and the divine, assuming the unbridgeable gulf between the two, becomes one of *authority* and *submission*—which, of course, is a purely exoteric and external approach to the matter. The searching out of the divine will thus become an intellectual problem. But when reduced to the flat, abstract terms of the intellect, the question of spiritual "authority" becomes an absurdity—and necessarily so, because faith and love, being spiritual realities, are not reducible to those terms. The absurdity consequent upon a reduction of a matter of dynamic faith and love to an accordance with the terms of the rational understanding is shown nowhere more completely than in the Sortini episode in *The Castle;* and it is in connection with this that Max Brod refers us to Kafka's deep interest in Kierkegaard's *Fear and Trembling:*

> The Sortini episode is literally a parallel to Kierkegaard's book, which starts from the fact that God required of Abraham what was really a crime, the sacrifice of his child; and which uses this paradox to establish triumphantly the conclusion that the categories of morality and religion are by no means identical.

It is strange, however, that no one has commented upon the full significance of this episode, which, put briefly, is a reduction to the limits of the Kafka universe of the fate of the Jewish race consequent upon their repudiation of Christ. The Barnabas family are held in high esteem in the village, the father has a high post in the fire-brigade (or priesthood), and on one occasion when a fete is to be held to commemorate the presentation by the Castle to the village of a new fire-engine (a new Law), Sortini, a very high official who "hardly ever comes into the open," but who, on this occasion, "took part in the ceremony of handing over the fire-engine," apparently falls in love with the Barnabas daughter, Amalia, and "leaps over the shaft" of the engine to get nearer to her. The following morning he sends her a note, couched in outrageously offensive terms, bidding her to come to him at once, but she tears up the note and flings it in the

349

messenger's face. From that time on the Barnabas family, without coming in any way under the direct condemnation of the Castle authorities, from whom they can get no word either of condemnation or forgiveness, begin to be ostracized and despised by the community, into which all their endeavours to reinstate themselves are unavailing. It is certainly true that this episode shows in a masterly way "what a gulf there is between human reason and divine grace" (Brod), although in a way which Kafka can hardly have intended. But we are misjudging Kafka if we assume that it is his purpose merely to demonstrate the existence of such a gulf. His is an attempt to puzzle out the meaning of the disparity, and if possible to overcome it. But because he is incapable of that free surrender of himself and of his worldly existence in the act of faith, and can only apply, to that which is beyond rational understanding, the measuring-rod of the skeptical intelligence, he is led to reduce the depth and complexity of a spiritual choice of destiny to the trivial and incomprehensible terms of fire-engines and midnight messengers.*

The endeavor to bring the skeptical intelligence to bear upon the problems of the spiritual life can only result in the dissolution of spiritual reality. To ask, skepticzlly and analytically, "What is personality?" or "What is love?" or even "What is truth?" and to analyse your findings recurrently back is to reach a point where these realities disintegrate into fragments, leading the enquirer into a dismembered, fragmentary, mechanistic world. The further back into the spiritual life you try to push the analytical method, the further the object of your investigation disintegrates, the more hallucinatory the world in which you discover yourself. This is so simply because spirit is not substance but motion, and

---

* Further, it is necessary to note Kafka's emphasis in this matter upon the *worldly* disgrace apparently consequent upon a spiritual delinquency, an emphasis which presumes an identification of earthly rewards with spiritual benefits. Yet the lesson, to the religious understanding, of the coming of Christ (translated in Kafka's symbolism to the presence of Sortini at the fete) is that the spiritual world is our world turned upside down, with all its values reversed. Kafka's emphasis upon Sortini's "authority" and Amalia's disobedience is also characteristic and characteristically beside the point.

350

the spiritual life exists only as it is dynamically and "subjectively" created. The absence of dynamic faith in Kafka's world accounts for the absence of personality and love.

How these aspects of Kafka are related to his spiritual impotence is to be seen from certain very marked features of the world into which his writings conduct us. First of all, it is necessary to remark the atmosphere of *isolation* in which the action of each of the novels and tales takes place. This action centers around one individual and one alone, and he is a patent representation of Kafka himself. It is solely his own obsessions which preoccupy him; other human beings enter the scene only in a subordinate relationship to the isolated hero, whose relationship with them is never one of equality, of personal communion. His interest in them is chiefly as means to an end: can they be used to subserve his over-riding purpose, to secure his acquittal from the Court, or to obtain for his activities the acknowledgment and sanction of the Castle authorities? This is a solipsistic universe. It is appropriate, therefore, that K., himself, in *The Trial* and *The Castle* is singularly deficient in personal qualities, remaining little more than a cipher, and given a character only by the compulsive nature of his quest: a moving anxiety, a question mark of guilt and impatience.

It is particularly noticeable how, with each succeeding work, the atmosphere of isolation increases. In *Amerika,* the least characteristic of the novels, there is some degree of average human equality among the characters, and Karl Rossman, a portrayal of natural innocence, and not of guilt, is not yet quite the cipher, K., while the social scene is given some attention for its own sake.* In *The Trial* we are in the metropolis, although it is a metropolis whose reality is cast into doubt by the enigmatic

* The progression of the novels and tales is as follows: In *Amerika* there is an acceptance of "normality," with a play upon an optimistic naturalism. In *The Trial* normality is menaced and undermined by the enigmatic forces of the supernatural which pursue the individual with a sense of outraged guilt. In *The Castle* the supernatural authority has been accepted unquestioningly, and the problem is of "advancing to the attack" in quest of its sanctions. But these sanctions are never achieved. The last stories represent a relapse to a hopeless condition of defeated, though whimsical, apathy.

351

presence in its midst of the Court with all its mysterious ramifications. But the characters to whom we are introduced—K.'s land-lady, K.'s uncle, Fraulein Burstner—have a solid aspect, as have the circumstances of K.'s existence, the Bank, his lodgings, the Cathedral. In *The Castle* all that is changed, and we are in the rarefied and spectral atmosphere of a feudal village high up on the mountains in winter. The sense of isolation is finely suggested by the pervading cold, the snow, the strangeness of everything and the remoteness of the Castle high up overhead, sometimes visible, sometimes obscured from view by mist and clouds. It is a world in which the isolation of personality draws it to the verge of unreality. Fantasy predominates over realism. And in the later stories, where isolation is carried to its conclusion, and the problem is no longer that of relating human efforts to divine law (the attempt having been abandoned as hopeless), dehumanization results, and the problems (as in "The Burrow" and "Investigations of a Dog,") are those, not of men, but of animals.

There seems little need to pursue this analysis of Kafka into these last stories—that is, the tales contained in the collection entitled *The Great Wall of China*. It is sufficient to remark that here we are confronted with the same preoccupations as have tortured Kafka throughout his writings—the problems of guilt and original sin, of a mysterious and inscrutable authority, with their overtones of anxiety and persecution. In "Investigations of a Dog," Kafka's own search for the divine is pathetically parodied, the apparent moral being that it is as absurd for a dog to attempt to comprehend the rules which govern the behaviour of its invisible masters as it is for a human being to seek to scrutinize the divine forces which govern his destiny. "The Burrow," ". . . a description," according to Mr. Muir, "of the shifts to which man is reduced in his isolation, and the fatal imperfection of his most astute devices," portrays Kafka's personal situation in its last extremity. But the burrow, with its ingenious passages and its central Castle Keep filled with its maker's "stores," is not only a parable of introspection and self-love. It is also Kafka's symbol for his intellectual activity, his writings, which have been a painful but absorbing game during which he has been able to forget his "enemy"—fate, life, death, or the reality beyond death—in pre-

352

paring the burrow as a refuge against him—battering the walls of the Castle Keep firm with his head and cementing the sand with his blood which results. Yet nothing can really protect him from the "enemy." And when at last this mysterious being is in prospect, the burrower can only reprove himself for his failure to take still further, more complicated, precautions against the attacker—

> Not the slightest attempt have I made to carry out such a plan, nothing at all has been done in this direction, I have been as thoughtless as a child, I have passed my manhood's years in childish games, I have done nothing but play even with the thought of danger, I have shirked really taking thought for actual danger. And there has been no lack of warning.

Or, to take the opening sentence from "Investigations of a Dog,"

> How much my life has changed, and yet how unchanged it has remained at bottom!

To conclude, a merely esthetic approach to Kafka is bound to lead to an illusory estimate of his work, unless it is based upon some such apprehension of the total pattern of his writings as I have here attempted to display. For Kafka was not primarily an "artist"—who is?—but an explorer of the human condition, and the character of his work must be related to the compulsions of his questioning mind. Kafka himself is the sole subject of his work, and it was certainly of no one but himself that Kafka wrote—

> A certain heaviness, a feeling of being secured against every vicissitude, the vague assurance of a bed prepared for him and belonging to him alone, keeps him from getting up; but he is kept from lying still by an unrest which drives him from his bed, by his conscience, the endless beating of his heart, the fear of death and the longing to refute it: all this will not let him rest and he gets up again. This up and down and

353

a few fortuitous, desultory, irrelevant observations made in the course of it, are his life.

And again:

The bony structure of his own forehead blocks his way; he batters himself bloody against his own forehead.

the fundamental revolution

egon vietta

"There is only a spiritual world; what we call the physical world is the evil in the spiritual one, and what we call evil is only a necessary moment in our endless development."

—FRANZ KAFKA.

"The genius is distinguished from the ordinary person," writes Kierkegaard, "in that he starts, within the framework of his historical situation, on as primitive a level as Adam, and discards, as it were, the perspective of world-history." Any understanding of Kafka must begin with this basic premise. In one of his aphorisms he himself declares: "The decisive moment in human development is a continuous one. For this reason the revolutionary movements which declare everything preceding them to be null and void are in the right, for nothing has happened yet." There is also the piece entitled "The Next Village":

> My grandfather used to say: "Life is amazingly short. Now as I look back at it, things are crowded so closely together that I can hardly understand, for example, how a young person can decide to ride into the next

355

village without being afraid—quite aside from unfortunate accidents—that even the span of the average happy life will not nearly be long enough for such a ride."

To the grandfather, in the retrospect of his life, a ride from his village to the next seems like a practically impossible undertaking, not to be completed in the course of one lifetime. Here time is shown as something incommensurable with spatial concepts.

Thus Kafka's problems cannot be rooted within the perimeter of everyday necessities, conflicts and opinions. Before proceeding to investigate them it is necessary to free one's perspective. Kafka's inquiry consistently calls everything into question; his work is marked by a radical, philosophical openness, in which it anchors as in something abysmal and bottomless. This openness is carried to the extreme. Like Spinoza who, Egon Friedell says, petrified into a pathologist of logic, Kafka is an extremist, except that in his case the logical mechanism is converted into its opposite: the mechanism of the irrational. For his work derives from no thought-process but simply from a unique creative potentiality. The area of his creative power, to be sure, contains no plethora of possibilities which the poet must strive to confine, but rather a single cast of the die which has been vested with poetic form. The arbitrarily achieved isolation which lends his work such an appalling intensity is at the same time a great limitation. Hugo Friedrich has already noted that "all of Kafka's processes are strictly predetermined," due to a hopelessness beyond redemption. In the final chapters of *The Trial* Kafka's creative intensity is revealed in astounding concentration; the chapters, that is, containing the conversation which K., pursued by the inviolable Court, holds with the priest in the twilit Cathedral. The visionary dialogue, projected into empty space, reaches its climax in the quasi-Biblical parable of the door-keeper, the Law, and the man from the country. Here is an almost Spinozistic argument, one sentence of which merely serves to invalidate the other. This impossibility of finding a way out, Kafka epitomizes in the aphorism: "The bony structure of his own forehead blocks his way." The hero K., thrown entirely on himself, tossing in a whirl-

356

pool of questions which vanish into emptiness because no one knows to whom they are addressed, dies by a murderous, mysterious destiny. Here Kafka's basic attitude is more than clear, namely: world-anguish (not to be confused with social suffering, the destiny of Job).

There are no solutions in Kafka's works. Wherever he sought them in reality (as in *Amerika,* for example), his poetic power proved inadequate. He himself was clear on this point. For Kafka's basic attitudes, abstractly derived, are of such a nature that they do not permit a direct answer. Is this blind-alley an absolute one? Or is there a leap, a break-through, perhaps, of which this "no-way-out" is merely the premise? Does the poet's work indicate a dramatic collapse of all metaphysical hope (a painful exception in a time of opposite tendencies) or does it bear the mark of the precursor? Does Kafka's echoless isolation indicate a fundamental defect in himself or in our era?

           ✲   ✲   ✲

Important critics of Kafka have sought to link his work to the Christian doctrine of salvation or to "theological reflections" (Willy Haas). But even the concept "Justice" has no validity in Kafka's sphere. In his "Penal Colony" he invents an absurd recording machine of justice. His "God," who might well be the engineer of this contraption, dwells in a "castle," isolated by a lesser bureaucracy from all who do not possess credentials. The doctrine "all are summoned" Kafka ironically re-christens "all are unauthorized" (with the additional flavor of a police prohibition). In a letter to his friend Klopstock, Kafka meditates on Abraham's sacrifice:

> I could think of another kind of Abraham who . . . would be ready at once, with the subservience of a waiter, to fulfill the demand of the sacrifice, and who would nevertheless be unable to make it come off, because he could not get away from home. . . . Another Abraham, one who intends to perform a thoroughly proper sacrifice, and in general has the right instinct for the whole thing, cannot believe that he is the one who is meant. . . . He fears that he may ride out with

357

his son as Abraham, but on the way become meta-morphosed into Don Quixote.

The Quixotism of current religious claims could hardly be brought home more clearly. If Kafka believed in a divine guidance of human destiny (which is what the theologians mean by "Grace," says Brod in his Postscript to *The Castle*), then his work would cancel itself out, remaining only a senseless blasphemy. "Grace" presupposes a supernatural answer to human endeavor, and it is precisely this presupposition which is given an ironical turn in *The Castle*. It is "man's eternal being-in-the-wrong before God, no matter how much-in-the-wrong God may be before man," as Willy Haas excellently characterizes Kafka's ontological position. Would it not, then, be better to approach this position directly as a phenomenon instead of talking of "being-in-the-wrong" or of "God" (as Kafka himself does in his aphorisms)? There is there-fore little point in what Hans Joachim Schoeps says of Kafka's special significance for the religious problem of the Jews. It is rather that questions are involved here which formerly belonged to the province of theology. From this coincidence (as is already apparent in Kierkegaard) derives the erroneous subordination of Kafka to religious determinants.

∗   ∗   ∗

And, of course, Kafka's problems are clarified even less by a literary-historical approach. His creative forces, rooted in that unfathomable world-anguish, lie beyond actuality. Neverthe-less his work is integrated with the present time, and only in this reference can it be understood. Except that in this case time signifies not historical sequences of datable events, but rather the revolutionizing of basic human attitudes: the accepted concept of time, everything basically part of the fabric, above all the domi-nant surface of our era, the "hierarchy of facts." What is peculiar in Kafka is that the revolution pervades his entire work consist-ently. Hence the ease with which he absorbed into his work the milieu of everyday life.* Using conventional forms and present-

* There has been much argument concerning Kafka's "reality-symbolism," as if he were plotting against reality with a grotesque magnifica-tion of reality. His early work especially caused him to be misrepresented as a poet of "small things, the powerful small things." (Süskind)

ing facts in the traditional manner, he seems to be faithfully portraying reality. Hence it was possible for him to be mistaken for a critic of the judicial system in its concrete forms (*The Trial*) and even for a brother of the oppressed (the short stories, "The Metamorphosis," K. in *The Castle* and *The Trial*). However touching and poetically unique in his use of social distress as a symbol of a completely different, fundamentally human oppression, he thereby confused the mass of readers, for each sentence, each statement of his work is saturated with this entirely different basic attitude. Thus he is able to elevate the most brutal theme of everyday life to a symbol, since he can dispense with mysterious incidents and supernatural interferences. He dares confront the self-sufficient hierarchy of facts with a single possibility, in order to upset its balance. This, in great part, is the technique of his short stories. He does not dispute the man of "facts"; rather by a magical displacement in time-space relationships he upsets the conception of the world held by the man of "facts." Each of his works substantiates the premise that time for him cannot be fixed by dates. *The Castle*, to take a drastic example, could take place in the fifteenth century as well as in the twentieth. Though in *Amerika* he focuses particularly happily on modern perspectives, the action could take place in 1890 or 1940, historical placement is unnecessary. Similarly he may prophesy about the social community and its leaders (as in "The Great Wall of China") as if he were talking to a worker of the Leuna factory. In spite of, or perhaps because of, the over-clarification of details, space is subtilized to a mere outline. By this process what we prize as actuality is really quite hollow within. K.'s torturesome inner developments in *The Castle* and *The Trial* prevent us from noting the absence of geographical location. Even the letter K. is symbolic, for the hero requires no historical identity. He is taken up at any arbitrary exterior point in his life-journey—but still, it is the decisive one. Everything that precedes or accompanies the new development can be disregarded. For the traditional world of fact as presented to ordinary consciousness is deprived of its values. Therewith collapses an essential support. A reality so deprived of its rights succumbs to the magic play of possibility, its forms can easily be interchanged, and it clings desperately to those "manias of the imagination" on account of which stories like "The Hunger-

Artist," "The Country Doctor," and "The Metamorphosis" or the impressionistic nihilism of "First Sorrow" were received with admiration and also with a sense of surprise at their oddness (the poet's preference for vaudeville numbers, distorted into symbol, is indicative). The prisms of Kafka's view of the world, often so perfect, refract pure nothingness in their splendid color-play. But this nothingness breathes, threatens, speaks and is silent; apparently its frightful destiny is to become accessible only by the negation of everything positive and real.

What Kafka thought of facts is made quite evident in one of his aphorisms: "He rushes after facts like a novice on skates, a novice, moreover, who is practicing in a place where it is forbidden to skate."

❉   ❉   ❉

"The senseless has been appointed the executor of sense; we have to deal with it to the end," said Martin Buber of Kafka.❉ In these very "tangled knots of absolute contradictions" Buber discovers "the sense which proves to be totally different from our kind." Brod believes this interpretation can be confirmed from Kafka's diaries. It seems quite plausible to consider this "collision of sense with the senseless" (Brod) Kafka's basic theme.

The meaning of this Kafka has shown in one of his aphorisms, which elucidate so many of his problems:

> He feels imprisoned on this earth, he feels constricted; the melancholy, the impotence, the sicknesses, the feverish fancies of the captive afflict him; no comfort can comfort him, since it is merely comfort, gentle head-splitting comfort glozing the brutal fact of imprisonment. But if he is asked what he actually wants he cannot reply, for that is one of the strongest proofs —he has no conception of freedom.

The "tangled knots of absolute contradictions" prove to be a state of being helplessly trapped. Therefore the question must be asked again and again whether there is no way out, or whether we have to

❉ Quoted by Max Brod in a book published in honor of Buber and containing extracts from Kafka's diaries.

do with a negligence which, a priori, blocks the way out? Kafka pursues this train of thought in the story "A Report to an Academy," being the report of an ape who "through an effort never again repeated on this earth" has acquired the average education of a European. The description of the gradual advancement of the ape also embodies the meaning of the aphorism. The transition from ape to man takes place in a cage en route to Europe on the deck of a Hagenbeck steamer. "No, freedom was not what I wanted. It was just some escape." But the "great sense of freedom without restriction from any side" is worthless for the ape, for freedom means only liberty of movement, one more concrete possibility—this is of no value to him. Then a way out occurs to him: that of becoming a man. Yet Kafka evades the colossal task of revealing, if only theoretically, the "qualitative jump" (Kierkegaard) into the human state. Rather he gives the story a charming, poetic twist: the ape does not advance to the human state; he only becomes a vaudeville performer, in other words, the average educated Central-European. However accurately the gibe finds its mark—even the Academy, anxious for knowledge, is part of the same vaudeville show—the solution is not successful. Here Kafka's "hopelessness beyond redemption" leads to a defective concept of freedom. Here is that limit beyond which Kafka did not penetrate, which he treated as something absolute. He was, however, aware that the break-through, the jump over one's own shadow, cannot be prevented. He writes:

> All that he does seems to him, it is true, extraordinarily new, but also, because of the incredible spate of new things, extraordinarily amateurish, indeed scarcely tolerable, incapable of becoming history, breaking short the chain of the generations, cutting off for the first time at its most profound source the music of the world, which before him could at least be divined. Sometimes in his arrogance he has more anxiety for the world than for himself.

But, to speak figuratively, instead of spading more deeply, in order to lay bare ever more boldly the roots of human existence, at this decisive turning point he seeks a way out in allegorizing

361

reality: the poetically perfect and moving solution takes shape in the "Nature Theater of Oklahoma," in a universal charter of man for this world, similar to the one he apparently had planned as the conclusion of *The Castle*. It is not accidental that *Amerika* is the novel of an emigrant. It would be erroneous to see in the Nature Theater—this celestial-terrestrial prospect of redemption—nothing but the idea of the brotherhood of man. Rather this is the geometrical point where all contradictions dissolve, where no further questions can or may be asked. But in order to understand Kafka's own writings, it is necessary to go beyond this last fragment, even though the public may shrink back. "Too many individuals live in fear of a restless mind, but it is the restless mind which means real rest before eternity." (Kierkegaard)

What the public fears is a radical skepticism toward its standard of uniformly accepted ideas. Kafka puts fundamental question marks behind this well-proven reality. The historic Russian Revolution undertook the complete reversal of the collective consciousness of a people numbering many millions; within the framework of historical-materialistic conception of history to shift the figures on the chessboard of reality. But here the official version of "reality" is never put in doubt. This revolutionary attitude is entirely foreign to Kafka. It is true that his heroes are the socially oppressed, but it would be absurd to find feudal contrasts in the "lords of the castle" or to take the riches of the American uncle for more than a fairy tale from *The Arabian Nights*. In Kafka's world the earthly hierarchy does not exist, for "before God all men are equal."

We therefore have to look elsewhere for Kafka's revolutionary attitude. Never is it expressed in the form of a program, never is it made into a postulate, but—and this weighs more heavily—it is simply there. For a long time modern painting included in its manifestoes the demand for a loosening up of the temporal-spatial structure of pictures and thus it opened the road to unfathomed possibilities. In the same sense the metamorphosis of the "new music" cannot be observed solely in the changed idiom of its forms. The only explanation for it can be found in a basic shift within the consciousness itself, a shift involving chiefly man's self and not a system. This metamorphosis destroys the most secure

362

and apparently most valid current concepts and, like all revolutionary movements, it is not confined within national boundaries. The effect of this, so to speak, syndicalist plot is calculated the more exactly in that the individual is left no escape, not even withdrawal into a political ideology. The loss of immediate success with the public—and this applies to modern art in all its forms—is an extremely effective serum against its early decay. It may appear bold to establish such an essential connection between the different phenomena and to see in it a natural growth, to detach it from the context of historical development. The most comprehensive attempt at such a panoramic view of the present situation we owe to Ortega y Gasset. In the plastic arts innumerable monographs have made it a matter of course. If the historians of literature until now have only charted trends, it is because the decisive factors have not yet entered their consciousness.

For this metamorphosis of consciousness throws out a fundamental challenge to man and to the validity of his traditional view of the world. This process of chemical conversion cannot be demonstrated here. It has taken programmatic shape in personalities like Massimo Bontempelli and Jean Cocteau and it can be discerned in Rilke's *Duino Elegies*, that majestic phantasmagoria of the space of the mind where the ground often gives way. A plastic example in both meanings of the word is interpreted by Franz Roh in his *Post Expressionism:* I am speaking of the exceptional generation of the *valori plastici* in Italy. These painters—for example Chirico, Funi, Carrà—discover the "existence of an objective world which calls for a new twist"; they discover "the quiet admiration of the magic of existence" which tends toward a recreation of the objective world. The conventional horizon is abolished in favor of a more fundamental existence. It is decisive that the usual horizon is overcome so to speak by its own means, through the most intensive utilization of its own materials. This is the same process which operates in Kafka's short stories, and in the unreal reality of his novels. Though philosophically not yet clarified, a more profound conception of existence here presses forward and authorizes an art which, "while remaining conscious of its own power to form, is intent on seizing reality as such and does not wish to miss it in thrusting

363

past it." But this manner of seizing reality uproots conventionally accepted reality. If Kafka's work is put into this context, it loses any appearance it may have of being accidental and becomes an excellent source of insight into the new attitude of the spirit.

To give a purely formal analysis of this metamorphosis is impossible; it would only obscure instead of clarifying (though it is true that in isolated cases, such as Joyce's *Ulysses* or Gide's *Prometheus Illbound*, the purely formal is absorbed into the total process of fermentation and is therefore of equal significance). The incompleteness of Kafka's novels, even though due to external causes, perhaps, is not felt to be a shortcoming, and justly so. Here is an unintentional similarity between Kafka and the generation of great European novelists like Dostoyevsky, Proust, even Gide, whose sensibility found fragmentariness a necessity, for a formal conclusion means nothing in these novels.

If Kafka's work cannot be divided into different phases and dismissed with a partial solution which would have validity only for him, this is due to the fundamental homogeneity of his work, even stylistically. This basic unifying element is a sustained feeling of oppression, a metaphysical anguish. Kafka visualized the resolution of dissonances almost concretely, but it was in the nature of his work that he could not achieve it. However from every side solutions were suggested to him which went beyond his questions (though the public had not yet caught up even with those) and which, in an incomparable, sparkling display of intuitions and possibilities illuminate his dominant anguish. Of this resolution of dissonances the great law-maker of modern music, Ferruccio Busoni, said in his "Outline" of a new aesthetics of music: "However young this child may be, one radiant quality can already be discerned which distinguishes it from its older companions: it floats in the air! It does not touch the earth. It is not subject to the law of gravity. It is almost incorporeal. . . . *It is free.*"

Philosophical methods cannot deal with this concept of freedom. It is a kind of graceful unimpeded ease, whose metaphysics is intimately acquainted with the fathomless. It is a magic game of catching all possibilities thrown in its way. Only from this point of view can we understand the much discussed lack of seriousness of modern artists. It is that esoteric and aristo-cratic elasticity whose beauty fascinated Nietzsche. To be sure we do not claim this to be the only possible solution, even though it has succeeded in creating the purest harmonies thus far. Nat-urally one cannot penetrate into Kafka's world if, owing to an acoustic illusion, as Nietzsche calls it, one does not understand the fundamental revolution.

Translated by Lienhard Bergel and F. Wood.

intuition

ezequiel martínez estrada

The work of Franz Kafka, aside from its great literary value, is framed within a very delicately adjusted metaphysical concept. The observing reader will realize this fact when he notes that in each one of Kafka's pieces—novel or story—the subject is connected with a theme of universal significance. Plot, incident and character, which in his stories have neither beginning nor end, seem to be concluded, explained and justified in the writer's vast hidden context. They are like brightly lighted cogs of a great machine which remains in darkness, but of whose existence and infallibly precise functioning we are certain.

Putting aside for the moment Kafka's merit as a writer and a poet, we must endeavor to reconstruct this vast system by means of the content implicit in his work, and with a thorough examination of metaphors, establish some points of reference and comparison.

The most direct route to an interpretation of Kafka is not that which leads straight to conclusions. It is the road which winds through the unmapped terrain of Kafka's world, a sphere in which the reality of the text is fused with the reality of our

367

world, a sphere in which the validity of reason itself is questionable. This world of Kafka's can be located within the orbit of the thought and sensitivity of the beginning of this century. Poets, philosophers and scientists worked separately and together to make knowledge and intuition more flexible, weakening or denying the heretofore unquestioned rights of the postulates of reason and the certitudes of common sense. Since the physical and biological worlds now scarcely preserve a trace of the past century's positive sciences, we feel that man is reborn into a more certain world, a world of new thought. The temple of this thought, an immense structure constructed by reason and logic, has been torn down almost to its foundations by reason and logic themselves, and replaced by an edifice solidly buttressed by the principles of statistical order and indetermination.° Man can now regard with equanimity the ruins of the former building and of the scaffolding for its continuation, and take pride in the absolute, mathematical security of the new one. The new technique for understanding and divining the nature of the world—intuition —created by the simultaneous functioning of new mental and sensory organs, was heralded by several extraordinary men, almost contemporary: Kierkegaard, Gauss and Poe. The others who followed—Nietzsche, Whitehead, Spengler; Lobatchevski, Einstein, Schrödinger; Dostoyevsky, Joyce, Kafka—perfected the instrumental use of the new reason and intuition. For them, objects and beings are located in an unexplored "area" where it is evident that relationships and functions are more certain and important than the objects and beings themselves, where man's existence is a story about to be written for the first time. Kafka, in a manner like no one before him, applies the new tool of pure intuition to the observation and chronicling of the reality of man in an alien world. Although it was forgotten by men in their first enthusiasm at exploring the world, this tool is a vital compass of long standing among animals and an old force among men in the ancient days when they created myths, extracted numbers

° Concerning these edifices, Louis de Broglie says ". . . they were not destroyed by progress, but enveloped within vaster structures." *The New Physics and Quantum Mechanics.*

and figures from objects, and used articulated sound for communication.

This world can no longer be negated. Nor can the existence of man as an entity within an "area" full of mysterious forces which determine his conduct, his biography and his destiny, be overlooked. Its investigation and explanation can be attempted by means of two methods: through pure reason or through pure intuition. Man has been progressing along the road of reason. Out of the ratiocination of myths, numbers, figures and sounds resulted a reality. So man abandoned the path of intuition, which had begun to point to "another reality." It was inevitable, and to man's credit, that only ratiocination could finally discover after centuries that reason was not an infallible exploratory organ, but simply an auxiliary tool. The use of intuition was necessary in investigation of the vegetable and animal worlds, whose cosmoses differ from ours to such an extent that they are absolutely irreconcilable through the sole use of ratiocination. We could systematize the insects, plants and mammals with reason, but nothing more. Linnaeus was the outstanding representative of this method of understanding nature through a classification system, and Darwin the extreme advocate of a rationalistic and mechanical interpretation of that same classifiable world. So reason at first rationally defined the world and was satisfied to understand and explain it rationally.

But now we can see that there is something else. There exists the "world" as it is conceived by the theory of relativity, and there exist other worlds even more complex—the world of living beings as the neo-vitalists have begun to conceive it; and, within the cosmos of relativity and the universe of neo-vitalism, the world of man. The character of this world cannot be itemized. It is divined by intuition and intuitively transmitted to others. No one else has gone so far in this as Kafka, because his intuition is within the structure of those systems, and this is why his works seem to be visible parts of a mysterious and vast reality. With him we return to Plato, to the author of the metaphysical and aesthetic dialogues, free from the contradictions of his pupil, Aristotle, and of his pseudo-teacher, Pythagoras. Above all,

369

we return to Lâo-tse, who, whether Kafka knew it or not, was perhaps his only teacher.[*]

This "world" of Kafka's is the world of all beings except man; but a world within which man has enclosed a human system of life and understanding; therefore it is not logical, but dramatic. It is an illogical, mythical and absurd world, the ancestral world of dreams which are not distinct from wakefulness, and which speak a long-forgotten language whose key must be discovered. In man's body, like still more dormant dreams, lie his millions of years in ignorance of his origin.

Therefore it is naïve to say that in Kafka everything is explained because with his infinite and casual arguments, his elastic time and his projection over the borders of the unfinished and the inexplicable, he adjusts the technique of dreaming dreams to the facts of ordinary life. This would not disturb us. This would be a technique and nothing more. Yet possibly this ingenuous explanation is necessary to form the image of its opposite, a method which is perhaps the only recourse of reason to delineate this world of structures and functions where an individual needs neither soul nor name; this world of intuitive understanding of the eternal and the universal; this world of the adjective and adverb (immensely more important and sure than verb and noun); this world of pure "taboo" which is yet the world of the quintessence of birds, lizards, rose-bushes and butterflies. It is a world which has not yet entirely disappeared for man, one which is contained within himself, which does not interrupt or accent his life with nights and days, and of which he has only occasional and fleeting flashes of intuition or memory.

From this forgotten world—this world which has disappeared like ancient cultures beneath the pavements of modern cities, and like the origins of theorems and syllogisms—Kafka brings to the surface of our conscience, to the thin gray cortex of

[*] In his work on Lâo-tse and Taoism, Richard Wilhelm lists the following translations into German of the Chinese philosopher: *Laotse, Taoteking, das Buch des Alten vom Sinn und Leben*. Jena, 1911; and *Laotses Buch vom Höchsten Wesen und vom Höchsten Gut*. Tübingen, 1910. Kafka could have read these works. Lâo-tse's thought is the only precedent I know of for his manner of conceiving the world.

our being, a direct and mystic message of strangeness and of awe, a message never before so clear and vivid in any writer. What Frobenius, Freud and Nietzsche tried to explain as an extreme case by this system (which only succeeded in obliterating our previous intuitive knowledge of it) Kafka expresses in the language of the problem itself—in words which create in turn myths and symbols. His world is, then, not that of beings and objects, of solid geometry, but is composed of perfectly structured hollows into which the objects and beings are inexorably and inexplicably fitted. Kafka uses nothing but intuition, the artist's only legitimate instrument of understanding. We read his tales and we see, far out beyond their hazy boundaries, an indistinct figure which envelops everything, within which the author, his story, and we ourselves are like characters in another tale. We read them and it is as if, with some organ distinct from those we are using, we perceived beneath the printed text blurred traces of our own lives. Whatever the episode we choose, we know that we are reading a chapter of the new history of man.

It is also wrong, moreover, to speak of absurdity in Kafka's novels and stories, for the absurd is carefully extracted from them (as in Poe) and projected into the outside and the beyond which surrounds them. Projected too beyond the text is his characters' reason—they scarcely reason—as well as their individuality, generally recognized by physiognomy or a name, which is here reduced to a mere initial letter—K. or A. or B. Nor do madness or the incomprehensible occur in his work in reference to beings or objects, but they too are incorporated into the hidden sense, into the context, into this world which escapes reason.

Does the work of Kafka then provide any guarantee that it is not based on that delirious world which Dostoyevsky as a protagonist without shape or role injects into his novels? Yes. Kafka's world is a perfectly logical world. It is guaranteed by reason, for it is constructed as if by an architect's hand; and it is guaranteed by deep intuition, for it is animated by symbols. Man's dreams and his deliriums, and the absolution of his guilt, are in the beyond; everything which formerly constituted man's tragedy—his vertigo at the fall into the deepest recesses of introspection—also remains on the outside, more so than in the trag-

371

edies of Sophocles, where fate finally penetrates the hearts of his heroes and there arouses terror or remorse. All this delineates the "areas," the hollows of a history without historian, of an empty honeycomb, of a structure to which life must conform, where human bodies with their accompanying psychological burdens must find their corresponding places—data for our understanding and intuition of the true reality of man.

Translated by Caroline Muhlenberg.

the negative capability

wladimir weidlé

A letter from Keats to his two brothers (December 21, 1817) contains a passage, often quoted by English critics, whose esthetic and historical relevance has not been duly emphasized. The poet says that he and his friend Dilke had been discussing what quality is most essential in a great man of letters, a great poet. This quality, which Shakespeare possessed "so enormously," Keats called *negative capability*, i.e., "when a man is capable of being in uncertainties, mysteries, doubts, without any irritable reaching after fact and reason." Any debilitation of this power may imperil poetry. This is an original, accurate and profound observation, of real significance in understanding the fate of poetry and art in general. It manifested itself in Keats' time, and has not ceased developing, manifesting itself most conspicuously during the first half of the twentieth century.

The negative capability is the gift of remaining faithful to an intuitive certainty, discarded by reason and precluded by common sense; of preserving a way of thinking which must seem insensate and illogical to reason and logic, but which from a deeper viewpoint may appear superior to reason and transcends

373

the logic of conceptual thought. If this gift is negative it is so only in opposing that other faculty, that other calculating and discursive technical and scientific tendency, that "irritable reaching after fact and reason" which, from the moment it crosses the boundaries assigned to it, destroys all art and poetry.

Truly nothing is more positive than the negative capability. To make use of it does not mean "remaining content with half-knowledge"; it means, on the contrary, the knowing of truths which, without it, would remain unknown.

Undoubtedly the development of abstract reasoning and conceptual dialectics is compatible, within certain limits, with that of artistic creation; yet if we were to call progress a development which ends with the triumph of rational and scientific knowledge over all the rest of the forms of knowledge and, in a general way, over spiritual activity, it is necessary to recognize that inevitably the time will come, whether one wants it or not, whether one is conscious of it or not, when progress will be the enemy of art and of culture in general, which a civilization exclusively technical and scientific will endeavor to replace.

Considered in its positive aspect, Keats' negative capability is the gift of seeing the miraculous face of things. In bygone days since such a gift was nothing exceptional there was little ado about it. The poet's imagination differed from that of simple men in its greater sharpness, amplitude and intensity. Only after the inevitable hour had sounded, and precisely because it occurred thus, Keats was able to feel so keenly the discovery of his uniqueness among men, of his family-bond with Shakespeare, of the qualities they had in common, of the danger with which the impatient exigencies of reason may beset a genius as arithmetical as Coleridge. The miraculous character of the things he saw and believed in, no one near him saw. Without negating "natural laws," that miraculous character merely reacted against scientific knowledge which, in the name of progress and technology, was trying to formulate and exploit those laws. At times the miraculous shone across the mathematical web of the world which seemed to be the only knowable thing and the only thing worth knowing, just as today the sun rises and sets on the immovable earth, regardless of Copernicus. Henceforth the poet and the

374

artist—and this is what Keats understood—will have to endeavor, above all, to acquire the virtue of living in this miraculous world, of breathing its air, for art and poetry will only asphyxiate in progress and pure reason. At present everyone feels and knows it —at least all those who are not contented with the reasonable and the useful, all those whom the negative capability inspires with nostalgia. The last century witnessed the artist's struggle to conquer the miraculous, to defend himself against the historical and biological development which threatened to deny him his most sacred right: that of creation.

Most of the artists of the last century who endeavored to react against the rationalist disintegration of their art were reactionaries not merely because they negated progress, more or less consciously, but because they wanted to retrogress to an earlier phase of mankind's historical development. Here lie the true roots of all primitivisms, so numerous from the Romantic period with its imitation of popular poetry to Gauguin's flight to Tahiti, from the appearance of the German Nazarenes and the English Pre-Raphaelites to our own day, with its admirers of Negro sculpture and Negro music. All these aspirations have the same background. Primitivism means the flight of the artist from his own period into another. He considers that this is the only way offered him by a world otherwise closed to him. The propagation of primitivisms did not cease with the post-World War I period but, on the contrary, they became more popular in the realm of artistic creation. Today in order to achieve this artificial return to the primitive, the artist recurs not only to phylogenesis but also to ontogenesis, i.e., the childhood of the individual interests him as much as the childhood of the species.

o　　o　　o

Among the many tortures which the contemporary world holds in store for the artist, the cruelest, perhaps, is the torture of light. The tormented one is like a prisoner locked in a cell in which high-power lamps burn day and night. To avoid the blinding glare he seeks a world free of this torment, and he dreams of a negative capability. The director of the Paris Observatory once declared that he hated poetry because it did nothing but lie and that scientists cannot bear poetical lies. While scientific creation in more ways than one resembles artistic and poetic creation, the artists' sentiment of the world remains irreconcilable with that which the scientists believe they can deduce from science with no other help. Logarithm tables shine with such marvelous clarity that the astronomer, fascinated by his calculations, feels inclined to curse the obscurantism of a Goethe or a Shakespeare. There are many worshipers of numbers in the contemporary world, and the religion of science apparently regards art as no more than a well-organized deceit, and poetry as a charlatan invention. A new Moses has come down from Mount Sinai and the Commandments he brings are the four rules of arithmetic. Of course the artist must also recognize that $2+2=4$ or 3 or 5, but—what can he do with such a truth which admits no other truth? He endeavors to escape from this sortilege by returning to bygone periods of mankind, but this remedy is none too certain, and his only recourse is to invoke the darkness, where there are neither calculations nor measurements, where 1000-watt lamps do not burn, where nothing can prevent him from extinguishing the intelligible world and sinking into the nocturnal world of sleep, of insanity, of sex and of the unconscious.

This road is not a new one; it was charted at least 150 years ago, at a time when "our age" was beginning to react violently against rationalism and the scientific spirit of the century of "lights." The German romanticists felt greatly drawn to "the nocturnal face of Nature"; Herder taught the young Goethe the "tactile" knowledge of the world by means of sentiment and intuition as opposed to diurnal and rational knowledge; and thus—as the author points out—in the second part of *Faust* the "*Lynkenslied*" to the beauty of visible things is sung in a "deep night." In the literature and art of the nineteenth century we find that leitmotiv of flight to the depths, to a realm inaccessible to intellectual consciousness, to a world beyond the reason which measures and differentiates. Experiences of this type may or may not be useful to this or that artist, but the problem now becoming urgent is whether this road is still open today or whether artists should henceforth consider it a road not to be trespassed. Nor does the nocturnal world seem destined to disintegrate under the pressure

376

of forces hostile to art, since these make us see art as a mechanical necessity, a determined causality. Psychoanalysis is the most systematized and broadly conceived attempt at "mechanizing" the unconscious, at reducing dreams, love, the creation of myths and the creative processes in literature, to the regular functioning of an internal mechanism. Under the influence of psychoanalysis or parallel to its evolution, this viewpoint keeps growing in the arts and letters of our time. The artist gulps down a soporific and sinks into darkness, but even in his sleep he is only a robot, and the world a machine.

The imagination of some painters, such as Chagall or Rouault, still provides them with visions which do not appeal to the tribunal of "exact science" nor to that of a psychology which derives its methods and postulates from this science; but the imagination of the surrealists—be their names Chirico, Max Ernst or Salvador Dalí—offers them only materials already exploited by reason: by a reason adapted to the methods of psychoanalysis. If inevitably their dreams become nightmares, it is because in the darkest corners of their refuge the hated electric lamp goes on automatically. In discussing them, one is inclined to invert the Sensualist formula: in the senses of these artists there is nothing which has not previously been in their intellect. What is found in the canvases or poems—even in those of an authentic poet, free from the formulas of any specific school, such as Pierre-Jean Jouve—is not primitive chaos, capable of engendering life and light, but the inorganic incoherence of a whole city or of a body torn by shrapnel. Even in the case of a magician of dreams as original as Marcel Jouhandeau, we nearly always feel that there is something calculated, artificial and distorted in him; the effort of the intellect has transformed his characters into statues of salt, and everywhere in his books we meet the same galvanized human beings, sacred images or wax dolls, resembling the mannequins in Prudence Hautechaume's show window. Even stranger from this viewpoint is the destiny of D. H. Lawrence. The pan-sexualism of Rozanov (which Lawrence did not know and would not have understood, perhaps) had already called for an immersion in the night, but still it was a night inducive of procreation, of birth, the tutelary night of every generation, and the nostalgia which inspired Rozanov, despite its carnal warmth, was not unlike Goethe's "*Selige Sehnsucht*." No doubt Lawrence would have wished that his pan-sexualism might have been something similar, that it might have been a blessing to life, and brought to man that elemental fullness of the individual for which he thirsted; but he did not know how to achieve it. The failure of *Lady Chatterley's Lover*, Lawrence's literary testament, his favorite work, which he rewrote three times, was due to this anomaly: that its author, almost in spite of himself, was forced to supplement his hymns to the love of soul and body—indivisible love—with a number of prescriptions for the normal functioning of the sexual mechanism.

As often happens, destructive forces which have actually constituted a hindrance to artistic creation have found, in spite of everything, artists who succeeded in expressing them exhaustively and even in reinforcing them and extracting from them their tragic beauty. In the realm of the dissolution of the personality and of the novel, this artist is Marcel Proust; in the mechanization of the unconscious, it is Franz Kafka. It is very difficult to appreciate Kafka from translations, for his first and foremost quality is his language—extraordinarily clear, transparent, musical—a classically harmonious style without which he could not have expressed the inexplicable oppression, the unspeakable anguish, which form the content of his unique books, so clear and at the same time so impenetrable, in which the darkest night is as if imprisoned in a crystal glass. They would not be what they are if Kafka's writing had been ornamental, oratorical or "romantic." Only the luminous sobriety of their verbal raiment allowed their intimate, strange and incomparable essence to be expressed.

This strangeness is by no means due to this or that preconceived artistic idea, to a search after originality at any cost. Rather it is due entirely to the sentiment of life inextricably bound up with Kafka's nature. The publisher of *Amerika*—one of his three unfinished novels—summarizes the book thus: "A young student, Karl, must, after a misadventure, leave his paternal home and Europe. Penniless and dependent upon nobody but himself, he becomes acquainted with the New York of the rich and of the poor. He leads a vagabond's existence, gets a job as elevator boy

378

in a big hotel, as servant to shady characters, but nevertheless he forges ahead in life thanks to his irreproachable honesty." It must be said of this resumé that it is at one and the same time completely accurate and perfectly false. The external facts are correct but they do not mean anything in relation to the real content of the novel, which is far from what the facts would have us suppose. All that the story, so limpid and serene, presents to us is phantasmagoria, it possesses only the incomplete and fleeting reality of dreams; the most elementary sensory qualities are missing. Reading Kafka, one constantly has the impression of attending a concert in which the pianist is running his fingers along a muted piano with the most natural air in the world, or of listening to a very animated conversation but one in which we suddenly notice that the lips of the interlocutors are not moving, and that in place of eyes they have deep black holes. All these characters, so natural at first sight, have lost their shadows and one feels that they could go through a wall or be diluted in a sun ray. The more we read the more we are convinced—and the impression becomes more acute until it attains unbearable proportions in the last chapter of *Amerika*—that we are attending the unfolding of an extremely subtle allegory whose hidden meaning we are about to guess. We need the meaning, we expect it to come; the suspense becomes painful, we are as if in the midst of a nightmare a few seconds before awakening—but we do not awaken and the end of the story explains nothing. We are condemned to the absurd, we must wander indefinitely in the exitless labyrinth of existence; and suddenly it dawns upon us that this and this alone was what Kafka meant.

Life is nothing but darkness; and here it is fitting to say once again that now it is not a matter of the penumbra of sex, birth, the original night, but rather a pitch-black darkness, of death. Kafka has delved into the unconscious to the point of insanity, and he has found but this: definitive, unappealable condemnation. The hero of *Amerika* is condemned to lovelessness and solitude; the hero of *The Castle*, to the impossibility of making himself understood and of ever finding a familiar world again; the hero of *The Trial*, to the perpetual awaiting of the verdict and the final punishment. The same sentiment is expressed with a maximum of intensity in the stories of *The Great Wall of China*,

379

especially in "Investigations of a Dog," where the vanity of all knowledge is demonstrated in implacable form. In like manner it is made evident in the dreadful unfinished story entitled "The Burrow": an unknown animal (who speaks in the first person) inhabits an ingeniously excavated burrow to escape a mortal danger which threatens him and which he cannot avoid. All that Kafka wrote merely verifies the inexorable law of absurdity. Man, he said, vainly beats his forehead against his own forehead. There is no salvation. The sensation of impending asphyxia, like that of a human being buried alive who awakens in a coffin, has never been described with greater intensity than in these books which are so clear, so polished and tranquilly perfect. Art exists here only to discover the nocturnal secret of existence; it does not lie, and what it reveals is not freedom but cold necessity and death. "Our art," Kafka said, "is a dazzled blindness before the truth: The light on the grotesque recoiling phiz is true, but nothing else." The gift with which Kafka was endowed was such that it permitted him to incarnate totally in his works his almost inhuman experience in its unilateral depth. His art is an authentic art, but mutilated and fenced in against nothingness. This author progressed farther than any other into the nameless country and brought from there only the same mechanical determinism which the art of our times tries desperately to avoid in order to be able to breathe freely, in order to be able to revive. Why has this happened? Hasn't it been, perhaps, because in our time mechanical causality dominates the spirit and the creative imagination of the artist to such an extent that it and it alone, is still the only thing that he knows how to distinguish in the realm of the unconscious, of dreams, and of mythical intuition? The nocturnal genius of Kafka only demonstrates, clearer than any other, the weight that he and others have had to bear. He obeyed only his narrow but infallible instinct in the direction which he irrevocably took; others have endeavored to erect into a principle, into a method, that which was for him an entirely personal and profound "expérience vécue"; and this explains why the destructive forces which he knew how to place at the service of his art and which he incarnated in his work, have destroyed the art of the others and even hindered them in achieving their work. The disaster in this case is principally the result of a tendency which is very prevalent

380

in our day and which assumes different forms; in essence it consists in replacing art by a magic, that is to say, by a system of procedures designed to react upon the unconscious in a premeditated way, to alter the inner life of the reader, the judge and the spectator in a specific direction. Artists who have such a conception about their art generally do not realize that magic differs from applied science only in the processes it uses and not in the goal it is aiming at, while in the realm of art it is not possible to speak of a motive beyond the work itself. Surrealism in some of its manifestations constitutes precisely such an attempt to replace art by an immediate magical reaction upon man or, to put it more accurately, upon the nervous system of man, since the new magic is inclined to take over from science the idea which the latter has about man and the world. It is for this reason and owing to a—so to speak—therapeutic orientation, that such a magic, instead of rejuvenating art, can only kill it. Danger besets art and this danger is extremely grave. In the first place there is danger in proclaiming as a model irregularity itself and of finding a new obligation in the arbitrary. The irrational as such, transformed into an abstract principle, is the worst of rationalist errors, and the modern world offers to us more than one example of the superlatively inhuman determinism which is deduced from irrational premises—not such, of course, because of their superiority to reason, but because they have been taken by means of an act of the will from the domain of intelligence. Art is asphyxiating in a world where technical and utilitarian thought reigns supreme, in a world tyrannized by the arithmetical spirit; but it will gain nothing if it applies this arithmetic—with equal rigor—to premises irrational by dint of their absurdity. The symbol of the modern world is not only the machine but also the god of the machine adored under the puerile guise of a mascot or a fetish. If the artist's eyes pain him because of the electric light, that does not mean that it is necessary to break the bulb or to replace it with a kerosene lamp; it only means that the moment has arrived for the prisoner to escape from his prison and to seek elsewhere for a little bit of fresh air and living brightness.

Translated by Arlene Harrow.

381

the economy of chaos

t. weiss

A study of the fashions in chaos—that is, its varying
dispositions in different times and different societies, might prove
extremely revelatory to an understanding of the history of civilization. Applied particularly to the work of one writer, say an artist
as tantalizing as Franz Kafka, such a study should help to define
his unique quality and his contribution as well as the specific
character of chaos in his age. We can at once remark the vast
divergences in the pagan, the Jewish and the Christian attitudes
toward chaos. In the Judaistic world the invisible was worshipped
till the visible nearly disappeared; even bushes went up in smoke.
Despite the various beliefs already articulated, we can realize
what a splendid moral monolith this tower of Babel was. Chaos
was ubiquitous. But it was regarded, with all its multiplicity and
by the very oneness of man's inability to translate it, as the single
voice of God. Everywhere uttered, this voice the Jews met by
falling prostrate before it, to worship what by its inscrutability
was terribly superior. Still the ego of man was supreme; in hum-
bling himself, he was elevating and worshiping a part of himself, that which he could not explain.

Among the Greeks, however, the visible, coming into

383

its own, was enjoyed to the point where the invisible almost emerges. Notwithstanding the idealism of men like Plato, the Greeks generally luxuriated in what they saw; stones became men; the sea was one of their most frequented temples, the passionate home of myriad maidens pure by inconstancy. Even Venus rose. For the Greeks, by embracing their element with gusto, had mastered it. To account for multiplicity, yet to keep it in all its profound particularity, they established their abundant family of gods. Generously graceful, the Greeks even deferred to the unknown god; a stranger in their midst must be welcomed, housed, naturalized. Again, the unknown was a certainty; chaos was accounted for.

As for the first Christians, since they were, largely, converts out of impoverishment and slavery, they were expert at dealing in the invisible, the only element in which they could be free and infinitely wealthy. For poverty and rejection have fierce prides that must also be satisfied. Accordingly, these Christians seized upon the unknown god, and as their company increased, he grew. For even as Christ was the invisible manifested in the shape of man, so the Christian God was the Judaistic deity, also an invisible (the Jews were not to worship idols), embodied, paradoxically, in the unknown god, but stript presumably of human imperfection. The consummation of all wishes, this Christian God nonetheless preserved the slightest nuance of ignorance and fear. The world was still, transparently, the inscrutable word and will of God. As the wealth of worshiping accumulated, however, the church, expanding, adapted an additional Greek practice; it populated itself with the rich embodiments of myriad hopes. Why not employ a host of venerable figures? With the apotheosizing of lowliness, Christianity's power and glory, the hierarchy of the saints came into being. Multiplicity was still maintained; chaos had become a well-mapped city.

So, basically, the acclimations to chaos have expressed themselves. But frequently, in a very short time, an attitude, like chaos itself, undergoes considerable alteration. In fact, occasionally in the same period, one man by his sensitivity to the root impulses of his world can in penetration readily outstrip all his contemporaries. Shakespeare, for example, looked over the shoul-

384

der of the later Milton far beyond the confines of Milton's world. In Milton's universe even infinity was tidy. The circle of eternity was drawn; a sufficiency of faith could, on clear evenings, discern its rondure. Struck as it was by conflicting beliefs, this universe stood—stood in the dogma of Milton's wish. For what more could he request than the architectural order the church prescribed? A closed world, carefully supervised, with chaos a convenient supply of building materials for whatever additional wings God might eventually plan. This was a world to live in—a universe in which one's esthetic and the world agreed! No wonder Milton fought so heroically in the crusade of this order.

The tremors in Shakespeare's world, however, were much mightier. What are Hamlet, Macbeth, Cleopatra and the rest but quintessentialized human beings questioning their day's world-picture, questioning, defying, threatening? The picture is saved, but only after stains and gashes mar its surface. Gradually other probing fingers enlarged these gashes. Some Renaissance men, resenting complete projection and a life of promises, began to study as substance what hitherto had been dismissed as shadow; humanity itself, as it was, not as it might be or would like to be, became their occupation, the world too as their senses knew it. The rent which Shakespeare's plays contain grew until the distance between the old world and the new became un-bridgeable for not a few. Still the majority insisted on or pas-sively accepted the old cosmological dispensation.

Perhaps the most ardent champion of this dispensation in recent times was Dostoyevsky. But an always spreading para-dox strikes across the heart of his work for us. Though the world he envisions is as tormented as a world can be, always, many miles below, he takes for granted the inexpungable foundation of faith. The frenzy of life, the changingness of his people, that he saw as clearly as any eye the world had, he presented mainly as proof of both the existence of and our need for such a faith. Of course, within such a stable framework many incidental chaoses can appear and even prosper. When a deep-sea diver is confident of the strength and rootedness of his life-line, he can attempt the blackest, most perilous depths. The paradox and irony of Dostoyevsky's work is that he has, for the most part, especially as we seem to come closer and closer to his characters, convinced us of the damnable accuracy of his details; this conviction has strengthened, for an always growing number, doubt of his foundation of belief rather than belief itself. Such a world is as unacceptable to many as Milton's.

Yet even among the most skeptical the nostalgia for the comforts and security of faith clings on. Though he may not be able to accept past mythologies, man is reluctant to abandon them; he is loath to deny his childhood and the proud childhood of his race. Science has battered the door down, exposed us to all the perils of the unknown which space contains. With the womb of wish violated, infinity has become its present self; and the prophecy that we should be as sands on the shore of eternity has been fulfilled. But few have the strength the present demands. Man, it would seem, has not been large enough in himself to support his own visions. Yet, contrarily, he has. For, after all, what is creation but man's creation, his dreams believed in?

But language changes. The dialect of today (language determines our thoughts probably as much as thought the language) for most of its inhabitants poorly contains yesterday's religions. Stuttering at best, this dialect cannot understand the religions or put much conviction in their utterance. The world, moving, has changed shape; the readymade answers can hardly fit. So man must move nakedly through his world (we see, in the album of beliefs, the ridiculousness of ancient costumes or customs) or weave together the pieces of the past. But though man cannot long do without explanations, ours is a time in which most answers are made of such inferior stuff they prove either flimsy or unfashionable even as we try them on. At this juncture the writer perhaps most agonizingly aware of his nakedness is Franz Kafka,* another example that men normally must live in projection; they must push themselves away, open their world before them. Religion or art, these are the principal worlds men try to rear around themselves.

Like Dostoyevsky, completely aware of the confusion

* I wish to thank Professor Paul Weiss for stimulation in talks with him about Kafka.

about him, Kafka in addition was partially taken in by it; he lacked the framework of faith. With a frightening precision he set about to build what he could. And always because perfection was his ambition, he failed. No wonder his books are incomplete. From such a realization, if his art was to be honest, picturing an open world, how could it achieve a conclusion? The inevitable dissatisfaction, however, made his desire that his work be destroyed plain enough. And yet, possessed as he was of a religious temperament, he refused to be victimized by it. He accommodated in his world the very thing modern man has striven to keep out; chaos, the unknown, became a common staple in his work.

As Austin Warren has put it in "Kosmos Kafka," Kafka is "not a moralist and reformer but a man of religion. The problem is one of accepting the universe, of learning, by means of pathos, humor, and irony, to tolerate it. The too painful sense of life as mystery can be transcended by reducing mystery to a kind of pattern. You don't solve the mystery, but you segregate it and give it status, you learn to live with it." This was Kafka's treatment, his economy of chaos. He did not solve chaos; rather he kept it in solution. Yet by the strength of his art, an awareness and so an order appeared. He did not reduce mystery, but by remarking its continuous presence in the most commonplace, eventually the most mysterious might be accepted as rather daily. Kafka captures the dream content of the homely; through him we come awake into the terrible dream of the ordinary that usually comforts us; we see this dream with the impact of clarity and intimacy strangeness alone can insist on, with the wide-awake eyes of the dreamer, for the cul-de-sac the supposed insulation of the ordinary is. It is the feeling of apartness, of being locked out, one occasionally gets in looking, say, at a dog. As it looks through us, we fear it because we do not know what it can do. Now imagine this attitude maintained toward oneself. Such mystery is luminously plain in Kafka's writing. He cannot dispose of it; but, after all, disposal is not his problem or his province; the realization of this mystery is quite enough. Speculation may try to dispose of it; art brings it back furiously alive and thriving. By his realization Kafka's art could not embarrass him. Unlike

most economies, it would not suddenly discover that it had not
made room for an unexpected, yet terribly important, guest. Generally, in other worlds confronted with such unexpectedness, the
entire structure must be leveled and a new one erected. Kafka,
on the other hand, does not try to persuade the world to accept
his terms. More than that, he does not try to wring meanings
(still terms or preconceptions) from the world he sees. That
world is enough, almost too much.

Of course Kafka shocks us, for, as we have suggested,
he shows us bits of ourselves we thought we had completely concealed, from ourselves as well as from others. Bereft of social
conventions and personal habits which normally give us our feeling of immortality, we are plunged into the racing crystal stream
of our own core changingness. For the first time we meet our
swift, fiery-cold perpetuity. His is the microscope that by the flaw
of vision, the bright obliquity, reveals in our daily conventions
and convictions the unsuspected horror; our world remains our
world, and yet it is terrible, more terrible and strange by this
intimacy, this remaining the same. Then can the nightmare be
horrified by what is really the daily. What is particularly frightening is the work's relentless logic, its unequivocal accuracy. We
are trapped in our logic. And suddenly we understand it. Think
of the momentary seen with the terrified eyes of eternity; think
also of eternity at the mercy of the transient as, in a sense, it is,
of the everlasting able to see itself in the shape of the speedily
passing, the human race. We too therefore see ourselves from the
outside snared in our vision. But possibly this insight is our only
freedom.

There are other logics, that of the insane and of orders
we cannot know. Naturally we impugn the existence of such
logics. For as men we are doomed to be logical, rational. Perhaps
in a universe not made so, that is our fall; for consciousness is
chaos. Kafka has described the logic of human chaos, of the very
Philadelphia we build around us to hide in, a world that deliberately mirrors only what we externally are. This city is a monument to loneliness, our solitudes made monolith. We need not be
surprised that we shudder at the threatening closeness of ourselves. As Kafka demonstrates again and again, whatever we are

at a particular moment, that is all we can be. The ape cannot know man as man cannot know the cockroach as the living cannot know the dead. In this exclusive oneness, our clutching of ourselves is hardly surprising. Who cares to surrender what he believes to be all that there is—at least for him as he at that moment is. We are dealing here with the tragedy of being; for whatever one is by the act of being, one surrounds oneself, becomes an infinity of non-being. But the tragedy is not the infinity perhaps so much as the surprises locked up in one's own being, the rack of oneself one is forced to live through. Once we are committed to a shape, we are exposed to the acute ruthlessness of change, of becoming busily acting within us. Little as we experience the outside, we know that we know ourselves less. Despite the urgency of survival, to escape the particular sharp presence of the infinite tightly imprisoned within us, we often yearn for this outside. But for such walls of writing, the externalization of ourselves, we, as Kafka, might be crushed, the weight of the world or ourselves upon us.

Much as we may dislike or gainsay it, for many art has become a surrogate religion: Matthew Arnold saw it as a hopeful prospect; it has proved an inevitable. Instead of accepting an ancient picture, prepared by writers of another world and underwritten by centuries of practice, we turn to the creation of the genius of one. The danger of worship, however, threatens us here also. Certainly it is more understandable than not a few other worships, say that of the state. (Today the world lurches—its own minotaur. What way other than mass-sacrifice, of putting flesh and blood on an abstraction as defiant as the state? Great writers have usually taken account of our carnivorous natures.) Dostoyevsky, for instance, knew the value of blood, realized for some it needed to be spilt; these unregenerates (even as the world bathed in Christ's blood) must experience such transfusion to come alive. But the Dostoyevskies exercise their appetites at second hand; their work is their laboratory of freedom. Art satisfies some; others need murder.

Kafka also could not accept any such absorption in the state; nor could he recommend social panaceas. Not because he did not care about his fellow men; he cared too much to encourage such superficial remedy. No remedy save expression with as much humility and honesty as the human spirit can endure. And the expression, if it is to be honest, meticulous and wise, must take advantage of the normal literary devices practice has established. More than has been appreciated, Kafka was an artist who, in the mirror of his art, did not conquer by cutting off the snake-writhing head of reality, but came to realize it and, never taming, to live with it. Nor did his work turn to stone as other arts and religions have done, a carving of dead monuments and blind edifices against life. For him the living was monument enough, the world his violent vision.

Of course he tried the impossible; with a patience and a care that might have broken the fortitude of a god, he stormed the ever-topless towers of his dream, perfection. He knew that he would fail, knew that the quest was futile, that he could never cross the threshold guarded by his own human flesh. Reality would not yield. He knew; nonetheless with the indefatigability of genius he tried. The quest was futile; yet because it was honest and illuminated by love, the roadway strewn with battle is our triumph; his trial rendered a sentence of knowledge we can enjoy. Ignorance mapped, the unknown delimited, is a kind of knowledge, perhaps the only kind we can expect. Though reality itself may never be seriously threatened, even as the quest turns up importances on the way, it especially endows us with knowledge of the seeker, defines his emotion, perseverence, humanity, and so our own.

Kafka might have attempted the castle by straight siege. But his persistent concern with the village below prevented such directness. This concern is, in good part, his achievement and his worth. Like a Hopkins', Kafka's work is the tension between these two worlds, the fierce longing for both and the further longing to make them one. For the ordinary man there is usually little conflict. In most cases, he sees these two worlds, thinks he occupies them, and keeps them—to him infinitely different—tidily separate. It was their awareness of this distance, smugly advocated by their respective ages, that galled Hopkins and Kafka. So they wandered in the Slough of Despond between. Yet failure, even as it is a fate, applied too diligently, can prove a most splendid occupation. Had they, for instance, made the heavenly world, we might have had nothing. Because of their remembrance of their human responsibility and their love, this world could not be denied; insofar as religion had drawn away from earthly reality, they could not accept it.

But what is it Kafka has done? In simplest terms, he has presented a German subject matter in a style and an exactness that is French. Such a union would be miracle enough. He has given us Job without God or a Job who must discover God or peace within himself, his world, and the fragments of his dream. Not heaven, but the earth, comes first. We shall not try to lasso the loftiest peak with coils of rhapsodic language. In terms of the village, in its sinuous by-ways, in the center of its common pleasures and pangs, the impossible must be grappled with. What more epic conflict when the beginning and the end of the world meet in one heart, when the grappling is so tight we must recognize the opponents as one? Only by clasping ourselves in the myriad shapes we must take can we arrive at grace.

As his clarity admits, unlike other writers of our time, Kafka is not absorbed in style *per se*. Though we must live in our breath, in the world our words construct, these words cannot forget their roots and the quarries they have come from. Kafka's hunger to describe the details of his harried world allowed him small time for ornamentation. In fact because of this desperation, lucidity was a cardinal aim; it was the only way he could survive. Nor did he sit back in the scholarly ivory tower of his work amid a waste land to count over, miserly fashion, the precious fragments of previous greatnesses he has managed to preserve. He was too desperate, and too much in love, to make his work a macaronic skein, say, of quotations lit up at odd angles by their sudden juxtapositions and their presence in a particular mind. Nor had he time or the desire to rival physical builders of cities. Not the naturalistic blueprinting of the brain, heart, and liver; not a listening in on the sputtering dots and dashes of the subconscious; there is another typography here—the hot geometry of anguish, nightmare, and desire immaculately surveyed, manscape. Not only did Kafka achieve the equilibrium that is art, the position midway between the poles of scheme and actuality, system and mindlessness, but he posited the mindlessness, cap-

391

tured the actuality itself into a kind of arithmetic of clarity; with the connotations as infinite and infinitely confusing as they are, he adhered to strict denotation. As the outer world shrinks, the inner must grow; we must live inside. But we must live. The furnishings of the heart and head cannot be changed into wooden pieces, dealt with as prosaically as the contents of a third-floor flat. As precisely as possible, the contents must be examined; yet they must be examined in action.

Indeed Kafka could turn his back to the world nowhere; for he must always see it; he was that world. There is guilt here, but admission that its source (like the god) is unknown. Is it perhaps our unwitting realization that each man makes his world; and, making it, the crime he sees in it, the brutality, the hatred, is his own doing, his own projection? Consciousness is chaos. No wonder, feeling responsible, guilty, man pauses in his making to study the maker. Yet the making ruthlessly continues, another likely reason for the incompleteness of Kafka's work. Possibly too, this incompleteness might suggest, at that point in his books he came too close to himself, look against eye, grasp within hand, too identical to see. The objectification dissolves; the castle, the trial, America, what is the other side of these? Caught in the human condition we cannot possibly break free to basic knowledge. Kafka, however, did not strive to make a god of this ignorance, nor an order to be worshiped. Caught we are, whether country doctor or surveyor, whether ape trying to be a man or man trying to be— Kafka had none of the arrogance of those who would explain God's ways to man; man himself was more than he could explain.

There are few preconceived critical terms we can apply to Kafka's world; they must come out of this world itself, out of the becoming that is art rather than out of the being that is most philosophy and criticism. Such speculation is a finished world, one seen from a distance. Dispassionately participating and detachedly passionate, the artist has one foot out and one in this changingness. To accuse Kafka of allegory is to lose sight of the world he so devotedly built; this world is itself, not a Platonic illustration. To think of Kafka or to try to "explain" him in terms, say, of Kierkegaard is to change Kafka into something he is not—

392

worse than a poem's paraphrase. We cannot abstract eternal
verities or absolutes from his work. In art worthy of the name,
the particulars do not exist for the values; rather, the values serve
the particulars. Such is the essence of time, of living, and of living—the complexus of it—heightened into art. Then the particulars themselves become a kind of absolute. Let the values, if they
are recognized at all, bring us deeper into life, deeper through
the compass of clarity art has, not away from life. Kafka knew
that feelings, thoughts, appearances, though ephemeral, in their
being offshoots of whatever reality there is, are symbols enough.
Language itself is a set of symbols. To make these symbols of
symbols, in addition, is to attenuate their worth. Kafka surprised
change, surprised it in the very act, so kept its pristine, shimmer-
ing shape.

But what is it that tinges the atmosphere of Kafka's
world with fear and unqualified foreboding? It is precisely this
openness, the frozen time yet infinite of solitude, the mesmerized
sound of silence and imminence, and the plethoric threat of possibility, a possibility further multiplied in that it is hatching in us.
We experience at once the fierce imprisonment of freedom.
Jostled by plenitudes of space, we endure the intimacy of meas-
ureless distances and the fearful nearness of loneliness. It is not
even the world that frightens us as much as our consciousness.
Think of the raw, violent meat impatient immediately under our
skins; think of the sudden spurt of blood, the hate and the lust
and the violence, that blinds our eyes. Then think of what waits,
in the ambush of our breath, under the skin of our thinking: the
sunken Atlantises in our minds and our veins, the pre-Edens and
the primordial slime, the middle-of-the-night remembers. Again,
this man who is Hamlet and Hamlet's father one, his own voice
and knowledge the poison pouring down his thirsty ear, again
this man clings with a frantic genius, with a devotion amounting
at times to idolatry, to details. If the problem is infinite, every
step is a further expression of prison. But he will not be swept
away; he will play secretary to the inner workings of chaos.

It is the grip of Kafka that is particularly precious;
whether it be angel or devil he is wrestling with, as long as he
can, he does not let go. It is his art that saves him from being

393

devoured. Latter-day versions of chaos rarely share this muscularity. Writers like Kenneth Patchen and Henry Miller, for instance, resenting the hidebound smugness of much of their time, have sought to break through it by encouraging chaos. Satire and diatribe are their major devices. But in their urgency to level hypocrisy, they have lashed out so violently that they have often destroyed the very ground under their feet. Why, a reader can well ask, should we prefer their limited confusion to the vaster chaos they accuse the world of? Satire, to prove effective, must be focused. Unless its employer has solid criteria, clear values, and a larger context he can either readily refer to or take for granted, this satire is doomed to fail.

Chaos, as we saw, can be used only when it achieves some definition, when it can be placed beside something that is patently not chaos. But when the world the writer describes is so baffled, even willfully, that one value cannot be distinguished from another, then what value can any part of it have? Probably, in considerable measure, anti-intellectualism is responsible for the rubble-heaps writers present. Attributing our present miseries erroneously to the failure of intellect, regarding this anguish as irrefutable testimony to the inadequacy of intellect, such writers have heartily jettisoned the intellect's claims. Certainly their books would suggest that they have abandoned whatever rationality they possess.

We can understand such a course; we can even applaud the ambition to recruit other sources of knowledge. With the world increasingly various and rich in grief as well as in culture, we can appreciate a denunciation of superficial harmony through the intellect. Nor would it be wise certainly to emphasize the intellect at the expense of other methods or systems of knowing. Still, to dump the intellect, aside from the fundamental impossibility of such an act, as well as to try to scrap the resources of tradition, is the very ultimate of folly. Sensations for their own sake, exclusive adulation of the ravenous present, rejection of cumulative knowledge, such a course rather than freeing man must kill a good portion of what he is. Art has usually been a catalyst to form and comprehension, not simply a further spice for appetites already living in the midst of explosion.

Perhaps modern writers are trying to discover a new art, a form meet to their day; perhaps, putting on the prophetic robes, they are anticipating the consequences of atomic developments! How absurd, as though they could ever vie with the multifarious frenzies and confusion of living itself. In any event, these writers are correct: intellect has failed, not because it was intellect but because it was not sufficiently so. If the eye, only partially trained, sees distant shapes vaguely, shall we, in a fit of impatience, contemning sight, gouge the eye and trample upon it? Of course the eye, like the body, by its limits is an obstacle—as knowledge itself is; but as long as we are men writing for men, little is to be gained by trying to thrust away what organs we have. Death alone can yield the kind of knowledge many writers seem to desire.

Carlyle, we remember, deplored the growth of consciousness as a symptom of distemper. So perhaps we can diagnose the development of chaos. The Greeks, we saw, had outlawed it. In Milton's world, after the earth was finished, there was little need for it. But we, become more and more scrutinous, increasingly call attention to chaos, so call it into being. Consciousness is chaos. Of course chaos may simply further witness human arrogance; for, as we have observed, chaos is surely of our own making. Earlier man made god out of his ignorance. Now we attribute our ignorance and our notion of chaos to our world. We assume that the perplexity we find in the world, by our finding, must inhere in that world and its objects. Kafka did not shirk the labyrinth; nor, of course, did he ever break through it. For it was his being, the very stuff of his living. But by bringing his best strengths to bear upon it, he peopled it with fearful splendors and the anguished dignity of his love. To suffer, to know that one suffers, and withal to love—that is man's prize heroism. The scientist, for instance, may give his life for the advancement of knowledge; in a moment then, he achieves immortality. The major artist also gives his life, but often in a much more agonizing way—over the protraction of years. He, as an awareness, is the test and witness. We can hardly share Carlyle's animus toward the development of consciousness. But we must be ready to pay the price for the growing burden of riches.

395

the endless labyrinth

bernard groethuysen

We live in only one of many worlds, our own. Those who belong to it move easily in it, since everywhere they go, in the moon as well as on the earth, they know its geometry, can count its minutes, and discuss its causes. It's quite simple: they pull out their watches wherever they are and measure the positions. But when we wish to attack some other world everything is confused and we breathe with difficulty. Not that there is anything surprising about this since we can only see and think in the way we've been taught in the methods of our own world. And since we must think and see, it is obviously agonizing not to know how to set about it. And so it is wise to stay at home and to count and measure the unknown without wanting to pass the limits of a world which is extensive enough for one always to find something to do.

But there are adventurers who have risked their lives to get out and have entered worlds which were not ready to receive them. Most of them have lost themselves there and have had to seek refuge in the asylums which the inhabitants of this world reserve for those who have exiled themselves. Nevertheless there are also those—rare individuals, it is true—who have been able to maintain a perfectly lucid state of mind throughout their journey. They have kept their eyes open while they slept.

So it was with Kafka who was absent from us while living among us all his life and who told us of a world which necessarily seemed very obscure to us since we could only see and think in our own way. But what did he see there? The infinite? God? Monsters? Nothing like that, but people like you and me speaking our language. Houses and roads such as we see every day, guardians of the peace, bureaucrats, assistant directors of banks, and stenographers. We could be in Paris or New York. And yet everything is different. Because time stands still there—or perhaps runs in a different way—and distances have changed and can no longer be measured in our way. And as for finding out the reason for what is happening—we cannot count on it. Not because of a lack of reasons, but because everything is reasoned backwards in some way and the reasoning goes on without stopping and without possible conclusion.

And so we are afraid to wake up and pretend to be dead. Because if we woke up we would have to ask someone—we would have to question everyone—and it is just this that we're afraid of. If only we could just live, knowing where we were going without having to ask the passersby. But we are tormented by the question which we don't know how to put and which we fear we haven't asked in time.

For those who have stayed at home and gone their way it is quite different. For them the reply comes before the question. And so they occasionally seek out problems to match their solutions all while staying in that world where nothing exists that does not respond to them. Thus they say: there I am—and being there they wonder why they are there. Evidently they cannot find a reply that will satisfy them completely. But also, being here what do they need to know to exist?

In that other world we question in order to exist. I question, therefore I don't exist. I put myself in question. All the same we cannot put off indefinitely the date of our birth. And in waiting for it, if anyone were to ask you what you had come to do there, what could you say? Because after all you have not come there naturally. You don't belong there. This is easily seen by your worried look and that way you have of excusing yourself to everyone and acting modest. You have a bad conscience. Your questions betray you. It is certain that this is not your own country. Your visitor's permit? I arrest you . . . unless this is precisely your country, our country. But that we cannot say.

It's not that we are not alone. But we cannot escape the presence of others. We follow them with our eyes and take note of their gestures. Again if we could be content with that, we could live without torment. But when they come towards you or when you question them everything is changed. You're in for it. Every advance binds you. It takes possession of you. You see yourself involved in a collection of gestures which are not yours. Then resist. For, after all, why follow?

This is when you began to reason. But he was in front of you and continued to gesture. You were bound to watch him. He held you by his presence. You are his prisoner. Torment seizes you. You would like to get the better of him. But presences do not argue. You cannot refute him. Presence becomes law.

You would therefore like to establish an acquaintance-ship with him. In that way you could explain yourself. But there is no explanation. You do not always understand what the other one says. There's no way of making him say more. And listening to his silence is terrible. You must definitely leave him. Say to him then: I think, therefore I am, or some such thing. Or simply say: I. But that you cannot say to him. For in saying it you would declare yourself guilty. You were beginning to go cheerfully on— I, I am I. But you were not alone. There was another with you. The "I" is only a slip of the tongue. He has followed you with his eyes and you haven't turned round. But his presence follows you. His absence makes him present to you.

Everything is made up in this way of presences and absences. We know nothing else. Obviously there must be the great Wherefore. But it is not of this world. And so you bury yourself deeper and deeper in your arguments. We never argue so well as in a dream. We never dispute better than about absurdities. Everything is connected and linked together there. Everything there is at the same time perfectly logical and in-

399

comprehensible. And so no line of reasoning can rid you of your torment. In vain will you look for the Law.

But everything proves that you are not free. Try to say "no" to anything at all. Everything is evident, everything is there. You can only go continually from one thing to another, and everything is dreadfully far apart. "All the same there's nothing to prevent me from going where I like." But can you? Is there nothing stopping you? Why do you stay fixed in one place? Because in front of you you see corridors upon corridors. And how will you find the way back again? Go up this staircase if you like. You will find yourself in front of other corridors through which you have to pass.

You must get out of the building then. But who knows its exit? There are doors on all sides. Will you give your three knocks? But you are mistaken. They are strangers who haven't risen at your approach. You will go out again then into the corridors, alone, or followed by the other one who climbs the stairs behind you.

In the world of Kafka there is no empty space where we can take refuge. The line is drawn. You follow it. And it shortens itself proportionately as you follow it. There is nothing either to the right or left, at least nothing for you, for you do not know how to reach the lines of the others. Nothing happens according to geometrical law, and everything that is is part of an infinitely complex geometry. Learn to see without understanding. The non-self comes before the self; geometry before the spirit.

There is then a geometrical order which nothing escapes. Those who belong to it and whom you see traveling there are resonant bodies. They have the gift of speech. It is curious to hear them talk. What do they say then? You have to know how to listen to them. And be satisfied with what they are saying. You must be careful not to attribute words to them that they haven't used under the pretext of knowing their thoughts. Thought obscures speech. Let us strangle psychology. Only speech counts.

But what do they say? They argue. Man is a resonant body that argues. They argue alone. They argue in twos and threes. They dispute with themselves or with others. It is a continual exchange of arguments. You count for little or nothing in this business. Is it even you who are arguing—or isn't it rather the argument that calls forth the argument without your having the power to put in your word?

There is a line of reasoning for minds in the same way as there is geometry for bodies. We are not free to think as we like, even as we are not free to move as we like. The argument carries you along in the same way that the road leads you. You cannot stop once you have started. There are the preambles, the arguments, the replies, the counter-arguments. There are the Ayes and the Noes, the Buts and the Ifs. All this existed before you began to think and will exist always. The argument makes the arguer, and the arguer is you. You will go then from argument to argument and will find in your arguments the corridors and stairways along which your resonant body moves. The whole thing goes up and down, goes off at an angle, forks, starts again, and goes on without stopping.

There is the movement of the resonant bodies, the goings and comings of human beings. There is the march of arguments. The world of geometry and logic. Both of them hold you. It's a large mechanism in which you are caught. You have to argue as far as you can see, just as you will have to go forward without stopping to follow the line that is marked out for you. All this is done without you. Once more: you count for nothing.

But you want to know what you have to do. Someone should stretch out his hand to you and call you by name. But you are nameless in a nameless world. This is what frightens you. You are horribly alone. And who are you? "I am the dreamer of a world where everything is perfectly ordered and where everything accuses me." But how is it that you are simultaneously part of this world and outside it? That you are absent and present in it at the same time? You say to yourself: I would like to wake up, because then I could say to him whom I see coming toward me arguing, and toward whom all my torments turn, since he is no other than myself: "Stop, I have something to say to you." What should I say to him? That we are not guilty and that everything will be explained? Obviously this is what he expects of me, and then everything would doubtless become easy. But how to tell him this? When we met and when we were only one person we argued and the torment was common to both of us. You said to me: "I'm guilty" and I couldn't tell you of what. Then you replied: "They will come to fetch me soon. I shall have to know how to clear myself." Then let us see if the two of us can rummage among our memories and find out what you can be guilty of. Still, what's the use? It's the accuser who makes you guilty. No one could know how to choose his own crimes.

Let us go before the judge then. But, you say, I've looked for him all my life. He's not to be found; and I no longer know which door to knock on. I shall never be judged. We are involved in an endless trial. The dead have been awakened a thousand times already, and the last judgment has always been put off. Some part concerning me—or someone else—was always missing. Or perhaps the judge was on his vacation. Or perhaps he never even existed. In the beginning everyone asked to go to Heaven; finally they asked only to go to Hell, so that all might be over. For their torments were becoming unbearable. At first they all had their sins and knew what they were going to be accused of. But little by little doubts came to them. Perhaps there were other sins that they would be questioned about. But what others? Perhaps quite insignificant offenses that they had paid no attention to. Some remembered that on meeting someone who wanted to tell them something, or who had just begged them with his eyes, they had brusquely left their companion without asking him what he wanted. One of them said to the others: "How did it happen? I had knocked at a door and then fled. But here is someone running after me. What can I say to him?" But another, who had just woken up, interrupted, saying in his turn: "What was she called, that woman, slight and rather plump, whom I have never seen again? Yet I must remember her name." But no one answered him. Everyone sought again for some misdemeanor which they had taken no notice of while they were alive.

At this point they were more and more troubled and their minds became greatly confused. They were afraid they had forgotten their mistakes and tortured themselves trying to find their lost sin. They no longer knew what they had done and there was no one there to tell them. This was the worst kind of damnation.

Man invented sins to free himself from his torments. He had to find all sorts of sins, big and little, and draw up a list of them so that he could take his choice. For he could not remain in guilt. So he made himself a code. This was his awakening.

But there are those who could not wake up and who live in torment. It is only in rare moments that they know any peace, and then a stupefying numbness comes over them. Their limbs relax and they seem to forget their worries. This is what they call love and is why they seek after a woman. Sometimes she is tall, sometimes small. Sometimes she is one and sometimes many. Sometimes she is quite close to you, and you can hear her breathing; sometimes she is in the next room or in a room that you can only reach by going upstairs. Sometimes she is alone, sometimes with another who goes or stays. She is there in your moments of supreme torment. You can count on meeting her at the turning of a long corridor; or open a door and there she is. At times too she is waiting for you at the end of an argument when you are trying to justify what you have done. (She can argue with you.)

Then you no longer think of anything. This is your deliverance. You have come home from a long journey. And talking to yourself alone when no one was listening you said: "Where was I during all this time? And what could I have been doing while I was away? Never mind, since I am back again. Who could still stop me and ask me questions?"

But are you really alone? Lift your head. There is the other one looking at the two of you through the window. You must drive him away. But what will you do if he is quite little and calls your woman with a look? He's your companion. Don't you recognize him? You must leave her to him. She belongs to him. Don't you see they are of the same build? Let them both go then. They will be happy in their corner.

But you are afraid of her going, for it is terrible to wake up all alone in a room that is not yours or in a corridor. You will have to start explaining yourself all over again to those who pass by. But how can you keep her and say to her: I love you? You said to yourself: When I am born we will speak intimately, we will call each other by our pet names. We will be alone to-

403

gether. You belong to me, and I to you. How good it will be to live together somewhere.

This is how those who are born talk. But there are also the others who are not born and have nothing by their birthright. They have no one, nothing. They are conscious of a great longing, a longing to exist and love, and of a great torment, to be born and then not to be able to say "I love you." So they would like to be dead without having lived, having skipped the stage which separates birth from death. Everything could have happened without them, and that is what they wish. They would not have been questioned and argued with; they would not have fallen over themselves trying to go forward. They would not have known the insomnia of living.

But how can they get to sleep again, once they have been imprudent enough to wake up? They beg in vain for their lost sleep from the arms of their mistress. She is not the earth. You cannot hide yourself in her. She is not able to give you shelter. And so you will wake up somewhere among people who are watching you. You will have to get up and go on your way again. You are in the street and everything has to be started over again. You will roll on the ground in vain, scratching the soil with your fingers. We cannot bury ourselves there as we would like.

We would have to live underground, which is not an easy life. Underground there are corridors, corners, and innermost recesses. You have to go up and down and turn at the right moment. You have to know the entrances and exits and not lose sight of the layout of the burrow. But underground you are master. You are at home there. It is your kingdom and only you know it. You can be silent there. There are, it is true, noises that you hear coming from above and often from beside or beneath you too. But however much they may bother you they are the sounds of another world. Occasionally too you look out and hear footsteps, but all that goes on without you. Sleep and let them be. You are at home.

But once you have left the underground and taken the risk of living on the surface everything changes. You run right and left and no longer know which way to go. Then great anxiety takes hold of you. Crossing undergrounds that are no longer

yours and passing along corridors that you haven't dug you will
always climb higher. Wouldn't it be better then to make yourself
quite small and creep along the ground? In that way the others
wouldn't see you and you may see them go by without their
noticing you. People don't bend down for insects. But take care
not to lift your head. Watch out for their feet. And how will you
escape them since there is no longer any way of going underground again?' 'If only we could fly!' 'Don't you see those almost
imperceptible dots way up high?' 'Those dots people? You make
me laugh. They're little balls with paws . . . Really very amusing
. . . Don't they ever come down to earth?' 'Yes, and they're considered very highly there. People admire their lightness. For coming from above and being filled with air they have remained completely aerial. And so they seem to be always flying while others
walk with difficulty and often get lost.'

    'Where am I then?' 'You are in a corridor where you
will meet people, towns, country, and occasionally a woman. You
must go straight ahead. There are walls on both sides that we
cannot penetrate. No one can dream more than one dream. But
once you are born it is no longer yours. You are in a strange
country. At each moment you risk getting yourself arrested. For
how should you know the law of the land?' 'I will find out and I
won't stop until I know where I am and what my position is.' 'But
who will be able to tell you?' 'I shall go and find the Law; I will
plead until someone opens the door to me. Then I will be in order
and no one will stop me any more. I will go along with the others
as one of them.' 'But who will open the door for you? The porter
watches and lets no one by.' 'I will ask forgiveness then.' 'But of
whom and for what? You will see many people go by on foot or
in cars and standing by the road you will say to yourself: it must
be that one, he looks important. He will know how to accept my
petition favorably, and armed with his pardon I will go and introduce myself to the others who cannot help accepting me. But
if he replies to you at all he will say: Who are you, Sir? You have
done nothing to me that I can forgive. There is some mistake.
And if you insist and implore him to say he forgives you he will
turn away his head and you will see him go busily on his way . . .
Listen, perhaps there is a message for you somewhere. The mes-

405

senger is coming to meet you. He has looked for you everywhere. He's quite out of breath, he is an such a hurry to join you.' 'I sit in my window waiting for him. I will wait for him always. Perhaps he has already gone by. For how should I recognize him? And what shall I do to find myself on his path? He came up the stairs while I was waiting for him, and while I was waiting he went down again without having found me. I heard him from my room. Now he goes along through the roads, I don't know where. I weep by my window for the message I have lost.'

"To be or not to be." The difficult thing is to be. It's quite simple when one is not yet born or when one is dead. No one asks you then what you are doing there. But to live is to do something, to commit oneself to something. If someone questions you, you can of course always say 'I have done nothing.' But you say it to clear yourself of blame, for after all you have done something. And so you have to say what. You are responsible for what you have done. You must answer..No one can escape his examination.

The inhabitants of this earth, which is not yours, have established distinctions between good and evil. They have thought that certain actions win rewards and others make them guilty. But what they have overlooked is the fact that their anxiety springs from having done something. That is why they have established their "I distinguish," seeking the reason for their actions and going to endless trouble to justify themselves.

When he thinks about it, no one can bear the burden of having done something. No one can bear to have his action noticed. No one can live without judgment. If he were judged he would be at ease. But the thing that robs you of your peace of mind is that everything counts, or something counts and there is no one to draw up the reckoning for you. And so men have created ways of establishing balance sheets to show clearly what must be written on one side or the other. What stories they have made up for themselves, what vices and virtues they have invented! They have been caught in their own game. You are good, you are bad. Oh, wonderful man! Oh, miserable creature! They have claimed to know the Law. But who has ever known the Law? And who could say what counts and what doesn't? The records of the trial remain blank, and at the end the signature is illegible. That's all we can know. What is written on your file doesn't depend on you.

But it's obvious that you have done something. Someone will say 'Who has done this?' and you will answer 'I did.' It is this "something" that is so terrible. For if you had done nothing you could stay quietly at home; but having done something you have to wait until the judge goes by. Everyone is watching you. They have a right to watch you. They say to each other: He did that. And when you ask what they are silent. They don't know, nobody knows. It is a great mystery, the mystery of your existence.

When you wake up from a nightmare you no longer make excuses for yourself. You have sought justification for yourself and you have collected arguments while you slept. But no one could acquit you. And now you are awake. You say to yourself: I have done nothing at all. You burn your case histories. The judge goes away in the morning. His accused has defaulted.

But once you are awake you are present. You are born. You exist. And to exist is to be judged. You are already written down on the list of the living. Will you say that you have no civic status? Certainly the worst of conditions in a world where everything is ordered. The judge will have nothing to do with you. You are a dead man among the living. What are you doing among them?

You came imprudently into the world without being born. You have stayed in an inner world while moving in the outer one. The inner world holds you and you can't get out. But when you try to retire completely and shut yourself up you can no longer rest there. You have hardly lain down and curled yourself up when you get up again and begin to pace up and down carrying your cage with you. Or rather the cage carries you and travels along while you only walk up and down or crouch in a corner waiting to get out as soon as possible to begin the same movement again indefinitely. The cage is small and outside it is the world of the living. It is not fixed anywhere and seems to roll across the earth. And you can't get out while it is going.

407

'But what would I do outside? There are people there going in all directions, some this way and some that. They retrace their steps, meet each other and part again. What should I do among them? There are corridors that they do not see and they go on as if they could always go further without having to turn round or stop in front of a wall. How can they live that way without knowing the Law?'

'But what is it that you want to know?' 'That which all the world should know, the plan according to which this building that we wander through is built. We wander without knowing whether we should go to the right or the left, upstairs or down. We would know where we were going. We would know which roads to take and would not be at a loss when we found ourselves at an impasse or halted by a stairhead.'

'But even though you know that, be careful that you do not lose yourself. For what are you looking for? Your judgment, that is why you just prostrated yourself before the porter so that he might let you in to the Law itself. Let me be judged, you say, and I will be free. And at the same time you are afraid of the judgment and try to escape from it in a thousand ways. What stratagems you have used! What excuses you invented when it was a question of being judged!'

This judge you flee from is a terrible one. Yet you are he who has not found his judge and not having obtained judgment remain a prey to your torments. You will have to die without being judged and without having found peace anywhere.

There is nothing more terrible than to have missed your judge and to stay in your cage all your life exposed to the gaze of the passersby. They point at you and say to each other: Do you see him in his cage? Why doesn't he get out? Nothing prevents him from getting out. The bars are wide apart. He could easily slip between them. But every time he comes near them he rushes back and retires into his corner where he stays as if stupefied. It's because he's waiting for his judge and he keeps himself imprisoned because he hasn't found him. But at the same time he is always in doubt that he is in prison since no one came to take him there or deliver his sentence, so he always looks as if he's going to come out and once out to stay there. He has no right to the prison since he has fled from his judge. He is both free and accused. There is no state worse than that.

But the man who doesn't leave his cage and mingle with the crowd preserves a strange clairvoyance. He sees everything while the others only see in part and imagine the rest. In dreams nothing is imaginary. Only the actuality counts. All is seen. All is there. Nothing else is. There are none of those things which may or may not be true, no possibilities. Everything exists and nothing exists, but all is one and the same thing. There is no in-between, nothing indefinite or fleeting. (Such things belong to the dreams of poets who have never dreamed.) But the dreamer stands face to face with things in such a way that nothing vanishes or becomes less real because everything simultaneously exists and doesn't exist.

The living have invented memory and they make plans for the future. As far as they're concerned nothing exists just like that. They don't recognize the presence of things. They say to what they see: You already no longer exist—and shut their eyes, keeping only a memory of it. They dispose of everything this way. This is what makes life easy for them. They mingle memories with everything and add conjectures to them. Everything that is here is always absent for them in some way, and nothing is so completely absent that it cannot be called to mind. That is why they are not afraid to see things there. Their imagination removes or replaces them in a thousand different ways. In this way they feel they have mastery over them and can fly over them with ease.

But the man who cannot turn round and look somewhere else knows no way of getting rid of them. Their existence frightens him and that makes living painful for him. Having to dream is what makes life so terrible. He knows that there is no freedom in dreaming. But he also sees realities more clearly since he cannot add anything or imagine anything else but what is part of him. It's only on awakening that we say to ourselves: 'Why did I forget this or that, or how could I have overlooked such a possibility?' But as long as we are dreaming we are outside the realm of possibility. Now he, knowing he will never wake up, lives face to face with reality.

409

Everything hangs together; there are no gaps. Everything is necessary. (This is the important thing, not truth.) Nothing is obliterated. There is a succession of presences. Everything is always fully lighted by the crude light of dreams. There is no way for objects which may exist and may not exist to hide in the shadow. There is no Perhaps for him. He cannot deny things that are. For what could he put in their place? He cannot tamper with realities.

He will say: I am not waiting for you; is there another who should come? But where is he; he is not here. You are here and it cannot be that you are he. We are together. Let us not argue further about why we are two. Neither of us has come here willingly. We will gain nothing by questioning each other. We are present to each other. You and I; our common presence unites us. What does it matter if I know you or you me? It would do no good to send you away under the pretext that you are a stranger. For where would you go, or where would I go myself to escape you since there is nothing beyond the present. We hold each other, or rather there is something else that holds us. Don't say it is fate that has reunited us. People who evade reality talk like that. We are *really* together. What more could we be? And what could be more terrible than to realize that we are both shut up in the same present?

Everything is there then, wholly there, in words and gestures. Everything is single and clear. Nothing passes, nothing disappears, nothing loses itself in the distance. Everything is there, quite close and strangely transparent. Everything is identical and contains nothing else that could modify its substance. Nothing lessens the reality, nothing is conducive to its confusion or loss in oblivion.

It is a world without sleep. The world of the sleeper who is wide-awake. Everything is clear with a terrifying clarity and nothing can be left out or hinted at even as nothing can be added to relate things to something that is not there. There is a lucidity which is lost as soon as one wakes up in a complex world whose changing aspects we know. Here everything is simple with a uniform simplicity. Everything counts equally. Everything must be said. How can we select or place this or that in a world where everything is present and nothing other than that can appear?

You are then wholly occupied by what is, and cannot turn your head to look elsewhere. Nothing is seen in a scattered way. Everything is 'exactly so'; nothing is 'almost.' Everything is in order. Things do not lose their shape while others are formed in their place in such a way that everything melts into everything else without definite outlines.

But who can bear his own presence and that of others? He dies who looks on God. The world of the living is not there, rich in all kinds of imaginings, the world of the awakened who move freely among things and change their viewpoints as often as they please, gathering impressions. They have left that other world and climbed to the surface. It is their way of life.

But the man who has not made the motion of changing his dwelling place has kept certain things that the others had to forget in order not to see themselves stopped in their goings and comings and so be frightened. He has stayed in a world that the others have left and which they only meet occasionally when they are drowsy and forget where they are. Then they hasten to tell themselves: 'I have been dreaming, I must get back to my job.' But those who live waiting for life, hesitating to be born, have no job. Kafka was one of these; his lucid mind could tell us of that abandoned world where he had lived.

Translated by Muriel Kittel.

max brod and herbert tauber

lienhard bergel

In 1937 Max Brod published a biography of his friend Kafka as a supplement to the six volumes of Kafka's *Collected Works*. This book is rather an accumulation of material for a biography than a fully developed picture of Kafka's life. The richness of source material (unpublished letters, diaries and sketches, fragments of conversations) constitutes the main value of the book; it leaves almost everything to be done in the utilization of this material. There are enough indications, however, to deduce the outlines of an "inner" biography of Kafka if Brod had gone beyond the stage of the merely anecdotal.

Brod is anxious to stress the "healthy" side of his friend's life and writings; he sees as the purpose of his book the modification of the impression of Kafka which his works and diaries create: "Left to himself, Kafka was perplexed and helpless—an impression which one rarely had of him in personal contact because of his strict self-discipline—but this impression is undoubtedly strengthened when one reads his diaries. His books and particularly his diaries create an entirely different, much more depressing picture than the one derived from daily inter-

413

course with him. To correct and complement this picture is one reason for my writing these recollections."

The discrepancy of which Brod speaks has two possible explanations. It may have been that Kafka did not lose his reticence even in his relations with his best friend. Perhaps Kafka purposely concealed from him some of his most intimate concerns, and presented instead a cheerful appearance as a cloak. There could have been many reasons for this, including a far-reaching difference between the two, in spite of their friendship. The reader of this biography cannot avoid the impression that Brod was not Kafka's equal in artistic and intellectual matters.

The other explanation is that even if he were unreservedly frank toward his friend, in his writings Kafka still would reveal a countenance different from the one which Brod knew from his personal contacts with Kafka. There always remains a difference between the "practical" and the "poetical" personality, a distinction which Benedetto Croce taught us to observe. The attitudes of an artist in his private conversations need not be identical with those longings and anxieties which find expression in his art, because here layers of personality are stirred up which lie deeper than those which come to the fore in his casual relations with other people.

Brod himself gives us an insight into those factors which probably stood between the two friends and which caused Brod to conceive a picture of Kafka which is not fully valid. Brod is a convinced Jewish nationalist: the "healthy" which he tries to discover in Kafka consists for him in being firmly rooted in a community of blood. Brod tells of his persistent efforts to convert his friend to the religion of nationalism and he claims to have finally succeeded in this. He admits, however, that in his zeal he was not always tactful. At a time when Kafka's relation with his fiancée had reached a crisis, he still insisted on discussing with him problems of Zionism, with the result that Kafka was on the verge of breaking with Brod. Brod is objective enough not to conceal Kafka's sharp reaction to these attempts at "education for integration into a community": "What do I have in common with the Jews? I hardly have anything in common with myself." "Kafka says that he has no feeling for community because his strength is barely sufficient for him alone." This is what Kafka thinks about the Chassidic rites which he attended together with Brod: "Looking at it closely was like observing a wild African tribe. Crude superstition."

The tendency to make Kafka a "Jewish" poet of "healthy" convictions permeates the whole book. As in his comments on Kafka's *Collected Works,* Brod sees him predominantly concerned with religious problems. In his notes to *The Castle* written in 1926, Brod had stressed the "incommensurability of earthly and religious aims" and man's helplessness before God as Kafka's main themes. In a chapter of this biography dealing with Kafka's religious development, Brod modifies this position. Now he discovers in Kafka "the basic recognition that man with his spark of reason, his will and his ethical insight is not at all a plaything of superior forces." "What I stress and what, I believe, distinguishes my interpretation of Kafka from those of others (for instance Schoeps, Vietta, Stumpf), is the fact that I see his final word spoken in favor of that which is positive, favorable to life and earthly activity and religious in this sense—but not in favor of helplessness, hostility to life, despair, 'tragic position.' " The allusion to an article by Hans Schoeps probably contains the explanation for the differences between Brod and his former collaborator in the editing of Kafka's writings, differences which Brod mentions in the notes to the fifth volume and which were responsible for ending their collaboration.

In his efforts to claim Kafka for a "healthy" philosophy of life Brod goes one step further: he identifies the religious problem in Kafka, as he sees it, with that of Jewish nationalism. " 'To live close to God' and 'to live right'—were identical for Kafka. But one cannot live right as a member of a 'nation without land.' " He believes that Kafka had a positive message, that he appealed for integration into a blood community, in this case the Jewish people. Hence Brod gives a special "Jewish" interpretation to some of Kafka's writings, particularly *The Castle.* It will be one of the main tasks of future critics of Kafka to refute Brod on this point. It is extremely questionable whether Kafka had a "message" and if so, whether it was one of such narrow scope. Great artists do not have "messages"; they stand or fall on the merits

415

of their art and not of their religious or philosophical convictions.

The other aspect of Brod's book which is open to question concerns only indirectly the interpretation of Kafka's writings. Brod attributes the unhappiness of Kafka's life and his premature death to the unfortunate relations between him and his father, and to the crushing burden imposed upon him by his profession, which consumed so much of his strength that he could write only at the sacrifice of his health. These are undeniable facts, but the conclusions which Brod draws from them require close scrutiny. In his effort to make Kafka a poet of the "healthy," he needs an explanation for those elements in his writings which do not fit into this preconceived notion. The easiest way out is to make external circumstances responsible for them, in this case the domineering attitude of the father, which produced timidity and a feeling of inferiority in the son, a state of mind which is reflected in his writings. This is a typical example of the "biografismo" which Benedetto Croce castigated. Undoubtedly the impressions of his youth were among the "sources" of Kafka's writings, but it is a crude method which tries to explain a work of art by its "sources." The private experiences of an artist do not enter into his "poetic" personality in as direct a way as Brod assumes; the somber features of Kafka's writings cannot be explained as mere reflexes of his private life. The errors in the interpretation of Leopardi should not be repeated in the case of Kafka.

A similar superficiality is revealed in Brod's manner of relating Kafka's premature death to his writings. Brod believes that "the harmful effects of his profession, which was forced upon him by outward circumstances, penetrated into metaphysical depths." If his parents had shown more understanding for their son by supplying him with the economic independence needed for his writing, if a different social order had made it unnecessary for an artist to earn his living in an ordinary profession, then helplessness and despair would not have become dominant in his writings. Then he would have suffered only from "noble," "metaphysical" misfortune, while the "ignoble" misfortune, that caused by the pettiness and drudgery of everyday life, would have been avoided. If Kafka's will power had not been so completely crushed by his parents, he would have made himself independent of them and not taken up a bourgeois profession in deference to their wishes, according to Brod. All this is purely speculative. If Kafka was really so anxious for integration into a blood community, if he valued family bonds as highly as Brod asserts, it would have been curious indeed if he had shown his high esteem for family life by breaking with his parents. It would be a strange thing to be rooted in a blood community and to have broken the closest blood ties. It is also absurd to try to avoid neatly all "ignoble" misfortune and to concentrate only on "noble," "metaphysical" misfortune. Kafka might have felt that all misfortune is "noble," simply because it is a part of reality. We do not disagree with Brod that the drudgery of his profession, the lack of understanding on the part of his parents, made writing immensely difficult for Kafka, and that he finally sacrificed his health to it; but we should not forget that in a more comprehensive sense his art gained by this sacrifice. Kafka is the poet of the metaphysics of everyday reality. He would not have been able to reveal to us new depths of this reality if he had avoided those aspects of it which are agonizing. No amount of metaphysical speculation, no leisurely study of Kierkegaard in a carefree economic situation could have been a substitute for his daily encounters with a sordid and inhuman reality and with an ever more encroaching illness. Those elements in his art which to some extent may be traced back to his personal misfortunes are not foreign matters and do not distort his art; they are rather the reason for its uniqueness. Brod's speculations on the different course Kafka's art would have taken if he had had an easier life are relics of the times which believed in the sovereignty and glory of the artist for the sake of being an artist.

Max Brod's biography of Kafka was followed five years later by the first attempt at a complete interpretation of his works. In the preface to his *Franz Kakfa, eine Deutung seiner Werke*, Herbert Tauber expresses the ambition of giving a running commentary to all of Kafka's writings; instead of drawing broad outlines, as all previous articles on Kafka had done, Tauber progresses from story to story. This was a necessary step forward, but the execution of this plan is rather uneven. It is impossible to interpret the six volumes of Kafka adequately in a book of 236 pages. Tauber often does not go beyond the most general indications; a story of the richness of "The Hunter Gracchus," for instance, is treated in six lines. Interpretations which are seemingly longer consist largely of a recapitulation of the contents. The book would have been more useful if Tauber had limited himself to a few of Kafka's writings, one of the novels, for instance, and if he had treated these more exhaustively, with constant reference to the whole of Kafka's work.

This book was written as a doctor's dissertation at the University of Zürich. It is true to its German origin in its emphasis on the "abstractly intellectual" content of Kafka's art. The author admits that the language, the style of Kafka, is just as essential to his understanding as the "content," but he leaves the investigation of this to others. This artificial separation, common to most German critics, this neglect of the artistic and "poetical" in Kafka, has seriously impaired the results of the interpretation. Kafka cannot be read as if he were a metaphysician who happened to express himself in narrative rather than in systematic form. Because he is in search of allegorical meanings which can be rationally formulated and because of his lack of artistic sensitivity, Tauber often goes astray; he sees for instance in the circus which "The Hunger-Artist" joins in his declining years a symbol for the all-embracing community of which Kafka supposedly wished to become a member! In this allegorical, intellectualistic interpretation, Tauber is largely dependent on Brod. Like Brod he sees in Kafka's works "the search for religious guidance in the sense of the theology of revelation" and he interprets them in the light of Kierkegaard. He also follows Brod in the tendency to find a specifically "Jewish" meaning in many of Kafka's stories. In one respect, however, Tauber goes beyond Max Brod, or rather approaches an earlier position of Brod. While he agrees with Brod that Kafka always longed for the "healthy" and positive, he discovers in him on the other hand "an unfruitfulness which breaks out in the work itself and shows its deadly face, symptomatic of all the barrenness of its time." These arguments about "fruitfulness," or the lack of it, in Kafka only illustrate the sterility of a method which confuses art with theology.

The greatest asset of the book is a number of passages from hitherto unpublished diaries of Kafka which Max Brod made accessible to the author.

Three unnamed drawings by Kafka

419

the cabalists

charles neider

I

Only a little more than twenty years ago there died in Europe a comparatively young man who wrote some of the most extraordinary books of modern times, books of great daring, brilliance and profundity. These books have been known and appreciated by a few; yet, they would, in my opinion, offer a rich experience for the many.

Take *The Castle*—a novel full of wonder and suspense, strange happenings and a moody and poetic atmosphere suggestive of a heath, a novel which sets up waves in the reader which affect him long after he has put it down; a novel of a man who dies of exhaustion from seeking logic and justice on earth. Or take *The Trial*—a great, novel-length detective story in which the hero's life is constantly threatened, in which he is pursued by an enemy whose nature is unclear to him but who stalks him unfalteringly and "with insidious intent" until he is slain; a novel full of strange houses and dim, dangerous apartments and queer and dangerous people.

421

These novels are beautifully wrought and almost deceptively simple; their profundity is unobtrusive, for they please primarily through their remarkable form and their sensory stimulation. Their symbolism is complex but, like much of great art, their effect is emotional and psychological and does not depend on intellectual intricacies and efforts. And yet they are unknown to many readers who would thoroughly enjoy them if they chanced upon them.

Kafka is an expert at contriving a complicated and effective plot and at generating an immense amount of suspense. He is not a conventionally realistic novelist who sprinkles his canvas with samples of humanity in the manner of Balzac and Tolstoy; nor is he, like James Joyce, a fine etcher of a few thoroughly realized individuals, although some of them possess outstanding individual traits. Kafka is not interested in delineating characters as such; his interest lies rather in the most profound and highly personal psychological factors. Yet his people are anything but drab and mechanical. They are as startling as Dostoyevsky's—probably because of Kafka's unflagging and uncanny interest in the hidden causes of certain types of abnormal behavior.

Kafka writes about "Everyman." He writes about him almost in the medieval allegorical sense and adds pungent irony and stunning psychological insight. But his characters are also symbols in the modern tradition; that is, they are symbolic on several levels at the same time. In fact, the entire texture of his novels is shot through with symbolism. Yet strangely enough, this does not overburden them or make them opaque or ineffective; on the contrary, under Kafka's hand it lends them an evocative and allusive quality rarely duplicated in modern literature, and this quality heightens the enjoyment of the reader as well as intensifies his sense of perceiving the truth. Allegoric and symbolic are unfortunate terms, however, for describing Kafka's characters if they make him seem formidable.

What about Kafka's style? It is brilliant and simple; it is classical. Perhaps Kafka's sole prose eccentricity is his occasional use of long paragraphs, in which dialogue may be presented without indentation. His settings are bizarre, not intrinsically but because of his poetic gift of selecting and heightening those elements in a normal environment which he wishes to employ to create a fantastic effect. One of his novels, *The Trial*, is laid in a city; another, *The Castle*, in a village; and the interesting thing is that they are at once both real and dreamlike environments. To a large extent Kafka's genius lies in this ability to fluctuate precariously between the solid and the insubstantial, between realism and distortion. The emotional effect on the reader of this talent of Kafka's is overpowering.

Kafka's father was a highly successful business man, a "regular" fellow whom Kafka, in his youth, despaired of emulating because of his physical fragility as compared with his father's robustness and because of his tendency toward the artistic. Kafka never got on with his father; his father was puzzled and antagonistic, while Kafka himself was full of guilt and resentment, a reaction which he never outgrew. Kafka was a Jew. He was also a civil servant, very familiar with the bureaucracy of the semi-feudalistic Austrian Empire. He leaned toward the Slavic factors in his environment and toward mysticism. And, finally, he was sickly—he died of tuberculosis in 1924. All of these elements are germane to an understanding of his work and of the fact that Kafka's protagonists are ridden by fears and guilt and beset by injustice, that they strive toward equilibrium until exhausted and smothered to death. His heroes live in a nightmare of reality, a reality responding to the laws, to the distortions of the dream world.

II

In view of the above, it is ironic that Kafka, who of all modern writers perhaps most bitterly satirized cabalism, should himself be the victim, after his death, of a number of cabalas whose proponents are increasing and, if anything, growing even more ardent and esoteric. The cabalists are not limited to country or school; their abundant literature flourishes; and only occasionally does one hear a voice in protest. Kafka has come close to becoming the exclusive literary property of esoteric readers; the fact is, regardless of whether he would have approved of it or not, that he is not getting through to his maximum audience potential. And undoubtedly an important reason for this is the abstruse literature on him.

Of the several cabalas the most prominent are the mystic and the psychoanalytic, while the Marxist method, beneficial in its skepticism and earth-bound approach, itself at times threatens to expand to the nebulousness of a cabala. The causes are not difficult to seek out. Much of the cabalism can be set down as the result of critical professionalism: over-complication and temporary blindness are the specialist's occupational hazards. Besides, there has been a critical tendency in the past few decades to write around a subject and to avoid a direct examination and discussion of works themselves, as though the latter were too simple a task to occupy a really worthwhile critical intelligence. It is something like the ancient Greek disdain for empirical methods compared to their love of speculation and philosophizing. In a world beset by chaos and faithlessness the search for meaning, for the "key," is particularly intense; since Kafka is a refreshing voice he has been seized upon by critics bored with an over-played realism; and since his manner is extremely allusive it is natural that the interpretations of his work and life should be so varied and passionate. Nevertheless the harm done him is often greater than the good.

The misinterpretation of Kafka is three-fold: literary, critical and philosophical. In the first place various conclusions have been formed regarding the structure, style and psychology of Kafka's works which are not warranted by the facts, such as the relation between Joseph K. of *The Trial* and K. of *The Castle* and such as the thematic and psychological differences between these two novels; in the second place critics have read into Kafka meanings unsupported by sufficient internal proof and in a number of cases have made interesting but unfounded comments based on poor reasoning and/or false stress and anachronisms; in the third place the philosophical issues in the Kafka quarrel have been obscured by the majority of the commentators, who have consequently fought blindly and in most cases have either overshot their targets or fallen short of them. The Kafka problem should be viewed in the light of the worldwide religious revival which

424

has been accelerating during the past several decades and which brought, to a large extent, the expressionist school, of which Kafka is a leading exponent, into being and which may (or may not, according to the point of view) have inspired Kafka's works. It is the revival which is responsible for the mystical interpretations of Kafka as exemplified by Brod and other of Kafka's mystical friends, by his excellent, but unfortunately mystical English translator, Edwin Muir, and by those converts to anti- or super-naturalism who have looked upon Kafka possessively as well as admiringly—Auden, Isherwood, Huxley and the rest. It is a mistake to regard the Kafka problem as something isolated in a hermetic sphere removed from non-literary matters. The philosophical and therefore the ethical and political implications of the religious revival, of the "failure of nerve," are deep and ramified, as John Dewey, Sidney Hook, Morris R. Cohen and other naturalists have made clear. It is natural enough that it has been the revivalists who have beaten the drum loudest for Kafka; they have sought far and earnestly for keystones for their movement and have come up with Kierkegaard and yoga and many other anti-naturalist gems; in the case of Kafka, however, they may have trundled a Trojan horse into their camp. It is only in the last few years that naturalist critics have attempted to save Kafka from his zealous well-wishers; but oddly enough they failed to see the issues clearly themselves, with strange and murky results.

The entire Kafka controversy has existed under incredibly turbulent conditions, with both sides occasionally wandering into enemy territory and, through sheer ignorance or confusion, sniping at their own positions. In the main the supernaturalists have come out best under such conditions, not because of superior logic but because, based on turmoil and the vague, the unempirical, they have fought the battle on their own ground; besides, and more important, they have in a sense laid down the rules of the game, with their "inside" knowledge as divulged by Kafka's intimates and disciples, their exegeses in terms of absolutes, divine, original sin and all the rest of the mystical baggage. And the naturalist critics, failing to recognize the philosophical issues and the moral consequences involved, lulled by the belief that the controversy was only "literary" and therefore sealed from the realm of ethics, fascinated by the fantastic logic of the mystics and lured by the "key," supinely accepting reports from the disciples as gospel, even when at variance with their own reasoning and the evidence in the works of Kafka, and even adapting some of the impedimenta of the supernaturalists, have failed to fix their sights and consequently have fired mightily but in vain. Their position should be: (1) If Kafka is found, on the basis of the best evidence, internal and external, to be supernatural, then he should be read simply for whatever artistic values he possesses apart from his ideas, presupposing that a divorce between these is possible; and his life and work should be studied for the light to be cast upon the failure of nerve in our century; (2) If, because of insufficient evidence, no conclusion can be formed concerning Kafka's philosophical position, it should be made clear that he is not the special province of the mystics and he should be read to advantage, for ethical as well as esthetic reasons, by the naturalists. But witness their silence, their uncertainty and their occasional gullibility. At best they deny the assertion of the mystics that Kafka is *solely* concerned with the incommensurability between man and God, and they proceed to suggest other relevant and illuminating matter; sometimes they ignore the business of the divine out of embarrassment; but generally they accept the premise and then struggle to get a firm grip on Kafka despite it. The supernaturalists abhor, of course, empirical method as a means of warranting assertions and they are consistent in neglecting it in their discussions of Kafka. It is all the more curious, then, that the naturalists have neglected the factors of observation, analysis, supposition, idealization and inference in their attempts to confute them.

Both the naturalist and the anti- or super-naturalist interpretations of Kafka are legitimate, the first on the basis of the absence of explicit references to supernatural beliefs and motifs in Kafka and the second on the basis of biographical data relating to Kafka's preoccupation with mystical doctrine. The naturalist approach significantly places first emphasis on Kafka's strange relations with his father, while the supernaturalist more or less neglects these in favor of disembodied "ideas," "impulses" and "beliefs." The naturalist approach may even grant the existence of the supernaturalist element in Kafka's work and then interpret it as a projection of his personal situation, in the light of its knowledge of the inception and development of religious myths; but it need not go so far, for the burden of proof lies with the supernaturalists as far as Kafka's works are concerned, since it is they who insist on meanings in Kafka which are not self-evident. (The works are a kind of no man's land between the naturalist and the supernaturalist positions and it is a question whether in the long run Kafka will benefit by his deliberately enigmatic method, which provides no safe bridge from his biography to his works.) It does not follow that a man necessarily writes about his beliefs, particularly where the novel form is concerned, whether he wishes to do so or not; therefore it remains for the mystics to prove that the works contain unified and fertile ramifications on the religious theme; their internal proof must be fruitful and germane to warrant serious rational consideration. To date they have failed in this; they are always pointing out the Emperor's finery when it is obvious he is naked, they are forever asking the reader to assume the existence of things which are not in the books but which they require to complete their text. The naturalist's position is much simpler and easier; his interpretation neglects no element of the Kafka problem; he deals with details as part of a whole and, rather than ask the reader to assume the existence of the non-existent, he offers him new light on both the man and his work by the careful examination of facts related to the whole. As for the question why Kafka did not make his religious notions explicit in his work, here again the burden of proof rests upon the mystics. The naturalist can content himself with the assumption that Kafka had sufficient (and perhaps anti-religious) reasons for remaining vague regarding his mysticism; at any rate he can peacefully accept the fact that the answer is unknown and can proceed to an examination of the known facts and a conclusion. Another aspect of the case favoring the naturalist is that even if Kafka did write about the divine and so on, it does not follow that his books do not possess a secular and more fruitful meaning; one can believe one is writing about God yet actually write about men; and this is a fair probability in any case, since one can write only in terms of one's mortal expe-

427

rience. The naturalist, then, can reach the conclusion that what Kafka is writing about is not the incommensurability between man and the divine but between Kafka and his father or Kafka and society, and that basically he is asserting that to reach a spiritual understanding with his father and/or society (possibly equating the two) is as impossible as reaching the Castle or the highest Courts. Nor must it be forgotten that a book is a public property and that it may (and quite often does) have an effect altogether different from the author's intention. For this added reason it is important to insist on Kafka's books speaking for themselves—that is, to insist on an internal examination of them for casting light on his meaning. At the present time each major book of his published in English contains material written either by Brod or by Muir, not to mention others, prejudicing the innocent reader in favor of the mystical point of view. Thus a sort of clandestine and probably quite involuntary proselytizing is carried on. If Kafka's books need prefaces and epilogues at all, then it is time that the naturalist had an opportunity to present his views side by side with the mystic, in order that the reader may come to his own conclusions after examining both sides of the case.

An interesting study, outside the scope of this essay, could be written on Kafka and the failure of nerve in our century, indicating Kafka's own failure of nerve together with that of the religious faction of the German expressionist movement, including such figures as Barlach, Werfel, Edschmid and Kornfeld. It would be interesting to view Kafka, also, from the perspective of such contemporary revivalists as Auden, Eliot, Huxley *et al.* and to examine his influence on them as well as the influence of the German religious revival upon supernaturalists in England and America. An investigation of Kafka's influence upon naturalists (mainly in terms of technique and psychology) as well as upon supernaturalists would also be illuminating. Finally, a detailed examination of the influence of the religious revival in relation to criticism and interpretation of Kafka would be valuable. But at present it is appropriate to indicate only that the expressionist movement was not solely religious (it included rational expressionists who wanted social and political reforms),

428

that it arose from a dissatisfaction with a stagnant, spiritless society as well as with current modes in art and literature and that Kafka avoided identifying himself—at least in his work—with either of the three or four factions of the movement.

III

The consequences of this literary turmoil are that there is a Kafka problem more than twenty years after his death, with little agreement regarding his basic meaning, and that he is being distorted for various ends without clear regard for his inherent value. It seems inevitable that one must go over the Kafka literature in an effort to clear at least some of the ground before proceeding to a discussion of Kafka with an emphasis on empirical method and the literary mechanism.

The chief advocates of the mystical school—by far the greatest cabala of them all—are Max Brod, Kafka's friend, literary executor and biographer, and Edwin Muir. It was Brod who first characterized *The Trial* and *The Castle* as "two manifested forms of the Godhead (in the sense of the Cabala), justice and grace" and indicated that they were religious novels dealing with the incommensurability between man and the divine. Muir carried Brod's suggestion to an extreme. To him the novels are definitely metaphysical or theological; he accepts the word "divine" literally; compares the novels to various religious works, among them *Pilgrim's Progress*; and sees Kafka's creations as elaborate religious allegories of a highly personal nature. Brod, however, does not wish to go so far: he makes it clear that a biographical understanding of the novels is more vital than theological explanations; and he says that "Nearness to God and right living were identical for Kafka." But Muir, apparently unsatisfied with this rather pragmatic view of the "divine," constructs case after case to implement his notion that Kafka's works are along the lines of mystical revelation. His skillfully formed cases are laborious to the rational mind; they seem like the hair-splitting of the schoolmen; and their foundation, the naturalist is convinced, is nonexistent.

A shrewd exegete in America for the mystical school is John Kelly. By the use of hindsight and careful selection of odd

429

bits from *The Trial* he builds up a case to show that Kafka was deliberately theological and neo-Calvinist, that at the same time that he was immersed in Kierkegaard he was also expressing, without knowing it, a parallel to Kierkegaard's disciple's, Karl Barth's, *Commentary on the Epistle to the Romans*. His constant implication is that Kafka's effects and suggestions are cerebral and purposive to an almost political degree. He does not discuss Kafka in biographical or social terms or literary or psychoanalytical ones. Kafka to Kelly is an automaton intent on a game of translating Kierkegaard into novelistic terms—he is not an artist at all, not autobiographical or intuitive but only cerebral and conscious. This sort of argument goes to such an extreme in Kelly's essay that it defeats itself; its value lies in the damage it creates in its own backyard. Those who like that kind of thing, well done though it is, are welcome to it; for those who don't, a good antidote may be found in Magny, Landsberg, Arendt, Lerner and the others of the naturalist group.

Not all the mystical apologetes, however, are as shrewd and closely-reasoned as Kelly. An essay by an English writer, R. H. Thomas, is an example of mystical mouthing at its worst. The subject of Kafka's work, claims Thomas in his "Franz Kafka and the Religious Aspect of Expressionism," is the attempt "to reconcile the Finite with the Infinite." He continues: "His work is symbolic because his aim is to express the Infinite in Finite terms." Thomas is quite a remarkable critic, for in the same breath that he talks seriously of the infinite in terms of the finite he calls "The Metamorphosis" "a significant document of the war period," claiming that "the sudden change in Samsa is to be regarded as the symbolical presentation of the dissolution of the prevailing order of things, such as took place under the impact of the war." Even the most historically-minded and sociological of the Kafka critics have hesitated to bludgeon the reader with a conclusion so gauche. Coming from one who accepts enthusiastically Brod's dicta of divine grace and justice, it makes one realize with startling clarity how confused is so much of the thinking about Kafka.

Nor is Thomas free of bald factual errors. For example: "In 1923 he went to Berlin where he suffered from malnutrition at the time of the deepest economic distress in Germany. He married (sic!) in the same year but he was already a hopeless invalid." Thomas makes another error, which caused some anguished soul to write "No!" in the margin of my library copy of the essay: he calls *Amerika* the last of Kafka's novels—that is, he does so for one sentence. In the next sentence he corrects himself chronologically, only to pile confusion on confusion by adding: "Although chronologically it precedes the other two (it was begun in 1912) it must be regarded, by virtue of its content, as following upon them." This is indeed a novel thought, overwhelming in its originality; Thomas does not even hesitate to spit upon the facts of time. But why does he make the statement? The answer is (begging pardon for a *non sequitur*): "For in this work Kafka suggests the possibility of a happy ending of fulfilment and thus it stands apart from most of his work."

I mentioned the factual error only in order to indicate the state of Kafka literature. Speaking of errors, here are two gems from *Transition Stories,* edited by Eugene Jolas and Robert Sage: "Franz Kafka was born in Czechoslovakia and died in Germany in 1924 at the age of thirty years."(!) "He published nothing during his lifetime."(!) And both Hannah Arendt and Janko Lavrin keep speaking of *Amerika* as Kafka's last novel, for some reason, probably because when it first appeared in 1927 it followed *Der Prozess* (1925) and *Das Schloss* (1926) and because these writers may have referred to those editions.

Whereas Kelly utilizes reason in an attempt to prove mysticism in Kafka, Ezequiel Martínez Estrada uses mysticism itself in a similar attempt. "The most direct route to an interpretation of Kafka is not that which leads straight to conclusions," says Estrada, making an observation correct only for himself and his colleagues. Then he proceeds to an orgy of wildest postulation, mainly about "pure" reason and "pure" intuition. He is full of historical oddities—e.g., he speaks of poets, philosophers and scientists at the beginning of this century as "weakening or denying the heretofore unquestioned rights of the postulates of reason and the certitudes of common sense," disregarding the contribution of Schopenhauer, among others, relating to the significance of the unconscious. He pronounces the "absolute, mathematical security"

431

of the new, modern world, which is the sort of thing said loudly in every boastful age, only to be exploded by the next major discovery. He calls intuition the "new technique for understanding and divining the nature of the world," as if the great artists and the saints and mystics of past centuries were not historical facts. Kafka, he asserts, "applies the new tool of pure intuition to the observation and chronicling of the reality of man in an alien world." This artificial dichotomy between "pure" reason and "pure" intuition has no valid connection with reality. The character of the "new" world of relativity and the universe of neo-vitalism can be divined only by intuition, says Estrada. But who operates in the higher mathematical realms of relativity—in, say, perceiving the fourth dimension—by intuition alone? Where would Einstein have gotten in his physical research early in the century without the empiricism of the Michaelson-Morley experiments and their failure to register "ether" drag—how could he have conceived of his relativity theory before being aware of the problem? And who achieves a solely intuitive grasp of a world of n dimensions, which only mathematics offers in pragmatic form? One of the lessons to be learned from Einstein is that we must never cease being skeptical of our "intuition," which is largely dependent on sense impressions and which therefore is more valid in terrestrial terms than in universal ones, in terms, say, of velocities far beyond human experience or "colors" beyond the range of human vision. On the other hand we must also be skeptical of "reason."

One thing about Estrada and the other mystics: they are not afraid to contradict themselves. "It is an illogical, mythical and absurd world," Estrada says of Kafka's works. A few paragraphs later he says: "It is also wrong, moreover, to speak of absurdity in Kafka's novels. . . ."

W. H. Auden, writing in *The New Republic*, begins by decrying the fact that Kafka belongs to the cultists and ends by discussing him with metaphysical hair-splitting in the best (or worst) manner of the cultists, at a time when Kafka needed a few blunt statements from appreciative sources. Auden has written one of the most interesting and self-revealing statements of the philosophical problem in Kafka as well as offered sugges-

432

tive literary hints, particularly in reference to the problem of the Quest. He sees Kafka from his particular prejudice, one aspect of which is an insistence that the true significance of a neurosis is teleological and that the questions with which Kafka dealt have very little to do with his relationship with his father. Auden sees in Kafka only what he wishes to see, his own Quest, his own torment between skepticism and a desire for faith. He sees in Kafka both more and less than the rational reader. Auden is proud of Kafka and eager to have him on his side, erroneously assuming that therefore Kafka belongs among the anti- or super-naturalists.

In the last analysis one may legitimately approach any artistic work solipsistically. But since Kafka's appeal is not limited to mystical minds and since his intended meanings have been obscured by his untimely death and since a rational interpretation sounds just as cohesive and related as the mystical, it is also legitimate to examine the mystical view from the vantage point of naturalism and to conclude that the naturalist approach has the advantages of intelligibility, closer relation to the facts of biography and literary method and, above all, closer relation both to the world which created Kafka and that which by a great majority received him. As Stephen Spender wrote, Kafka is not interested in discovering a metaphysic but in penetrating reality to discover a system of truth. The verbiage of the "divine" approach serves only as a fog to distort the truth.

As for the psychoanalytical (or perhaps it should be termed the Freudian-materialist) school, possibly its most prominent member in America is Harry Slochower, who, while he has written on other topics with admirable insight and logic, in his approach to Kafka is psychoanalytical not only in content and interpretation but in method as well. That is, he tends to develop his thesis associationally rather than logically. His essay "Franz Kafka: Pre-Fascist Exile" is illuminating, however, despite this handicap. It is particularly good in dealing with Kafka's social background and in the relation of the three novels (*Amerika, The Trial* and *The Castle*) to the varying times which produced them. It is unfortunate, therefore, that Slochower is often guilty of quite irrelevant statements which muddy the waters so sorely in need of purification—such statements as the following: "The

433

negative, repressive form of the sex act is the characteristic of Franz Kafka's writings." "The motif of sinning against the world of the Fathers is further symbolized by Karl's loss of his father's trunk when he lands in the new world. According to Stekel, luggage is 'the burden of sin by which one is oppressed.' " "In Freud, the number three is symbolic of the male genitalia." (This last in reference to the fact that in *The Trial* Joseph K. is led away to his execution by two men, one on each side of him.) "Thomas Mann's Castorp, similarly suffering from lack of air (*there is even the parallel of the k-sound in his name*), 'resolves' his dilemma by physical action on a communal battlefield." (The italics are mine.)

In relating the novels to the times which produced them, Slochower makes out a case that Kafka grew progressively mature and therefore progressively gloomy from *Amerika* to *The Trial* to *The Castle*. He calls *Amerika* Kafka's "pre-war dream of a free country," a dream shattered by the First World War, and proceeds to build up his case. Now this case, while laudable and unquestionably true in part, achieves error through false stress. As valid a case can be constructed on the basis of the literary mechanism. One can say, for example, that Kafka was feeling his literary oats in *Amerika* and that therefore it is not as rich an expression of his tortuous, questioning dream-world as *The Trial* and *The Castle*. He was sounding out his theme and still depending, to a considerable extent, on conventional realism for his effects. Later, when he mastered style and theme, he was able to achieve greater individuality and therefore originality. It is not only possible but quite probable that *The Trial* and *The Castle* would have been written without the First World War and its aftermath because their creation was dependent not so much on large-scale social events as on Kafka's inner torment, which, moreover, found expression not in ordinary realistic documentation but through allegory. The basic psychology of our century may have been deepened by the war but it was not created or challenged by it. The war was a symptom, not a cause. Thus Slochower is sometimes guilty of over-simplification on the social level and obscurantism on the psychoanalytic.

Also guilty and along similar lines, in an otherwise ex-

434

cellent and comprehensive essay, is a critic of the Marxist school, Edwin Berry Burgum, who unfortunately makes many unfounded and unsupported assertions—e.g., ". . . his attempt to escape a dominating father left his adolescence stranded upon the fluctuating shoals of the Weimar Republic"; "his own diseased personality symbolized the disease at the heart of German society"; "he takes us into the personality structure itself, remaining unconscious of its nature since he shares it"; "since Kafka's last stories are almost exclusively devoted to his hallucinations"; "that Kafka's anxieties have passed the norm and become psychotic in 'The Burrow' is obvious"; "this rare example ['The Burrow'] of successful communication of psychotic content"; "K.'s murder symbolizes the final ascendancy of fascism . . ."

Burgum makes a great point of the influence of the Weimar Republic on Kafka's works; but the Republic was not established until the end of the war, when Kafka was thirty-five and when he had only six years to live. Therefore when Burgum speaks of the inefficiency of the Weimar Republic and of the effect of its bureaucracy on Kafka and *The Trial,* he misuses his terms; it was the empire bureaucracy of feudalistic Austria which bred Kafka, not that of the Weimar Republic. Also, Burgum claims that Kafka grew progressively psychotic and that "his own diseased personality symbolized the disease at the heart of German society." (This, incidentally, is the thesis of his essay, "Franz Kafka and the Bankruptcy of Faith.") But his elaborate analysis does not convince because he fails to explain how it was, if Kafka was growing progressively psychotic (in fact as well as fiction), that in his last years, in the words of Max Brod, "his whole life took an unforeseen turn for the better, a new, happy, and positive turn which cancelled out his self-hatred and Nihilism." Certainly there was nothing in the ominous growth of fascism (to use Burgum's own method) to warrant Kafka's new optimism and happiness. Burgum, unfortunately, never mentions these last years. His weakness, like Slochower's, is his too-great dependence on social reference frames in explaining Kafka and his works. Such an interpretation is as basically misleading as the implication of the mystics that Kafka was not at all influenced by the problems of his time.

435

A similar critic, Philip Rahv, in two otherwise illuminating essays, fluctuates in confusion between cerebration and intuition, picking up most of the mystical baggage of his predecessors and only occasionally and then faint-heartedly permitting an intuitive suspicion that Kafka was quite a good old rationalist after all. In "The Hero as Lonely Man" he says outright that Kafka is "the most genuine mystic in modern literature" and adds: "The relationship of Kafka to K. is dramatic: within the latter he isolates his own rationalism for the purpose of purging himself of its impiety." Thus he contradicts an earlier statement in the same essay: "The application of Freudian ideas to literature has often been gratuitous, but in Kafka's case it seems to me quite necessary. He is a writer who cannot be explained adequately by a strictly literary analysis, in terms of his literary qualities alone—and the methods of Freud are superior, I think, to the metaphysical flights which he has inspired in his German critics." That is, although Rahv uses the methods of rationalism in exploring Kafka, he begins with the fallacious assumption that Kafka himself is not rational and never seriously challenges this assumption.

This first essay of Rahv's is, however, more cautious than his second, "*The Death of Ivan Ilyich* and Joseph K.," in which he swallows the mystical line with almost complete innocence, speaking of the tendency in *The Trial* as "against rationalism, against civilization, against the heresies of the man of the city whose penalty is spiritual death" and speaking of Kafka's "all-absorbing belief in the incommensurability of the human and divine orders" and proceeding to the following sample of mystical verbiage: "But from the chrysalis of the Kafkian self there also emerges another figure, who, by means of a psychic transformation, assumes the role of judge and avenger. This dread antagonist summarily lifts K. out of his rationalist sloth and plunges the metaphysical knife into his breast. However, this antagonist is not a character we can recognize, he is not a living actor in the drama of K.'s fate. He is, rather, a transcendental emanation taking shape in the actual plot against K.'s life—and, in the final analysis, against the human faith in visible reality." But perhaps the zenith of Rahv's ethereal flight is reached in his statement that "He, the perverted modern man, can never adapt himself to the conditions of the absolute; he commits the most ludicrous errors and, though guilty, he thinks himself innocent. As he enters the Court he feels stifled in its pure air; its magnificent chambers he mistakes for dingy tenement rooms. Blinded by the fierce light of Moira, he can never experience the unity of justice and necessity, but must ever divide one from the other." Near the conclusion of the essay, however, Rahv experiences a moment of doubt which he instantly suppresses: "Yet from another standpoint is it not possible to say that, objectively, Tolstoy and Kafka were really protesting against the irrational masquerading as the rational?"

In the second essay Rahv explores the so-called parallelism between the deaths of Ivan Ilyich and Joseph K., asserting that their authors punished them for their rationalism and typicality by torturing them with unknown afflictions, preparing them for death by arousing their consciences and then executing them. This thesis is interesting but it contains several errors of fact, the most important of which are: (1) While it is true that Ivan Ilyich's conscience is aroused by his impending death, Joseph K.'s conscience is already aroused when the novel opens—Ivan Ilyich is smug and self-assured in the beginning, while Joseph K. is uneasy and suffers guilt feelings always; (2) While Ivan Ilyich is typical, Joseph K. is distinctly not—as a matter of fact it is precisely his atypicality which ruins him, for instead of being a "regular guy" and accepting his situation he insists on questioning and fighting "the system"; (3) As for the rationalism of the two protagonists, which Rahv equates, it is clear that Ivan Ilyich is an irrational character who calls upon rationalism (in the form of science and doctors) only when he is in trouble, while rationalism, skepticism and, above all, integrity are the very bases of Joseph K.'s existence.

Certain aspects of the cabalas have become the common property of all the schools. What a dither, for example, has resulted from the fact that in *The Trial* and *The Castle* the heroes are anonymous, in *The Trial* being Joseph K. and in *The Castle* simply K. "*Amerika* is the only novel in which the hero *has a name*," says Slochower. (The italics are his.) Elsewhere he says,

437

"The initial 'K.' suggests the stifling element in his life. Like the anonymous and standardized people in the expressionistic works, Kafka's unheroic hero lacks a name." And Klaus Mann, in his preface to *Amerika*, says: "Both of these remain strangely anonymous—or rather, they hide their mysterious identity with the author behind the obvious initial 'K.' . . ." Max Lerner, writing in the *Saturday Review of Literature,* cautions: ". . . note the progressive attenuation of the name." And Burgum writes of *Amerika,* "Its hero, Karl Rossman, is the only one among his writings to whom Kafka gave a name. The others are unnamed or generalized into 'K.'" And Estrada says: ". . . their individuality, generally recognized by physiognomy or name, . . . is here reduced to a mere initial letter . . ."

Now it happens that Brod explicitly states, in a note to the English edition of *The Castle,* that the novel "seems to have been begun as a story in the first person, the earlier chapters being altered by the author, 'K.' being inserted everywhere in place of 'I,' and the later chapters written straight out in the third person." And in his epilogue to the English edition of *The Trial,* Brod reports that in his preparation of the manuscript he transcribed in full "the innumerable contractions (for instance, instead of F.B., Fräulein Bürstner; instead of T., Titorelli. . . ." We have here, I think, sufficient information regarding the manuscripts to enable us to judge for ourselves whether the excitement is justified or whether it is simply another aspect of the cabalas. This information is in the form of insights into Kafka's creative mechanism; we see that he was in the habit of identifying his characters by their initials (probably for economy of time and effort) and that he identified himself, at least in an earlier stage of the work, with the K. of *The Castle,* or in other words used himself as the model for the protagonist. Besides, there is the element of tradition in the use of abbreviation. At various times during the last century it was fashionable to write in the following manner: "On the morning of the 16th day of May 18–, I came upon P—— in the town of Y——." Incidentally, Kafka is hardly unique in his methods. Numerous authors have used abbreviations in their early drafts and in some cases, prominent among them Dostoyevsky, have employed real names to help call the models to mind, just as Kafka used the initial of his surname to aid him in identifying his protagonists with himself. (It is also interesting to note that the F.B. in *The Trial* manuscript corresponds to the F.B. to whom Kafka was twice engaged.) All this indicates the possibility—one could even conservatively say probability—that had Kafka lived to arrange for the publication of his last two novels he would have given his protagonists fictitious names, just as he did in works published during his lifetime.

IV

It has been seen, then, that the shortcomings of much of the literature on Kafka stem from too specialized views, from a lack of an understanding of the underlying issues in the Kafka quarrel, from a neglect of the "merely" literary and from the failure to see the Kafka details as parts of a whole including biography, sociology, philosophy and the literary art. It remains now to indicate what has been missed in the Kafka search. For the purposes of this essay we shall concentrate on one aspect, Kafka's basic theme—his critical analysis of cabalism, defined loosely as any social tradition with the force no less than that of folkway which has lost its meaning or which is harmful to the majority and which rests on the irrational rather than on reason.

The irrational is a great motif in Kafka. Not only do his books suggest overpoweringly the irrationality of existence and its dominance over reason and order but their basic fiber is the irrationality of dream-logic. He deals with the irrational not only as the container but also as the thing contained—his very approach to his truth is through the irrational. He does not look down into the irrational, as did the literary precursors of Freud, but up from it. It is to the discredit of the surrealists that they go down into disorder to wallow there, using the license granted by the new awareness of the unconscious and the irrational, while it is Kafka's distinction that, caught in the web of disorder, he desperately and courageously seeks order, at the cost of his life. To him disorder is sin, it is a bohemia from which he would flee in terror, yet he suffers it, studies and catalogues it for the benefit of light and health. The surrealists wend an easy and shallow way to hell and beat their breasts in exultation half-way before arriving, convinced they have arrived; theirs is the thrill of schoolboy sin; while Kafka is too familiar with sin, disorder and disease to find them amusing or tolerable; he collects and codifies only for the ascent to the world. The surrealists are playboys let loose in a clinic, while Kafka is rabbi and doctor, Talmudist and scientific skeptic in one.

He is forever plagued by the irrational. First there is the dilemma of existence, the confused and blurred glimpse of the universe vouchsafed to man, the knowledge of death plus the ignorance of its meaning. Then there is the irrationality of society, the absence of reason in an age which calls itself enlightened, the operation of maxims such as might is right as witnessed in the continued force of such concepts as national sovereignty, states' rights, individual possession of portions of the earth's crust. And finally there is the irrationality of the individual, of Kafka himself, with his monstrous torments and impulses. Often Kafka seems to be trying to show that there is no absolute truth, that truth depends on the point of view and that points of view cancel each other out. Life, in short, is a torturous enigma. His work, too, in reproducing life as he knows it, is enigmatic.

To people who have sat on American juries, much of the argumentative and hair-splitting side of Kafka will be familiar—particularly if they have sat on one of those numerous and typical civil cases where both sides present absolutely contradictory assertions and witnesses and where it is almost always impossible to decide rationally where the truth is, since the truth depends on the credibility of the witnesses and the varying points of view. A verdict in these cases is usually brought in on the basis of "intuition" or "faith" as to who is telling the truth. So it is in Kafka, where contradictory cases are elaborately developed concerning simple and seemingly obvious incidents and where no "absolute" truth is ever achieved. This is the legal tone, the heritage of Kafka's law studies; and it is also his Talmudic heritage. In this connection it is apparent that the Hebraic tradition in Kafka is overwhelmingly stronger than the Hellenistic; the sensuous element in him is meager compared to the moral and ratiocinative. One feels that he is ashamed of the sensuous as

440

if it were pagan and amoral. There is nothing of the musical in him, nor of the mythical, and little of the usual literary ornamentation.

Yes, Kafka is plagued, for he cannot accept the irrational; no matter how he strives to do so, no matter what mental gymnastics he attempts he cannot succeed. Kierkegaard in the end is no solace, nor is the Kabbala, nor the mid-European mysticism of his friends. Therefore he despairs—of understanding his father, his family, society, of realizing himself, of marrying—and so on endlessly; and his despair is forever heightened by his illness. There are men who learn to accept the irrational, but Kafka was too Talmudic, too modern for that. He was too thoroughly grounded in the Hebraic virtues of morality, order and restraint to permit himself the Hellenistic and sensualist, the Dionysiac luxury of accepting the irrational. If one may use Arnold's terms loosely, one may say that the nineteenth century was Hellenistic, with emphasis on the individual and the sensual, and that the twentieth is Hebraic, with emphasis on moral and political responsibility. Kafka was caught in a trap between the two. A possible reason for his inability to extricate himself from his Talmudic leanings is that he was the epitome of minority—he was Czech, Jew, intellectually *raffiné*, diseased. It is the minority which seeks safety in law and reason; and this being in a minority of one was Kafka's curse.

This extreme isolation is best symbolized in Kafka by the use of the number two (as suggested to me by Vivien B. Neider), by duality, the glaring opposite of singularity. It is two as completion, the opposite of aloneness. There are the two assistants, the two inns and the two sisters in *The Castle,* the two warders at the beginning and the two executioners at the end of *The Trial,* the two mechanics (Robinson and Delamarche) in *Amerika,* the two bouncing balls, two girls and two assistants in "Blumfeld, An Elderly Bachelor," the two young female assistants in "My Neighbor," the two horses in "A Country Doctor," etc. An examination of the relation of Kafka's protagonists to the two is quite illuminating. The two, which stand for the norm, for society, are invariably irrational and rather mad from the viewpoint of the protagonists, who use utmost logic upon them in an

441

effort at communication but who invariably fail. The protagonists feel superior to the foolish pair and yet they realize that the pair have a strength they themselves noticeably lack and yearn for—they have company, they have each other. The two are always presented as so similar in behavior as to be taken as identical twins. Who can be better adjusted than such twins, who are conscious of no singularity, each possessing a perfect compatriot and comrade? Psychological studies have amply made this clear and no doubt Kafka understood this intuitively. A question arises: Why is it that he chose identical twins to represent unity and completion rather than the more conventional and widespread symbol of mates? Can it be that he preferred a homosexual completion to a heterosexual one? The known facts are insufficient to make a conclusion. But we know, of course, that Kafka described sex relations in his novels—yet he always presented them as awkward and abortive; women there are more truly mothers and comrades than mistresses. And we know too that Kafka had affairs with women; yet he was incapable of bringing himself to marry; he broke off an engagement in panic at the last moment and once charged his father with having made him incapable of marriage. Is it possible that a father-complex predisposed him to homosexual relations for basically psychic reasons? And is this the key to the narcissistic tone of all his writings? In short, perhaps what Slochower calls the onanistic feature of Kafka's work is in reality the homosexual.

To Kafka, cabalism meant the secretive and superficial. When he spoke smilingly and enigmatically of "a secret cabala" in his works he meant, in my opinion, an attack on cabalism, an attack apparent in his works. His friends and critics, however, have generally accepted his words at face value, mainly because they were impressed by his interest in Kierkegaard, his study of the Kabbala and by his genuinely shy, poetic and "religious" nature; and they have proceeded to split hairs upon chimerical foundations almost as deliriously as the Court and Castle functionaries in Kafka's major works. But they failed to reckon with his profound skepticism and his fondness for the enigmatic; also his training as a lawyer and his ability to build up sound-seeming cases at the same time that he was secretly tearing them down. It is strange how esoteric critics strive to find philosophers in artists and artists in philosophers. Kafka is a man primarily of intuitions, emotions and images—an artist—who presented more vividly than anyone else certain aspects of his experience common to his age. He is not a thinker, nor did he pretend that he was; and his works are in reality, for all their actual complexity, simpler than they have been made out to be.

Kafka in his fiction projected his personal deficiencies upon the society which seemed deliberately to exclude him; it was a way of striking back. There is evidence that he was aware of this projection and suspicious of it, and that at times he felt that society was justified in its treatment of him and that he and not it was evil; and perhaps it was for this reason that he asked Brod to destroy his unpublished works, thus renouncing them and thereby acknowledging the justifications of society's case against him. From this point of view it is clear that Kafka's works may have induced great guilt feelings in him, just as his assertions before his father did; in a sense his works were aggressive acts, to be followed, in the neurotic pattern, by self-abasement. According to Brod, Kafka complained that "what he had already written, not to say published, led him astray in his further work." Perhaps it is for this reason that Kafka was so reluctant to publish his work in his lifetime and so insistent in his will that his unpublished manuscripts be destroyed.

Kafka's works are an assault upon the reader; he deliberately teases and mystifies; it is his aggression at play. At the same time they are a kind of hara-kiri on the doorstep of society, only and paradoxically, he lives to regret them. They are the final insult as well as the final self-abasement; and they are a romantic wooing by the mutant of the norm, the romantic self-slaying for the unobtainable beloved in the manner of Werther. And always there is the symbolic commingling of society and the Father, the rejection by the healthy and authoritarian. The key is Kafka's neurotic and trapped ambivalence, his hypochondriacal paradoxicality which makes him incapable of leaving his wound alone, which makes him probe it masochistically with never-ending pain and delight, which makes him value the wound as a

443

sign of difference, of heightened and heightening spirituality, and proudly expose it while ashamed of it.

"In how many conversations," Brod has written, "I tried to make my friend see . . . his over-estimation of his father, the senselessness of his self-distrust. It was entirely useless, the flood of arguments with which Kafka defended his stand (if he did not prefer to say nothing) left me shaken and at a loss." And again: "This need [for his father's approval] was a fact, an irrefutable feeling. It continued to affect Kafka to the end as 'the general burden of fear, weakness, and self-distrust.'" And yet the supernaturalists do not realize that Kafka's writings are extremely autobiographical. "I had lost my self-confidence with you, and exchanged a boundless sense of guilt for it," Kafka wrote his father. "Remembering this boundlessness, I once wrote fittingly about someone: 'He fears that his feeling of shame may even survive him.'" This last refers to the concluding words of *The Trial*. A man writes a highly neurotic and amazingly lengthy and complex "letter" to his father at the age of thirty-six and still the mystics refuse to admit that Kafka's feelings toward his father were dominant in his thought and work and that his work is secular in meaning. They refuse to admit this even though Kafka said, in the letter, that he wanted to group everything he wrote under the collective title of *The Attempt to Escape from Father*. Brod lightly passes over this, commenting ". . . as if his love of art, his creative joy had not existed in its own right and strength," forgetting, apparently, that the attempt to escape from the father and creative joy are not necessarily mutually exclusive or contradictory.

His "Letter to My Father," one of Kafka's most revealing works, much of which has been suppressed by Brod "for reasons of a personal nature," contributes importantly to the understanding of cabalism as Kafka's basic theme. Kafka says to his father: "For me you began to have that mysterious quality which all tyrants have, whose privilege is based on their personality, and not on reason," and this is what he meant by the laws of the nobles, the Courts, the Castle and all the other symbols of outdated shibboleths which he presented. In addition to

444

the bureaucracy under which he lived and the reactionary laws promulgated by the aristocracy, Kafka had another and perhaps most important example of cabalism in his immediate family life —in the Judaism of his father, which included a vast amount of flummery such as chants and readings in the synagogue in a language few understood and symbolic manipulation of items which had ceased to have a vital significance thousands of years ago. Kafka wrote to his father: ". . . I failed to understand how you, with that mere nothing of Judaism you could muster, could criticize me for not exerting myself (at least out of respect for tradition, as you put it) to achieve a similar nothing. . . . You went to synagogue on four days of the year; there you were, to say the least, closer to the indifferent ones than to those who took it seriously. . . ." Kafka goes on at length, speaking derisively of the ceremony of the Bar Mitzvah as "a silly memory test" and of the first Seder night as "a farce with spasms of giggling." He adds: "And it was impossible to convince a child, over-observant from excessive fear, that the few trifling rituals you observed in the name of Judaism, with an indifference corresponding to their emptiness, could have a higher meaning."

It is a mistake to suppose that Kafka in his writings is primarily the intellectual or that the intellectual element is the source of his inspiration. The intellectual is only a symbol and a vessel. Even if we grant that Brod is correct in saying that Kafka wrote of the incommensurability between the Absolute, between God, and the human, this in itself does not explain the passionate return to the wound, nor is it a fruitful concept to one so steeped in skepticism—after all, if the two are incommensurable what can be done about it, what more can be said? But to Kafka's neurotic torment it is a perfect dilemma on the horns of which he may impale himself with remarkable variation. His reaction is neurotic, out of proportion to the stimulus. In an autobiographical sketch he once wrote: "It was like receiving a tap with a brush, not intended to hurt, but only as a warning; but one reacted by separating the bristles, drawing their points singly into one's body and beginning to prick and scratch one's inside according to one's own design, while the other's hand is still calmly holding the handle of the brush." Of course Kafka is diseased and this is

445

the source of his inspiration, as it is in Dostoyevsky, Nietzsche, Schiller and Novalis.

One can hardly blame society for reacting as it did to Kafka or as he imagined it did, for society, the "norm," must protect itself against the mutant, the genius, which it occasionally thrusts up. In the proud artistic revolt so characteristic of the nineteenth century it was fashionable to scorn society yet secretly to envy and woo it, and in many cases rebellious artists who nevertheless wished admittance paid for their entry by creating works of beauty and nobility, often even while attacking society. But in Kafka's case he created in fiction, by projection, only the dubious paradoxes which plagued him, offering no token as a plea for peace and grace, and it may well be that these very acts of aggression drove him further from adjustment, so that in his last years, when he canceled out his former nihilism, as Brod has said, and achieved an easier frame of mind, he wanted to destroy the unpublished works which lay heavily on his overactive conscience.

At times Kafka seems to equate cabalism with society in general and at times limits it to the irrational excesses of society which result in widespread suffering. But his basic attack is against unnecessary suffering—not the suffering of existence itself and the tragedy of life culminating in death—but that entailed by man's relations with his fellows. There is enough suffering in that we *are*, Kafka says, in that we lead a blind existence upon a planet spinning blindly into nowhere among millions of stars and planets more important than our own; there is enough suffering in that—let us at least recognize that we are making a trip together and arrange it as pleasantly for each other as we can. Kafka is appalled by the blindness of his fellows, who stoutly refuse to recognize that life is a tragic journey and who refuse to see the value of acting decently on it. Such acute consciousness, such awareness of the basic element of suffering in highly reflective life, is typical of all reflective men who suffer bitterly, either from some personal tragedy or from a sense of alienation. It is the *weltschmerz* of the romantic. In the case of Kafka it is heightened by his Hebraic-Slavic moral tone. And it is in this moral tone that he is superior to most of the other expressionists, many of whom found the art form a game of irresponsibility and who delighted in its element of incommunicability, which is too often merely an excuse to spit upon the bourgeois, a hangover from the days of Baudelaire and his compatriots.

In Kafka the personal tragedy was mingled with the sense of alienation—he was both a tubercular and a Jew; and in addition he suffered from a neurotic relationship with his father. It is easy, from these, to understand the psychology of the outcast which he developed and presented. Because of these he understood the plight of minority groups, particularly of the oppressed; he understood how the oppressed slowly come to think themselves monstrous and guilty under the powerful and unrelieved suggestion of the oppressors. What gave him the insight was his apartness—to be apart is to question, while to belong is to be able to act irrationally without guilt pangs, provided the action conforms to the social conscience. "I had always questioned myself over every trifle; in every trifle you convinced me, by your example and by the way you brought me up . . . of my incapability," wrote Kafka to his father, speaking also of his "nerve-destroying fear and sense of guilt." There is no absolute morality and sense of guilt; it is all relative: witness how the SS officials in Germany did not as a rule feel guilty about acts which to the rest of the world were monstrous; they had the support of the groups, they acted within their cabala. (Hitler was perhaps the greatest cabalist of them all.) For the same reason it is possible to order men to kill each other through the devices of armies, uniforms and slogans without having them suffer overwhelming pangs of guilt.

To be apart is to question; and to be thrown upon oneself means to have to create one's own conscience and therefore to seesaw between the criminal and the over-ethical, both of these, like conscience itself, relative factors differing widely in varying cultures. Man is so gregarious by nature that to be set apart entails a strong sense of guilt; retaliation is possible on the non-criminal level by superior reason and insight. The criminal and the over-ethical: the first defies the society from which one is an outcast and the second both woos and attacks it with superior reason and morality. The over-ethical implies the over-

447

scrupulous, the psychoneurotic—and we know from Brod how scrupulous Kafka was. And from his work we are aware of the other element, the criminal, in the horrible, the monstrous, the outrageous in his work. The over-scrupulous implies, in turn, perfectionism. May it not be that Kafka's literary perfectionism was an aspect of his neurosis? A perfectionism which urges one to destroy one's work and to be ashamed of it despite the assurances of objective critics is certainly abnormal; and perfectionist personalities are generally recognized as psychoneurotic.

To question: that is Hamlet's burden and an enormous one. How much easier, safer to belong. In this sense Kafka's theme is the incommensurability between the genius and society or the genius and the cabalism. Still he realizes that forms of behavior are necessary, for life is too complex for us to act scrupulously and consciously all the time, weighing each action on the basis of reason and "absolute" justice. We require conditioning to face the business of living. The problem is: how to prevent a divorce between the form and the spirit of the cabala. The form without the spirit is obviously evil—it entails indifference to suffering, venality in administering justice, all under the pretense of spirit while the spirit is dead. It is good, therefore, to have mutants, the maladjusted like Kafka, to attack them from without.

It is interesting to note that the philosophy of naturalism stands in relation to anti-naturalism or supernaturalism as Kafka does to cabalism. For naturalism wishes to examine social myths or cabalisms from the point of view of evidence and reason and to define and categorize so that it is possible to determine when a myth is form without spirit—in short, to promote the better life within the capability and dignity of man.

V

In *The Trial*, cabalism is epitomized by the Law and the Courts, by their irrational, unjust and deliberately clandestine and capricious nature, which places the burden of proof on the accused, then leads him from one psychological trap into another and by a process of alternating encouragement and discouragement enervates him until he is ready to accept spiritual execution.

But the Courts could not exist without a general belief in their existence and power. Therefore the people, who support the mores and effect the social pressures, are a party to the continuation of the cabalism. Kafka is not an anarchist decrying governments or bureaucracies, but he is indeed decrying those which are capricious and unjust, particularly to the sensitive individual. While Hans Christian Anderson would have adults experience a revelation because of a child's insight, Kafka would have the adults hound the child until it too believes, against the evidence of its fresh senses, that the emperor is clothed. In a fairy tale the hero conquers obstacles until he lives happily ever after; in Kafka obstacles conquer the hero until he dies or lives miserably ever after. Kafka's devices are basically quite mechanistic and capable of inversion. It would be easy enough to make any of them pleasant fairy tales with happy endings simply by making the obstacles inspire the heroes to new confidence and strength. Kafka's fable in *The Trial* as well as in the rest of his work is the education of all youthful idealists into adjusted middle-aged "realists." The escape from the Courts is belief in oneself, in one's integrity, one's senses and one's logic. This belief, plus the courage of aggressiveness, will avoid disaster.

A similar satire on cabalism permeates *The Castle*, only there the accused is an entire group, the Barnabas family. In *The Trial* social pressures are presented directly in only one instance, in Joseph K.'s uncle's attitude toward K., while all others are stated indirectly or hinted at; while in *The Castle* the various forms of pressure are described in detail, such a procedure being consonant with the author's new purpose, an examination of the communal aspects of his theme.

This interpretation of Kafka may also be applied to religion, not in any mystical sense of personal revelation but rather in the sense of faith in God, which inevitably means faith in the eventual triumph of goodness and order in man. In such an application it would appear that religious bureaucracies are the cabalism, that one needs no advocate to plead one's case with God, that God can be reached only by direct and simple communion, and that the door to God is always wide open. All one needs is the courage to disregard the hocus-pocus of the door-keeper and to pass through. The Cathedral in *The Trial*, with its verger, priest and barbaric ornamentation, emphasizes Kafka's conception of organized religion as a cabalism. It is significant that the priest calls himself the prison chaplain and that he and the Cathedral are instruments of the Courts, which is to say that the Church is playing secular power politics. K. is supposed to show an Italian around the Cathedral, suggesting Romanism or the extreme of religious orthodoxy. All the window blinds around the Cathedral square are commonly drawn, an indication that the Cathedral is remote from the people, that it has no vital relation to their lives. This notion of religion as cabalism may or may not have been one aspect of what Kafka meant, although I suspect it was. But in any case it has relevance, particularly if one is inclined to equate the concept of God with justice based on reason. It seems to me apparent that my inclusion of this point as a possibility in no way invalidates my disagreement with the mystical interpretation, since my point of difference still hinges on the concept of God and the divine.

The essence of both Kafka's portrayal of cabalism and his ironic and implied comment on it can be found in the final chapter of *The Trial* in Joseph K.'s conversation with the priest in the Cathedral. The latter encourages the confused K. with his tale of the doorkeeper and the Law, giving him the clue for his salvation, but when K. leaps at the suggestion the priest, who is a Court functionary, immediately proceeds to smother K. in a fog of Jesuitical and Talmudic quibbling, further confusing K., who all along has been filled with feelings of inferiority and guilt and who therefore has not been able to trust his intuitions against the mumbo-jumbo of authority. In this final confusion K. completely accepts his fate, so that later, when he is being led to his death by his two executioners (who, incidentally, have not been given definite orders relating to their task and are obviously instruments of K.'s will rather than of the Court's), K., on coming upon a policeman in the street, a man that might help him, actually sprints away, carrying his executioners with him. But just before his death he is again ambivalent, this time bitterly so; but by now his will has been completely sapped and he is destroyed. Kafka's use of the cathedral and the priest relates his theme here more closely than elsewhere to religion but again not in the sense of mystical revelation, rather in faith in one's intuition, logic and sense of justice.

Kafka's attitude toward cabalisms is revealed in these insights in Brod's biography of him: "In all things Kafka came in touch with, he sought that which was significant, rooted in the world of truth. . . . His attitude ignored completely all literary hierarchies, ranks and classifications. Everywhere he grasped essentials. . . . He was prejudiced neither into accepting nor into rejecting a general opinion on principle. The refreshing thing about him was the absence of any preoccupation with paradox. He was, in fact, preoccupied by its antithesis. His judgment had an elementary simplicity, naturalness and obviousness; it was easy and sure in spite of the caution with which he gave it, and the willingness, the almost passionate willingness with which he admitted error."

Yet Brod writes, in his note to *The Castle:* "The essential thing to be noted is that the hero in *The Trial* is persecuted by an invisible and mysterious authority and summoned to stand his trial, and that in *The Castle* he is prevented from doing exactly the same thing." This is a misreading of the facts and it has been accepted by many critics who have simply picked it up from Brod. (It is unfortunate, for example, that Thomas Mann has lent his considerable influence to the mystical theory in his introduction to the American edition of *The Castle*. It should be noted, however, that his conception of the divine is sharply at variance with Muir's and somewhat with Brod's; his God is conceived in terms of the human.)* Joseph K. stands trial not because he is summoned but only because he believes in the accusation and in his basic guilt, unfounded as these may be; he is never forced to stand trial. And the K. of *The Castle* is not prevented from standing trial by anything except his own timidity and his own

---

* In answer to this Thomas Mann wrote me: "Concerning my own occasional utterance about Kafka, I did not really want to classify him with the mystics when I characterized him as a 'religious humorist.' Religious allusion and symbolism cannot be denied in his works, particularly in *The Trial* and *The Castle*, but for a mystic even his style is too clear and rational."

willingness, despite his being a stranger with perspective, to accept the nonsensical cabala that the Castle is powerful and unapproachable. In both instances the cause of the plot development lies in the protagonists themselves. Brod fails to understand this probably because he does not have sufficient perspective over European super-respect for authority and tradition, something that Kafka attained only through his fantastic sense of isolation.

I am willing to agree that K.'s efforts to become a member of the village community represent a search for grace, for belonging, but I can't agree that the Castle represents either the dispensation of grace or the divine. In not one instance does the Castle manifest real power; its power is purely suggestive, it resides only in the superstitions of the villagers; in this sense it is similar to the Court of *The Trial*. Only the villagers can dispense grace, only they can accept or ostracize. Therefore the irony of the novel, as well as the implied criticism of the "divine" school, lies in the fact that K.'s sole possibility for grace rests in himself, in his willingness to become like the villagers in order to be accepted by them, in his readiness to accept the village superstitions, the Castle cabalism. In short, he must give up his dependence on justice related to logic. Obviously this is not what Kafka advocated; therefore the book can be read only as a satire on what he did *not* advocate, a satire on the particular search for grace which K. represents. This the mystical school does not see, since it is blinded, by its obsession with the Castle as the divine, into as ready an acceptance of the Castle cabalism as the villagers themselves. The mystical interpreters, in short, manage to adjust themselves very nicely to the village; and it is they who find the state of grace, not K. Nor does the fact that Kafka yearned to belong controvert my explanation. At the same time that he yearned to belong he despised belonging.

Muir's nebulous note in *The Castle* is simply a rationalization of Brod's categories of divine law and divine grace. In it he contradicts Mann by saying that Kafka "avoided scrupulously the pose of the spectacular wrestler with God." Mann, in the same volume, says of *The Castle*, "It is the most patient, obstinate, desperate 'wrestling with the angel' that ever happened. . . ." Muir's short note is replete with such nonsense as the following: "While following the adventures of his heroes we seem to be discovering—almost without being fully aware of it—various things about those entities, divine powers, which we had never divined before, and could never perhaps have divined by ourselves."

The story, "Investigations of a Dog," which is perhaps Kafka's last work, is also one of his most explicit. Here the symbolism is least involved and opaque and the tone and content most confessional. It is as if the tired and very ill Kafka is writing his last testament—not in the complicated and dramatic manner of the novels but rather in an essayistic mood, although still within a limited framework of expressionism. For these reasons and because Kafka kept repeating his themes it is extremely enlightening regarding Kafka's meaning. The mystics, however, must postulate the existence of the non-existent to explain Kafka in their terms. Thus Muir writes, in the introduction to *The Great Wall of China:* "To understand it properly one must assume that the human race are invisible though still operatively present, roughly fulfilling toward the dog world the role of divine and incomprehensible powers." This sort of approach might well have postulated the existence of an invisible but "operatively present" moon between us and our visible one to explain the discrepancies in Newton's gravitational theory. But from the rational, naturalist point of view, no such postulation as Muir's is necessary—one is required only to look facts in the face and weigh the evidence in a manner which is generally and rationally verifiable.

Note the essayistic and autobiographical elements in the beginning of the story. The protagonist dog, which I shall call the K-dog from now on, is queer, yet not exempt from the laws of his species: ". . . somewhat cold, reserved, shy and calculating, but all things considered a normal enough dog." The K-dog makes an ironic commentary on non-dog species (including man): "But one thing is too obvious to have escaped me; namely how little inclined they are, compared with us dogs, to stick together, how silently and unfamiliarly and with what a curious hostility they pass each other, how mean are the interests that suffice to bind them together for a little in ostensible union, and how often these very interests give rise to hatred and conflict." As

453

for dogs: "We are drawn to each other and nothing can prevent us from satisfying that communal impulse; all our laws and institutions, the few that I still know and the many that I have forgotten, go back to this longing for the greatest bliss we are capable of, the warm comfort of being together. But now consider the other side of the picture. . . ." And the K-dog shows how dogs are separated from each other by "distinctions of class, of kind, of occupation, distinctions too numerous to review at a glance . . ." Then he cries out against himself because he cannot live as the others, accepting in silence whatever disturbs the harmony—that is, the divisive forces.

Soon the K-dog describes a remarkable experience in his youth which set him upon his endless investigations—the meeting with the seven "musical" dogs. The important elements of the incident are (a) whenever the K-dog is skeptical or critical or curious about the behavior of the seven, he is instantly knocked flat by their music, in short he is conditioned against skepticism, criticism and curiosity and (b) the seven are compulsive in their behavior or forced into it for some reason unknown to the K-dog. The reason is the irrational cabalism. The K-dog cannot understand the cause or meaning of the horrible music and he longs to shout to the seven and to beg them to enlighten him—but before he can speak the violent music flagellates him mercilessly. At first the K-dog is impressed by the courage of the seven and their power to endure the music calmly but on closer study he sees it is not calmness that characterizes the seven as much as extreme tension. In short, they are not behaving naturally but are following a pattern imposed on them. Why are they afraid, the K-dog, wonders and he shouts out questions but the seven carefully pay no attention to the innocent mutant. Then the K-dog notices that the seven "had flung away all shame" and were walking on their hind legs—were acting like humans. Inverted (and inversion here, as in Butler's *Erewhon* and Swift's *Gulliver's Travels* is a satiric device) this reads: humans acting like animals, crawling on all fours. The K-dog tries to keep them from committing further sin but the music again overpowers him—that is, the cabalism cudgels him.

Talmudic rationalizations of the incident from contradictory points of view follow in the usual Kafka manner. Later the K-dog inquires into the question: What does the canine race nourish itself upon? He accepts certain facts relating to the question and is happy to agree with the majority in this. "Quite honestly I have no ambition to be peculiar, or to pose as being in the right against the majority; I am only too happy when I can agree with my comrades, as I do in this case." But, not content, he goes still further and asks where the earth procures the food it thrusts up, a taboo question which usually elicits the answer, "If you haven't enough to eat, we'll give you some of ours." The reaction to this question is two-fold: on the one hand dogs find it stupid; yet they are attracted to it—the attraction of the norm for the genius mingled with the fear of him.

It becomes increasingly clear that what the K-dog wants admitted is the knowledge of the basic tragedy of life— this would be some consolation for his alienation and a point of comradeship between him and the others—as well as the basic irrationality of cabalistic behavior and the lack of reason and originality of the devotees. But he meets only silence. Finally he says of his kind: "We are the dogs who are crushed by the silence, who long to break through it, literally to get a breath of fresh air; the others seem to thrive on silence: true, that is only so in appearance, as in the case of the musical dogs, who ostensibly were quite calm when they played, but in reality were in a state of intense excitement . . ."

To the mystical school I can offer only the rebuke of Zeus to men in the *Odyssey*: "Lo, you now, how vainly mortal men do blame the gods! For of us they say comes evil, whereas they even of themselves through the blindness of their own hearts, have sorrows beyond that which is ordained."

The above might well stand as the motto over Kafka's works.

VI

This view—in terms of cabalism—of Kafka's life and work is so central to both that it illuminates even structural or formalistic difficulties in his major works (let alone his minor) which otherwise cannot be dealt with intelligently or at best must

455

be discussed in the mumbo-jumbo of mysticism and what-not. The difficulties throw light, in their turn, upon Kafka's essential meaning. For form is indissoluble from meaning in genuine artistic works and one cannot properly examine one without the other. Let me then discuss one of the most enlightening as well as puzzling structural discrepancies in Kafka—the structural difference between the tightly-knit *Trial* and the loose, rambling *Castle*, a difference involving a serious discrepancy of psychology.

In *The Trial* one notes the wealth of subjectivism and is fascinated by the dream-distortion technique, the irrational and neurotic, which are intimately revealed through the mind and reactions of Joseph K. These, in my opinion, are responsible for the novel's impact, its drama and its experiential value. But one looks for them quite often in vain in *The Castle*, at any rate until the major and key chapter, fifteen, in which Olga relates her story to K. The result of this failing is that *The Castle* is a spotty book, a novel with a confused focus; consequently it is not as satisfying emotionally as *The Trial*. What are the causes of this discrepancy? First, while Kafka was interested in the K. of *The Trial* as an individual he was interested in the K. of *The Castle* as a device with which to view the village. Second, in *The Trial* he was concerned with individual psychology in relation to his theme, in *The Castle* with communal psychology. And third, *The Castle* is more poorly constructed than *The Trial* from the point of view of what he was trying to accomplish.

Only by making these distinctions between Kafka's purposes in these two novels can one avoid falling into the error of regarding both Joseph K. and K. as heroes. Joseph K. *is* a hero, for the action of *The Trial* revolves around him and the theme is based on him; but K. is little more than a device. The real hero of *The Castle* is the Barnabas family, which suffered the extremely unpleasant relations with the Castle and the village. Between this family and Joseph K. there is a real affinity but between K. and Joseph K. the kinship is only slight. To go a step further, there is a greater affinity between the Barnabas family and the villagers than between the family and K., even though the family are outcasts. The reason is that both the family and the villagers accept the cabalism of the Castle. The Barnabas family, like Joseph K., is convinced of its guilt; they worry not about the absolute state of things but only about the fact that misfortune befell *them*. As for K., he is the device of the outsider, used by the author to bring perspective and skepticism to bear upon the hypnotized people of the village. In this sense he is similar to Hans Castorp in *The Magic Mountain* and Tchitchikov in *Dead Souls*. In *The Magic Mountain* European society is the real hero, in *Dead Souls* it is Russian society. But beyond this there is no deep similarity, for both Mann and Gogol, unlike Kafka, profoundly explore the minds of their brain-children.

The Castle is, on the whole, a disappointing book compared with *The Trial*, as I have indicated. It rambles, is atomistic in construction and many of the conversations are overwritten and could have been replaced by meaningful action. At times Kafka contents himself with exploiting K. as a device with which to examine the village traditions and psychology through such people as the landlady, Frieda and the teacher but at others he turns his attention—but only skimpily—to developing the psychology of K. The communal psychology is interesting but is presented in external terms only; therefore it is difficult to make the necessary identification with it. The result of all this is largely unfortunate. Yet it seems obvious that the problems which Kafka failed to solve were not beyond his powers. Perhaps the simplest explanation is that *The Castle* was the least completed of his major works and that he would have revised it extensively had he lived and cared to go on with it. Taken as it stands, however, it suffers from an ambivalence of focus and from poor construction: the two are interrelated. It develops along two parallel lines which should be interwoven—the line of K.'s attempts to reach the Castle and that of the village's domination by the Castle cabalism. Confusion results; until chapter fifteen, one effect cancels out another, leaving the reader quite bored at times. In addition, the psychology of frustration is inadequately dramatized and in this too the novel falls short until chapter fifteen. And the wonderful, oppressive dream psychology is also missing in great part, so that too often the style limps along on the crutches of mere realism, something that Kafka can afford less than more

457

conventional authors, since his chief distinction lies in presenting the truth by means of distortion.

On the other hand there are a number of aspects in which *The Castle* excels *The Trial* and which account for its relative popularity. The prose is of a finer texture, more calm and more pure, and the atmosphere more poetic. The characters are closer approximations to individuals than the types and symbols of *The Trial*. And the conception is on a more magnificent scope, with a sulky landscape playing an important role. *The Castle* is a rural novel, *The Trial* an urban one. Since the village acts as a microcosm *The Castle* is able to capture more truthfully the breath of social life. In addition, chapter fifteen is the most sustained and effective writing in Kafka. It is almost a book in itself. By sheer volume it dominates *The Castle:* it is 77 pages long in a book of 328, or almost a quarter of the entire work. The average chapter is only about 18 pages long.

The nature of Kafka's reaction to the cabalism of his day may perhaps be seen most clearly when viewed in the perspective furnished by a contrast between Kafka and the nineteenth-century Samuel Butler, another victim and antagonist of cabalism. In order to clear the ground for an examination of the striking similarities in their lives and work, let me first acknowledge their very real differences.

Butler's tendencies were toward science and rationalism, Kafka's toward philosophy and art. Butler was a rather arid character who haunted the British Museum and worried about posterity's appraisal of him; Kafka was feminine, poetic, chaotic and was so little concerned about posterity that he failed to finish his three major works and requested that they be burned after his death. Butler was the product of nineteenth century formalism; Kafka was a typical twentieth century character: neurotic and ironical and full of outward as well as inward turmoil. Butler had only a thin love for the accepted masters of art and for art in general and he cared little for the German masters, for example, with the exception of Handel, occasionally even sneering at Goethe and Beethoven (he distrusted the romantics and suspected anyone with a large reputation); while Kafka loved the romantics and revered Goethe. Butler belonged to the British world of science and materialism and flourishing empire of the nineteenth century while Kafka's world was the decadent, out-moded, bureaucratic and feudalistic world of pre-war Austria, a world writhing with psychoanalysis and mysticism in revolt against the extremes to which nineteenth-century rationalism had gone.

Yet in spite of these differences their patterns are basically similar. Butler barely escaped the life of a churchman, Kafka that of a lawyer; and the church plays a large role in Butler's works and the law in Kafka's. Both men hungered for acceptance by the cabalisms of their times and both were re-jected; both, in consequence, retaliated through their works; and in doing so reproduced the cabalisms in order to satirize them. In the process they portrayed the essence of cabalas with such a ring of truth and at the same time so ambivalently and allusively that they seemed to have created cabalas of their own when in reality they were merely giving vent to the scorn and bitterness of their rejection. The cabalisms they attacked were dissimilar—Butler lashed out at the cabalism of scientific professionalism and smug professionalism in general, Kafka at the social, ethical and philosophical cabalism best symbolized for him by the bureauc-racy with which he was so disastrously familiar—but the causes of their attacks were approximately the same: father-troubles re-sulting in feelings of inferiority, in the psychology of the outcast, which lent them the fresh view of the stranger pressing his nose against the window of contemporary life. Butler's attack was for the most part rationalistic (he was an island of rationalism in the romantic stream of nineteenth-century English literature), while Kafka's was psychological. As for the more apparent similarities, both were lifelong and neurotic bachelors, both suffered from father complexes, both were ridden by feelings of guilt and in-feriority, both had their major work published posthumously and both were the products of authoritarianism which found expres-sion in the father. Butler, the product of Victorian rigidity and arrogance, revolted openly against his father and made his final and most exhaustive attack on him in *The Way of All Flesh*. Kafka, the product of Austrian feudalism, of a bureaucratic, paperwork empire, revolted negatively by withdrawing into a shell of pain and developing anxiety and guilt. Apparently Butler's father was more susceptible to direct attack than Kafka's, for he cut a rather ludicrous figure with his excessive discipline mixed with extreme sentimentality; on the other hand Kafka's father stood in Franz's eyes, for a long time, as the personification of extrovertive success and acceptance of and by the world.

In the works themselves there are numerous and fertile centers of comparison. To mention only one, there is the similarity between Butler's *Erewhon* and *Erewhon Revisited* to *The Trial* and *The Castle*. Butler comments on the problems of his day through the medium of fantasy, in which he has an excellent opportunity to display his love of intellectual perversity, of turning things inside out. The two books are reminiscent of *Gulliver's Travels* in their caustic and shrewd examination of society. Kafka also uses fantasy to examine society and to exercise his love of *emotional* perversity. Thus he handles the subjective element of criticism, for in a sense he is more interested in effect than cause, being primarily an artist rather than a thinker like Butler.

VII

One often has the feeling in Kafka that he is describing the spiritual state of the majority of people, their slavery to fad, attitude, tradition. His great social truth is acceptance of cabalism—e.g., of the might and isolation of the Castle and the existence and authority of the Courts. Even K., the outsider, never asks Olga the direct question and the only meaningful one: why hasn't she gone to the Castle directly and physically to plead her family's case? K. himself gives up trying to reach the Castle directly after one minor attempt, thereafter losing himself in the morass of indirection. But basic questions are, of course, taboo in any cabalism. And so how true is Kafka's portrayal of the process of pyramiding rationalization upon rationalization in the ceaseless and shrewd explanations which give the effect of actuality to the baseless and the nonexistent. In this sense his works form a skeptical spiritual fable of modern man. In his view modern man is a neurotic with a sapped will, which is a matter of a bad con-

460

science and social insecurity. His exemplifications of the physical results of mental conditions, in such characters as Block in *The Trial* and Olga's father in *The Castle,* are in line with the conceptions of the psychosomatic school in medicine.

When the student carries off the Law-Court Attendant's wife to the latter's obvious pleasure in *The Trial,* Joseph K. slowly follows them and realizes that this is his first unequivocal defeat from these people attached to the Courts. But he tells himself that he received the defeat only because he insisted on giving battle. "While he stayed quietly at home and went about his ordinary vocations he remained superior to all these people and could clear any of them out of his path with a hearty kick," says Kafka. This is one of the purest dramatizations of Kafka's guilt motif. K. suffers a defeat because he gives battle; he gives battle because of a heavy sense of guilt which urges him to defend himself against a baseless charge; he feels this guilt because of his overdeveloped conscience; his conscience is the result of his sensitivity; and his sensivity, inevitably, has been overstimulated by the injustice everywhere evident in society. K. could have avoided defeat by denying his guilt, by staying at home, in other words by looking the other way in the face of injustice, by stifling his conscience.

Therefore it becomes apparent that K. is not simply a neurotic who defends himself against any charge, no matter how foolish; he is also, because of his own suffering, a man of compassion with a fine regard for the rights of others. And so he is, on the one hand, a Don Quixote character tilting with windmills of his own creation and on the other a neurotic genius who insists on fighting his case with logic and conscience. He is a genius despite his neurosis and because of his strange methods; and yet in the end he suffers the unnecessary fate of all the accused because of his neurosis: he is executed—symbolically by two men but psychologically by himself—and thereby he establishes his identity with the common man. He is not able to tear out of his mind the hypnotic web of guilt and accusation which subtly strangles him; he is the victim of auto-suggestion.

What are we to deduce from this? We can deduce that neurosis is a societal phenomenon and that society must be held responsible for it. We can also deduce that the remedy for a man like K., who is after all a typical specimen, is to free himself of his neurosis either by himself, beginning by defying any hints of auto-suggestion, or with professional help. But his cure must not lead simply to an ability to scorn baseless accusations but also to a defiance of the social structures which create the neuroses which in turn incapacitate those of sensitivity and conscience to deal with the structures. In other words, it is not enough for him to emerge as the normal citizen with the latter's normal callousness in political affairs; he must, because of his greater vision and compassion, defend the rights of all men by attacking the political and economic, the reactionary cabalas which stifle man's development. He must emerge as the unneurotic genius. This is a striking example of art as wish-fulfillment.

Kafka, for all his modernity of manner and technique, is a psychological primitive in the same sense that Freud is, giving new meaning to adulthood by exploring the layers of childhood which adhere. But he is not a primitive in anything approaching the anthropological meaning, of course; his characters are, rather, highly civilized people who, like modern man in general, are profoundly childlike. Kafka seems to be reminding us that childhood and dreams are closely related, dreams being childish and childhood dreamlike. And he seems to be recalling that following western man's development since the Renaissance, has come his constantly greater understanding and appreciation of childhood, of both its beauties and its terrors. Clearly as man develops horizontally in broadening his world view he also, because of his increasing feeling of isolation in a mechanistic and power-mad society, extends himself vertically in his psychology for better and for worse, reaching down into the wells of dream, childhood and myth. In his artistic exploitation of these motifs Kafka is the descendant of Schopenhauer, who was among the earliest thinkers to emphasize the power of the unconscious. Unlike Dostoyevsky, who is a master of abnormal psychology in adults, and Henry James, Marcel Proust and Thomas Mann, who are masters of societal psychological subtleties, Kafka is a master of the psychology of the dream: the irrational, distorted and primitive. And while the psychology of the trio is highly societal

462

even when individualized, Kafka is extremely individual even when socialized. He stands, because of his psychology, in the romantic tradition despite his classic style; while such a novelist as Proust, on the other hand, remains a classicist for all his stylistic eccentricities.

One of Kafka's basic themes is none other than the one so prevalent in his time and so rich in blood-brothers both before and after—the portrait of the artist as outcast. If in Kafka's case the outcast seems also to be a psychoneurotic, it is only because of his greater isolation. Like Thomas Mann's early artistic protagonists (especially Tonio Kröger) Kafka's heroes yearn for identification and acceptance by the "regular" and the "normal," the extrovertive pillars of society. This is clear throughout Kafka's work and is particularly explicit in "Investigations of a Dog," as we have seen. This theme in Kafka is to be viewed, therefore, as part of a well-traveled stream rather than as some isolated rivulet; his use of expressionism rather than impressionism or realism should not be permitted to obscure this point. Expressionism, which came into favor in certain quarters as a reaction to the deadening photographic quality of an over-exploited realism, served Kafka's needs well. However, while it gives him the advantage of being able to deal more readily with the essences of character and experience, freeing him of the burden of cataloguing and conscious observation which is inherent in the technique of realism, nevertheless it lends his work an opaqueness and indetermination which in the last analysis may be harmful to it, for it is possible that Kafka would not have achieved such stature if his meaning had been transparent. If his enigma is responsible for his influence currently, in the long run, once his novelty wears off, it may injure rather than aid him. But it does not follow, of course, that the use of expressionism need necessarily create enigma; in other hands it has offered freshness of treatment not incompatible with transparency.

Lacking the aggressiveness of a James Joyce, who could strike back at the regular in no uncertain terms through Stephen Dedalus, Kafka found the new form an adequate veil of modesty to cover his spiritual disrobing. Touches of realism he employed only to keep his autobiography from soaring altogether

463

into the realm of incommunicable fantasy, spicing the result with symbolism for artistic effect as well as intelligibility. Thus, beginning more extremely than Joyce in medium, he did not go as far as Joyce's quasi-schizophrenic meanderings; on the contrary, his effects grew increasingly explicit. As for Mann, who picked up realism at its point of perfection, he saved himself from enslavement to it by the use of symbolism and musical devices. Mann is the type of writer, like Goethe and Tolstoy, who writes autobiographically and who builds around an emotion or an idea; in short he externalizes. Kafka, like all sick geniuses, internalizes, writing in the language of the wound itself; he does not try to exorcise the pain by verbalizing it; on the contrary he prolongs it excruciatingly, encouraging it to father new pain. If Kafka at times crosses over into the psychopathic in his work, it does not follow that he himself is psychopathic. It is well known that the psychoneurotic has psychotic tendencies. All that can be said is that at times Kafka gives vent to these tendencies, sublimating them; the biographical facts are too clear to allow any other assertion.

Kafka's books are full of marvelous externalized as well as inner psychology. It is this psychology which is his forte, for after all his intellectual message is negligible and his qualities as a man dealing with beauty are negligible too. But his bits of psychological business are truly remarkable; together with his dream-method they create a lasting effect. This effect is proof of the broad base of his theme and method. While reading him we are impressed by the feeling that the world as we know it, like Kafka's dream-suggestions, is largely irrational; in other words, living in an irrational world is like living in a dream, with all the uncertainties, frustrations and fears of the latter. But quite often Kafka's people are abnormal, so that sometimes one wonders whether his novels are studies in the psychology of failure and paranoia: how is it, then, that the reader can identify himself with them? The answer is that we, even in our "normality," being the products of our society, are, like Kafka, basically neurotic: driven, anxious, inhibited. This fact, together with Kafka's powers of evocation, makes him one of the most effective modern practitioners of the literature of catharsis.

Of the many aspects of neurosis, Kafka stresses one, the understanding of which came late in the history of psychiatry: that delicate neurotic balance between loving and hating oneself, between protecting and destroying oneself which often has its predominant expression in the form of severe masochism. Straightforward masochism is mainly interesting from a medical viewpoint; it lacks the drama of conflict and ambivalence found in more subtle forms. It is, therefore, the latter which Kafka treats so tellingly in his novels, in those twilight states of mind in which the will to protect barely flickers before the choking will to destroy oneself. Such a state is beautifully evoked in the empty interrogation chamber in the third chapter of *The Trial*, in which Joseph K. fights desperately against a hypnotic desire to succumb to willessness and to the clutches of the Court tenement-catacombs, which are really the catacombs of K.'s masochistic tendencies. He even desperately attempts to escape into a forgetfulness of himself, willing to accept any insults in order to achieve this salvation. This powerful urge to destroy oneself, which K. barely escapes, is the inner villain of Kafka's novels, the outer being the Courts and the Castle—or the cabalisms—which are largely responsible for the urge. Masochism is obviously an expression of one's feelings of worthlessness, which in severe cases is cultivated for the pleasure it offers as sheer feeling. In Kafka's case this feeling stemmed from his comparison of himself with his father as well as his consciousness of his irregularity in society. His father is the outer but absent villain of the novels, the inner being Kafka himself, or at any rate his excessive sensitivity or attenuation, which deprived him of the normal aggressiveness necessary to assert himself before his father's ego. For Kafka his father was a personification of the cabalism of his day.

The other side of the coin of masochism is sadism and both are the poles of the neurotic's ambivalence. Kafka emphasizes the aspect of sadism importantly; *The Trial* and "The Penal Colony" in particular reek of the atmosphere of a concentration camp. Usually sadism emanates from the cabalisms (Court and Castle) but quite often it is distinctive of his protagonists' behavior, particularly of Joseph K. The latter, for example, is obviously sadistic toward his landlady and toward Block, the pitiful

465

commercial traveler. And in the startling scene in which his two former warders are being whipped he is again sadistic, shoving one of them when the latter screams in pain. Viewed in social terms, Kafka seems to be saying that sadism is equivalent, in democracies, to the free-for-all quest for success and power which allows the devil to take the hindmost and which encourages every man to step on the face of the one beneath him on the ladder; in the monarchic, semi-feudalistic countries such as Austria it is equivalent to the existence of the rigid autocracy which sits as legislator as well as judge upon the people, averting its eyes from the sight of mass suffering and degradation.

It is Kafka's distinction that he realized the universal implications of his exaggerated sense of guilt and that he was able to apply this realization to a penetrating evocation of the ramifications of guilt in modern man. Is there then a great residue of guilt in us all and does our age differ from others in this respect? In most other times the categories of behaving and thinking were more strictly drawn and bounded; it was therefore easier to know the "right" way of life. Today everything is fluid and ambivalent, the "right" way far from certain. Compromise is the general rule, compromise between "idealism" and "realism," compromise which, in sensitive persons who already share the general neurosis of the age, leads to profound feelings of guilt. Someone once said that irony is the factor which differentiates the twentieth century mind from all others. That touches the problem but does not explore it. For what is the cause of this irony? It is based on the dualism and ambivalence which are the result of the interplay of a heightened skepticism with a heightened idealism, the result of a struggle between a more firm vision of the ideal, particularly of the social ideal, with a growing despair of achieving it. There is another approach. If irony is the philosophic or artistic result of the struggle, what is the psychological? A sense of guilt. Greater knowledge, by its expansion of the conscience, involves the possibility of greater sin. Therefore a sense of guilt and ambivalence are characteristic of our time. And Franz Kafka is unique because he perceived these facts, so completely on the imaginative, emotional, poetic planes, giving us, through his conscious dreams, a more intense and complete

466

and above all experiential awareness of these factors in ourselves.

Kafka is basically a poet—in terms of imagination, conception and meaning—despite his medium. He sinks his shafts deeply into the unconscious, fetching up symbols which are often erotically evocative, like those in dreams. His debt to dream-life is incalculable; this is not accidental, for he was aware of dreams acutely and in addition possessed an unusually fertile and vivid dream life. In his diaries he describes dreams in great length and detail, in absolutely coherent prose and with no little literary merit.

It is extraordinary how he manages to balance himself between chaos and reason; this extends an enormous tension to his situations and his prose. It would be easy to fall into complete distortion, into automatic writing, into the thoroughly undisciplined; but Kafka remains disciplined in the midst of his disorder. His tact and taste invariably save him; and what are these but his absolute skepticism, his unwillingness to indulge in sentimentality either of the realistic or surrealistic variety. With this in mind his insistence on the use of conventional, "classic" prose is understandable and commendable.

Kafka's long paragraphs, running on at times without regard for dialogue or change of pace or mood, at first puzzle and annoy, but soon one realizes that their effect is not, as in Proust and Mann, that of density and architectural solidity but rather that of breathlessness. This quality is typical of Kafka and is also a feature of the German expressionist school; but it is only one facet; indiscrimination is another; together they create a kind of wonderful buzzing in the reader's ear, which suggests irony, irrationality and dissonance—in short, the modern temper.

In certain nightmares we experience the torment of being unable to flee in the face of danger; this is a recurring motif in Kafka. The feet of his protagonists are likely to stick and their bodies grow sluggish precisely when their anxiety is at its height. This feeling of hysteria also occurs in serious illness, which brings to mind the thought that much of Kafka can be described as the psychology of disease—the helplessness, the incomprehension of the healthy, the distortion, the inaccessibility, the narcissism, the dependence. Almost invariably characters act toward Kafka's protagonists as nurses toward invalids, somewhat patronizingly, with an excessive show of health and with a certain obliviousness to suffering. All of which recalls Kafka's neurasthenia, frailty and tuberculosis. The explicit absence of air in many Kafka situations also can be viewed as an objectification of a personal situation—in this instance of Kafka's neurotic breathlessness, also of the chest awareness of the tubercular.

The world of Franz Kafka is sometimes reminiscent of Hemingway because of its sadism but Kafka's sadists are never Hemingwayish outlaws; as a matter of fact there is no element of the lawless in the sense of "wild" in all of Kafka. The most refined cruelties are part of some established program; the atmosphere is closed in, one is weighed down by the sense of tradition, there is a palpable heaviness of spirit in the air. It is the stale air of Europe, of course. Even the humor is a little desperate; everything is desperate, everything trembles with exaggeration; the healthy is a little too healthy. One feels that the books could easily have been written by a Japanese, in a land exhausted by topheavy and bloodless tradition.

The world of Franz Kafka. . . . It *is* a world, consistent and rare, the inspiration genuine; the nether world, the lower depths of the spirit, where the deepest truths, the hidden truth, reside, from which they move the puppets of the upper regions. It is a world of sustained visions; Kafka was able to plunge into the creative unconscious and remain with his muse in that breathless twilight longer than most.

Strange: he who was an expert at rejection, who rejected even himself as a human being and at times rejected the notion that he possessed talent, by his example restated the truth of the maxim that greatness can be attained only by being oneself. In his writings he finally accepted himself, accepted the ugly and tormented duckling, accepted the sick, irrational and castoff, all elements of his remarkable world; and by so doing reached the rare atmosphere of universal truths which stands above the cabalisms in which his feet were enmeshed; here he belonged, here he breathed at last, with the noblest and the best, the pure uncompromising air of art and truth.

Kafka's Works in English —
A Complete List

Kafka's Works in English — A Complete List

by Angel Flores

KEY OF ABBREVIATIONS:

D 1910—13—*The Diaries of Franz Kafka 1910—1913*. Edited by Max Brod. Translated by Joseph Kresh. New York: Schocken Books, Inc., 1948.

D 1914—23—*The Diaries of Franz Kafka 1914—1923*. Edited by Max Brod. Translated by Martin Greenberg, with the co-operation of Hannah Arendt. New York: Schocken Books, Inc., 1949.

DF—*Dearest Father, Stories and Other Writings*. Translated by Ernst Kaiser and Eithne Wilkins. New York: Schocken Books, Inc., 1954.

DS—*Description of a Struggle*. Translated by Tania and James Stern. New York: Schocken Books, Inc., 1958.

GW—*The Great Wall of China. Stories and Reflections*. Translated by Willa and Edwin Muir. New York: Schocken Books, Inc., 1946.

P—*Parables*. In German and English. Translated by Willa and Edwin Muir, and Clement Greenberg. New York: Schocken Books, Inc., 1947.

PC—*The Penal Colony. Stories and Short Pieces*. Translated by Willa and Edwin Muir. New York: Schocken Books, Inc., 1948.

QRL—*Quarterly Review of Literature*, Vol. II, No. 3 (1945).

SS—*Selected Short Stories of Franz Kafka*. Translated by Willa and Edwin Muir. New York: The Modern Library, 1952.

Abraham (Abraham). P, 37—41.

Absent-minded Window-gazing (Zerstreutes Hinausschaun). PC, 33. Also tr. by Muriel Kittel as "Fleeting Glimpse." QRL, 174—75.

The Advocates (Fürsprecher). DS, 210—214.

The Aeroplanes at Brescia (Die Flugzenge von Brescia). GW, 299—311. Also tr. by G. Humphreys Roberts, in Max Brod: *Franz Kafka.* New York: Schocken Books, Inc., 1947, 221—30.

Alexander the Great (Alexander der Grosse). P, 81.

Amerika (Amerika). Tr. by Willa and Edwin Muir. New York: New Directions, 1938—1946; same, as *America.* London. Routledge & Kegan Paul, 1938; same, as *Amerika.* New York: Doubleday (Anchor Books), 1955.

The Angel (Ein Engel). D 1914—23, 62—64.

At Night (Nachts). DS, 202.

Autobiographical Sketch (Skizze einer Selbstbiographie). Tr. by Sophie Prombaum in *A Franz Kafka Miscellany.* New York: Twice a Year Press, 1940, 51—54.

Bachelor's Ill Luck (Das Unglück des Junggesellen). PC, 30.

Bauz the Director (Bauz, der Direktor). D 1914—23, 73—75.

Before the Law (Vor dem Gesetz). P, 45—63; PC, 148—50. Also tr. by Philip Horton, in Horace Gregory (ed.): *New Letters in America.* New York: Norton, 1947, 145—50.

Blumfeld, an Elderly Bachelor (Blumfeld, ein älterer Junggeselle). Tr. by Philip Horton. *Partisan Review,* Fall, 1938, Vol. VI, No. 1, 54—65, and Winter, 1939, Vol. VI, No. 2, 96—102; DS, 97—145.

The Bridge (Die Brücke). GW, 231—32.

Bruder, a City Official (Der Magistratsbeamte Bruder). D 1914—23, 44—46.

The Bucket Rider (Der Kübelreiter). GW, 233—37; PC, 184—87 Also tr. by G. Humphreys Roberts as "The Scuttle-Rider." *Life and Letters* (London), Dec., 1938, 49.

The Building of the Temple (Der Tempelbau). P, 42—43.

The Burrow (Der Bau). GW, 79—147; SS, 256—304.

The Cares of a Family Man (Der Sorge des Hausvaters). PC, 160—61.

The Castle (*Das Schloss*). Tr. by Willa and Edwin Muir. London: Secker & Warburg; New York: Knopf, 1930, 1941 1954.

Children on a Country Road (Kinder auf der Landstrasse). PC, 21—25. Also tr. by Muriel Kittel as "Children on the Highway." QRL, 175—77.

The City Coat of Arms (Das Stadtwappen). GW, 245—47; P, 31—35.

Clothes (Kleider). PC, 36.

The Coming of the Messiah (Das Kommen des Messias). P, 65.

A Common Confusion (Eine alltägliche Verwirrung). GW, 229—30; SS, 157—58.

The Conscription (Fragment zu *Beim Bau der chinesischen Mauer*). Tr by Olga Marx. QRL, 209—10.

The Conscription of Troops (Die Truppenaushebung). DS, 229—233.

Conversation with the Supplicant (Gespräch mit dem Beter). PC, 9—17.

A Country Doctor (Ein Landarzt). PC, 136—43; SS, 148—56. Also tr. by M. B. [Mimi Bartel]. QRL, 183-88.

Couriers (Kuriere). P, 117.

The Dancer Eduardova (Die Tänzerin Eduardowa). D 1910—13, 9—10.

Dearest Father (Hochzeitsvorbereitungen auf dem Lande und andere Prosa aus dem Nachlass). Tr. by Ernst Kaiser and Eithne Wilkins. New York: Schocken Books, Inc., 1954; same, as *Wedding Preparations in the Country*. London: Secker & Warburg, 1954.

The Departure (Der Aufbruch). DS, 200.

Description of a Struggle (Beschreibung eines Kampfes). DS, 9-96.

Diaries (Tagebücher). Vol. I, 1910—1913. Tr. by Joseph Kresh. New York: Schocken Books, Inc.; London: Secker & Warburg, 1948. Vol. II, tr. by Martin Greenberg with the co-operation of Hannah Arendt. New York: Schocken Books, Inc, London: Secker & Warburg, 1949.

A Dream (Ein Traum). PC, 170—72.

The Eight Octavo Notebooks (Die Acht Oktarhefte). DF, 50—135.

Eleven Sons (Elf Söhne). PC, 161—67.

Ernst Liman (Ernst Liman). D 1910—13, 280—84.

Everything theater (Lautes Theater). D 1910—13, 142—44.

Excurson into the Mountains (Der Ausflug ins Gebirge). PC, 29—30.

Fellowship (Gemeinschaft). DS, 217—218.

The First Long Train Journey (part of a novel *Richard and Samuel*, written in collaboration with Max Brod). CW, 281—98.

First Sorrow (Erstes Leid). PC, 231—34. Also tr. by Lilian F. Turner as "First Grief." *Life and Letters* (London), Summer, 1937, 57-59.

Fragments from Notebooks and Loose Pages (Fragmente aus Heften und losen Blättern). DF, 198—376.

A Fratricide (Ein Brudermord). PC, 167-70; SS, 165-67.

The Giant Mole (Der Riesenmaulwurf). GW, 174-201.

Give It Up! (Gibs auf!). DS, 201.

473

The Great Wall of China (Beim Bau der chinesischen Mauer).
GW, 148—73; SS, 129—47.
The Great Wall of China [Fragment] (Fragment sum Bau der
chineischer Maur). DS, 226—228.
The Great Wall of China and Other Pieces (*Beim Bau der
chinesischen Mauer*). Tr. by Willa and Edwin Muir. Lon-
don: Martin Secker, 1933; New York: Schocken Books, Inc.;
London: Secker & Warburg, 1946.
Gustav Blenkelt (Gustav Blenkelt). D 1910—13, 276—77.
Hans and Amalia (Hans und Amalia). D 1914—23, 148—52.
He (Er). GW, 263—77.
The Helmsman (Der Steuermann). DS, 203—204.
Home-Coming (Heimkehr). DS, 215—216.
A Hunger Artist (Ein Hungerkünstler). PC, 243—56; SS, 188—
201. Also tr. by H. Steinhauer, in H. Steinhauer and Helen
Jessiman (eds.) : *Modern German Short Stories*. New York &
London: Oxford University Press, 1938, 203—17; and by M. L.
Nielsen. *Rocky Mountain Review*, Winter, 1946, 80—89.
The Hunter Gracchus (Der Jäger Gracchus). P, 91—103; GW,
205—14; SS, 181–87.
The Hunter Gracchus, A Fragment (Der Jäger Gracchus, Ein
Fragment). P, 105—15; D 1914—23, 170, DS, 234—241.
Hyperion (Hyperion). GW, 315—17.
"I walked through a long row of houses"—a dream (Ich ging
durch eine lange Häuserreihe). D 1910—13, 88—90.
An Imperial Message (Eine kaiserliche Botschaft). P, 14—17;
PC, 158—59.
In the Penal Colony (In der Strafkolonie). PC, 191—227; SS,
90—128. Also tr. by Eugene Jolas. *Partisan Review* (New
York), March—April, 1941, 98—107, 146—58, and *Horizon*
(London), March, 1942, 158—83.
In the Penal Colony, Fragments (In der Strafkolonie, Frag-
mente). D 1914—23, 178—81.
In the Theater (Im Theater). D 1910—13, 153—56.
The Invention of the Devil (Die Erfindung des Teufels). P, 89;
D 1910—13, 264—65.
Investigations of a Dog (Forschungen eines Hundes). GW, 3—
78; SS, 202—55.
Jackals and Arabs (Schakale und Araber). PC, 150—54. Also tr.
by Mimi Bartel. *New Directions Yearbook*. Norfolk, Conn.,
1942, 408—12.
Joseph the Coachman (Der Kutscher Josef). D 1914—23, 31—33.
Josephine, the Singer, or the Mouse Folk (Josefine, die Säng-
erin, oder Das Volk der Mäuse). PC, 256—77; SS, 305—28.

Also tr. by Clement Greenberg as "Josephine the Songstress or The Mice Nation." *Partisan Review* (New York), May—June, 1942, 213—28.

The Judgment (Das Urteil). PC, 49—63; SS, 3—18. Also tr. by Rosa M. Beuscher and Kate Flores. QRL, 189—98.

The Knock at the Manor Gate (Der Schlag ans Hoftor). GW, 242—44.

The Landlady (Die Nermieterin). D 1914—23, 36—37.

Letter to His Father (Brief an den Vater). DF, 138—96.

Letters to Milena (Briefe an Milena). Edited by Willy Haas. Tr. by Tania and James Stern. London: Secker & Warburg; New York: Schocken Books, Inc., 1953.

A Little Fable (Kleine Fabel). GW, 260.

A Little Woman (Eine kleine Frau). PC, 234—43. Also tr. by Francis C. Golffing. *Accent* (Urbana, Ill.), Summer, 1943, 223—27.

The Married Couple (Das Ehepaar). GW, 215—24.

Memoirs of the Kalda Railroad (Erinnerung an die Kaldabahn). D 1914—23, 79—91.

The Merchant Messner (Der Kaufmann Messner). D 1910—13, 312—14.

The Metamorphosis (Der Verwandlung). PC, 67—132; SS, 19—89. Also tr. by Eugene Jolas. *Transition* (Paris), Fall, 1936, No. 25, 27—38; Winter, 1937, No. 26, 53—72; April—May, 1938, No. 27, 79—103. Also tr. by A. L. Lloyd as *Metamorphosis*. New York: The Vanguard Press, 1946, and as *The Metamorphosis* in the original edition, London: The Parton Press, 1937.

My education has done me great harm (Meine Erziehung in mancher Richtung sehr geschadet hat). D 1910—13, 14—22.

My Neighbour (Der Nachbar). GW, 225—28; D 1914—23, 37—38.

My Visit to Dr. Steiner (Mein Besuch bei Dr. Steiner). D 1910—13, 57—59.

The New Advocate (Der neue Advokat). PC, 135—36; SS, 159—60. Also tr. by Clement Greenberg as "The New Attorney." P, 83—85.

New Lamps (Neue Lampen). Tr. by Olga Marx. QRL, 207—8.

The News of the Bulding of the Wall, A Fragment (Die Nachricht vom Mauerbau, Ein Fragment). Tr. by Clement Greenberg. P, 19—21.

The Next Village (Das nächste Dorf). PC, 158.

A Novel about Youth (a book review of *Die Geschichte des*

475

jungen Oswald, by Felix Sternheim). Tr. by Clement Greenberg. GW, 312—14.

An Old Manuscript (Ein altes Blatt). PC, 145—47; SS, 161—64. Also tr. by Sophie Prombaum as "An Old Page" in *A Franz Kafka Miscellany.* New York: Twice a Year Press, 1946, 67—69.

On Kleist's "Anecdotes" (Kleists "Anekdote"). Tr. by Clement Greenberg. GW, 314—15.

On Parables (Von den Gleichnissen). GW, 258—59; P, 11.

On the Tram (Der Fahrgast). PC, 35—36.

Parables (Parabolen). German and English text. Tr. by Willa and Edwin Muir, and Clement Greenberg. New York: Schocken Books, Inc. 1947.

Paradise (Das Paradies). P, 25—29.

Paralipomena (Paralipomena). DF, 378—93.

Passers-by (Die Vorüberlaufenden). PC, 34—35. Also tr. by Muriel Kittel as "The Runners." QRL, 182.

The Penal Colony. Stories and Short Pieces (In der Strafkolonie). Tr. by Willa and Edwin Muir. New York: Schocken Books, Inc., 1948 and 1949.

Poseidon (Poseidon). P, 71—73, DS, 195—197. Also tr. by Joseph Kresh. *New Directions No. 9.* Norfolk, Conn.: New Directions, 1946, 140—41.

The Problem of Our Laws (Zur Frage des Gesetze). GW, 254—57; P, 119—23.

Prometheus (Prometheus). GW, 251—52; P, 68—69.

Reflections for Gentlemen-Jockeys (Zum Nachdenken für Herrenreiter). PC, 37—38.

Reflections on Sin, Pain, Hope and the True Way (Bertachtungen über Sünde, Leid, Hoffnung und den wahren Weg). GW, 278—307; DF, 34—48.

Rejection (Die Abweisung). PC, 37. Also tr. by Joseph Kresh as "The Refusal." *New Directions No. 9.* Norfolk, Conn.: New Directions, 1946, 141—45, DS, 179—191.

A Report to an Academy [Fragments] (Fragmente zum Bericht für eine Akademie). DS, 219—225.

A Report to an Academy (Ein Bericht an eine Akademie). PC, 173—87; SS, 168—80. Also tr. by William A. Drake as "A Report for an Academy." *The Literary World* (New York), July, 1934, 4—5. Also tr. by Rosa M. Beuscher and Kate Flores. QRL, 199-206.

Resolutions (Entschlüsse). PC, 28—29; D 1910—13, 229—30.

Robinson Crusoe (Robinson Crusoe). P., 126—27.

476

Seeking Advice (Ich will dich um Rat bitten). D 1914—23, 175—77.

Selected Short Stories of Franz Kafka. Tr. by Willa and Edwin Muir. New York: The Modern Library, 1952.

The Silence of the Sirens (Das Schweigen der Sirenen). P, 74—77; GW, 248—50.

A Singular Judicial Procedure (Sonderbarer Gerichtsgebrauch). D 1914—23, 162—63.

The Sirens (Die Sirenen). P, 78—79.

A Sport (Eine Kreuzung). GW, 238—41.

The Street Window (Das Gassenfenster). PC, 39.

The Sudden Walk (Der plötzliche Spaziergang). PC, 27—28; D 1910—13, 214.

The Sword (Das Schwert). D 1914—23, 109—10. Also tr. by Olga Marx. QRL, 208.

Temptation in the Village (Verlockung im Dorf). D 1914—23, 48—58.

The Test (Die Prüfung). DS, 207—209

The Thief (Dieb!). D 1914—23, 71—72.

The Top (Der Kreisel). DS, 205—206.

The Tower of Babel (Der Turm zu Babel). P, 30—31.

The Tradesman (Der Kaufmann). PC, 31—33.

The Trees (Die Bäume). PC, 39—40. Also tr. by Muriel Kittel. QRL, 181.

The Trial (Der Prozess). Tr. by Willa and Edwin Muir. London: Gollancz, New York: Knopf, 1937; London: Secker & Warburg, New York: Knopf, 1945.

The Tricycle and the Automobile (Das Tricycle und die Automobile). D 1914—23, 283—87.

Trip to Friedland and Reichenberg (Reise Friedland und Reichenberg). D 1914—23, 237—43.

Trip to Switzerland, Italy, Paris, and Erlenbach (Reise Lugano-Paris-Erlenbach). D 1914—23, 244—83.

Trip to Weimar and Jungborn (Reise Weimer-Jungborn). D 1914—23, 287—315.

The Truth about Sancho Panza (Die Wahrheit über Sancho Pansa). P, 125; GW, 253.

Unhappiness (Unglücklichsein). PC, 40—45. Also tr. by Muriel Kittel as "Being Unhappy." QRL, 178—81.

Unmasking a Confidence Trickster (Entlarvung eines Bauernfängers). PC, 25—27.

Up in the Gallery (Auf der Galerie). PC, 144—45.

The Urban World (Die städtische Welt). D 1910—13, 47—54.

A Visit to a Mine (Ein Besuch im Bergwerk). PC, 155—58.

477

The Vulture (Der Geier). Tr. by G. Humphreys Roberts. *Twice a Year* (New York), No. 1, Fall—Winter, 1938, 129—31. Also tr. by Joseph Kresh. *New Directions No. 9.* Norfolk, Conn.: New Directions, 1946, 140; DS, 198—199.

The Warden of the Tomb (Der Gruftwächter). DS, 147—178.

The Way Home (Der Nachhausweg). PC, 34. Also tr. by Muriel Kittel. QRL, 182.

Wedding Preparations in the Country (Hochzeitsvorbereitungen auf dem Lande). DF, 2—31.

The White Horse (Das weisse Pferd). D 1914—23, 34—35.

Wilhelm Menz, A Bookkeeper (Wilhelm Menz, ein junger Buchhalter). D 1910—13, 306—7.

A Wish To Be a Red Indian (Wunsch, Indianer zu werden). PC, 39. Also tr. by Muriel Kittel as "A Wish To Be an Indian." QRL, 174.

"You," I said, and gave him a little shove with my knee . . . ("Du," sagte ich und gab ihm einen kleinen Stoss mit den Knie). D 1910--13, 22—29.

Franz Kafka:
Biography & Criticism —
A new, up-to-date Bibliography

Franz Kafka: Biography & Criticism — A new, up-to-date Bibliography

by Angel Flores

Because the number of writings on Kafka has grown to such vast proportions, the present bibliography concentrates only on the more substantial contributions, emphasizing the last decade or so. My own bibliography in *Franz Kafka Today* (University of Wisconsin Press, 1958), pp. 259—285, and Harry Järv's *Die Kafka-Literatur* (Malmö-Lund: Bo Cavefors Verlag, 1961) take account of the innumerable short essays in periodicals, book-reviews, and other details.

***

Aarnes, Asbjorn S. "Franz Kafka," *Vinduet* (Oslo), May, 1950, No. 4, 293—298.

Ackermann, Paul K. *A Descriptive Bibliography of Franz Kafka,* Columbia, University, M. A. thesis, 1947; "A History of Critical Works on Franz Kafka," *German Quarterly,* XXIII (March 1950,) 105—113.

Adams, Robert M. "Swift and Kafka" in his *Strains of Discord.,* Cornell University Press, 1958. 146—179.

Adeane, Louis. "The Hero Myth in Kafka's Writing," *Focus One* (London), 1945, 48—56.

Adorno, Theodor W. "Aufzeichnungen zu Kafka," *Neue Rundschau* (Frankfurt) LXIV (July—September 1953), 325—353; reprinted in his *Prismen,* Frankfurt: Suhrkamp, 1955, 302—342.

Albérès, R. M. "La 'fortune' de Kafka," *Revue de Paris,* LXVII (March 1960), 107—113.

—. and Pierre de Boisdeffre. *Franz Kafka,* Paris: Editions Universitaires, 1960, 126pp.

Albrect, Erich, A. "Zur Entstehungsgeschichte von Kafkas Landarzt," *Monatshefte,* XLVI (April—May 1954), 207—212.

481

Allusion à Kafka. Short essays in Arabic and French by Lev Gillet, Messadie, Magdi Wahba, Kamel Zeheiry, Ahmed Abou Zeid, Georges Henein, and F. W. J. Hemmings. Cairo: La Part du Sable, 1954.

Anceschi, Luciano. *Poetica Americana e altri studi contemporanei di poetica,* Pisa: Nistri-Lischi, 1954, 111—122.

Anders, Gunther. *Kafka, Pro und Contra,* Munich: C. H. Beck, 1951, 109pp.; *Franz Kafka,* New York: Hillary House, 1960, 104pp.

Aranguren, José-Luis. "Franz Kafka," *Arbor* (Madrid), XX (1951), 222—233.

Arendt, Hannah. "The Jews as Pariah: A Hidden Tradition," *Jewish Social Studies* VI (April 1944), 99—122; "Franz Kafka: A Revaluation," *Partisan Review,* XI (Fall 1944), 412—422; *Sechs Essays,* Heidelberg: L. Schneider, 1948, 128—149.

Aschka, Friedrich. "Vergleich mit Kafkas *Prozess,*" in his *Die Zeit und die Erscheinung des Menschen im dichterischen Weltentwurf,* Erlangen University dissertation 1959, 118—126 [typewritten].

Asher, J. A. "Turning Points in Kafka's Stories," *Modern Language Review,* LVII (1962), 47—52.

Babler, O. F. "Frühe tschechische Kafka-Publikationen," *Das Antiquariat* (Vienna), XII, (1956), 181—182.

Bachler, Karl. "Kafka-Bildnis 1959," *Schweizer Rundschau* (Zurich), October 1959, 369—373.

Baker, James R. "*The Castle*: A Problem in Structure," *Twentieth Century Literature,* III (1957), 74—77.

Bänziger, Hans. "Der Bau," *Merkur* (Stuttgart), VIII (1957), No. 1, 38—49.

Bataille, Georges. "Kafka," in his *La Littérature et le Mal,* Paris: Gallimard, 1957, 159—182.

Bauer, Roger. "Kafka à la lumière de la religiosité juive," *Dieu Vivant* (Paris), IX (1947), 105—120.

Baumer, Franz. *Franz Kafka,* Berlin: Colloquium Verlag, 1960, 96pp.

Baumgaertel, Gertrud. "Franz Kafka: Transformation for Clarity," *Revue des Langues Vivantes* (Brussels), XXVI (1960), 266—283.

Beissner, Friedrich. *Der Erzähler Franz Kafka,* Stuttgart: W. Kohlhammer, 1952, 51pp.; *Kafka der Dichter,* Stuttgart: W. Kohlhammer, 1958, 44pp.; "Kafka the Artist," in R. Gray (ed): *Kafka,* Englewood Cliffs, N. J.: Prentice-Hall, 1962, 15—31.

Belgion, Montgomery. "The Measure of Kafka," *The Criterion* (London), October 1938, 13—28.

Bense, Max. *Die Theorie Kafkas,* Cologne & Berlin: Kiepenheuer & Witsch, 1952, 115pp.

Benson, Ann Thornton. *The American Criticism of Franz Kafka, 1930—1948,* University of Tennessee dissertation 1957/1958; "Franz Kafka: An American Bibliography," *Bulletin of Bibliography* (Boston), XXII (1958), 112—114.

Berendsohn, Walter A. "August Strindberg und Franz Kafka," *Deutsche Vierteljahrsschrift* (Stuttgart), XXXV (1961), 630—633.

Bergel, Lienhard. *"Amerika*: Its Meaning," in A. Flores & H. Swander (eds): *Franz Kafka Today,* University of Wisconsin Press, 1958, 117—125.

Blanchot, Maurice. *La Part du feu,* Paris: Gallimard, 1949 (4th ed), 9—34, 80—91; *L'Espace littéraire,* Paris: Gallimard, 1955, 52—81; "The Diaries: The Exigency of the Work of Art," in A. Flores & H. Swander (eds): *Franz Kafka Today,* University of Wisconsin Press, 1958, 195—200; "Le dernier mot de Kafka," *Nouvelle Revue Française,* VII, (February 1959), 294—300, (March 1959), 481—488.

Bo, Carlo. *Rifflessioni Critiche,* Florence: Sansone, 1953, 149—169.

Boden, Gérard. *Franz Kafka: Aspects de son oeuvre,* Algiers: Librairie Chaix, 1947, 55pp.

Boisdeffre, Pierre de. "Kierkegaard et Kafka," *Revue de Paris,* LXII (1955), 138—142; "La tragédie de la solitude chez Kierkegaard et chez Kafka," *Civitas* (Immensee), XI (March—April 1956), 341—346; "Kafka, face au mariage," *Table Ronde* (Paris), No. 150 (1960), 65—73.

Borchardt, Alfred. *Kafkas zweites gesicht. Der Unbekannte, das grosse Theater von Oklahoma.* Nuremberg: Glock & Lutz, 1960, 203pp.

Born, Jurgen. "Max Brod's Kafka," *Books Abroad,* XXXIII (1959), 389—396.

Braybrooke, Neville. "Celestial Castles: An Approach to Saint Teresa and Franz Kafka," *Dublin Review,* CCXXIX (1955), 427—445; "The Geography of the Soul: Saint Teresa and Kafka," *Dalhousie Review* (Halifax, N. S.), XXXVIII (1958), 324—330.

Bröckerhoff, Bernhard. *Seinserfahrung und Weltverstädnis des Dichters Franz Kafka,* Bonn University dissertation, 1957 [typewritten].

Brod, Max. *Franz Kafka, eine Biographie,* Berlin: S. Fischer,

1954, 360pp.; English translation, New York: Schocken, 1957, 270pp.; *Franz Kafkas Glauben und Lehre,* Winterthur: Mondial Verlag, 1948, 195pp.; *"The Castle*: Its Genesis," in A. Flores & H. Swander (eds) : *Franz Kafka Today,* University of Wisconsin Press, 1958, 161—164; *Verzweiflung und Erlösung im Werk Franz Kafkas,* Frankfurt, 1959, 88pp.; "Leben mit Franz Kafka," in his *Streibares Leben,* Munich, 1960, 228—290;

Buber, Martin: *Two Types of Faith,* London & New York: Macmillan, 1951, 162—169; "Schuld und Schuldgefühle," *Merkur* (Stuttgart) , VIII (1957) , 704—729.

Burns, Wayne. " 'In the Penal Colony:' Variations on a Theme by Octave Mirbeau," *Accent* XVII (1957) , 45—51.

Busacca, Basil. "A Country Doctor," in A. Flores & H. Swander (eds) : *Franz Kafka Today,* University of Wisconsin Press, 1958, 45—57.

Butler, E. M.: "The Element of Time in Goethe's *Werther* and Kafka's *Prozess,*" *German Life* & *Letters,* XII (1959) , 248—258.

Cáceres, J. A. *Panoramas del Hombre y del Estilo,* Bogotá: Ediciones Espiral, 1949, 31—35.

Camus, Albert. *The Myth of Sisyphus,* New York: Knopf, 1955, 124—138.

Carrouges, Michel. *Franz Kafka,* Paris: Labergerie, 1948, 162pp.; "La machine-célibataire selon Franz Kafka et Marcel Duchamp, *Mercure de France,* CCCXV (June 1952) , 262—281, rep. in *Les Machines célibataires,* Paris: Arcanes, 1954, 245pp.; *Kafka contre Kafka,* Paris: Plon, 1962, 182pp.

Caspel, J. van. "Josephine und Jeremias," *Neophilologus* XXXVII (1953) , 241—245; "Totemismus bei Kafka," *Neophilologus,* XXXVIII (1954) , 120—127.

Church, Margaret. "Time and Reality in Kafka's *The Trial* and *The Castle,*" *Twentieth Century Literature* II (July, 1956) , 62—69; "Kafka and Proust: A Contrast in Time," *Bucknell Review,* 1957, 107—112; "Kafka's 'A Country Doctor,' " *The Explicator* XVI (May 1958) , Item 45.

Clive Geoffrey. "The Breakdown of Romantic Enlightenment: Kafka and Dehumanization," in his *The Romantic Enlightenment: Ambiguity and Paradox in the Western Mind,* New York: Meridian, 1960, 170—184.

Cohn, Ruby. "Watt in the Light of *The Castle,*" *Comparative Literature,* XII (1961) , 154—166.

Collignon, Jean. "Kafka's Humor," *Yale French Studies,* Winter 1955—1956, No. 16, 53—62.

Collins, Hildegard Platzer. *A Study of the Relationship between Technique and Theme in the Shorter Works of Kafka.* University of Southern California dissertation, 1961; "Kafka's View of Institutions and Traditions," *German Quarterly,* XXXV (November 1962), 492—503.

Cook, Albert S. "Romance as Allegory: Melville and Kafka," in his *The Meaning of Fiction,* Wayne State University Press, 1960, 242—259.

Cook, Mary J. *The Women Characters in the Novels of Franz Kafka,* Columbia University M. A. thesis, 1947.

Cooperman, Stanley. "Kafka's 'A Country Doctor,'" *University of Kansas City Review,* XXIV (October 1957), 75—80.

Dalmau Castañon, Wilfredo. "El caso clínico de Kafka en 'La Metamorfosis,'" *Cuadernos Hispanoamericanos* (Madrid), March 1952, No. 27, 385—388.

Daniells, Roy. "In the Labyrinth: A Note on Franz Kafka," *Manitoba Arts Review,* III (Spring 1942), 3—13.

Daniel-Rops. "A French Catholic Looks at Kafka," *Thought* (New York), XXIII (September 1948), 401—404; "L'Univers désesperé de Franz Kafka," *Cahiers du Sud* (Marseilles), XVI (March 1937), 161—176.

Darzins, J. "Transparence in Camus and Kafka," *Yale French Studies,* 1960, No. 25, 98—103.

Dauvin, René. "*Le Procès* de Kafka," *Etudes Germaniques* (Lyons), III (January—March 1948, 49—63; "*The Trial:* Its Meaning" in A. Flores & H. Swander (eds): *Franz Kafka Today,* University of Wisconsin Press, 1958, 145—160.

Delesalle, Jacques. *Cet Etrange secret,* Paris: Desclée de Brouwer, 1957, 60—97.

Dell'Agli, A. M. "Problemi Kafkiani nella critica dell'ultimo decennio," *Annali A.I.O.N.* (Sezione Germanica, Istituto Universitario Orientali) (Naples), 1958, 77—105.

Demetz, Peter. "Franz Kafka a cesky národ," in *Franz Kafka a Praha,* Prague: V. Zikes, 1947, 43—53; "Franz Kafka a Herman Melville," *Casopis pro Moderni Filologii* (Prague), XXXI (1947/1948), 183—185, 267—271; "Zur Interpretation Franz Kafkas," *Plan* (Vienna), II (1948), 370—378; "Kafka in England," *German Life & Letters,* IV (October 1950), 21—30; "Kafka, Freud, Husserl: Probleme einer Generation," *Zeitschrift für Religions-und Geistesgeschichte* (Leyden), VII (1955), 59—69.

Dentan, Michel. *Humour et création littéraire dans l'oeuvre de Kafka.* Geneva: Groz, 1962.

D'Haen, Ch. "Franz Kafka," *Nieuw Vlaams Tijdschrift* (Antwerp) , XII (1953) , 1260—1291.

Doss, Kurt. "Ist Kafka eine geeignete Lektüre im Deutschunterricht der Obesstufe?", *Pädagogische Provinz* (Frankfurt) , 1957, 7/8, 358—364; "Die Gestalt des Torens in Grimmelhausens *Simplicissimus* und Kafkas *Amerika*," *Pädagogische Provinz* (Frankfurt) , 1959, 319—330.

Dresler, Jaroslav. "Die Verwirrung der Zungen. Franz Kafka im Spiegel kommunistischer Kritik," *Osteuropa* (Stuttgart) , 1960, 7/8, 473—481; "Kafka and the Communists," *Survey* (London) , 1961, No. 36, 27—32.

Dutourd, Jean. "Un Auteur tragi-comique," *La Nouvelle NRF* (Paris) , III (1955) , No. 36, 1081—1090.

Dyson, A. E. "Trial by Enigma, Kafka and Lewis Carroll," *Twentieth Century* (London) , CLX (July 1956) , 49—64.

Edel, Edmund. "Franz Kafka: 'Die Verwandlung.' Eine Auslegung," *Wirkendes Wort* (Dusseldorf) , VIII (1957/1958) , No. 4, 217—226; "Franz Kafka: 'Das Urteil,'" *Wirkendes Wort*, IX (1959) , No. 4, 216—225.

Edfelt, Johannes. "Franz Kafka," in A. Lundkvist (ed) : *Europas Litteraturhistoria*, Stockholm, 1946, 557—563.

Eisner, Pavel. *Franz Kafka and Prague*, New York: Arts, Inc., 1950 (Golden Griffin Books) , 100pp.; "Analyse de Kafka," *La Nouvelle Critique* (Paris) , 1958, No. 92, 92—109 and No. 93, 66—82; "Franz Kafkas *Prozess* und Prag," *German Life & Letters* XIV (October, 1960—January, 1961) , No. 1/2 16—25.

Emrich, Wilhelm. *Franz Kafka*, Bonn: Athenäum, 1958 (2nd ed, 1960) , 445pp.; "Franz Kafkas Bruch mit der tradition und sein neues Gesetz" and "Die Bilderwelt Franz Kafkas" in his *Protest und Verheissung*, Frankfurt: Athenäum Verlag, 1960, 233—248 and 249—263.

Erlich, Victor. "Gogol and Kafka: Note on 'Realism' and 'Surrealism,'" in Morris Halle (ed) : *For Roman Jakobson. Essays on the Occasion of his Sixtieth Birthday*, The Hague: Mouton, 1956, 100—108.

Falk, Walter. *Leid und Verwandlung, Rilke, Kafka, Trakl.* Salzburg: O. Müller 1961, 499pp.

Falke, Rita. "Biographisch-literarische Hintegründe von Kafkas 'Urteil,'" *Germanisch-Romanische Monatschrift* (Heidelberg) , 1960, No. 2, 164—180.

Fauchery, Pierre: "Faut-il bruler Kafka?" and replies by 29 writers, *Action* (Paris) , 1946, Nos. 90, 93, 94, 95, 96, 97, 98, 99 and 100 May 24 to August 2.

Flores, Angel (ed) : "Homage to Kafka," *The Literary World*

(New York), July 1934, 1—4; "Franz Kafka," in S. J. Kunitz
& H. Haycraft (eds) : *Twentieth Century Authors,* New York:
H. W. Wilson, 1942, 740—741; *Franz Kafka: A Chronology
and Bibliography,* Houlton (Maine) ; Bern Porter, 1944; "Light
on the Hideous," *New York Herald Tribune,* August 10,
1947, section VII, p. 4; "The Art of Kafka," *Yale Review,*
Winter, 1949, 365—367; *Franz Kafka Today,* University of Wisconsin Press, 1958, 290pp.

Flores, Kate. "The Judgment," *Quarterly Review of Literature,*
III (1947), No. 4, 382—405; "The Judgment", in A. Flores
& H. Swander (eds) : *Franz Kafka Today,* University of Wisconsin Press, 1958, 5—24; "La Condena," *Etcaetera* (Guadala-
jara, Mexico), V (September 1956), 133—151.

Florman, Samuel C. *American Criticism of Franz Kafka, 1930—
1946,* Columbia University M. A. thesis, 1947.

Fondane, Benjamin. "Kafka et la rationalité absolue," *Deucalion*
(Paris), 1947, No. 2, 125—140.

Fontana, Oskar Maurus. "Nya tyska böcker," *Bonniers Literära
Magasin* (Stockholm), February 1938, 125—135.

Fortini, F. "Gli uomini di Kafka e la critica delle cose," *Ras-
segna d'Italia* (Milan), IV (1949), 148—154.

Fraiberg, Selma. "Kafka and the Dream," *Partisan Review,*
XXIII (Winter 1956), 47—69.

Freedman, Ralph. "Kafka's Obscurity: The Illusion of Logic in
Narrative," *Modern Fiction Studies,* VIII (1962), 61—74.

Friedrich, Heinz. "Heinrich von Kleist und Franz Kafka," *Ber-
liner Hefte für geistiges Leben,* IV (November 1949), No. 11,
440—448.

Fromm, Erich. *The Forgotten Language,* New York: Rinehart,
1951, 213—224.

Frynta, Emanuel. *Franz Kafka Lebte in Prag,* Prague: Artia,
1960, 146pp.

Fürst, Norbert. *Die offenen Geheimtüren Franz Kafkas,* Heidelberg: W. Rothe, 1956, 86pp.

Gabel, Joseph. "Kafka, romancier de l'aliénation," *Critique*
(Paris), IX (November 1953), 949—960.

Gaillard, J. M. "Une Mythologie du désespoir: 'La Métamor-
phose' de Franz Kafka," *Helvetia* (Bern), June 1961, 151—158.

Gándara, Carmen R. L. de. *Kafka o el pájaro y la jauta,* Buenos
Aires: Ateneo, 1944, 133pp.

Gerlach, Kurt. "Die Mangelhaltung des modernen Menschen in
Kafkas Werk," *Pädagogische Provinz* (Frankfurt), 1956, No. 3,
117—128.

Gibian, George. "Dichtung und Wahrheit: Three Versions of

Reality in Franz Kafka," *German Quarterly*, XXX (January 1957), 20—31; "Karel Capek's Apocrypha and Franz Kafka's Parables," *American Slavic and East European Review*, XVIII (April 1959), 238—248.

Giesekus, Waltraud. *Franz Kafkas Tagebucher*, Bonn University dissertation. 1954, 227pp. [typewritten].

Girard, Alain. "Kafka et le problème du Journal Intime," *Critique* (Paris), I (1946), 23—32.

Girard, René. "Franz Kafka et ses critiques," *Symposium* (Syracuse, N. Y.), VII (May 1953) 34—44.

Glaser, Hermann. "Franz Kafka: 'Auf der Galerie,'" in *Interpretationen Moderner Prosa,* ed. by Fachgruppe Deutsch-Geschichte im Bayerischen Philoloverband, Frankfurt., Verlag Moritz Diesterweg, 1956 (4th ed., 1959), 40—48.

Glatzer, Nahum N. "Franz Kafka and the Tree of knowledge," *Between East and West*, 1958, 48—58.

Goldschmidt, H. L. "Key to Kafka," *Commentary*, VIII (August 1949), 129—138.

Goodman, Paul. *Kafka's Prayer*, New York: Vanguard, 1947, 265pp.; "Plot Structure of *The Castle*" in his *The Structure of Literature,* University of Chicago Press, 1954, 173-183.

Goth, Maja. *Franz Kafka el les lettres françaises (1928—1955)*, Paris: Corti, 1957, 288pp.

Grangier, Edouard. "Abraham, oder Kierkegaard, wie Kafka und Sartre ihn sehen," *Zeitschrift für Philosophische Forschung* (Meisenheim/Glan.), 1949, No. 3, 412—421.

Gravier, Maurice. "Strindberg et Kafka," *Etudes Germaniques* (Lyons), VIII (1953), 118—140.

Gray, Ronald. *Kafka's Castle,* Cambridge University Press, 1956, 147pp.; "The Structure of Kafka's Works," *German Life & Letters*, XIII (1959), 1—17; (ed): *Kafka,* Englewood Cliffs, N. J.: Prentice-Hall, 1962, 182pp. which contains his essay "Kafka the Writer," 61—73.

Greenberg, Clement. "At the Building of the Great Wall of China," in A. Flores & H. Swander (eds): *Franz Kafka Today,* University of Wisconsin Press, 1958, 77—81.

Grenzmann, Wilhelm. "Franz Kafkas Werk und geistige Welt," *Universitas* (Stuttgart), 1953, No. 8, 797—803.

Groethuysen, Bernard. "A propos de Kafka" and "Phénoménologie de Kafka" in his *Mythes et Portraits,* Paris: Gallimard, 1947, 121—143 and 145—159.

Guadagnino, L. M. "La giustizia di Kafka," *Letterature Moderne* (Milan), (1954), 626—630.

Guardini. Romano. "Zum Geleit," Introduction to the German

version of Robert Rochefort's *Kafka ou L' Irréductible espoir,*
[Kafka oder Die unzerstörbare Hoffnung], Vienna & Munich,
1955, 9—20.

Hass, Willy. *Die Literarische Welt. Erinnerungen.* Munich: P.
List, 1957 (new ed. 1960) , 315pp.

Hahn, Ludwig. "Franz Kafkas 'Der Kübelreiter,' " in *Interpretationen Moderner Prosa,* ed. by Fachgruppe Deutsch-Geschichte im Bayerischen Philologenverband, Frankfurt/M., Verlag
Moritz Diesterweg. 1957, 49—54.

Hajek, Siegfried. "Franz Kafka: 'Der Nachbar,' " *Deutschunterricht* (Stuttgart) , VII (1955) , 5—12.

Hasselblatt, Dieter. *Zauber und Logik. Zur Struktur des Dicterischen bei Kafka.* Freiburg i. Br. University dissertation, 1959
154pp. [typewritten].

Hebel, Franz. "Kafka: Zur Frage der Gesetze und Kleist: Michael
Kohlhass," *Pädagogische Provinz* (Frankfurt.) , 1956, No. 12,
632—638.

Hecht, M. B. "Uncanniness, Yearning and Franz Kafka," *American Imago,* IX (April 1952,) , 45—55.

Heiseler, Bernt von. "Sonnenfinsternis," *Zeitwende* (Munich) ,
XXIII (Jan. 1, 1952) , 436—440, rep. in his *Ahnung und Aussage,* Gütersloh: Bertelsmann, 1952, 232—240.

Heldmann, Werner. *Die Parabel und die parabolischen Erzählformen bei Franz Kafka,* Münster University dissertation, 1953,
201pp. [typewritten].

Heller, Erich. *The Disinherited Mind,* New York: Farrar, Straus
& Cudahy, 1957, 199—231.

Heller, Peter. "The Autonomy of Despair," *The Massachussetts
Review* (Amherst) , Winter 1960, 231—253.

Hemmerle, Rudolf. *Franz Kafka. Eine Bibliographie,* Munich:
Robert Lerche, 1958, 140pp.

Hennecke, Hans. *Kritik. Gesammelte Essays zur modernen Literatur.* Gütersloh, 1958, 209—216.

Hermsdorf, Klaus. "Zu den Briefen Franz Kafkas," *Sinn und
Form* (Berlin/Potsdam) , 1957, No. 4, 653—662; "Hinweis auf
einen Aufsatz von Franz Kafka, "*Weimarer Beiträge,* 1958,
545—556; *Franz Kafkas Roman fragment "Der Verschollene"*
["*Amerika*"], Humboldt-Universitat zu Berlin dissertation.
1961; *Kafka—Weltbild und Roman,* Berlin: Rütten & Loening, 1961.

Heselhaus, Clemens. "Kafkas Erzählformen," *Deutsche Vierteljahrsschrift* (Stuttgart) , XXVI (1952) , 353—376.

Hesnard, A. L. M. "Le Message incompris de Kafka," *Psyché*
(Paris) , II (1947) , 1161—1173.

489

Hesse, Hermann. *Gesammelte Schriften,* Berlin: Suhrkamp, 1957, Vol. VII, 469—471.

Heuer, Helmut. *Die Amerikavision bei William Blake und Franz Kafka,* Munich University dissertation, 1960, 139pp.

Hodin, J. P. *The Dilemma of Being Modern,* London: Routledge, 1956, 3—22.

Hoffman, Frederick J. *Freudianism and the Literary Mind,* Louisiana State University, 1945, 181—192; "Kafka's *The Trial*: The Assailant as Landscape," *Bucknell Review,* IX (May 1960), 89—105.

Hoffman, Leonard R. *Melville and Kafka,* Stanford University thesis, 1951.

Hofrichter, Laura. "From Poe to Kafka," *University of Toronto Quarterly,* XXIX (July 1960), 405—417.

Holland, Norman N. "Realism and Unrealism: Kafka's 'Metamorphosis,'" *Modern Fiction Studies,* IV (Summer 1958), 143—150.

Hoog, Armand. "Kafka et la grande peur," *La Nef* (Paris), 1945, No. 13, 107—112.

Hubben, William. *Four Prophets of Our Destiny: Kierkegaard, Dostoevsky, Nietzsche, Kafka.* New York: Macmillan, 1952, 129—144 (2nd ed. 1954).

Ide, Heinz. "Existenzerhellung im Werke Kafkas," *Jahrbuch der Wittheit zu Bremen* (Bremen & Hanover), 1957, 66—104.

Jacobi, Walter. "Kafkas Roman *Amerika* im Unterricht: Eine Untersuchung seiner Motive und Symbole und deren Bedeutung für Kafkas Gesamtwerk," *Deutschunterricht* (Stuttgart), XIV (1962), 63—78.

Jahn, Wolfgang. *Stil und Welbild in Kafkas Roman "Der Verschollene"* [*Amerika*], Tübingen University dissertation, 1961; "Kafka und die Anfange des Kinos," *Jahrbuch der deutschen Schillergesellschaft* (Stuttgart), VI (1962).

Janouch, Gustav. *Conversations with Kafka,* New York: F. A. Praeger, 1953.

Järv, Harry. *Konsten som livssurrogat. Kafkas analys av konstnärskapets problematik,* [A Report to an Academy] Upsala University thesis, 1953, 123pp. [Typewritten]; *Die Kafka-Literatur,* Malmö & Lund: Bo Cavefors Verlag, 1961, 380pp.

Jens, Inge. *Studien zur Entwicklung der expressionistischen Novelle,* Tübingen University dissertation, 1954, 318pp [typewritten] [Description of a Struggle, 80—108].

Jonas, Klaus W. "Franz Kafka: An American Bibliography" *Bulletin of Bibliography* (Boston), XX (September—December 1952). 212—216; (January—April 1953), 231—233.

490

Juliet, Charles. "La litterature et le theme de la mort chez Kafka et Leiris," *Critique* (Paris), 1957, No. 126, 933—945.

Kaiser, Gerhard. "Franz Kafkas *Prozess*. Versuch einer Interpretation," *Euphorion* (Heidelberg), CII (1958), No. 1, 23—49.

Kaiser, Helmuth. *Franz Kafkas Inferno. Ein psychologische Deutung seiner Strafphantasie,* Vienna: Internationaler Psychoanalytischer Verlag, 1931, 65pp., originally published in *Imago* (Vienna), XVII (February 1931), 41—104.

Kartiganer, Donald M. "Job and Joseph K: Myth in Kafka's *The Trial,*" *Modern Fiction Studies,* VIII (1962), 31—43.

Kassner, Rudolf. "Stil und Gesicht. Swift, Gogol, Kafka," *Merkur* (Baden-Baden/Stuttgart), VIII (1954), 737—752, and 834—845, and reprinted in his *Der goldene Drachen,* Erlenbach/Zurich: E. Rentsch, 1957.

Kauf, Robert. "Once Again—Kafka's 'Report to an Academy,'" *Modern Language Quarterly,* XV (December 1954), 359—366.

Kerkhoff, Emmy. "Franz Kafka," *Levende Talen* (Groningen), December 1953, No. 172, 488—509.

Klarman, Adolf. D. "Franz Kafkas 'Der Heizer': Versuch einer stilkritischen Studie," *Bibliotheque de la Faculté de Liège,* Fasc. CLXI (1961), 287—289.

Knieger, Bernard. "Kafka's 'The Hunter Gracchus'." *Explicator,* XVII (March 1959), Item 39.

König, Gerd. *Franz Kafkas Erzählungen und kleine Prose,* Tübingen University dissertation, 1954, 234pp. [typewritten].

Korst, Marianne Ruth. *Die Beziehung zwischen Held und Gegenwelt in Franz Kafkas Romanen,* Marburg University dissertation. 1953. 138pp. [typewritten].

Kosta, Oskar. "Wege Pragen deutscher Dichter zum tschechischen Volk," *Aufbau* (Berlin), XIV (1958), 556—581.

Kowal, Michael. *Franz Kafka: Problems in Interpretation,* Yale University dissertation, 1962, 304pp.

Kraft, Werner. *Wort und Gedanke,* Bern: Francke, 1959, 115—116, 129—131, 192, 321—322.

Krieger, Murray. *The Tragic Vision,* New York: Holt, Rinehart & Winston. 1960, 114—144.

Krüger, Hans-Peter. "Franz Kafkas Dramenfragment 'Der Gruftwacher,'" *Proceedings of the Department of Foreign Languages and Literatures,* University of Tokyo, IX (1962), No. 5, 27pp.

Kuhr, Alexander. "Neurotische Aspekte bei Heidegger und Kafka," *Zeitschrift fur Psychosomatische Medizin* (Göttingen), I (1955), No. 3, 217—227.

Kyler, Ingrid E. *The Pilgrimage of Franz Kafka,* Columbia University M. A. thesis, 1948.

Lachmann, Eduard. "Das Türhütergleichnis in Kafkas *Prozess,*" *Innsbrucker Beiträge zur Kulturwissenschaft,* 1959, 265—270.

Ladendorf, Heinz. "Kafka und die Kunstgeschichte," *Wallraf-Richartz Jahrbuch* XXIII (1961), 293—326.

Lainoff, Seymour. "The Country Doctors of Kafka and Turgenev," *Symposium* (Syracuse) 1962, No. 2.

Lamprecht, Helmut. "Mühe und Kunst des Anfangs. Ein Versuch über Kafka und Kleist," *Neue Deutsche Hefte* (Gütersloh), 1960, No. 66, 935—940.

Lancelotti, Mario A. *El Universo de Franz Kafka,* Buenos Aires: Argos, 1950.

Lawson, Richard H. "Kafka's 'Der Landarzt,' " *Monatshefte* XLIX (October 1957), 265—271: *"Ungeheures Ungeziefer* in Kafka's 'Die Verwandlung,' " *German Quarterly,* XXXIII, (1960), No. 3, 216—219; "Kafka's Use of the Conjunction *Bis* in the Sense of *As Soon As,*" *German Quarterly,* XXXV (March 1962), 165—170.

Ledgard, Rodolfo. "La realidad de Franz Kafka," *Tres* (Lima), March—June 1941, 84—91.

Léger, François. "De Job a Kafka," *Cahiers du Sud* (Marseilles), April 1945, No. 22, 161—165.

Leiter, Louis H. "A Problem in Analysis: Franz Kafka's 'A Country Doctor,' " *Journal of Aesthetics & Art Criticism* (Baltimore), XVI (March 1958), 337—347.

Lenz, Hermann. "Franz Kafka und die 'Mächte,' " *Welstimmen* (Stuttgart) XVIII (1949), No. 12, 1—8.

Leopold, Keith. "Franz Kafka's Stories in the First Person," *AUMLA, Journal of the Australasian Universities Language and Literature Association,* 1959, No. 11, 56—62.

Lesser, Simon O. "The Source of Guilt and the Sense of Guilt—Kafka's *The Trial,*" *Modern Fiction Studies* VIII (1962), 44—60.

Li, Chu-Tsing. *Franz Kafka's Theory of Literature,* State University of Iowa, M. A. thesis, 1949.

Lindsay, J. M. "Kohlhas and K, Two Men in Search of Justice." *German Life* & *Letters* XIII (April 1960), 190—194.

Lion, Ferdinand. *Die Geburt der Aphrodite,* Heidelberg: W. Rothe, 1955, 130—135.

Litterair Paspoort (Amsterdam) —Franz Kafkanummer, August —September 1949.

Loeb, Ernst. "Bedeutungswandel der Metamorphose bei Franz

Kafka und E.T.A. Hoffmann: Ein Vergleich," *German Quarterly,* XXXV (January 1962), 47—59.

Loeblowitz-Lennard, Henry. "Some Leitmotifs in Franz Kafka's Works Psychoanalytically Explored," *University of Kansas City Review,* XIII (1946), 115—118.

Lührsen, Hans Detlef. "Franz Kafka. Einführung und Bibliographie," *Europa-Archiv,* (Frankfurt), V (1950), 3527—3534.

Lukács, Georg. *Wider den misverstandenen Realismus,* Hamburg: Claasen, 1958, 49—96.

Luke, F. D. "The Metamorphosis," in A. Flores & H. Swander (eds): *Franz Kafka Today,* University of Wisconsin Press, 25—44.

Macklem, M. "Kafka and the Myth of Tristan," *Dalhousie Review* XXX (1950), 335—345.

Madden, William A. "A Myth of Mediation: Kafka's 'Metamorphosis,'" *Thought* XXVI (Summer 1951), 246—266.

Magny, Claude-Edmonde. *Les Sandales l' Empédocle,* Neuchâtel: Baconnière 1945, 173—266.

Mahler, Karl W. *Eigentliche und uneigentliche Darstellung der moderne Epik. Der parabolische Stil Franz Kafkas.* Marburg University dissertation, 1958 [typewritten].

Maier, Anna. *Franz Kafka und Robert Musil als Vertreter der ethischen Richtung des modernen Romans.* University of Vienna dissertation, 1949, 185 pp. [typewritten].

Maione, Italo. *Franz Kafka,* Naples: Libreria Scientifica Editrice, 1952, 81pp.

Mallea, Eduardo. "Introduccion al mundo de Franz Kafka," *Sur* (Buenos Aires), December 1937, No. 39, 7—37.

Mann, Thomas. "Homage," *The Literary World* (New York), July 1934, p. 1; "Homage" in Franz Kafka: *The Castle,* New York: Knopf, 1941, v-xvi.

Margeson, John. "Franz Kafka, a Critical Problem," *University of Toronto Quarterly,* XVIII (October 1948), 30—40.

Margolis, Joseph. "Kafka vs. Eudaimonia and Duty," *Philosophy and Phenomenological Research* (Buffalo, N. Y.), 1958, No. 1, 27—42.

Marson, E. L. "Franz Kafka's 'Das Urteil,'" *AUMLA* Journal of the Australasian Universities Language and Literature Association, 1961, No. 16, 167—178.

Martin, Peter A. "The Cockroach as an Identification; with Reference to Kafka's 'Metamorphosis,'" *American Imago,* XVI (1959), 65—71.

Martin, W. B. J. "Significant Modern Writers: Franz Kafka," *Expository Times* (Edinburgh), LXXI (1960), 309—331.

493

Martinez Estrada, Ezequiel. "Intento de señalar los bordes del 'Mundo' de Kafka," *La Nacion* (Buenos Aires), May 14, 1944, Section II, p. 1; "Acepcion literal del mito en Kafka," *Babel* (Santiago de Chile), Año XI, 1950, No. 13, 24—28.

Martini, Fritz. "Franz Kafka: *Das Schloss*. Text und Interpretation," in his *Das Wagnis der Sprache*, Stuttgart: Klatt, 1954, 287—335; "Ein Manuskript Franz Kafkas: 'Der Dorfschullehrer,'" *Jahrbuch der Deutschen Schillergesellschaft* (Stuttgart), 1958, 266—300.

Masini, Ferruccio. "La dialettica esistenziale in Kafka," *Aut-Aut* (Milan), XLV (1958), 116—137.

Matteucci, Benvenuto. "Franz Kafka o l'allegoria del Vecchio Testamento," *Vita e Pensiero* (Milan), III (1952), 157—164.

Mauer, Otto. "Kommentar zu zwei Parabeln von Franz Kafka ['Eine kaiserliche Botschaft' and 'Der Schlag ans Hoftor']," *Wort und Wahrheit* (Freiburg), I (1946), 29—34.

Mauriac, Claude. *The New Literature*, New York: Braziller, 1959, 15—34.

Meissner, Frank A. "A Social Ecology of the German Jews in Prague," *Dalhousie Review* (Halifax, N. S.), XXXIX (1960), 309—331.

Micha, René. "Le Fantastique kafkaien sur le plan de l'art," *L'Arche* (Paris), June 1946, No. 16, 43—50.

Michel, Kurt. *Adalbert Stifter und die transzendente Welt*, Graz: Stiasny Verlag, 1957, 160pp. [contains an analysis of "In the Penal Colony pp. 135—146].

Middelhauve, Friedrich. *Ich und Welt im Frühwerk Franz Kafkas*. University of Freiburg i. Br. dissertation, 1957 [typewritten].

Miller, J .H. "Franz Kafka and the Metaphysics of Alienation," in Nathan A. Scott, Jr. (ed): *The Tragic Vision and the Christian Faith*, New York: Association Press, 1957, 281—305.

Misslbeck, Maria. "Franz Kafka: 'Ein Landartzt,'" *Deutschunterricht* (Stuttgart), VI (1958), 36—46.

Mittner, Ladislao. "Kafka ohne Kafkaismen," in *La letteratura tedesca del Novecento e altri saggi*, Turin: G. Einaudi, 1960.

Molitor, Jan [André van Santen]. *Asmodai in Praag. Franz Kafka, zijn tidj en Werk*, 's Graveland: De Driehoek, 1950, 141pp.

Motekat, Helmut. "Franz Kafkas 'Ein Landartz,'" in *Interpretationen moderner Prosa*, ed. by Fachgruppe Deutsch-Geschichte im Bayerischen Philologenverband, Frankfurt.: Verlag Moritz Diesterweg, 1957, 7—27 [4th ed. 1959]

Mounier Guy-Fernand H. *Etude Psychopathologique sur l'écrivain Kafka*, University of Bordeaux dissertation, 1951.

494

Moyer, Patricia. "Time and the Artist in Kafka and Hawthorne," *Modern Fiction Studies* IV (1958), 295—306.

Mueller, William R. "The Theme of Judgment: Franz Kafka's *The Trial*," in his *The Prophetic Voices in Modern Fiction*, New York: Association Press, 1959, 83—109.

Mühlberger, Josef. *Hugo von Hofmannsthal—F. Kafka. Zwei Vorträge*, Esslingen: Bechtle Verlag, 1953, 31—70; "Zum 75. Geburtstag Franz Kafkas," *Sudetenland* I (1958—1959), 38—48.

Musurillo, Herbert. "Healing Symbols in Kafka," *The Month*, XIX (1958), 334—340.

Nadeau, Maurice. "Kafka et 'L'Assaut contre les frontières,'" *Les Lettres Nouvelles* (Paris), XXIV (February 1955), 260—267.

Navarro, Oscar. *Kafka, la crisi della fede*, Turin: Taylor, 1949, 109pp.

Neider, Charles. *The Frozen Sea*, New York: Oxford University Press, 1948, 195pp.

Németh, Andre. *Kafka ou Le Mystère juif*, Paris: Jean Vigneau, 1947, 201pp.

Neumann, Erich. "Aus dem ersten Teil des Kafka-Kommentars: 'Das Gerich.' Das Domkapitel," in *Geist und Werk. Aus der Werkstatt unserer Autoren. Zum 75. Geburtstag von Dr. Daniel Brody*. Zurich: Rhein-Verlag, 1958, 175—196.

Nicholson, Norman. *Man and Literature*, London: Student Christian Movement Press, 1943, 162—178.

Olafson, Frederick A. "Kafka and the Primacy of the Ethical," *Hudson Review*, XIII (Spring 1960), 60—73.

Ong, Walter J. "Kafka's Castle and the West," *Thought*, XXII (September 1947) 439—460; "Finitude and Frustration," *Modern Schoolman* (St. Louis), 1948, 173—182.

Parry, Idris F. "Kafka and Gogol," *German Life & Letters*, VI (January 1953), 141—145.

Pascal, Roy. *The German Novel*, University of Toronto Press, 1956, 215—257; "Dickens and Kafka," *The Listener* (London), April 26, 1956, 504—506.

Pasley, J. M. S. "Franz Kafka Mss., Description and Select Inedita," *Modern Language Review*, LVII January (1962), 53—59.

Paulsen, Wolfgang. "Franz Kafka," *Monatshefte*, XXIX (December 1937), 373—388.

Pearce, Donald. "*The Castle*: Kafka's Divine Comedy," in A. Flores & H. Swander (eds): *Franz Kafka Today*, University of Wisconsin Press, 1958, 165—172.

495

Pfeiffer, Johannes. "Franz Kafka: 'Eine kleine Frau.' Eine para-
bolisches Selbstgespräch," in his *Wege zur Erzählkunst,* Ham-
burg: Wittig, 1953, 108—116 [4th ed, 1958]; "Uber Franz
Kafkas Novelle 'Die Verwandlung,' " *Die Sammlung* (Gött-
tingen), XIV (1959), 297—302; " 'The Metamorphosis,' " in
R. Gray (ed) : *Kafka,* Englewood Cliffs, N. J.: Prentice-Hall,
1962, 53—59.

Pingaud, Bernard. "La doute de Kafka," *Table Ronde* (Paris),
1955, No. 89, 91—94.

Podestà, Giuditta. "Kafka e Pirandello." *Humanitas* (Brescia),
XI (1956), 230—244; *Franz Kafka e i suoi fantasmi nell'itiner-
ario senza meta,* Genoa: Libreria Universitaria Pacetti, 1957,

Poggioli, Renato. *Pietre di Paragone,* Florence: Parenti, 1939,
161—173.

Politzer, Heinz. "Letter to His Father," in A. Flores & H. Swander (eds) : *Franz Kafka Today,* University of Wisconsin Press,
1958, 221—237; "Der Prozess gegen das Gericht: Zum Ver-
ständnis von Franz Kafkas Roman *Der Prozess,*" *Wort und
Wahrheit* (Vienna), XIV (1959), 279—292; "Ein gefirmter
Kafka?," *Wort und Wahrheit,* XV (1960), 721—722; "Franz
Kafka's Language," *Modern Fiction Studies,* VIII (1962), 16—
22; *Franz Kafka, Parable and Paradox.* Cornell University
Press, 1962, 376pp.

Pongs, Hermann. *Franz Kafka, Dichter des Labyrinths,* Heidelberg: W. Rothe, 1960, 136pp.

Pott, Hans-Günther. *Die aphoristischen Texte Franz Kafkas. Stil
und Gedankenwelt.* Freiburg i. Br. University dissertation,
1958 [typewritten].

Pratt, Audrey E. (McKim). *Franz Kafka und sein Vater*: *des
Verhältnis der beiden und dessen Einwirkung auf Kafkas
Werk,* McGill University dissertation, 1949, [typewritten].

Rahv, Philip. *Image and Idea,* New York; New Directions. 1949,
105—139.

Rang, Bernhard. "Franz Kafka. Versuch eines Hinweises," *Die
Schildgenossen* (Augsburg), XII (1932) No. 2/3, 107—119;
"Der weltanschauliche Roman," *Welt und Wort* (Tübingen),
1951, 131—134.

Raynoschek, Gustav. *Realismus und Symbolismus im Werke
Franz Kafkas.* Vienna University dissertation, 1956, 278pp.
[typewritten].

Reed, Eugene L. "Moral Polarity in Franz Kafka's *Der Prozess*
and *Das Schloss,*" *Monatshefte,* XLVI (November 1954), 317
—324; "Franz Kafka: Possession and Being," *Monatshefte,* L
(December 1958), 359—366.

Rehfeld, Werner. *Das Motiv des Gerichtes im Werke Franz Kafkas. Zur Deutung des "Urteils", der "Strafkolonie," des "Prozesses."* Frankfurt University dissertation, 1960, 212pp. [typewritten].

Reimann, Paul. "Die gesellschaftliche Problematik in Kafkas Romanen," *Weimarer Beiträge*, III (1957), No. 4, 598—618, reprinted in his *Von Herder bis Kisch. Studien zur Geschichte der deutsch-österreichisch-tschechischen Literaturbeziehungen*, Berlin: Dietz, 1961, 150—173.

Reiss, Hans Siegbert. "Franz Kafka's Conception of Humour," *Modern Language Review*, XLIV (October 1949), 534—542; "Zwei Erzählungen Franz Kafkas. Eine Betrachtung," 'Der Schlag ans Hofter' and 'Der Prüfung'], *Trivium* (Zurich), VIII (1950) No. 3, 218—242; *Franz Kafka. Eine Betrachtung seines Werkes*. Heidelberg: Schneider, 1952, 195pp. [new ed. 1956, 223pp.].

Rhein, Philip Henry. *A Comparative Study of Franz Kafka's "Der Prozess" and Albert Camus' "L'Etranger"* University of Michigan dissertation, 1961.

Richter, Helmut. "Im Masstab der Klassik. Zu einigen Prosastücken Franz Kafkas," *Sinn und Form* (Berlin/Potsdam), 1959, No. 5/6, 837—871; *Werk und Entwurf des Dichters Franz Kafka. Eine literaturkritische Untersuchung*. Leipzig University dissertation, 1959, 408pp. [typewritten]; *Franz Kafka—Werk und Entwurf*, Berlin: Rütten & Loening, 1962, 348pp.

Robbe-Grillet, Alain. "Kafka discredité par ses descendants," *L'Express* (Paris), January 31, 1956.

Robert, Marthe. *Introduction à la lecture de Kafka*, Paris: Edition du Sagittaire, 1946, 46pp.; "L'Humour de Franz Kafka," *Revue de la Pensée Juive* (Paris), 1951, No. 6, 61—72; "La Lecture de Kafka," *Temps Modernes* (Paris), VIII (October—November 1952), Nos. 84/85, 646—660; *Kafka*, Paris: Gallimard, 1960, 292pp. [La Bibliotheque Ideale]; "L'Imitation souveraine," *Temps Modernes*, XVI (March 1961), 1124—1149.

Rochefort, Robert. *Kafka ou L'Irréductible espoir*, Paris: R. Julliard, 1947, 254pp.; "La culpabilité chez Kafka," *Psyché* (Paris) III (1948), 483—495.

Rohl, Freda Kingsford. *A Study of Kafka's Irony*, Manchester University M. A. thesis, 1955/1956; "Kafka's Background as the Source of his Irony," *Modern Language Review*, LIII (1958), 380—392.

Rohner, Wolfgang. *Franz Kafkas Werkgestaltung*. Freiburg i. Br. dissertation, 1950, 357pp. [typewritten].

497

Rougemont, Denis de. *Les Personnes du drame,* New York: Pantheon Books, 1945, 105—126.

Rubinstein, William C. "A Hunger Artist," *Monatshefte,* XLIV (January 1952), 13—19; "A Report to an Academy," in A. Flores & H. Swander (eds): *Franz Kafka Today,* University of Wisconsin Press, 1958, 55—60.

Ruland, Richard F. "A View from Back Home: Kafka's *Amerika,*" *American Quarterly* XIII (1961), 33—42.

Russell, Francis. *Three Studies in Twentieth Century Obscurity,* Aldington, Ashford, Kent: The Head and Flower Press, 1954, 45—65.

Salinger, Herman. "More Light on Kafka's 'Landarzt,'" *Monatshefte,* LIII (1961), 97—104.

Sarraute, Nathalie. "De Dostoievski à Kafka," *Temps Modernes* (Paris), III (October 1947), No. 25, 664—685, reprinted in her *L'Ere du soupçon,* Paris: Gallimard, 1956, 7—52.

Schaufelberger, Fritz. "Kafkas Prosafragmente," *Trivium* (Zurich), VII (1949), 1—15; "Kafka und Kierkegaard," *Reformation* (Schauffhausen, Zurich), July 1959, 387—400, and August 1959, 451—456.

Scherer, Michael. "Das Versagen und die Gnade in Kafkas Werk. Zu Kafkas Erzählung 'Ein Landarzt,'" *Stimmen der Zeit* (Freiburg/Br) 157 Bd. 81Jg. 1955/1956, No. 2, 106—117.

Schoeps, Hans-Joachim. "Theologische Motive in der Dichtung Franz Kafkas," *Neue Rundschau,* LXII (January—March 1951), 21—37; "Franz Kafka und der Mensch unserer Tage," *Universitas* (Stuttgart), XVI (January—February 1961), 163—171.

Schouten, J. H. "Franz Kafka," *Duitse Kroniek* (The Hague). 1952, No. 4, 91—97; "Kafka's brief aan zijn vader," *De Gids* (Amsterdam), CXVII (1954), No. 2, 359—372.

Schüddekopf, Jürgen, "Rätsel der Faszination. Zu Franz Kafkas Erzählung 'Die Verwandlung,'" *Athena* (Berlin), II (1947/1948), No. 7, 40—43.

Schwartzmann, Félix. "Fantasía y realidad en Kafka," *Babel* (Santiago de Chile), Año XI (1950), Vol. 13, 61—68.

Scott, Nathan A., Jr. *Rehearsals of Discomposure,* New York; King's Crown Press, 1952, 11—65.

Seidler, Manfred. *Strukturanalysen der Romane "Der Prozess" und "Das Schloss" von Franz Kafka,* Bonn University dissertation, 1953, 166pp. [typewritten]; "Franz Kafka: Leben, Dichtung und Bedeutung," *Die Kirche in der Welt* (Münster), 1954, Lfg. 1, 119—122.

Servotte, Hermann. "Franz Kafka: 'Der Landarzt,'" *Deutschun-*

terricht für Ausländer (Munich), 1958, No. 2, 33—38.

Seyppel, Joachim H. "The Animal Theme and Totemism in Franz Kafka," *American Imago*, XIII (Spring 1956), 69—93.

Sgorlon, Carlo. *Kafka narratore*, Venice: Neri Pozza, 1961 [Biblioteca di Cultura, 26]

Slochower, Harry. *A Franz Kafka Miscellany*, New York: Twice a Year Press, 1940, 96pp. [enlarged ed. 1946, 120pp.], contains also "Franz Kafka, Pre-Fascist Exile," 7—30; *No Voice Is Wholly Lost*, New York: Creative Age Press 1945, 103—125; "The Use of Myth in Kafka and Mann," in Stanley R. Hopper (ed): *Spiritual Problems in Contemporary Literature*, New York: Harper 1952, 117—126.

Sokel, Walter. "Kafka's 'Metamorphosis,' Rebellion and Punishment," *Monatshefte*, XLVIII (April—May 1956), 203—214.

Sommavilla, Guido. "Kafka era un santo," *Letture* (Milan), XII (1957), 485—489; "La disperazione religiosa di Franz Kafka," *Letture*, XVI (1961), 323—338.

Sonnenfeld, Marion. "Die Fragmente *Amerika* und *Der Prozess* als Bildungsromane," *German Quarterly*, XXXV (January 1962), 34—46.

Spahr, Blake Lee. "Kafka's 'Auf der Galerie': A Stylistic Analysis," *German Quarterly*, XXXIII (1960), 211—215; "Franz Kafka: The Bridge and the Abyss," *Modern Fiction Studies*, VIII (1962), 3—15.

Spann, Meno. "Die beiden Zettel Kafkas," *Monatshefte*, XLVII (November 1955), 321—328; "Franz Kafka's Leopard, ['A Hunger Artist'] *Germanic Review*, XXXIV (April 1959), 85—104; "Don't Hurt the Jackdaw," ['A Hunger Artist'] XXXVII (1962), 68—78.

Spector, Donald Robert. "Kafka's 'The Stoker' as Short Story," *Modern Fiction Studies*, II (May 1956), 80—81; "Kafka and Camus: Some Examples of Rhythm in the Novel,"*Kentucky Foreign Language Quarterly*, V (1958), 205—211.

Spilka, Mark. *Dickens and Kafka: A Mutual Interpretation*, Indiana University dissertation, 1956: "*Amerika*: Its Genesis," in A. Flores & H. Swander (eds): *Franz Kafka Today*, University of Wisconsin Press, 1958, 95—116; "Kafka's Sources for the 'Metamorphosis,' " *Comparative Literature* XI (1959), 289—307; "David Copperfield as Psychological Fiction," *Critical Quarterly* (Hull/London) I (1959), 292—301; "Kafka and Dickens: The Country Sweetheart," *American Imago*, XVI (1959), 367—378; "Dickens and Kafka: The Technique of the Grotesque," *Minnesota Review*, I (1961), 441—458.

Stallman, Robert W. "A Hunger Artist," in A. Flores & H.

Swander (eds) : *Franz Kafka Today,* University of Wisconsin Press, 1958, 173—192;

Standaert, Eric. *Franz Kafka. Van mens tot werk,* University of Ghent dissertation, 1954, 153pp. [typewritten]; "Psychografie van Kafka," *Nieuw Vlaams Tijdschrift* (Antwerp) , 1956, No. 2, 166—183.

Starobinski, Jean, "Kafka et Dostoievski," *Cahiers du Sud* (Marseilles) , XXXII (1950) , 466—475.

Stefani, Giuseppe. "Franz Kafka, impiegato delle Generali," *Bollettino delle Assicurazioni Generali* (Prague) , December 1952; "Kafka e l'Italia," *Nuova Antologia* (Rome) , 1957, No. 470, 67—68.

Steinberg, Erwin R. "The Judgment in Kafka's 'The Judgment,' " *Modern Fiction Studies,* VIII (1962) , 23—30.

Steinberg, M. W. "Franz Kafka: The Achievement of Certitude," *Queen's Quarterly* (Kingston, Ontario) , LXVIII (1961) , 90—103.

Steinhauer, Harry. "Hungering Artist or Artist in Hungering: Kafka's 'A Hunger Artist' " *Criticism, IV* (Winter 1962) , 28—43.

Stern, Guy. "Explication de texte: 'Der Heizer,' " *Modern Language Journal,* XLI (1957) , 37—38.

Storz, Gerhard, "Uber den 'Monologue Intérior' oder die 'Erlebte Rede' " [*The Trial*], *Deutschunterrich* VII 1955, 41—53.

Strauss, Walter A. "Franz Kafka: Between the Paradise and the Labyrinth," *Centennial Review of Arts and Sciences* (Michigan State College) , V (1961) , 206—222.

Strelka, Joseph. *Kafka, Musil, Broch und die Entwicklung des modernen Romans.* Vienna-Hanover-Basel, 1959, 110pp.

Strich, Fritz. "Franz Kafka und das Judentum," in *Festschrift des Schweizerischen Israelitischen Gemeindebundes,* Basel 1954, 273—289, and in his *Kunst und Leben. Vorträge und Abhandlungen zur deutschen Literatur,* Bern & Munich, 1960, 139—151.

Susman, Margarete. "Das Hiob-Problem bei Franz Kafka," *Der Morgen* (Berlin) V (1929) , 31—49, reprinted in her *Gestalten und Kreise,* Stuttgart: Diana Verlag, 1954, 348—366.

Swander, Homer. "*The Castle*: K's Village," in A. Flores & H. Swander (eds) : *Franz Kafka Today,* University of Wisconsin Press, 1958, 173—192.

Tauber, Herbert. *Franz Kafka, eine Deutung seiner Werke,* Zurich: Oprecht Verlag, 1941, 237pp.; *Franz Kafka, An Interpretation of His Works,* Yale University Press, 1948, 252pp.

Tedlock, E. W. Jr. "Kafka's Imitation of *David Copperfield*," *Comparative Literature,* VII (Winter 1955), 52—62.

Thomas, R. H. "Franz Kafka and the Religious Aspect of Expressionism," *German Life & Letters,* II (October 1937) 42—49.

Thurston, Jarvis. "The Married Couple." in A. Flores & H. Swander (eds) : *Franz Kafka Today,* University of Wisconsin Press, 1958, 83—91.

Tilton, John W. "Kafka's *Amerika* as a Novel of Salvation," *Criticism,* III (Fall 1961), 321—332.

Timmer, Charles B. "Kafka in de spiegel van de Russische critiek," *Litterair Paspoort* (Amsterdam), August—September 1949, 115—116.

Timmermans, R. *Franz Kafka. De mens-zijn werkzijn betekenos.* Leuven University dissertation 1954, 199pp. [typewritten].

Tindall, William York. *The Literary Symbol,* Columbia University Press, 1955, 63—64, 139, 142, 174—176.

Tramer, Friedrich. "August Strindberg und Franz Kafka," *Deutsche Vierteljahrsschrift* (Stuttgart), 1960, No. 2, 249—256.

Tyler, Parker. "Kafka and the Surrealists," *Accent,* VI (Autumn 1945), 23—27; "Kafka's and Chaplin's Amerika," *Sewanee Review,* Spring 1950, 299—311.

Ulshöfer, Robert. "Die Wirklichkeitsauffasung in der modernen Prosadichtung," *Deutschunterricht* (Stuttgart) VII (1955) 13—40 ['Die Verwandlung,' 27—36].

Untaru, V. *Esquisse pour une phénomenologie de la littérature noire: Dostoievski, Kafka, Lautréamont, James Joyce,* Sorbonne University thesis, 1949.

Urzidil, Johannes. "Meetings with Franz Kafka," *Menorah Journal,* April—June 1952, 112—116; "Das Reich des Unerreichbaren: Kafka-Deutungen," *Germanic Review,* XXXVI (October 1961), 163—179; "Edison and Kafka," *Monat* (Munich), XIII (1961), 31—35, also as "L'Amérique rêvée par Kafka.," in *Preuves* (Paris), 1962, No. 137, 31—35.

Uyttersprot, Herman. *Zur Struktur Kafkas "Der Prozess",* Brussels: Didier, 1953; 44pp.; *Zur Struktur von Kafkas Romanen,* Brussels: Didier, 1954, 20pp.; *Eine neue Ordnung der Werke Kafkas?,* Antwerp 1957, 85pp.; "The Trial: Its Structure," in A. Flores & H. Swander (eds).: *Franz Kafka Today,* University of Wisconsin Press, 1958, 127—144; *Kleine Kafkaiana* [containing: *Franz Kafka, de "Abermann",* and *Franz Kafka of de processie te Echternach*], Brussels: Didier, 1955, 22pp.

Victoroff, David. "Quelques aspects de la personne dans l'oeuvre de Kafka," *Etudes Philosophiques* (Paris), 1957, No. 3, 471—473.

Vigée, Claude. "Les artistes de la faim," *Table Ronde* (Paris), April 1957, 43—64; also in *Comparative Literature*, 1957, No. 2, 43—64; *Les Artistes de la faim. Essais*, Paris, 1960, 211—248.

Vivas, Eliseo. *Creation and Discovery.* New York: Noonday Press, 1955, 29—46.

Volkening, Ernesto. " 'La Metamorfosis' de Kafka," *Revista de las Indias* (Bogotá), March—May 1948, 465—475.

Volkmann-Schluck, K. H. "Bewusstsein und Dasein in Kafkas 'Prozess,'" *Neue Rundschau* (Frankfurt) LXII (January—March 1951), 38—48.

Vordtriede, Werner. "*Letters to Milena*: The Writer as Advocate of Himself," in A. Flores & H. Swander (eds.): *Franz Kafka Today*, University of Wisconsin Press, 1958, 239—248.

Wagenbach, Klaus. *Franz Kafka. Eine Biographie seiner Jugend (1883—1912)*, Bern: Francke Verlag, 1958, 345pp.

Waidson, H. M. "The Starvation Artist and the Leopard," *Germanic Review*, XXXV (December 1960), 262—269; "Kafka: Biography and Interpretation," *German Life & Letters*, XIV (October 1960—January 1961), 26—33.

Waismann, F. "A Philosopher Looks at Kafka," *Essays in Criticism* (Oxford), III (April, 1953), 177—190.

Waldmeir, Joseph J. "Anti-Semitism as an Issue in *The Trial* of Kafka's Joseph K," *Books Abroad*, XXXV (1961), 10—15.

Walker, Augusta. "Allegory, A Light Conceit," *Partisan Review*, XXII (Fall 1955), 480—490.

Walser, Martin Johannes. *Beschreibung einer Form*: Franz Kafka, Munich. Hanser, 1961, 156pp.

Warren, Austin. *Rage for Order*, University of Chicago Press, 1948, 104—142.

Waterman, Arthur E. "Kafka's 'Hunger Artist,'", *College English Association Critic*, XXIII (1961), 9.

Webster, Peter Dow. "Arrested Individuation or The Problem of Joseph K. and Hamlet," *American Imago*, V (1948), 225—245 "A Critical Fantasy or Fugue" [Shakespeare's "Venus and Adonis" and Kafka's "A Country Doctor"] *American Imago*, VI (1949), 297—309. " 'Dies Irae' in the Unconscious, or The Significance of Franz Kafka," *College English*, XII (1950), 9—15; "A Critical Examination of Franz Kafka's *The Castle*," *Americn Imago*, VIII (1951), 36—60; "Franz Kafka's 'In the Penal Colony,'" *American Imago*, IX (1951) No. 4; "Franz Kafka's 'Metamorphosis' as Death and Resurrection Fantasy," *American Imago*, XVI (1959), 349—365.

Weigel, Hans. "Vitamin K oder Ist Kafka von Kafka?" *Morgen* (Vienna), X (1954), 7—8.

Weinstein, Leo. "Kafka's Ape: Heel or Hero?" *Modern Fiction Studies,* VIII (1962), 75—79.

Weltsch, Felix. "The Rise and Fall of the Jewish-German Symbiosis: the Case of Franz Kafka," *Leo Baeck Institute Yearbook,* London 1956, Vol. I, 255—276. *Religion und Humor im Leben und Werk Franz Kafkas,* Berlin-Grunewald: F. A. Herbig, 1957, 95pp.; *Franz Kafka* [in Hebrew], Jerusalem, 1959, 128pp.

West, Rebecca. "Kafka and the Mystery of Bureaucracy," *Yale Review,* XLVIII (1957—1958), 15—35; *The Court and the Castle,* Yale University Press, 1957, 279—305.

Wiese, Benno von. "Franz Kafka. Ein Hungerkünstler," in his *Die deutsche Novelle von Goethe bis Kafka,* Düsseldorf: A. Bagel, 1956, Vol I, 325—342, "Der Künstler und die moderne Gesellschaft," *Akzente* (Munich), 1958, No. 2, 112—123; "Franz Kafka. Die Verwandlung," in his *Die deutsche Novelle von Goethe bis Kafka,* Düsseldorf: A. Bagel 1962, Vol. II, 319—345

Wilson, A. K. " 'Null and Void': An Interpretation of the Significance of the Court in Franz Kafka's *Der Prozess*," *German Life & Letters,* XIV (1961), 165—169.

Wood, Frank. "Hofmannsthal and Kafka: Two Motifs," *German Quarterly,* 1958, 104—113.

Woodring. Carl R. "Josephine the Singer or the Mouse Folk," in A. Flores & H. Swander (eds): *Franz Kafka Today,* University of Wisconsin Press, 1958, 71—75.

Zimmermann, Werner. "Franz Kafka: Auf der Galerie—Eine kaiserliche Botschaft—Vor dem Gesetz" in *Deutsche Prosadichtungen der Gegenwart. Interpretationen für Lehrende und Lernende. Düsseldorf:* Pädagogischer Verlag Schwann, 1954, 159—174 [3rd revised ed., 1956].

Zolla, Elémire. "Franz Kafka," *Letterature Moderne* (Milan), I (December 1950), 495—507; "La maschera e il volto di Franz Kafka," *Letterature Moderne,* V (1954), No. 2, 151—159.

53872